THE FOOTBAL

MATCH BY MATCH

1927/28

Edited by Tony Brown

A SoccerData Publication

Published in Great Britain by Tony Brown,
4 Adrian Close, Beeston, Nottingham NG9 6FL.
Telephone 0115 973 6086. E-mail soccer@innotts.co.uk
www.soccerdata.com

First published 2004

Please write to or email the publisher for news of future publications.

Printed by 4edge, Hockley, Essex

ISBN 1 899468 28 5

FINAL TABLES 1927/28

Division One

		p	w	d	l	f	a	w	d	l	f	a	pts
1	Everton	42	11	8	2	60	28	9	5	7	42	38	53
2	Huddersfield Town	42	15	1	5	57	31	7	6	8	34	37	51
3	Leicester City	42	14	5	2	66	25	4	7	10	30	47	48
4	Derby County	42	12	4	5	59	30	5	6	10	37	53	44
5	Bury	42	13	1	7	53	35	7	3	11	27	45	44
6	Cardiff City	42	12	7	2	44	27	5	3	13	26	53	44
7	Bolton Wanderers	42	12	5	4	47	26	4	6	11	34	40	43
8	Aston Villa	42	13	3	5	52	30	4	6	11	26	43	43
9	Newcastle United	42	9	7	5	49	41	6	6	9	30	40	43
10	Arsenal	42	10	6	5	49	33	3	9	9	33	53	41
11	Birmingham	42	10	7	4	36	25	3	8	10	34	50	41
12	Blackburn Rovers	42	13	5	3	41	22	3	4	14	25	56	41
13	Sheffield United	42	12	4	5	56	42	3	6	12	23	44	40
14	Sheffield Wed.	42	9	6	6	45	29	4	7	10	36	49	39
15	Sunderland	42	9	5	7	37	29	6	4	11	37	47	39
16	Liverpool	42	10	6	5	54	36	3	7	11	30	51	39
17	West Ham United	42	9	7	5	48	34	5	4	12	33	54	39
18	Manchester United	42	12	6	3	51	27	4	1	16	21	53	39
19	Burnley	42	12	5	4	55	31	4	2	15	27	67	39
20	Portsmouth	42	13	4	4	40	23	3	3	15	26	67	39
21	Tottenham Hotspur	42	12	3	6	47	34	3	5	13	27	52	38
22	Middlesbrough	42	7	9	5	46	35	4	6	11	35	53	37

Division Three (North)

		p	w	d	l	f	a	w	d	l	f	a	pts
1	Bradford Park Ave.	42	18	2	1	68	22	9	7	5	33	23	63
2	Lincoln City	42	15	4	2	53	20	9	3	9	38	44	55
3	Stockport County	42	16	5	0	62	14	7	3	11	27	37	54
4	Doncaster Rovers	42	15	4	2	59	18	8	3	10	21	26	53
5	Tranmere Rovers	42	14	6	1	68	28	8	3	10	37	44	53
6	Bradford City	42	15	4	2	59	19	3	8	10	26	41	48
7	Darlington	42	15	1	5	63	28	6	4	11	26	46	47
8	Southport	42	15	2	4	55	24	5	3	13	24	46	45
9	Accrington Stanley	42	14	4	3	49	22	4	4	13	27	45	44
10	New Brighton	42	10	7	4	45	22	4	7	10	27	40	42
11	Wrexham	42	15	1	5	48	19	3	5	13	16	48	42
12	Halifax Town	42	11	7	3	47	24	2	8	11	26	47	41
13	Rochdale	42	13	4	4	45	24	4	3	14	29	53	41
14	Rotherham United	42	11	6	4	39	19	3	5	13	26	50	39
15	Hartlepools United	42	10	3	8	41	35	6	3	12	28	46	38
16	Chesterfield	42	10	4	7	46	29	3	6	12	25	49	36
17	Crewe Alexandra	42	10	6	5	51	28	2	4	15	26	58	34
18	Ashington	42	10	5	6	54	36	1	6	14	23	67	33
19	Barrow	42	10	8	3	41	24	0	3	18	13	78	31
20	Wigan Borough	42	8	5	8	30	32	2	5	14	26	65	30
21	Durham City	42	10	5	6	37	30	1	2	18	16	70	29
22	Nelson	42	8	4	9	50	49	2	2	17	26	87	26

Division Two

		p	w	d	l	f	a	w	d	l	f	a	pts
1	Manchester City	42	18	2	1	70	27	7	7	7	30	32	59
2	Leeds United	42	16	2	3	63	15	9	5	7	35	34	57
3	Chelsea	42	15	2	4	46	15	8	6	7	29	30	54
4	Preston North End	42	15	3	3	62	24	7	6	8	38	42	53
5	Stoke City	42	14	5	2	44	17	8	3	10	34	42	52
6	Swansea Town	42	13	6	2	46	17	5	6	10	29	46	48
7	Oldham Athletic	42	15	3	3	55	18	4	5	12	20	33	46
8	West Bromwich Alb.	42	10	7	4	50	28	7	5	9	40	42	46
9	Port Vale	42	11	6	4	45	20	7	2	12	23	37	44
10	Nottingham Forest	42	10	6	5	54	37	5	4	12	29	47	40
11	Grimsby Town	42	8	6	7	41	41	6	6	9	28	42	40
12	Bristol City	42	11	5	5	42	18	4	4	13	34	61	39
13	Barnsley	42	10	5	6	43	36	4	6	11	22	49	39
14	Hull City	42	9	8	4	25	19	3	7	11	16	35	39
15	Notts County	42	10	4	7	47	26	3	8	10	21	48	38
16	Wolverhampton Wan.	42	11	5	5	43	31	2	5	14	20	60	36
17	Southampton	42	11	3	7	54	40	3	4	14	14	37	35
18	Reading	42	9	8	4	32	22	2	5	14	21	53	35
19	Blackpool	42	11	3	7	55	43	2	5	14	28	58	34
20	Clapton Orient	42	9	7	5	32	25	2	5	14	23	60	34
21	Fulham	42	12	7	2	46	22	1	0	20	22	67	33
22	South Shields	42	5	5	11	30	41	2	4	15	26	70	23

Division Three (South)

		p	w	d	l	f	a	w	d	l	f	a	pts
1	Millwall	42	19	2	0	87	15	11	3	7	40	35	65
2	Northampton Town	42	17	3	1	67	23	6	6	9	35	41	55
3	Plymouth Argyle	42	17	2	2	60	19	6	5	10	25	35	53
4	Brighton & Hove A.	42	14	4	3	51	24	5	6	10	30	45	48
5	Crystal Palace	42	15	3	3	46	23	3	9	9	33	49	48
6	Swindon Town	42	12	6	3	60	26	7	3	11	30	43	47
7	Southend United	42	14	2	5	48	19	6	4	11	32	45	46
8	Exeter City	42	11	6	4	49	27	6	6	9	21	33	46
9	Newport County	42	12	5	4	52	38	6	4	11	29	46	45
10	Queen's Park Rgs.	42	8	5	8	37	35	9	4	8	35	36	43
11	Charlton Athletic	42	12	5	4	34	27	3	8	10	26	43	43
12	Brentford	42	12	4	5	49	30	4	4	13	27	44	40
13	Luton Town	42	13	5	3	56	27	3	2	16	38	60	39
14	Bournemouth	42	12	6	3	44	24	1	6	14	28	55	38
15	Watford	42	10	5	6	42	34	4	5	12	26	44	38
16	Gillingham	42	10	3	8	33	26	3	8	10	29	55	37
17	Norwich City	42	9	8	4	41	26	1	8	12	25	44	36
18	Walsall	42	9	6	6	52	35	3	3	15	23	66	33
19	Bristol Rovers	42	11	3	7	41	36	3	1	17	26	57	32
20	Coventry City	42	5	8	8	40	36	6	1	14	27	60	31
21	Merthyr Town	42	7	6	8	38	40	2	7	12	15	51	31
22	Torquay United	42	4	10	7	27	36	4	4	13	26	67	30

Football League attendances are taken from the official ledgers, with permission of the Football League.

Match details are based on contemporary accounts, Football League ledgers, complete record books and correspondence with club experts. Computer validation has been used to check line-ups and scorers, but any remaining errors are probably the fault of the editor!

Acknowledgements are due to all those people that have helped with this volume, particularly Kit Bartlett (for Colindale research), Brian Tabner (attendances), Michael Joyce (player details) and Barry Spencer.

Accrington Stanley

9th in Division Three (North)

	Date	Opponent	Score	Scorers	Att.	Armstrong JD	Barclay IB	Brooke P	Butler R	Carrick J-H	Chadwick J	Clarkson R	Curran AE	Dodds C	Finnigan RP	Hall R	Lee PF	Martin J	McLaughlan G	Parkin JT	Parry FT	Slater F	Tootill A	Whittaker T
1	Aug 27	Nelson	4-1	McLaughlin 2, Parkin 2	8007		11	2	8	4			5		1		6		10	9	7			3
2	Sep 3	WIGAN BOROUGH	2-4	Butler, Parkin	8331		11	2	8	4			5		1		6		10	9	7			3
3	10	Doncaster Rovers	0-0		6143	2	11		8	4			5		1		6		10	9	7			3
4	17	DARLINGTON	0-0		7392	2	11		8	4			5		1		6		10	9	7			3
5	24	Ashington	1-1	Clarkson	2853	2	11		8	4		9	5		1		6		10		7			3
6	27	HARTLEPOOLS UNITED	2-2	Armstrong (p), McLaughlin	6353	2	11			4		9	5		1		6	10	8		7			3
7	Oct 1	CREWE ALEXANDRA	5-0	Parkin 2, Butler, McLaughlin, Armstrong (p)	3675	2	11		8	4			5		1		6		10	9	7			3
8	8	Halifax Town	1-3	Butler	7173	2	11		8	4			5		1		6		10	9	7			3
9	15	BRADFORD CITY	1-1	Parry	7428	2	11		8	4			5		1		6		10	9	7			3
10	22	Southport	0-5		2655	2	11		8	4	10		5		1		6			9	7			3
11	29	ROTHERHAM UNITED	3-1	Carrick, Parkin, Clarkson	4930	2	11			4		9	5		1		6		10	8	7			3
12	Nov 12	DURHAM CITY	2-0	Parkin 2	4459	2	11			4		8	5				6		10	9	7		1	3
13	19	Wrexham	1-0	Clarkson	2070	2	11			4		8	5				6		10	9	7		1	3
14	Dec 3	Bradford Park Avenue	3-3	McLaughlin, Clarkson, Parkin	10337	2	11			4		8	5		1		6		10	9	7			3
15	10	CHESTERFIELD	0-0		3771	2	11			4		8	5		1		6		10	9	7			3
16	17	Stockport County	3-3	Parkin 2, Parry	4020	2	11		8	4			5	6	1				10	9	7			3
17	24	BARROW	5-1	Parkin, Armstrong, McLaughlin, Barclay (p), Parry	3129	2	11		8	4			5	6	1				10	9	7			3
18	26	NEW BRIGHTON	2-1	Laycock (og), Martin	5644	2			8	4			5	6	1			11	10	9	7			3
19	27	New Brighton	1-3	McLaughlin	5384	2			8	4			5	6	1			11	10	9	7			3
20	31	NELSON	7-1	Parkin 3, Butler, McLaughlin, Curran, Martin	4207	2			8	4			5	6	1			11	10	9	7			3
21	Jan 2	LINCOLN CITY	1-0	Martin	5682	2			9	4	8		5	6	1			11	10		7			3
22	7	Wigan Borough	0-2		2756	2	11		9	4	8		5	6	1				10		7			3
23	14	Chesterfield	1-3	Parkin	3358	2	11		8	4			5	6	1				10	9	7			3
24	21	DONCASTER ROVERS	1-3	Parkin	4931	2	11			4		8	5	6	1				10	9	7			3
25	28	Darlington	0-3		3132	2	11					9	5	4	1		6		10	8		7		3
26	Feb 4	ASHINGTON	3-1	Butler, Ridley (og), Parkin	2526	2	11		8				5	4	1		6		10	9		7		3
27	11	Crewe Alexandra	3-2	Parkin, Barclay (p), McLaughlin	2576	2	11		8				5	4	1		6		10	9	7			3
28	15	TRANMERE ROVERS	2-3	Barclay (p), Butler	2017	2	11		8				5	4	1		6		10	9	7			3
29	18	HALIFAX TOWN	3-2	Dodds, Butler, Parkin	3241	2	11		8	5				4	1		6		10	9	7			3
30	25	Bradford City	0-2		10930	2	11		8	5				4	1		6		10	9	7			3
31	Mar 3	SOUTHPORT	4-1	Butler 2, Parkin 2 (1p)	4593	2			8				5	4	1		6	11	10	9	7			3
32	10	Rotherham United	1-2	Curran	3763	2	11		8				5	4	1		6		10	9	7			3
33	17	ROCHDALE	1-0	Barclay (p)	3885	2	11						5	4	1		6		10	9	8	7		3
34	24	Durham City	1-2	Parkin	1343	2	11			5				4	1		6		10	9	8	7		3
35	31	WREXHAM	2-0	McLaughlin, Parkin	3188	2	11		8				5	4	1		6		10	9	7			3
36	Apr 6	Lincoln City	1-3	Barclay	8810	2	11		8					4	1	5	6		10	9	7			3
37	7	Tranmere Rovers	2-3	Parkin 2	6169	2	11		8				5	4	1		6		10	9	7			3
38	9	Hartlepools United	2-0	Parry, Parkin	2245	2	11		8				5	4	1		6		10	9	7			3
39	14	BRADFORD PARK AVE.	2-1	Parry, Lee	4948	2	11				8		5	4	1		6		10	9	7			3
40	28	STOCKPORT COUNTY	1-0	Chadwick	5225	2	11				8		5	4	1		6		10	9	7			3
41	May 1	Rochdale	2-3	Barclay (p), Barber (og)	1443	2	11				8		5	4	1		6		10	9	7			3
42	5	Barrow	0-1		6561	2	11				8		5	4	1		6		10	9	7			3

	Armstrong JD	Barclay IB	Brooke P	Butler R	Carrick J-H	Chadwick J	Clarkson R	Curran AE	Dodds C	Finnigan RP	Hall R	Lee PF	Martin J	McLaughlan G	Parkin JT	Parry FT	Slater F	Tootill A	Whittaker T
Apps	40	37	2	28	27	7	9	38	27	40	1	33	6	41	38	40	4	2	42
Goals	3	6		9	1	1	4	2	1			1	3	10	27	5			

Three own goals

F.A. Cup

	Date	Opponent	Score	Scorers	Att.	Armstrong JD	Barclay IB	Brooke P	Butler R	Carrick J-H	Chadwick J	Clarkson R	Curran AE	Dodds C	Finnigan RP	Hall R	Lee PF	Martin J	McLaughlan G	Parkin JT	Parry FT	Slater F	Tootill A	Whittaker T
R1	Nov 26	LINCOLN CITY	2-5	Clarkson, Parkin	7245	2	11			4		8	5				6		10	9	7		1	3

Arsenal

10th in Division One

	Date		Opponent	Score	Scorers	Att	Baker A	Barley JC	Blyth WN	Brain J	Buchan CM	Butler JD	Clark AW	Cope HW	Hapgood EA	Hoar S	Hulme JHA	John RF	Kennedy AL	Lambert J	Lewis D	Moody J	Parker TR	Paterson W	Peel HB	Roberts H	Seddon WC	Shaw J	Thompson L	Tricker RW
1	Aug	27	Bury	1-5	Brain	17614	4		10	9	8	5					7	6	3		1		2		11					
2		31	BURNLEY	4-1	Brain 2, Buchan, Blyth	19910	4		10	9	8	5		3		11	7	6			1		2							
3	Sep	3	SHEFFIELD UNITED	6-1	Buchan 2, Hulme, Blyth, Brain, Parker	30910	4		10	9	8	5		3		11	7	6			1		2							
4		5	Burnley	2-1	Blyth, Brain	14668	4		8	9		5		3		11	7	6		10	1		2							
5		10	Aston Villa	2-2	Blyth 2	42136	4		10	9	8	5		3		11	7	6			1		2							
6		17	SUNDERLAND	2-1	Baker, Brain	45501	4		10	9	8	5		3		11	7	6			1		2							
7		24	Derby County	0-4		16539	4		10	9	8	5				11	7	6	3			1	2							
8	Oct	1	WEST HAM UNITED	2-2	Brain 2	34931	4		10	9	8	5		3		11	7	6				1	2							
9		8	Portsmouth	3-2	Blyth, Hulme, Brain	27261	4		10	9	8	5		3		11	7	6			1		2							
10		15	LEICESTER CITY	2-2	Brain, Hoar	36640	4		10	9	8	5		3		11	7	6			1		2							
11		22	Sheffield Wednesday	1-1	Buchan	12698			6	9	8	5		3		7				10	1		2		11		4			
12		29	BOLTON WANDERERS	1-2	Buchan	35787			10	9	8	5		3		11	7	6			1		2				4			
13	Nov	5	Blackburn Rovers	1-4	Parker (p)	9656			8		9		4	3		11	7	6			1		2				5			10
14		12	MIDDLESBROUGH	3-1	Buchan 2, Hulme	25921				10	9	5		3		11	7	6			1		2			4				8
15		19	Birmingham	1-1	Hoar	10030	4		10	9		5			3	11	7	6			1		2							8
16	Dec	3	Huddersfield Town	1-2	Brain	15140	4			10	9	5		3		11	7	6			1		2							8
17		10	NEWCASTLE UNITED	4-1	Hulme, Brain, Parker, Hoar	42630	4		10	9	8	5		3		11	7	6			1		2							
18		17	Manchester United	1-4	Wilson (og)	18120	4		10	9		5		3		11	7	6			1		2							8
19		24	EVERTON	3-2	Hulme, Buchan, Blyth	27995	4		10	9	8	5		3		11	7	6			1		2							
20		27	Liverpool	2-0	Hoar, Brain	41024	4		10	9		5		3		7		6		8	1		2		11					
21		31	BURY	3-1	Lambert, John, Parker (p)	20742	4		10	9		5		3		7		6		8	1		2		11					
22	Jan	2	TOTTENHAM HOTSPUR	1-1	Hoar	13518	4		10	9	8	5			3	11	7	6				1	2							
23		7	Sheffield United	4-6	Hoar 2, Brain 2	18158	4	10		9					3	11	7	6		8		1	2			5				
24		21	ASTON VILLA	0-3		32505	4	10	8	9		5		3		11	7	6			1		2							
25	Feb	4	DERBY COUNTY	3-4	Brain 3	21405	4		10	9	8	5		3		11	7						2	1			6			
26		11	West Ham United	2-2	Brain 2	28086			4	9	8	5		3		11	7	6		10	1		2							
27		25	Leicester City	2-3	Hoar, Buchan	25835	5		4	9	8			3		11	7	6		10	1		2							
28	Mar	7	LIVERPOOL	6-3	Brain 3, Hulme, Buchan, Lambert	14037	4		6	9	8	5					7	3		10	1		2		11					
29		10	Bolton Wanderers	1-1	Buchan	15546	4		6	9	8	5				7		3		10			2	1	11					
30		14	Sunderland	1-5	Lambert	9478	4		6		8	5				9	7	3		10	1		2		11					
31		17	BLACKBURN ROVERS	3-2	Buchan 2, Hoar	33446	4		6	9	8	5				11	7	3		10			2	1						
32		28	PORTSMOUTH	0-2		15416	4		6		9	5		3		7				8	1		2		11				10	
33		31	BIRMINGHAM	2-2	Buchan 2	13990	4		6	9	8	5		3		7		11		10	1		2							
34	Apr	6	CARDIFF CITY	3-0	Hulme, Buchan, Brain	36828	4		6	9	8	5				11	7	3		10	1		2							
35		7	Tottenham Hotspur	0-2		39193	4		6	9						11	7	3		10	1		2			5		8		
36		9	Cardiff City	2-2	Tricker 2	17699	4		6	9	8	5				11	7	3					2	1						10
37		14	HUDDERSFIELD T	0-0		38707	4		6	9	8	5				11	7	3			1		2							10
38		18	Middlesbrough	2-2	Baker, Hulme	16731	4		6	9		5				11	7	3			1		2		10			8		
39		21	Newcastle United	1-1	Shaw	22819	4		6	9		5				11	7	3			1		2		10			8		
40		28	MANCHESTER UNITED	0-1		22452	4		6	9		5				11	7	3			1		2		10			8		
41	May	2	SHEFFIELD WEDNESDAY	1-1	Brain	15818	4		6	9		5					7	3		10	1		2		11			8		
42		5	Everton	3-3	Shaw 2, O'Donnell (og)	48715	4		6	10	8	5					7	3					2	1	11			9		
						Apps	37	2	39	39	30	38	1	24	3	38	36	39	2	16	33	4	42	5	13	3	4	6	1	7
						Goals	2		7	25	16					9	8	1		3			4					3		2

Two own goals

F.A. Cup

	Date		Opponent	Score	Scorers	Att	Baker A	Barley JC	Blyth WN	Brain J	Buchan CM	Butler JD	Clark AW	Cope HW	Hapgood EA	Hoar S	Hulme JHA	John RF	Kennedy AL	Lambert J	Lewis D	Moody J	Parker TR	Paterson W	Peel HB	Roberts H	Seddon WC	Shaw J	Thompson L	Tricker RW
R3	Jan	14	WEST BROMWICH ALBION	2-0	Brain, Hulme	43322	4		10	9	8	5		3		11	7	6			1		2							
R4		28	EVERTON	4-3	Hulme 2, Brain, Buchan	44328	4		10	9	8	5		3		11	7	6			1		2							
R5	Feb	18	ASTON VILLA	4-1	Brain 2, Lambert, Hulme	58505			4	9	8	5		3		11	7	6		10	1		2							
R6	Mar	3	STOKE CITY	4-1	Blyth 2, Hoar 2	41974	4		10	9	8	5		3		11	7	6			1		2							
SF		24	Blackburn Rovers	0-1		25633	4		10	9	8	5		3		11	7	6			1		2							

SF at Filbert Street, Leicester

Ashington

18th in Division Three (North)

	Date	Opponent	Score	Scorers	Att.	Ball S	Best E	Bradley W	Carlton J	Chipperfield F	Coombs JR	Ferguson E	Gaffney P	Graham E	Grieves J	Hamilton G	Hepple J	Hopper M	Johnson GA	Kirkup R	Laverick W	Moore D	Noble JF	Price J	Randall J	Richardson W	Ridley RH	Robinson C	Robson GA	Robson JW	Turnbull HW	Watson WT
1	Aug 27	BRADFORD CITY	2-2	Randall, Ball	3841	9				6		2			4	3		7	8					5	10		1					11
2	29	CREWE ALEXANDRA	0-2		1825	9			4	6		2				3		7	8			1		5	10							11
3	Sep 3	New Brighton	0-6		5489	9			4	5		2				3		7	6			1			10						8	11
4	5	Halifax Town	1-6	Ball	4944	9			4			2	5			3			6			1			10			7			8	11
5	10	LINCOLN CITY	4-5	Ball, Watson, Johnson (p), Turnbull	3066	9	3	1	4	5						2		7	6						10						8	11
6	12	HALIFAX TOWN	3-3	Lees (og), Ball 2	1665	9	2	1	4	5						3		7	6						10						8	11
7	17	Hartlepools United	1-4	Ball	4294	9	2	1	4	5						3		7	6						10						8	11
8	24	ACCRINGTON STANLEY	1-1	Turnbull	2853	9	3	1	4	6								7	5						10				2		8	11
9	Oct 1	Wigan Borough	0-0		1696	9	3	1	8	6					5			7	4		11				10				2			
10	8	DONCASTER ROVERS	1-2	Johnson	2655	9	3	1		6					5			7	8		11			4	10				2			
11	15	Darlington	1-5	Ball	4902	9	3		6									7		4	11			5	8		1		2			10
12	22	Bradford Park Avenue	0-5		7315	8	3		6									7		4				5	11		1		2	9		10
13	29	CHESTERFIELD	0-0		2310	9	3		8	6								7		4				5	11		1		2			10
14	Nov 5	Wrexham	1-5	Randall	3531		3		4					9	6			7					8	5	11		1		2			10
15	12	TRANMERE ROVERS	3-0	Johnson, Randall, Graham	1785	9	3		4	6				8				7	5						11	2	1					10
16	19	Stockport County	0-3		6590		3		4	6				8				7	5						11	2	1			9		10
17	Dec 3	Nelson	5-1	Randall 2, Watson, Johnson 2	2936		3		4	6		2		8				7	9					5	11		1					10
18	10	BARROW	1-0	Randall	1680		3		4	6		2		8				7	9					5	11		1					10
19	17	Rotherham United	1-1	Johnson	4420		3		4	6		2		8				7	9					5	11		1					10
20	24	SOUTHPORT	1-3	Hopper	1703		3		4	6		2		8				7	9					5	11		1					10
21	31	Bradford City	0-5		5415				4	6		2				3			9	8				5	11		1	7				10
22	Jan 2	DURHAM CITY	2-2	Johnson 2	2099				4	6		2				3			9	8				5	11		1	7				10
23	7	NEW BRIGHTON	3-2	Graham, Johnson 2	1619					6	4	2		8		3			9					5	11		1	7				10
24	14	ROCHDALE	5-1	Wood (og), Chipperfield, Johnson, Graham 2	1223					6	4	2		8		3			9					5	11		1	7				10
25	21	Lincoln City	1-3	Watson	5768					6	4	2		8		3			9					5	11		1	7				10
26	28	HARTLEPOOLS UNITED	3-1	Robinson, Chipperfield, Randall	1407	8				6	4	2			5	3			9						11		1	7				10
27	Feb 4	Accrington Stanley	1-3	Johnson	2526	8				6	4	2			5	3			9						11		1	7				10
28	11	WIGAN BOROUGH	6-3	Ball 3, Johnson 3	1380	8	3			6	4	2			5				9						11		1	7				10
29	18	Doncaster Rovers	2-3	Ball, Robinson	6553	8				6	4	2			5	3			9						11		1	7				10
30	25	DARLINGTON	2-3	Ball 2	4232	9				6	4	2			5	3			8						11		1	7				10
31	Mar 3	BRADFORD PARK AVE.	0-3		4052	9				6	4	2				3			8					5	11		1	7				10
32	10	Chesterfield	0-3		2422			1		6	4	2		8	9	3	10							5	11			7				
33	17	WREXHAM	2-1	Robinson, Chipperfield	1369	8		1		6	4	2				3			9					5	11			7				10
34	24	Tranmere Rovers	3-5	Watson, Randall 2	3749	8		1		3	4	2					10		9					5	11			7				6
35	31	STOCKPORT COUNTY	4-1	Watson 2, Randall, Johnson	2053	8		1		6	4				2	3			9					5	11			7				10
36	Apr 6	Crewe Alexandra	0-3		5874	8		1		6	4				2	3			9					5	11			7				10
37	7	Rochdale	2-2	Johnson, Robinson	3309	8		1		6	4				2	3			9					5	11			7				10
38	14	NELSON	5-1	Johnson 3, Randall, Robinson	1410	8		1		6	4	2				3			9					5	11			7				10
39	18	Durham City	0-0		931	8		1		6	4	2				3			9					5	11			7				10
40	21	Barrow	1-1	Graham	7273			1		6	4			8	2	3			9					5	11			7				10
41	28	ROTHERHAM UNITED	6-0	Graham, Johnson 2, Watson, Randall, Price	1464			1		6		2		8	4	3			9					5	11			7				10
42	May 5	Southport	3-3	Randall, Johnson 2	1749			1		6		2		8	4	3			9					5	11			7				10
					Apps	27	17	17	20	38	18	26	1	14	16	27	2	19	37	5	3	3	1	28	42	2	22	23	7	2	6	39
					Goals	13				3				6				1	24					1	13			5			2	7

Two own goals

F.A. Cup

	Date	Opponent	Score	Scorers	Att.	Ball S	Best E	Bradley W	Carlton J	Chipperfield F	Coombs JR	Ferguson E	Gaffney P	Graham E	Grieves J	Hamilton G	Hepple J	Hopper M	Johnson GA	Kirkup R	Laverick W	Moore D	Noble JF	Price J	Randall J	Richardson W	Ridley RH	Robinson C	Robson GA	Robson JW	Turnbull HW	Watson WT
R1	Nov 26	Crewe Alexandra	2-2	Ball 2	4800	9	3		4	6				8				7	5						11	2	1					10
rep	30	CREWE ALEXANDRA	0-2		3000	9	3		4	6		2		8				7	5						11		1					10

Aston Villa

8th in Division One

No	Date	Opponent	Score	Scorers	Att	Armfield WCW	Beresford J	Bowen SE	Brittleton JT	Capewell LK	Chester RA	Cook GW	Dorrell AR	Gibson JD	Goddard H	Harris WH	Hickman J	Jackson T	Johnson WWF	Kingdon WIG	Milne VE	Mort T	Moss F (snr)	Olney BA	Smart T	Stephenson GT	Talbot AD	Tate JT	Tully FA	Walker WH	Waring T	Yates J	York RE
1	Aug 27	LEICESTER CITY	0-3		47288							9	11	4				1			5	3			2	8	6			10			7
2	31	Portsmouth	1-3	Walker	32050							9	11	4				1		6		3			2	8	5			10			7
3	Sep 3	Liverpool	0-0		42196		8	2				9	11	4				1			5	3	6							10			7
4	5	PORTSMOUTH	7-2	Beresford 3(1p),Cook 2,Dorrell,Walker	20624		8	2				9	11	4					1	6	5	3								10			7
5	10	ARSENAL	2-2	Beresford, Cook	42136		8	2				9	11	4				1		6	5	3								10			7
6	17	Burnley	2-4	Cook 2	19523		8	2				9	11	4				1		6	5	3								10			7
7	24	BURY	1-0	York	25538		8	3				9	11	4				1		6	5				2					10			7
8	Oct 1	Sheffield United	3-0	Dorrell, Cook, Beresford	12327		8	3				9	11	4				1		6	5				2					10			7
9	8	MIDDLESBROUGH	5-1	Cook 3, Dorrell, Walker	38180		8	3				9	11					1		4	5		6		2					10			7
10	15	SUNDERLAND	4-2	Walker 2, Cook, York	38116		8	3				9	11					1		4	5		6		2					10			7
11	22	Huddersfield Town	1-1	Cook	14679		8	3				9	11	4				1		6	5				2					10			7
12	29	NEWCASTLE UNITED	3-0	Dorrell, Walker, Spencer (og)	50797		8	3				9	11					1		4	5		6		2					10			7
13	Nov 5	Birmingham	1-1	Walker	47605		8	3				9	11	4				1		6	5				2					10			7
14	12	TOTTENHAM HOTSPUR	1-2	Cook	30759		8	3				9	11	4				1			5		6		2					10			7
15	19	Manchester United	1-5	Cook	25991		8	3		9		10	11			7		1		4	5		6		2								
16	26	BLACKBURN ROVERS	2-0	Walker, Beresford	27281		8	3			7	9	11					1		4	5		6		2					10			
17	Dec 3	Cardiff City	1-2	Cook	14264		8	3			7	9	11					1		4	5				2					10		6	
18	10	EVERTON	2-3	Cook, Chester	40353		8	3			7	9	11					1		4	5				2					10		6	
19	17	Bolton Wanderers	1-3	Dorrell	14852		8	2			7	9	11		1					4	5	3								10		6	
20	24	SHEFFIELD WEDNESDAY	5-4	Beresford 3, Cook 2	12345		8	3			11	9					1			4	5		6		2					10			7
21	26	Derby County	0-5		23303		8	2			11	9					1			4		3						5		10		6	7
22	27	DERBY COUNTY	0-1		43228		8				11	10							1	4		3	6		2			5	7				9
23	31	Leicester City	0-3		25233		8				7	9	11							4		3	6	1	2			5		10			
24	Jan 7	LIVERPOOL	3-4	Chester 2, Capewell	29505		8			9	7		11							4	5	3	6	1	2					10			
25	21	Arsenal	3-0	Dorrell, Cook, Smart (p)	32505		8	3				9	11							4	5		6	1	2					10			7
26	Feb 4	Bury	0-0		9814		8	3		9		10	11							4	5		6	1	2								7
27	8	BURNLEY	3-1	Capewell 2, Cook	18602			3		9		8	11	4							5		6	1	2					10			7
28	11	SHEFFIELD UNITED	1-0	Cook	27231			3		9	11	8		4						6	5			1	2					10			7
29	25	Sunderland	3-2	Cook, Waring, York	29444				3			8	11							4	5		6	1	2					10	9		7
30	Mar 10	Newcastle United	5-7	Waring 2, Cook, Dorrell, York	23053				3			8	11	4							5		6	1	2					10	9		7
31	17	BIRMINGHAM	1-1	Smart (p)	59367							8	11	4						6	5	3		1	2					10	9		7
32	21	Middlesbrough	0-0		15698						7	8	11	5						4		3		1	2					10	9	6	
33	24	Tottenham Hotspur	1-2	Capewell	21537			3		9		8	11							4	5		6	1	2				7	10			
34	31	MANCHESTER UNITED	3-1	Waring, Cook, Smart (p)	24691			3				8	11							4	5			1	2					10	9	6	7
35	Apr 6	West Ham United	0-0		31469			3				8		4							5			1	2				11	10	9	6	7
36	7	Blackburn Rovers	1-0	Armfield	21432	7	8	3					11	4							5			1	2					10	9	6	
37	9	WEST HAM UNITED	1-0	Dorrell	31059	7	8						11	4							5	3		1	2					10	9	6	
38	14	CARDIFF CITY	3-1	Beresford, Waring, Smart (p)	22428		10	3				8	11	4							5			1	2						9	6	7
39	21	Everton	2-3	Waring, Gibson	39825		8	3					11	4							5			1	2					10	9	6	7
40	28	BOLTON WANDERERS	2-2	Walker, Armfield	22895	7	8	3						4							5			1	2			6	11	10	9		
41	May 2	HUDDERSFIELD T	3-0	Walker, Dorrell, Waring	30173		8	3					11	4						6	5			1	2				7	10	9		
42	5	Sheffield Wednesday	0-2		36636		8	3					11	4						6	5			1	2				7	10	9		
					Apps	3	31	32	2	6	11	35	36	24	1	1	2	17	2	31	37	14	17	20	36	2	2	4	6	38	13	11	28
					Goals	2	10			4	3	23	9	1											4					10	7		4

One own goal

F.A. Cup

Rd	Date	Opponent	Score	Scorers	Att	Armfield WCW	Beresford J	Bowen SE	Brittleton JT	Capewell LK	Chester RA	Cook GW	Dorrell AR	Gibson JD	Goddard H	Harris WH	Hickman J	Jackson T	Johnson WWF	Kingdon WIG	Milne VE	Mort T	Moss F (snr)	Olney BA	Smart T	Stephenson GT	Talbot AD	Tate JT	Tully FA	Walker WH	Waring T	Yates J	York RE
R3	Jan 14	Burnley	2-0	Walker, Beresford	26150		8				7	9	11							4	5	3	6	1	2					10			
R4	28	CREWE ALEXANDRA	3-0	Cook 3	41000		8	3				9	11							4	5		6	1	2					10			7
R5	Feb 18	Arsenal	1-4	Cook	58505		8	3				9	11							4	5		6	1	2					10			7

Barnsley

15th in Division Two

	Date	Opponent	Score	Scorers	Att.	Allen F	Ashton E	Baines CE	Baker LH	Batty W	Brook EFG	Caddick GFR	Curran J	Dixon C	Eaton F	Fletcher B	Gale T	Godderidge AE	Hodgkinson H	Jones WD	McDonagh P	Morton R	Proudfoot J	Richards A	Scott JW	Stark JW	Tilson SF	Wilshaw J
1	Aug 27	HULL CITY	1-1	Eaton	10830	4		6			11	5	7	2	9	8	1		3								10	
2	29	Leeds United	2-2	Tilson, Fletcher (p)	21219	4		6			11	5	7	2	9	8	1		3								10	
3	Sep 3	Preston North End	2-1	Fletcher (p), Curran	20431	4		6			11	5	7	2	9	8	1		3								10	
4	10	SWANSEA TOWN	3-3	Eaton 2, Curran	13643	4		6			11	5	7	2	9	8	1		3								10	
5	17	Fulham	1-3	Tilson	16924	4		6			11	5	7	2	9	8	1		3								10	
6	24	CLAPTON ORIENT	4-2	McDonagh 2, Fletcher, Curran	11951	4		6			11	5	7	2		8	1		3		10						9	
7	26	LEEDS UNITED	2-1	Tilson, Brook	13038	4		6			11	5	7	2		8	1		3		10						9	
8	Oct 1	WOLVERHAMPTON W.	2-2	Fletcher, Brook	9082	4		6			11	5	7	2		8	1		3		10						9	
9	8	Port Vale	1-2	Fletcher (p)	10010	4		6			11	5	7	2		8	1		3		10						9	
10	15	SOUTH SHIELDS	0-0		10611	4		6			11	5	7	2		8	1		3		10						9	
11	22	Stoke City	0-0		8323	4		6			11	5	7	2		8	1		3		10						9	
12	29	BRISTOL CITY	2-3	Fletcher (p), Baines	10079	4		6			11	5	7	2		8	1		3		10						9	
13	Nov 5	West Bromwich Albion	1-1	Fletcher	18129	8		6			11	5	7	2		10	1		3	4							9	
14	12	SOUTHAMPTON	0-1		7621	8		6			11	5	7	2		10	1		3	4							9	
15	19	Notts County	0-9		9382	8		6	5	3	11		7	2		10	1			4							9	
16	26	READING	2-0	Eaton, Tilson	7181	4		6			11	5	7	2	9		1		3		8						10	
17	Dec 3	Grimsby Town	1-3	Brook	10421	4		6			11	5	7	2	9		1		3		8						10	
18	10	OLDHAM ATHLETIC	0-1		4944	4		6			11	5	7	2		8	1		3							9	10	
19	17	Blackpool	3-1	Tilson 2, Curran	7629			6			11	5	7	2	9		1		3	4			8				10	
20	24	CHELSEA	3-1	Tilson, Curran (p), Proudfoot	5634			6			11	5	7	2	9		1		3	4			8				10	
21	26	MANCHESTER CITY	0-3		17252				6	3	11	5	7	2	9		1			4			8				10	
22	31	Hull City	1-2	Eaton	9569				6		11	5	7	2	9		1			4			8	3			10	
23	Jan 2	Manchester City	3-7	Curran 2 (1p), Tilson	38226				6		11	5	7	2	9		1			4			8	3			10	
24	7	PRESTON NORTH END	2-1	Curran, Brook	7967	4		6			11	5	7	2	9			1					8	3			10	
25	21	Swansea Town	0-3		6420	4		6	3		11	5	7	2	9			1					8				10	
26	28	FULHAM	8-4	Eaton 4, Curran 2, Brook 2	4563	4		6			11	5	7	2	9	8		1	3								10	
27	Feb 4	Clapton Orient	0-2		8985	4		6			11	5	7	2	9	8		1	3								10	
28	11	Wolverhampton Wan.	1-2	Tilson	7151	4		6			11	5	7	2	9	8		1	3								10	
29	20	PORT VALE	4-2	Tilson, Eaton, Brook, Curran	5423	4		6			11	5	7	2	9			1	3				8				10	
30	25	South Shields	0-0		5513	4		6			11	5	7	2	9			1	3								10	8
31	Mar 10	Bristol City	0-2		12662			6	4		11	5	7	2	9			1	3							8	10	
32	17	WEST BROMWICH ALB.	2-4	Fletcher 2	8144	4		6	5				7	2	10	8		1	3						11			9
33	19	STOKE CITY	3-1	Scott 2, Eaton	4658			6				5	7	2	9	8		1	3	4			10		11			
34	24	Southampton	1-6	Fletcher	10528			6				5	7	2	9	8		1	3	4			10		11			
35	31	NOTTS COUNTY	0-0		5619			6	4			5	7	2	9	8		1	3				10		11			
36	Apr 7	Reading	1-1	Curran	10659			6	4			5	7	2	9			1	3				10		11	8		
37	9	Nottingham Forest	1-1	Morton	11640		7	6	5					2	9	8		1	3	4		11	10					
38	10	NOTTM. FOREST	2-1	Curran, Eaton	7688	4		6	5				7	2	9	8		1	3						11	10		
39	14	GRIMSBY TOWN	1-4	Fletcher	4516	4		6	5				7	2	9	8		1	3				10		11			
40	21	Oldham Athletic	1-0	Baker	7036				6			5	7	2	9	8	1		3	4			10		11			
41	28	BLACKPOOL	2-1	Eaton, Scott (p)	4949				6	4		5	7	2	9	8	1		3				10		11			
42	May 5	Chelsea	2-1	Eaton 2	13707		7	6		4		5		2	9	8	1		3				10		11			
					Apps	28	2	37	14	4	31	37	40	42	31	29	26	16	36	12	9	1	17	3	10	4	31	2
					Goals			1	1		7		13		15	11					2	1	1		3		10	

F.A. Cup

	Date	Opponent	Score	Scorers	Att.	Allen F	Ashton E	Baines CE	Baker LH	Batty W	Brook EFG	Caddick GFR	Curran J	Dixon C	Eaton F	Fletcher B	Gale T	Godderidge AE	Hodgkinson H	Jones WD	McDonagh P	Morton R	Proudfoot J	Richards A	Scott JW	Stark JW	Tilson SF	Wilshaw J
R3	Jan 14	Port Vale	0-3		13162	8		6			11	5	7	2	9			1		4				3			10	

Barrow

19th in Division Three (North)

						Adams W	Agar A	Brown D	Brown N	Chalcroft H	Cochrane AF	Dixon WH	Gore T	Harwood JA	Hatch TH	Letham C	Maconnachie JSJ	MacDonald E	McGuire A	Melville J	Miller W	Mortimer R	Nairn J	Parsons J	Parton J	Postlethwaite TW	Roebuck F	Smith W	Walker H	Wharton CN
1	Aug 27	ROCHDALE	1-3	D Brown	7783		7	9			1	4	5		2			11			6						3	10	8	
2	29	Halifax Town	2-5	McDonald, Mortimer	7769		7	9			1	4	5		2			11			6	8					3	10		
3	Sep 3	Rotherham United	0-3		4227		7	9			1	4	5		2			11			6							10	8	
4	10	SOUTHPORT	3-1	D Brown, Agar, Smith (p)	6154		7	9			1	4	5		2			11			6						3	10	8	
5	12	Nelson	0-4		4928		7	9			1	4	5		2			11			6						3	10	8	
6	17	Durham City	1-4	Walker	1895		7	9			1	2	5					11			6	4					3	10	8	
7	24	WREXHAM	2-2	Smith, Agar	4426		7	9			1	6	2			4		11			5						3	10	8	
8	29	NELSON	3-1	D Brown 2, Agar	4306		7	9			1	6	2			4		11		10							3	5	8	
9	Oct 1	Chesterfield	0-6		2338		7	9			1	6	2			4		11				10					3	5	8	
10	8	BRADFORD PARK AVE.	0-0		8316		7	9			1	6	2			4		11		10							3	5	8	
11	15	Tranmere Rovers	0-5		5666		7	9			1		2	5		4		11		10							3	6	8	
12	22	BRADFORD CITY	0-0		4673		7	9		8			2	5		4		11									3	10	6	1
13	Nov 5	LINCOLN CITY	3-3	Agar 2, Chalcroft	5131		7	9		8			2	5		4		11									3	10	6	1
14	19	CREWE ALEXANDRA	1-1	Mortimer	3869		7				1	6	2		3	4		11		10		9						5	8	
15	Dec 3	DARLINGTON	2-0	D Brown, Mortimer	4327		7	8					5		2	4		11			6	9					3	10		1
16	10	Ashington	0-1		1680		7	8					5		2	4		11			6	9					3	10		1
17	17	WIGAN BOROUGH	6-2	Mortimer 2,Smith 2,McDonald,D Brown	4110		7	8					5		2	4		11			6	9					3	10		1
18	24	Accrington Stanley	1-5	Smith	3129		7	8					5		2	4		11			6	9					3	10		1
19	26	Stockport County	0-4		8697		7	9			1		5		2	4		11			6						3	10	8	
20	27	STOCKPORT COUNTY	2-3	Letham, McDonald (p)	6225		7	9			1		5		2	4		11			6						3	10	8	
21	31	Rochdale	0-3		3973			8				6	2		7	4		11	10		5	9			3					1
22	Jan 2	Hartlepools United	2-6	McDonald, D Brown	3377			8			1	6				4		11	10		5				3	9			2	
23	7	ROTHERHAM UNITED	1-1	Dixon	2804			8				6	2		3	4		11			5	9						10		1
24	14	Doncaster Rovers	0-4		6120				5			6	2		3	4		11		9	10					7		8		1
25	21	Southport	0-4		3051				5			6	2		3	4		11			10	9				7		8		1
26	28	DURHAM CITY	1-2	Smith	3117		7					6	2		3	9		11		10	4							5	8	1
27	Feb 4	Wrexham	0-5		2438		7	8				6	2		3	4	9	11			5							10		1
28	11	CHESTERFIELD	2-0	Miller, Gore	3166		9						5		2	4	7	11			10				6	8	3			1
29	18	Bradford Park Avenue	1-1	Miller	11176		7						5		2			11			10			9	6	8	3	4		1
30	25	TRANMERE ROVERS	2-1	Parsons, Miller	5119		7						5		2			11			10			9	6	8	3	4		1
31	Mar 3	Bradford City	1-4	Nairn	10084								5		2			11			10		7	9	6	8	3	4		1
32	10	NEW BRIGHTON	2-1	Parsons, McDonald	6232				5				2					11			10		7	9	6	8	3	4		1
33	17	Lincoln City	0-5		5202	2	7						5					11			10		8	9	6		3	4		1
34	24	HALIFAX TOWN	6-2	Parsons 3, Miller, McDonald(p), Smith	4470	3	7						5		2	4		11			10			9	6			8		1
35	31	Crewe Alexandra	1-4	Nairn	3536	3							5		2	4		11			10		7	9	6			8		1
36	Apr 6	HARTLEPOOLS UNITED	2-0	Parsons, Miller	7059	3							5		2	4		11			10		7	9	6			8		1
37	7	DONCASTER ROVERS	0-0		7989	3							5		2	4		11			10		7	9	6			8		1
38	14	Darlington	1-1	Agar	1904	3	7						5		2	4		11			10		9	8	6					1
39	18	New Brighton	3-3	Miller, McDonald, Agar	1575	3	7						5		2	4		11			10		9	8	6					1
40	21	ASHINGTON	1-1	Nairn	7273	3	7						5		2	4		11			10		9		6			8		1
41	28	Wigan Borough	0-1		3355	3	7								2	4		11			10		9	8	6			5		1
42	May 5	ACCRINGTON STANLEY	1-0	Parsons	6561	3							5		2	4		11			10		7	9	6	8				1
					Apps	10	31	23	3	2	15	18	40	3	31	31	2	42	2	6	35	11	11	13	17	9	24	36	17	27
					Goals		7	7		1		1	1			1		7			6	5	3	7				7	1	

Played in one game: M Purcell (3, at 3).

Played in games 22 and 23 at 7: P Rawlinson

F.A. Cup

						Adams W	Agar A	Brown D	Brown N	Chalcroft H	Cochrane AF	Dixon WH	Gore T	Harwood JA	Hatch TH	Letham C	Maconnachie JSJ	MacDonald E	McGuire A	Melville J	Miller W	Mortimer R	Nairn J	Parsons J	Parton J	Postlethwaite TW	Roebuck F	Smith W	Walker H	Wharton CN
Q4	Nov 12	Workington	1-3	Agar			7	9		8			2	5		4		11									3	10	6	1

Birmingham

11th in Division One

	Date	Opponent	Score	Scorers	Att	Barton PH	Bloxham A	Bond B	Bradford J	Briggs GR	Bruce H	Coxford J	Cringan JA	Crosbie JA	Curtis ER	Dale RA	Davies SC	Ellis WT	Firth J	Harris WN	Hibbs HE	Johnson A	Leslie AJ	Liddell GM	Morrall GR	Pike TE	Randle J	Smith J	Stainton RG	Threlfall W	Tremelling RD	Womack F
1	Aug 27	Tottenham Hotspur	0-1		37408	3		7	9	10			5							8			6	4						11	1	2
2	29	HUDDERSFIELD T	3-1	Bradford 2, Harris	16432			7	9	10			5							8			6	4				2		11	1	3
3	Sep 3	MANCHESTER UNITED	0-0		25863			7	9	10			5							8			6	4				2		11	1	3
4	7	Sunderland	2-4	Bond, Bradford	23007			7	9	10	4					5				8		11	6					2			1	3
5	10	Everton	2-5	Bradford. Briggs	37386			7	9	10						5				8		11	6	4				2			1	3
6	17	CARDIFF CITY	1-3	Bond	23723			7	9	10	3			8		5				11			6	4				2			1	
7	24	Blackburn Rovers	4-4	Bradford 4	15331			7	9	10	3	5								8			6	4				2		11	1	
8	Oct 1	BOLTON WANDERERS	1-1	Harris	15988			7	9	10		5								8			6	4				2	3	11	1	
9	8	Sheffield Wednesday	3-2	Briggs 2, Bradford	19974	3	7		9	10		5								8		11	6	4				2			1	
10	15	MIDDLESBROUGH	3-2	Bradford, Bloxham, Briggs	17143		7		9	10		5				4				8		11	6	3				2			1	
11	22	BURY	2-2	Harris, Bradford	11925			7	9	10			5			4				8		11	6					2			1	3
12	29	Sheffield United	1-3	Bond	17128	5		7	9	10						4			8			11	6					2			1	3
13	Nov 5	ASTON VILLA	1-1	Crosbie	47605			7	9	10			5	8		4						11	6					2			1	3
14	12	Burnley	1-2	Bradford	14648			7	9	10			5	8		4						11	6				3	2			1	
15	19	ARSENAL	1-1	Crosbie	10030			7	9	10			5	8			4					11	6				3	2			1	
16	26	Portsmouth	2-2	Crosbie 2	18549			7		10		5	4	8			9	11					6				3	2			1	
17	Dec 3	LEICESTER CITY	0-2		24272		7			9		4	5	8			10	11			1		6				3	2				
18	10	Liverpool	3-2	Davies, Briggs 2	24255				9	7			5	8			10	11					6	4			3	2			1	
19	17	WEST HAM UNITED	1-2	Bradford	18206				9	7			5	8			10	11					6	4			3	2			1	
20	24	Derby County	1-4	Bradford	8535			7	9				5	8			10	11					6		4		3				1	2
21	26	SUNDERLAND	1-1	Davies	20120	4			9	7			5	8			10	11			1		6				3					2
22	31	TOTTENHAM HOTSPUR	3-2	Bradford 2, Briggs	11603	4		11	9	7			5	8			10				1		6				3					2
23	Jan 2	Newcastle United	1-1	Briggs	34434			11	9	7			5	8			10				1		6		4		3					2
24	7	Manchester United	1-1	Briggs	16853			8	9	7			5				10	11			1		6		4		3					2
25	21	EVERTON	2-2	Ellis, Briggs	33675				9	7			5	8			10	11					6		4		3				1	2
26	Feb 4	BLACKBURN ROVERS	2-1	Bradford 2	21425				9	7			5	8			10	11			1		6		4		3	2				
27	11	Bolton Wanderers	2-3	Bradford, Crosbie	11747				9	7			5	8			10	11			1		6	4			3	2				
28	22	Cardiff City	1-2	Briggs	10758				9	7			5	8				11	10		1		6		4		3	2				
29	25	Middlesbrough	1-1	Firth	18329				9	7			5	8				11	10				6	2	4		3				1	
30	Mar 3	Bury	3-2	Bradford 2, Briggs	13164	5			9	7				8				11	10				6	2	4		3				1	
31	7	SHEFFIELD WEDNESDAY	1-0	Ellis	12076	5			9	7				8				11	10				6	2	4		3				1	
32	10	SHEFFIELD UNITED	4-1	Briggs 3, Bond	22860	5		7		9			4	8	10			11					6				3	2			1	
33	17	Aston Villa	1-1	Bradford	59367	5			9	7			4	8	10			11					6	2			3				1	
34	24	BURNLEY	4-0	Bradford 3, Crosbie	23689	5			9	7			4	8	10			11					6	2			3				1	
35	31	Arsenal	2-2	Crosbie, Ellis	13990	5		7					4	8	10		9	11					6	2			3				1	
36	Apr 7	PORTSMOUTH	2-0	Bond, Ellis	32996	5		7		9				8	10			11					6	4			3	2			1	
37	9	Huddersfield Town	0-2		28779			11	9	7		5		8	10								6	4			3	2			1	
38	10	NEWCASTLE UNITED	0-2		23436	5		11	9	7					10				8				6	4			3				1	2
39	14	Leicester City	0-3		17558				9	7		5		8	10			11					6	2	4		3				1	
40	21	LIVERPOOL	2-0	Bradford 2	16063	5			9	7				8	10								6	4		11	3	2			1	
41	28	West Ham United	3-3	Bradford 2, Briggs	17917	5			9	7				8	10								6	4		11	3	2			1	
42	May 5	DERBY COUNTY	2-1	Curtis, Carr (og)	16430	5		7	10	9					8								6	4		11	3	2			1	

	Barton PH	Bloxham A	Bond B	Bradford J	Briggs GR	Bruce H	Coxford J	Cringan JA	Crosbie JA	Curtis ER	Dale RA	Davies SC	Ellis WT	Firth J	Harris WN	Hibbs HE	Johnson A	Leslie AJ	Liddell GM	Morrall GR	Pike TE	Randle J	Smith J	Stainton RG	Threlfall W	Tremelling RD	Womack F
Apps	16	3	24	37	40	3	8	25	28	11	8	14	20	6	11	8	9	42	25	10	3	29	27	1	5	34	15
Goals		1	5	29	16				7	1		2	4	1	3												

One own goal

F.A. Cup

	Date	Opponent	Score	Scorers	Att	Barton PH	Bloxham A	Bond B	Bradford J	Briggs GR	Bruce H	Coxford J	Cringan JA	Crosbie JA	Curtis ER	Dale RA	Davies SC	Ellis WT	Firth J	Harris WN	Hibbs HE	Johnson A	Leslie AJ	Liddell GM	Morrall GR	Pike TE	Randle J	Smith J	Stainton RG	Threlfall W	Tremelling RD	Womack F
R3	Jan 14	PETERBRO' & FLETTON U	4-3	Davies, Bradford 3	38128			7	9				5	8			10	11					6		4		3				1	2
R4	28	Wrexham	3-1	Randle (p), Davies 2	12228				9	7			5	8			10	11			1		6		4		3	2				
R5	Feb 18	Manchester United	0-1		52568				9	7			5	8			10	11			1		6	4			3	2				

Blackburn Rovers

12th in Division One: FA Cup Winners

							Campbell AF	Cope H	Crawford JC	Harper EC	Healless H	Holland PB	Hutton J	Jones H	McIntyre JMcG	McLean T	Mitchell T	O'Dowd JP	Puddefoot SC	Rankin W	Rigby A	Roscamp J	Roxburgh R	Shaw GA	Thornewell G	Walter JD	Whyte J
1	Aug	27	BURNLEY	2-1	McLean, Puddefoot	32441			1	9	4		2	3		10			8	5	11					7	6
2	Sep	3	Bolton Wanderers	1-3	Harper	25711			1	9	4		2	3		10			8	5	11					7	6
3		5	CARDIFF CITY	0-0		14343			1	9	4	7	2	3			11		8	5	10						6
4		10	SHEFFIELD WEDNESDAY	3-1	Whyte 2, McLean	17877			1	9	4	7	2	3		10			8	5	11						6
5		12	Cardiff City	1-1	Harper	15955	6		1	9	4	7	2	3		10			8	5	11						
6		17	Middlesbrough	0-2		28300	6		1	9	4	7	2	3		10			8	5	11						
7		19	MANCHESTER UNITED	3-0	Puddefoot 2, Harper	18243	6		1	9	4	7	2	3		10	11		8	5							
8		24	BIRMINGHAM	4-4	Harper 3, Healless	15331	6		1	9	4	7	2	3		10	11		8	5							
9	Oct	1	Newcastle United	1-0	Harper	30869	6		1	9	4	7	2	3		10			8	5							11
10		8	HUDDERSFIELD T	1-1	Puddefoot	28032	6		1	9	4	7	2	3		10			8	5	11						
11		15	Tottenham Hotspur	1-1	Rigby	23020			1	9	4	7	2	3		10			8	5	11						6
12		22	LEICESTER CITY	0-0		11115			1	9	4		2			10			8	5	11		3			7	6
13		29	Liverpool	2-4	Puddefoot 2	28489			1		4			3		10	9		8	5	11	7	2				6
14	Nov	5	ARSENAL	4-1	Mitchell 3, Rigby	9656			1		4		2	3		10	9		8	5	11	7					6
15		12	Portsmouth	2-2	Mitchell, Puddefoot	18078			1		4	7	2			10	9		8	5	11		3				6
16		19	WEST HAM UNITED	1-0	Mitchell	14040	5		1		4	7	2			10	9		8		11		3				6
17		26	Aston Villa	0-2		27281	6		1		4	7	2	3	11	8	9			5	10						
18	Dec	3	SUNDERLAND	0-0		16175	6		1		4	7	2	3	11	8	9			5	10						
19		10	Derby County	0-6		10612	6		1		4	7	2	3		10	9			5	11	8					
20		17	SHEFFIELD UNITED	1-0	Healless	12588	6		1		4		2	3		10	9		8	5	11	7					
21		24	Bury	3-2	McLean, Mitchell, Roscamp	12855	6		1		4		2	3		10	9		8	5	11	7					
22		26	Manchester United	1-1	Rigby	38131	5		1		4		2	3		10	9		8		11	7					6
23		31	Burnley	1-3	Mitchell	28354	5		1		4		2	3		10	9		8		11				7		6
24	Jan	2	EVERTON	4-2	Puddefoot 2, Mitchell, Rigby	39300	5	1			4		2	3		10	9		8		11				7		6
25		7	BOLTON WANDERERS	1-6	Mitchell	14660		1			4		2	3		10	9		8	5	11				7		6
26		21	Sheffield Wednesday	1-4	Holland	36094	5		1		4	9	2			10			8		11		3		7		6
27	Feb	4	Birmingham	1-2	Mitchell	21425	6		1		4			3			9		8	5	11	7	2	10			
28		11	NEWCASTLE UNITED	1-0	Mitchell	12504	6		1		4		2			10	9		8	5	11	7	3				
29		23	MIDDLESBROUGH	3-0	Roscamp 2, Puddefoot	12855	5		1		4	7	2	3			10	6	8		11	9					
30		25	TOTTENHAM HOTSPUR	2-1	Mitchell , Roscamp	20890	5		1		4	7		3			10	6	8		11	9	2				
31	Mar	10	LIVERPOOL	2-1	McLean , Roscamp	16249	5		1		4	7	2			10		6	8		11	9	3				
32		14	Huddersfield Town	1-3	Roscamp	10890	6		1		4	7		3		10	8	5			11	9	2				
33		17	Arsenal	2-3	Puddefoot, Rigby	33446	6		1					3		10		4	8	5	11	9	2		7		
34		31	West Ham United	3-4	Roscamp 2, Thornewell	17917	6		1			10	2					4	8	5	11	9	3		7		
35	Apr	6	Everton	1-4	Holland	48521	6		1			10	2	3			8			5	11	9			7		4
36		7	ASTON VILLA	0-1		21432	6		1			10	2	3			8			5	11	9			7		4
37		14	Sunderland	0-1		12577	6		1		4		2	3		10	8			5	11	9			7		
38		24	PORTSMOUTH	6-0	Puddefoot 2, Roscamp 2, Rigby, Campbell (p)	35516	6		1		4		2	3		10			8	5	11	9			7		
39		26	DERBY COUNTY	3-2	Mitchell , Rigby, Campbell (p)	21438	6		1		4		2	3			10		8	5	11	9			7		
40		28	Sheffield United	3-2	Mitchell 2, Roscamp	25239	6		1		4		2	3		10	11	5	8			9			7		
41		30	Leicester City	0-6		14914	6		1		4	9	2	3		10	11	5	8						7		
42	May	5	BURY	0-1		16836	6		1		4	9	2	3			10		8	5	11				7		
						Apps	32	2	40	12	38	24	37	35	2	33	28	8	35	31	37	20	12	1	14	3	18
						Goals	2			7	2	2				4	15		13		7	11			1		2

F.A. Cup

							Campbell AF	Cope H	Crawford JC	Harper EC	Healless H	Holland PB	Hutton J	Jones H	McIntyre JMcG	McLean T	Mitchell T	O'Dowd JP	Puddefoot SC	Rankin W	Rigby A	Roscamp J	Roxburgh R	Shaw GA	Thornewell G	Walter JD	Whyte J
R3	Jan	14	NEWCASTLE UNITED	4-1	Mitchell 2, Puddefoot, Thornewell	27652	6		1		4		2			10	9		8	5	11		3		7		
R4		28	Exeter City	2-2	Rigby, Roscamp	17330	6		1		4		2			10			8	5	11	9	3		7		
rep	Feb	2	EXETER CITY	3-1	Mitchell, Puddefoot, Roscamp	28348	6		1		4		2			10	9		8	5	11	7	3				
R5		18	PORT VALE	2-1	Mitchell, Roscamp	43700	6		1		4		2	3		10	9		8	5	11	7					
R6	Mar	3	MANCHESTER UNITED	2-0	Puddefoot 2	42312	6		1		4	7	2	3			10		8	5	11	9					
SF		24	Arsenal	1-0	Roscamp	25633	6		1		4	10	2	3					8	5	11	9			7		
F	Apr	21	Huddersfield Town	3-1	Roscamp 2, McLean	92041	6		1		4		2	3		10			8	5	11	9			7		

SF at Filbert Street, Leicester. Final at Wembley Stadium.

Blackpool

19th in Division Two

No	Date	Opponent	Res	Scorers	Att	Ayres GA	Barnett LH	Benton WH	Brookes S	Browell T	Cowan W	Crompton L	Crook MS	Downes P	Fishwick AE	Grant WM	Grimwood JB	Hampson J	Hughes RA	Malpas E	McIntyre JMcG	Meredith J	Mobbs FW	Neal RM	Oxberry J	Purdy A	Ramsay SH	Thorpe P	Tilford A	Tremelling WR	Tufnell SJ	Watson A	Williams H	Wright R
1	Aug 27	SWANSEA TOWN	2-2	Tremelling, Downes	15771	5		6		8		1	10	11								7						2	3	9		4		
2	29	OLDHAM ATHLETIC	1-2	Adlam (og)	16690	5		6		8		1	10	11								7						2	3	9		4		
3	Sep 3	Chelsea	0-3		36529	5		6		8		1	10	11								7						2	3	9		4		
4	5	Oldham Athletic	0-6		14542			6		8		1	10	11						5		7						2	3	9		4		
5	10	CLAPTON ORIENT	0-1		12337			6		8	9		10	11			5					7	1					2	3			4		
6	17	West Bromwich Albion	3-6	Tufnell 2, Williams	19605			6		8				11			5					7	1					2	3		10	4	9	
7	24	BRISTOL CITY	6-2	Browell 3, Watson, Williams, Tufnell	12507			6		8				11			5					7	1					2	3		10	4	9	
8	Oct 1	Stoke City	0-2		9293			6		8				11			5					7	1					2	3		10	4	9	
9	8	SOUTHAMPTON	1-0	Williams	11875			6		8				11			5					7	1					2	3		10	4	9	
10	15	Notts County	1-3	Hampson	11885	5		6						11				8				7	1					2	3		10	4	9	
11	22	MANCHESTER CITY	2-2	Hampson 2	17013		5	6		8				11				9				7	1					2	3		10	4		
12	29	Hull City	2-2	Neal, Hampson	9067		2	6		8								9				7	1	11				5	3		10	4		
13	Nov 5	PRESTON NORTH END	4-1	Benton 2 (2p), Meredith, Tufnell	10789		2	6		8								9				7	1	11				5	3		10	4		
14	12	Nottingham Forest	1-4	Hampson	8602		2	6							8			9				7	1	11				5	3		10	4		
15	19	LEEDS UNITED	0-2		9008		2	6										8				7	1	11				5	3	9	10	4		
16	26	Wolverhampton Wan.	4-2	Hapson 3, Downes	13200			6		10				11				9				7	1					5	3		4	8		2
17	Dec 3	PORT VALE	1-6	Hampson	7662			6		10				11				9				7	1					5	3		4	8		2
18	10	South Shields	2-2	Downes, Hampson	5130				10	8				11		5		9					1	7				2	3		6	4		
19	17	BARNSLEY	1-3	Hampson	7629			8	10					11		5		9				7	1					2	3		6	4		
20	24	Fulham	2-2	Hampson, Neal	10853		3	4	10					11	8	5		9				7	1					2			6			
21	26	READING	3-1	Fishwick 3	13233			4					10		8	5		9				7	1	11				2			6			3
22	27	Reading	0-1		11841		3		10						8		5	9				7	1	11							6	4		2
23	31	Swansea Town	0-1		9185		3	6					10		8		5	9				7	1	11				2				4		
24	Jan 2	GRIMSBY TOWN	4-5	Crook 2 (1p), Hampson, Ayres	10347	6							10		8	5		9	4			7	1	11				2	3					
25	7	CHELSEA	2-4	Browell, Tremelling	8704	6	3			10						5		9	4			7	1	11						8				2
26	21	Clapton Orient	5-2	Neal 2, Browell, Hampson 2	11401		3	4		8						5		9			10	7	1	11						6				2
27	28	WEST BROMWICH ALB.	4-3	Hampson 2, Benton (p), McIntyre	8102		3	4		8						5		9			10	7	1	11						6				2
28	Feb 4	Bristol City	2-2	McIntyre, Browell	11395		3	4		8						5		9			10	7	1	11						6				2
29	11	STOKE CITY	3-1	Meredith, Hampson, Browell	8744		3	4		8						5		9			10	7		11		1				6				2
30	18	Southampton	0-2		12229		3			8						5		9			10	7		11		1				6	4			2
31	25	NOTTS COUNTY	3-3	Fishwick, Neal, Meredith	9423		3			8					9	5					10	7		11		1				6		4		2
32	Mar 3	Manchester City	1-4	Hampson	40906		3	4								5		9				7		11	8	1	10			6				2
33	10	HULL CITY	2-1	Oxberry, Downes	9988	5	3							11				9				7			8	1	10	2		6		4		
34	17	Preston North End	1-2	Benton (p)	22341	5	3	6						11				8				7			9	1	10	2				4		
35	24	NOTTM. FOREST	5-3	Hampson 4, Ramsey	8977	5	3					1		11				9				7			8		10	2		6		4		
36	31	Leeds United	0-4		19630	5	3					1		11				9				7			8		10	2		6		4		
37	Apr 6	Grimsby Town	3-3	Tremelling, Hampson 2	15097								7			5		9						11	8	1	10	2	3	6		4		
38	7	WOLVERHAMPTON W.	3-0	Neal, Browell, Oxberry	18030		3			10		1	7			5		9						11	8			2		6		4		
39	14	Port Vale	0-3		5321		3			10		1	7			5		9						11	8			2		6		4		
40	21	SOUTH SHIELDS	4-1	Tremelling, Hampson 2, Browell	8539		3			10			7			5		9						11	8	1		2		6		4		
41	28	Barnsley	1-2	Hampson	4949		3			10			7			5		9						11	8	1		2		6		4		
42	May 5	FULHAM	4-0	Hampson 3, Oxberry	14466		3			10			7			5		9						11	8	1		2		6		4		
					Apps	10	25	27	4	27	1	8	14	20	7	19	7	32	2	1	6	35	24	23	11	10	6	33	21	22	18	32	5	12
					Goals	1		4		9			2	4	4			31			2	3		6	3		1			4	4	1	3	

One own goal

F.A. Cup

Rd	Date	Opponent	Res	Scorers	Att	Ayres GA	Barnett LH	Benton WH	Brookes S	Browell T	Cowan W	Crompton L	Crook MS	Downes P	Fishwick AE	Grant WM	Grimwood JB	Hampson J	Hughes RA	Malpas E	McIntyre JMcG	Meredith J	Mobbs FW	Neal RM	Oxberry J	Purdy A	Ramsay SH	Thorpe P	Tilford A	Tremelling WR	Tufnell SJ	Watson A	Williams H	Wright R
R3	Jan 14	OLDHAM ATHLETIC	1-4	Neal	10349		3	4		8		1				5		9				7		11						10	6			2

Bolton Wanderers

7th in Division One

	Date	Opponent	Score	Scorers	Att.	Blackmore HA	Boston HJ	Butler W	Cope JW	Finney A	Gibson GB	Gill JJ	Gough H	Greenhalgh HW	Haworth R	Jack DBN	Jack RR	Jennins W	McClelland J	Murphy L	Nuttall H	Picken AH	Pym RH	Round JH	Seddon J	Smith JR	Thornborough EH	Vizard ET	Wagstaffe JT	Wright WB
1	Aug 27	Cardiff City	1-2	Smith	24107			7		3	10			2							4		1		5	9	6	11		
2	Sep 3	BLACKBURN ROVERS	3-1	Smith 2, Picken	25711			7		3	10			2							4	11	1		5	9	6			
3	5	EVERTON	1-1	R Jack	18734			7		3	10			2							4	11	1		5	9	6			
4	10	Bury	0-1		24593			7		3	10				2						4	11	1		5	9	6			8
5	14	Everton	2-2	Butler, Picken	22726			7	4	3	10				2							11	1		5	9	6			8
6	17	Sheffield Wednesday	0-3		19111			7	4	3	10				2						6	11	1		5	9				8
7	24	MIDDLESBROUGH	0-0		21720		7	8			10				2			6			4	11	1		5	9			3	
8	Oct 1	Birmingham	1-1	D Jack	15988	9		7		3	10				2	8					4	11	1		5		6			
9	8	NEWCASTLE UNITED	1-2	D Jack	30676	9		7		3	10				2	8					4	11	1		5		6			
10	15	Huddersfield Town	0-1		19818	9		7		3	10					8		2			4		1	5			6	11		
11	22	LIVERPOOL	2-1	Vizard, Blackmore	12024	9		7	4	3	10					8		2					1	5			6	11		
12	29	Arsenal	2-1	Gibson, Vizard	35787	9		7	4	3	10					8		2			6		1	5				11		
13	Nov 5	BURNLEY	7-1	Blackmore 4 (1p), D Jack 3	14340	9		7	4	3	10					8		2			6		1	5				11		
14	12	Leicester City	2-4	Wright, Blackmore	21249	9		7	4	3						8		2			6		1	5				11		10
15	19	PORTSMOUTH	3-1	D Jack, Wright, Blackmore	14302	9		7	4	3		1				8		2			6			5				11		10
16	26	Sunderland	1-1	D Jack	20406			7	4	3		1				8		2			6			5		9		11		10
17	Dec 10	West Ham United	0-2		18926			7	4	3		1				8		2			6			5		9		11		10
18	17	ASTON VILLA	3-1	Finney, Smith, Vizard	14852			7	4	3	10	1				8		2			6			5		9		11		
19	24	Sheffield United	3-4	D Jack 3	10503			7	4	3	10	1			2	8					6			5		9		11		
20	26	TOTTENHAM HOTSPUR	4-1	D Jack 2, Nuttall, Gibson	25229	9		7	4		10	1			2	8		3			6			5				11		
21	31	CARDIFF CITY	2-1	D Jack, Blackmore	15748	9		7	4	3	10	1			2	8					6			5				11		
22	Jan 2	DERBY COUNTY	1-3	Gibson	23569	9		7	4	3	10	1				8					6			5			2	11		
23	7	Blackburn Rovers	6-1	D Jack 2, Gibson 2, Smith 2	14660			7	4		10	1			2	8		3			6	11		5		9				
24	21	BURY	2-1	D Jack, Smith	23497			7	4		10	1			2	8		3		11				5		9				6
25	Feb 4	Middlesbrough	5-2	D Jack 2, Smith, Butler, Murphy	21109			7	4	3	10	1			2	8				11	6			5		9				
26	6	Tottenham Hotspur	2-1	Smith 2	18183			7	4	3	10	1			2	8				11				5		9				6
27	11	BIRMINGHAM	3-2	D Jack 2, Gibson	11747			7	4	3	10	1			2	8				11	6			5		9				
28	18	Newcastle United	2-2	D Jack, Murphy	28932			7		3	10	1			2	8				11	4				5	9				6
29	25	HUDDERSFIELD TOWN	0-1		44082			7		3	10	1			2	8				11	4				5	9				6
30	29	SHEFFIELD WEDNESDAY	2-0	D Jack 2	9786			7		3	10	1			2	8	9			11	4			5						6
31	Mar 3	Liverpool	2-4	D Jack, Gibson	37115			7	4	3	10	1			2	8	9			11	6				5					
32	10	ARSENAL	1-1	R Jack	15546		7	8	4		10		1		2		9	3		11	6				5					
33	17	Burnley	2-2	Butler, McClelland	15865			7	4	3	10		1		2	8			9	11	6				5					
34	24	LEICESTER CITY	3-3	McClelland 2, Butler	18142			7	4		10		1			8		3	9		2				5			11		6
35	31	Portsmouth	0-1		21846			7			10				2	8		3	9	11	4		1		5					6
36	Apr 6	MANCHESTER UNITED	3-2	McClelland, Vizard, Round	23795			7		3	10				2		8		9		4		1	5				11		6
37	7	SUNDERLAND	1-2	McClelland (p)	18064			7	4		10		1		2	8		3	9						5			11		6
38	9	Manchester United	1-2	McClelland	28590	9	11	7	4	3	10				2				8				1	5			6			
39	14	Derby County	0-1		12378		7		4	3	10				2		8		9		6		1		5			11		
40	21	WEST HAM UNITED	4-0	McClelland, Murphy, Butler, Nuttall	8520			7	4		10				2	8		3	9	11	6		1		5					
41	28	Aston Villa	2-2	Gibson, Boston	22895		7		4	3	10				2	8			9	11	6		1		5					
42	Mar 5	SHEFFIELD UNITED	1-1	McClelland	7958		7			3	10				2	8			9	11	4		1		5		6			
					Apps	12	6	39	28	33	38	17	4	3	28	33	6	18	10	14	36	9	21	21	21	18	21	18	1	16
					Goals	8	1	5		1	8					24	2		8	3	2	2		1		10		4		2

F.A. Cup

	Date	Opponent	Score	Scorers	Att.	Blackmore HA	Boston HJ	Butler W	Cope JW	Finney A	Gibson GB	Gill JJ	Gough H	Greenhalgh HW	Haworth R	Jack DBN	Jack RR	Jennins W	McClelland J	Murphy L	Nuttall H	Picken AH	Pym RH	Round JH	Seddon J	Smith JR	Thornborough EH	Vizard ET	Wagstaffe JT	Wright WB
R3	Jan 14	LUTON TOWN	2-1	Butler, Smith	20266			7	4		10	1			2	8		3						5		9	6			11
R4	28	Stoke City	2-4	Round, Murphy	23050			7	4	3	10	1			2	8				11	6			5		9				

Bournemouth & Boscombe Ath.

14th in Division Three (South)

						Baynham DM	Blair J	Bradford J	Buchanan J	Butt LG	Clifford P	Crumley JB	Crump LV	Drummond RC	Eyre CR	Halliwell JC	Hayward JW	Jones E	Maidment HW	McKay N	Miles WP	Pike TE	Robson JH	Saxton E	Smith CF	Stringfellow JF	Taylor FE	Threlfall W	Tyler W	Walker RG	Young A
1	Aug 27	SWINDON TOWN	2-0	Clifford, Eyre	10208		3				7		11		9	4	2				5		1		6	10	8				
2	31	SOUTHEND UNITED	2-3	Eyre, Taylor	5874		3				7		11		9	4	2				5		1		6	10	8				
3	Sep 3	Brentford	1-2	Stringfellow	11108		3				7		11		9	4	2				5		1		6	10	8				
4	7	Southend United	0-3		5631		3				7				9	4	2		11				1		6	10	8				5
5	10	LUTON TOWN	2-2	Eyre 2	6040	3					7				9	4	2		11		5		1		6	10	8				
6	17	Millwall	0-2		14371		3				7				9	4	2				5	11	1		6	10	8				
7	21	QUEEN'S PARK RANGERS	1-2	Pike	4440		3				7				9	4	2				5	11	1		6	10	8				
8	24	CRYSTAL PALACE	2-2	Eyre, Stringfellow	5933		3				7	1	11		9	4	2								6	10	8				5
9	Oct 1	Exeter City	1-4	Eyre	6136		3				7	1		8	9	4	2				5	11			6	10					
10	8	TORQUAY UNITED	1-1	Taylor	5781		3				7	1		8	9	4	2					11				10	5		6		
11	15	Norwich City	3-3	Stringfellow, Eyre, Campbell (og)	9675		3			4	7	1			9	6	2				10	11				8	5				
12	22	GILLINGHAM	3-0	Eyre, Miles, Pickering (og)	4119		3			4	7	1			9	6	2				10	11				8	5				
13	29	Coventry City	2-3	Miles, Eyre	10933		3	6		4	7	1			9		2				10	11				8	5				
14	Nov 5	NEWPORT COUNTY	0-0		5324		3	6			7	1			9	4	2				10	11				8	5				
15	12	Walsall	3-2	Eyre, Taylor 2	3917		3	6			7	1			9	4	2					11			5	8	10				
16	19	MERTHYR TOWN	2-1	Eyre 2	2077		3	6			7	1			9	4	2				5	11				8	10				
17	Dec 3	BRISTOL ROVERS	4-3	Eyre 2, Clifford, Pike	4414	3				4	7	1			9	6	2				5	11					8				
18	17	WATFORD	1-0	Eyre	3798		3	6			7	1			9	4	2				5	11				8	10				
19	24	Queen's Park Rangers	0-2		6260		3	6			7	1			9	4	2				5	11				8	10				
20	26	BRIGHTON & HOVE ALB	3-1	Maidment, Halliwell, Eyre	2288	2	3	6			7	1			9	4			11		5					8	10				
21	27	Brighton & Hove Albion	2-3	Stringfellow, Eyre	6380	2	3	6			7	1			9	4			11		5					8	10				
22	Jan 7	BRENTFORD	1-0	Taylor	4796	3		6			7	1			9	4				8	5	11		2			10				
23	21	Luton Town	3-3	Taylor, Maidment, Miles	6453		3	6				1			9	4	2		7		5	11				8	10				
24	28	MILLWALL	5-0	Miles 2, Taylor, Pike, Eyre	4695		3	6			7	1			9	4	2				5	11				8	10				
25	Feb 4	Crystal Palace	1-6	Eyre	10862		3	6			7	1			9	4	2				5					8	10	11			
26	11	EXETER CITY	2-0	Taylor 2	5863		3	6			7	1			9	4	2				5					8	10	11			
27	18	Torquay United	2-2	Eyre, Taylor	4236		3	6			7	1			9	4	2	8			5						10	11			
28	25	NORWICH CITY	2-1	Eyre, Hayward (p)	6041		3	6			7	1			9	4	2	8	11		5						10				
29	Mar 3	Gillingham	1-2	Hayward	6817		3	6			7	1			9	4	2	8	11		5						10				
30	10	COVENTRY CITY	2-3	Jones, Eyre	4493		3	6			7	1			9	4	2	8	11		5					10					
31	17	Newport County	3-4	Jones, Stringfellow, Eyre	3754		3	6			7	1			9	4	2	8	11		5					10					
32	21	Swindon Town	2-3	Stringfellow, Eyre	2685		3	6			7	1			9	4	2	8	11		5					10					
33	24	WALSALL	3-1	Eyre, Miles, Hayward (p)	4549		3	6			7	1			9	4	2		11		5					8	10				
34	31	Merthyr Town	1-1	Clifford	1039	2	3	6			7	1			9	4			11						5	8	10				
35	Apr 7	CHARLTON ATHLETIC	3-1	Stringfellow, Eyre 2	5764		3	6			7	1			9	4	2		11		5					8	10				
36	9	NORTHAMPTON T	1-1	Stringfellow	9099		3	6			7	1		11	9	4	2				5					8	10				
37	10	Northampton Town	1-1	Stringfellow	11693		3		8		7			11	9	4	2				5		1		6	10					
38	14	Bristol Rovers	0-3		5681		3	6	10		7			11	9	4	2						1		5	8					
39	16	Charlton Athletic	1-1	Drummond	1227			6	10		7			11	9	4	2				5		1			8				3	
40	21	PLYMOUTH ARGYLE	2-2	Eyre 2 (1p)	5495		3	6	10		7	1		11	9	4					2					8	5				
41	25	Plymouth Argyle	1-3	Eyre	5519		3	6	10		11				9	4					5		1			8				2	
42	28	Watford	0-2		5102	2	3	6	10		11				9	4							1		5	8	7				

Played in one game: W Chivers (17, at 10), TC Johnstone (41, 7)

	Baynham DM	Blair J	Bradford J	Buchanan J	Butt LG	Clifford P	Crumley JB	Crump LV	Drummond RC	Eyre CR	Halliwell JC	Hayward JW	Jones E	Maidment HW	McKay N	Miles WP	Pike TE	Robson JH	Saxton E	Smith CF	Stringfellow JF	Taylor FE	Threlfall W	Tyler W	Walker RG	Young A
Apps	7	38	28	6	4	41	30	4	7	42	41	35	6	13	1	35	16	12	1	14	37	34	3	1	2	2
Goals						3			1	30	1	3	2	2		6	3				9	10				

Two own goals

F.A. Cup

						Baynham DM	Blair J	Bradford J	Buchanan J	Butt LG	Clifford P	Crumley JB	Crump LV	Drummond RC	Eyre CR	Halliwell JC	Hayward JW	Jones E	Maidment HW	McKay N	Miles WP	Pike TE	Robson JH	Saxton E	Smith CF	Stringfellow JF	Taylor FE	Threlfall W	Tyler W	Walker RG	Young A
R1	Nov 26	Coventry City	2-2	Pike 2	13627		3	6			7	1			9	4	2				5	11				8	10				
rep	30	COVENTRY CITY	2-0	Pike, Eyre	5566		3	6			7	1			9	4	2				5	11				8	10				
R2	Dec 10	BRISTOL ROVERS	6-1	Taylor 2, Clifford 2, Miles, Eyre	9098		3	6			7	1			9	4	2				5	11				8	10				
R3	Jan 14	Sheffield Wednesday	0-3		26297		3	6	7			1			9	4	2				5	11				8	10				

Bradford City

6th in Division Three (North)

No	Date	Opponent	Score	Scorers	Att	Bancroft A	Barkas S	Bauld R	Burkinshaw R	Byrne D	Cairns T	Campbell J	Ewart J	Fowler JC	Harvey E	Hobson RGE	Islip E	Johnson J	Lloyd JE	Moore C	Poole JS	Ray GB	Richardson GE	Russell SR	Scriven A	Senior H	Shirlaw WP	Spence W	Summers W	Ward J	Watson W
1	Aug 27	Ashington	2-2	Bauld (p), Cairns	3841	5		6	9		10		1		7		8		4					2	11						3
2	31	DARLINGTON	0-1		15334	5		6	9		10		1		7		8		4					2	11						3
3	Sep 3	CREWE ALEXANDRA	4-1	Scriven 2, Burkinshaw, Moore	17491	5		6	9		10		1		7				4	8				2	11						3
4	10	Halifax Town	1-2	Burkinshaw	19935	5			9		10	6	1		7				4	8				2	11						3
5	17	BRADFORD PARK AVE.	2-3	Burkinshaw, Moore	37059			6	9		10		1		7				4	8			11	2					5		3
6	24	NEW BRIGHTON	3-1	Scriven, Harvey, Cairns	11701			6	8		10		1		7		9		4					2	11				5		3
7	Oct 1	Lincoln City	2-2	Burkinshaw, Harvey	6049			6	8		10		1		7		9		4					2	11				5		3
8	8	HARTLEPOOLS UNITED	2-1	Bauld 2	13762			9	8		10		1		7	4			6					2	11				5		3
9	15	Accrington Stanley	1-1	Burkinshaw	7428			9	8		10		1		7	4			6					2	11				5		3
10	22	Barrow	0-0		4673			9	8		10		1		7	4			6					2	11				5		3
11	29	STOCKPORT COUNTY	2-2	Bauld, Scriven	13582			9	8				1		7	4	10		6					2	11				5		3
12	Nov 5	Tranmere Rovers	1-2	Richardson	4882			6	8		10		1		7	4				9			11	2					5		3
13	12	NELSON	9-1	Cairns, Richardson 2, Moore 5, Harvey	15638			6	8		10		1		7	4				9			11	2					5		3
14	19	Rochdale	3-3	Harvey, Richardson, Summers	5952			6	8		10		1		7				4	9			11	2					5		3
15	Dec 3	Southport	1-5	Byrne	3841				8	9	10		1		7	4			6					2		11			5		3
16	17	Wrexham	0-1		4072				6	9	10		1	3	7	4				8			11	2					5		
17	24	CHESTERFIELD	3-3	Burkinshaw 2, Harvey	7236			6	8	9	10			3	7	4								2	11				5	1	
18	26	WIGAN BOROUGH	3-0	Scriven, Harvey, Burkinshaw	13748				8		10			3	7	4			6	9				2	11				5	1	
19	27	Wigan Borough	2-2	Islip, Scriven	4100	5			4		8			3	7		10			9	6			2	11					1	
20	31	ASHINGTON	5-0	Moore 2, Hobson, Burkinshaw, Cairns	5415	5			8		10		1	3	7	4			6	9				2	11						
21	Jan 2	Darlington	2-1	Moore, Harvey	5248	5			8		10		1	3	7	4			6	9				2	11						
22	7	Crewe Alexandra	1-2	Moore	5993			6	8		10			3	7				4	9				2	11				5	1	
23	14	DURHAM CITY	4-0	Harvey, Burkinshaw, Moore 2	4422			6	8		10			3	7				4	9			11	2					5	1	
24	21	HALIFAX TOWN	0-0		18747			6	8		10		1	3	7				4	9			11	2					5		
25	28	Bradford Park Avenue	0-5		21876				8		10		1	3	7	4			6	9			11	2					5		
26	Feb 4	New Brighton	1-1	Moore	2939		2		8		10		1		7	4			6	9			11						5		3
27	11	LINCOLN CITY	3-1	Cairns, Harvey, Richardson (p)	7229		2		8		10		1		7	4			6	9			11						5		3
28	18	Hartlepools United	3-2	Richardson, Burkinshaw, Hobson	4475		2		8		10		1		7	4			6	9			11						5		3
29	25	ACCRINGTON STANLEY	2-0	Burkinshaw, Harvey	10930				8		10		1		7	4			6	9			11	2					5		3
30	Mar 3	BARROW	4-1	Moore 2, Cairns, Richardson	10084				8		10		1		7	4			6	9			11	2					5		3
31	10	Stockport County	0-3		9984			10	5		8		1		7	4			6	9			11	2							3
32	14	ROTHERHAM UNITED	3-1	Cairns, Richardson, Scriven	3821	5		6			10		1		7				4	8			11	2	9						3
33	17	TRANMERE ROVERS	3-1	Bancroft, Scriven, Bauld (p)	9717	5		6			10				7				4	8				2	9	11	1				3
34	24	Nelson	3-0	Bauld, Harvey, Spence	5085	5		6			10				7				4	8				2		11	1	9			3
35	31	ROCHDALE	2-2	Scriven, Cairns	10565	5					10				7	4			6	8				2	9	11	1				3
36	Apr 6	Doncaster Rovers	1-2	Bauld	16134			6			10				7	4			5	8			11	2	9		1				3
37	7	Durham City	2-3	Harvey 2	2135			6			10		1		7	4			5	8			11	2	9						3
38	9	DONCASTER ROVERS	1-0	Cairns	13375			6			10				7	4			5	8			11	2			1	9			3
39	14	SOUTHPORT	2-0	Johnson, Richardson	9072	5					10				7	4		8	6	9			11	2			1				3
40	21	Rotherham United	0-0		2775	5			8		10				7				6	9		4	11	2			1				3
41	28	WREXHAM	2-0	Senior, Scriven	6844	5			4		10				7				6	8		2			9	11	1				3
42	May 5	Chesterfield	0-2		2152	5	2		4		10				7				6	8			11		9		1				3
					Apps	15	4	24	34	3	41	1	28	10	42	24	6	1	37	32	1	2	21	37	23	5	9	2	23	5	32
					Goals	1		7	12	1	9				13	2	1	1		16			9		10	1		1	1		

F.A. Cup

Rd	Date	Opponent	Score	Scorers	Att	Bancroft A	Barkas S	Bauld R	Burkinshaw R	Byrne D	Cairns T	Campbell J	Ewart J	Fowler JC	Harvey E	Hobson RGE	Islip E	Johnson J	Lloyd JE	Moore C	Poole JS	Ray GB	Richardson GE	Russell SR	Scriven A	Senior H	Shirlaw WP	Spence W	Summers W	Ward J	Watson W
R1	Nov 26	WORKINGTON	6-0	Cairns, Moore, Richardson 2, Burkinshaw 2	14579			6	8		10		1		7	4				9			11	2					5		3
R2	Dec 10	ROTHERHAM UNITED	2-3	Harvey, Richardson	9503				6	9	10		1	3	7	4				8			11	2					5		

Bradford Park Avenue

Champions of Division Three (North): Promoted

No	Date	Opponent	Score	Scorers	Att	Cartwright HP	Clough JH	Croot J	Davis H	Dickinson S	Duckett DT	Duffield A	Fell G	Hart I	Hawes AR	Little J	Lloyd T	Manderson R	Matthews RW	McDonald K	McLean G	Millership W	Quantrill AE	Rawlings A	Schofield HW	Smith IA	Taylor HW	Turnbull G
1	Aug 27	DURHAM CITY	4-0	McDonald 3, Lloyd	14040		1			6					10		3	2	5	9	8		11	7			4	
2	30	Southport	1-2	Hawes	6457		1			6					10		3	2	5	9	8		11	7			4	
3	Sep 3	Wrexham	1-1	Hawes	7579		1	4							10		3	2	5	9	8		11	7		6		
4	5	SOUTHPORT	5-3	McDonald 3, McLean, Rawlings	10429		1	4							10		3	2	5	9	8		11	7		6		
5	10	CHESTERFIELD	1-0	McLean	12816	7	1			6					10		3	2	5	9	8		11				4	
6	17	Bradford City	3-2	McLean, McDonald, Quantrill	37059	7	1			6					10		3	2	5	9	8		11			4		
7	24	Tranmere Rovers	2-2	Hawes, McDonald	5370	7	1			6					10		3	2	5	9	8		11			4		
8	Oct 1	STOCKPORT COUNTY	2-0	McDonald, Hawes	9838	7	1			6					10		2		5	9	8		11			4		3
9	8	Barrow	0-0		8316	7	1			6					10		3	2	5	9	8		11			4		
10	15	NELSON	3-2	Quantrill, McLean, McDonald	14833	7	1						4		10		3	2	5	9	8		11			6		
11	22	ASHINGTON	5-0	McLean, McDonald 2, Lloyd, Hawes	7315	7	1								10		3	2	5	9	8		11			6	4	
12	29	Crewe Alexandra	3-1	Quantrill, McDonald 2	5207	7	1								10		3	2	5	9	8		11			6	4	
13	Nov 5	HALIFAX TOWN	3-2	Hawes, Smith, McDonald	15727	7	1								10		3	2	5	9	8		11			6	4	
14	12	Darlington	3-1	Hawes, Cartwright, McDonald	7976	7	1								10		3	2	5	9	8		11			6	4	
15	19	DONCASTER ROVERS	0-2		22202	7	1								10		3	2	5	9	8		11			6	4	
16	Dec 3	ACCRINGTON STANLEY	3-3	Little, Davis, Smith	10337	7	1		8						10	11	2		5	9						6	4	3
17	17	LINCOLN CITY	3-0	McLean 2, Cartwright	10977	7	1		9	6					10		3	2	5		8		11				4	
18	24	New Brighton	2-1	Macdonald (og), Hart	2589	7	1			6				9	10		3	2	5		8		11				4	
19	27	ROCHDALE	4-1	Taylor, Quantrill, Hart 2	21762		1			6				9	10		3	2	5		8		11	7			4	
20	31	Durham City	1-0	McLean	2262		1			6				9	10	11	3	2	5		8			7			4	
21	Jan 3	Rochdale	4-0	Quantrill, Hart 3	5481		1		7	6				9	10		3	2	5		8		11				4	
22	7	WREXHAM	2-0	Hart, Hawes	13060		1		7	6				9	10		3	2	5		8		11				4	
23	14	Hartlepools United	1-1	Matthews	5023		1		7	6				9	10		3	2	5		8		11				4	
24	21	Chesterfield	0-0		6465		1		7	6					10		3	2	5	9	8		11				4	
25	28	BRADFORD CITY	5-0	McDonald 2, McLean, Hawes, Lloyd	21876		1		7		6				10		3	2	5	9	8		11				4	
26	Feb 1	Wigan Borough	3-1	McLean 2, Quantrill	2406		1		7	6					10		3	2	5	9	8		11				4	
27	4	TRANMERE ROVERS	6-2	McLean 2, McDonald 3, Hawes	13815		1		7		6				10		3	2	5	9	8		11				4	
28	11	Stockport County	2-2	McLean, Matthews	15775		1		7		6				10		3	2	5	9	8		11				4	
29	18	BARROW	1-1	Hawes	11176		1		7	6					10		3	2	5	9	8		11				4	
30	25	Nelson	2-1	McDonald 2	8096		1		7		6				10		3	2	5	9		8	11				4	
31	Mar 3	Ashington	3-0	McDonald 2, Davies	4052		1		7		6				10		3	2	5	9	8		11				4	
32	10	CREWE ALEXANDRA	2-0	McLean 2	9504		1		7		6				10		3	2	5	9	8		11				4	
33	17	Halifax Town	1-1	Hawes	15842		1		7		6				10		3	2	5	9	8		11				4	
34	24	DARLINGTON	6-3	Hawes, McLean, Quantrill 3, McDonald	16294		1		7		6				10		3	2	5	9	8		11				4	
35	31	Doncaster Rovers	0-2		14176		1		7		6				10		3	2	5	9	8		11				4	
36	Apr 7	HARTLEPOOLS UNITED	3-0	Millership, McDonald, McLean	12715		1		7		6						3	2	5	9	8	10	11				4	
37	9	Rotherham United	0-1		6288		1		7		6							2	5	9	8	10	11		3		4	
38	10	ROTHERHAM UNITED	3-1	Hart 2, McLean	14311		1		7	6	4			9	10		3	2	5		8		11					
39	14	Accrington Stanley	1-2	Hawes	4948		1		7		6			9	10		3	2	5		8		11				4	
40	21	WIGAN BOROUGH	5-1	McLean 3, McDonald 2	11236		1		7		6				10		3	2	5	9	8		11				4	
41	28	Lincoln City	0-2		9785		1		7		6				10		3	2	5	9	8		11				4	
42	May 5	NEW BRIGHTON	2-1	McLean, McDonald	9538		1		7		6	2			10		3		5	9	8		11				4	
					Apps	14	42	2	24	18	16	1	1	8	40	2	41	39	42	33	40	3	40	6	1	13	34	2
					Goals	2			2					9	14	1	3		2	29	23	1	9	1		2	1	

Two own goals

F.A. Cup

Rd	Date	Opponent	Score	Scorers	Att	Cartwright HP	Clough JH	Croot J	Davis H	Dickinson S	Duckett DT	Duffield A	Fell G	Hart I	Hawes AR	Little J	Lloyd T	Manderson R	Matthews RW	McDonald K	McLean G	Millership W	Quantrill AE	Rawlings A	Schofield HW	Smith IA	Taylor HW	Turnbull G
R1	Nov 26	Nelson	3-0	Cartwright 2, Hawes	9000	7	1								10	11	2		5	9	8					6	4	3
R2	Dec 10	SOUTHPORT	0-2		9226	7	1								10		3	2	5	9	8		11			6	4	

Brentford

12th in Division Three (South)

							Bailey H	Beacham AJ	Berry WG	Butler CJW	Cairns J	Craddock CW	Dearn S	Donnelly J	Douglas EAC	Drinnan JMcK	Ferguson JS	Fletcher AW	Hodge W	Lane JW	Lawson H	McCafferty J	Phillips J	Price WJ	Stevenson A	Ward S	Watkins ET	Wiggins JA	Winship E
1	Aug	27	Brighton & Hove Albion	2-5	Phillips, Drinnan	13164		4					6		11	10	1	5		8	7		9		2				3
2		29	NORTHAMPTON T	3-0	Phillips 3	8280				2			6		11		1	5	4	8	7		9				10		3
3	Sep	3	BOURNEMOUTH	2-1	Fletcher, Douglas	11108				2			6		11		1	5	4	8	7		9				10		3
4		5	Northampton Town	2-3	Lane, Watkins	7220				2			6		11		1	5	4	8	7		9				10		3
5		10	Queen's Park Rangers	3-2	Watkins, Lane, Phillips	18826		5		2			6		11		1		4	8	7		9				10		3
6		14	Bristol Rovers	3-1	Phillips, Watkins, Lawson	2578		5		2			6		11		1		4	8	7		9				10		3
7		17	Luton Town	2-5	Lawson 2	9182		5		2			6		11		1		4	8	7		9				10		3
8		24	MILLWALL	6-1	Douglas, Watkins (p), Phillips 2, Lawson 2	12513				2			6		11		1	5	4	8	7		9				10		3
9	Oct	1	Crystal Palace	2-0	Phillips, Lane	11552				2			6		11		1	5	4	8	7		9				10		3
10		8	EXETER CITY	1-1	Lawson	11326				2			6		11	10	1	5	4	8	7						9		3
11		15	Torquay United	1-2	Lawson	4185				2			6		11		1	5	4	8	7		9				10		3
12		22	COVENTRY CITY	4-1	Craddock 2, Hodge, Lane	4666		5		2		9			11		1	6	4	8		7					10		3
13		29	Newport County	0-3		5790		5		2		9			11		1	6	4	8	7						10		3
14	Nov	5	SWINDON TOWN	1-4	Lane	9527		5		2			6		11		1		4	8	7		9				10		3
15		12	Gillingham	1-2	Lawson	3293		4					6		11	10	1	5		8	7				2		9		3
16	Dec	3	PLYMOUTH ARGYLE	0-2		7537		4		2			6		11	10	1	5		8	7						9		3
17		5	WALSALL	3-2	Watkins, Dearn (p), Lane	2202				2			6		11		1		4	8	7					5	10	9	3
18		10	Merthyr Town	1-3	Craddock	2465		4	11	2		8	6				1	5			7						10	9	3
19		17	CHARLTON ATHLETIC	1-1	Berry	5245	1		11	2		8	10					6	4		7					5	9		3
20		24	Watford	1-1	Craddock	5226	1		11	2		9	10					6	4	8	7					5			3
21		26	Southend United	2-3	Craddock 2	3540	1		11	2		9	6						4	8	7					5	10		3
22		31	BRIGHTON & HOVE ALB	1-3	Lane	6061	1		11	2		9	6						4	8	7					5	10		3
23	Jan	7	Bournemouth	0-1		4796		5	11	2		10	6				1		4	8	7						9		3
24		21	QUEEN'S PARK RANGERS	0-3		10430		5	7	2		9	6		11		1	4		8							10		3
25		28	LUTON TOWN	4-2	Wilson 4	3291		4	7	2		8	6		11	10	1									5	9		3
26	Feb	4	Millwall	0-3		16885		5	7	2		8	6		11	10	1	4									9		3
27		11	CRYSTAL PALACE	2-1	Beacham, Drinnan	7580		5	7	2			6		11	10	1	4		8							9		3
28		18	Exeter City	1-0	Drinnan	7420		5	7	2			6		11	10	1	4		8							9		3
29		25	TORQUAY UNITED	1-2	Lane	8355		5	7	2			6		11	10	1	4		8			9						3
30	Mar	3	Coventry City	0-0		8188		5	7	2			6		11	10	1	4		8			9						3
31		10	NEWPORT COUNTY	3-1	Berry 2, Phillips	5759		5	11	2			6			10	1	4		8	7		9						3
32		17	Swindon Town	1-1	Phillips	6500	1	5	11	2			6			10		4		8	7		9						3
33		24	GILLINGHAM	2-0	Lane 2	6107	1	5	11	2			6			10		4		8	7		9						3
34		31	Walsall	2-4	Drinnan, Phillips	4750	1	5	11	2			6			10		4		8	7		9						3
35	Apr	6	NORWICH CITY	3-1	Berry, Price, Wiggins	11814	1	5	11	2			6					4		8	7			10				9	3
36		7	BRISTOL ROVERS	5-1	Wiggins, Cairns, Drinnan 2, Lawson	7894	1	5	11	2	8		6			10		4			7							9	3
37		9	Norwich City	1-1	Berry (p)	10848	1	5	11	2			6			10		4		8	7		9						3
38		14	Plymouth Argyle	0-1		5940	1	5	11	2			6			10		4		8	7		9						3
39		21	MERTHYR TOWN	4-0	Phillips 2, Berry, Lane	4583	1	5	11	2			6			10		4		8	7		9						3
40		23	SOUTHEND UNITED	2-2	Phillips 2	4889	1		11	2			6	3				4		8	7		9			5	10		
41		28	Charlton Athletic	2-3	Watkins, Phillips	7122	1	5	11	2			6					4		8	7		9				10		3
42	May	5	WATFORD	1-1	Phillips	4775	1	5	11	2			6					4		8	7		9				10		3
						Apps	15	29	25	40	1	11	40	1	24	18	27	33	19	37	34	1	23	1	2	7	29	4	41
						Goals		1	6		1	6	1		2	6		1	1	11	9		18	1			10	2	

F.A. Cup

							Bailey H	Beacham AJ	Berry WG	Butler CJW	Cairns J	Craddock CW	Dearn S	Donnelly J	Douglas EAC	Drinnan JMcK	Ferguson JS	Fletcher AW	Hodge W	Lane JW	Lawson H	McCafferty J	Phillips J	Price WJ	Stevenson A	Ward S	Watkins ET	Wiggins JA	Winship E
R3	Jan	14	Manchester United	1-7	Jones (og)	18538		5	7			10	6		11		1		4	8							9		2

Played at 3: Hendrie

Brighton & Hove Albion

4th in Division Three (South)

	Date	Opponent	Score	Scorers	Att	Chamberlain HG	Cook TER	Curran JJ	Hopkins J	James D	Jenkins J	Jennings S	Little WJ	Mace RS	Mooney P	Oswald W	Readman JA	Simpson TM	Smith R	Sykes EAA	Thomson NS	Wilkinson RG	Williams RG	Wilson E
1	Aug 27	BRENTFORD	5-2	Wilson, Jennings 3, Thomson	13164			3	10			9	6		5			7	2		8	4	1	11
2	Sep 1	Newport County	1-3	Thomson	6146			3	10			9	6		5			7	2		8	4	1	11
3	3	Luton Town	5-2	Cook, Simpson, Mooney 2, Hopkins	9468		9	3	10			8	6		5			7	2			4	1	11
4	10	MILLWALL	3-1	Cook 3	12984		9	3	10			8	6		5			7	2			4	1	11
5	14	NEWPORT COUNTY	1-4	Cook	3700		9	3	10			8	6		5			7	2			4	1	11
6	17	Crystal Palace	1-1	Hopkins	13557		9	3	10			8	6		5			7	2			4	1	11
7	24	EXETER CITY	0-2		10076		9	3	10			8	6		5			7	2			4	1	11
8	Oct 1	Torquay United	1-1	Wilson	2156		9				3		6		5	10	8	7	2			4	1	11
9	8	NORWICH CITY	1-0	Oswald	9286			3				8	6		5	10	9	7	2			4	1	11
10	15	Northampton Town	0-1		13214		10	3				8	6		5		9	7	2			4	1	11
11	22	WALSALL	0-0		2737		10	3		7		8	6		5		9		2			4	1	11
12	29	Gillingham	1-0	Jennings	4681	3	9		10	7		8	6		5				2			4	1	11
13	Nov 5	COVENTRY CITY	3-0	Cook, Jennings, Wilson	7153		9	3	10	7		8	6		5				2			4	1	11
14	12	Merthyr Town	2-4	James, Hopkins	3111		9	3	10	7		8	6		5				2			4	1	11
15	19	PLYMOUTH ARGYLE	4-1	Wilson, James, Cook, Smith	5552		9	3	10	7		8	6		5				2			4	1	11
16	Dec 3	CHARLTON ATHLETIC	2-2	Jennings, Cook	7992		9	3	10	7	2	8	6		5							4	1	11
17	17	QUEEN'S PARK RANGERS	1-3	Cook	5835		9	3	10	7	2	8	6		5							4	1	11
18	24	Swindon Town	3-4	Cook 2, Simpson	7455		9	3	10	8	2		6		5			7				4	1	11
19	26	Bournemouth	1-3	James	2288		9	3	10	8	2		6		5			7				4	1	11
20	27	BOURNEMOUTH	3-2	Simpson, Cook, Hopkins	6380		9	3	10	8	2		6	5				7				4	1	11
21	31	Brentford	3-1	Hopkins, Cook, Simpson	6061		9	3	10	8	2		6	5				7				4	1	11
22	Jan 7	LUTON TOWN	3-1	Cook 2, Wilson	5707		9	3	10	8	2		6	5				7				4	1	11
23	14	Watford	3-3	Hopkins, Cook 2	5912		9	3	10	8	2		6	5				7				4	1	11
24	21	Millwall	0-6		20696		9	3	10	8	2		6	5				7				4	1	11
25	28	CRYSTAL PALACE	4-2	James, Wilson 2, Cook	4494		9	3	10	8	2				5		7			6		4	1	11
26	Feb 4	Exeter City	3-0	Cook, Hopkins 2	6916		9	3	10	8	2				5			7		6		4	1	11
27	11	TORQUAY UNITED	3-0	Cook, Hopkins, Jenkins (p)	7430		9	3	10	8	2				5			7		6		4	1	11
28	18	Norwich City	0-0		8131		9	3	10	8	2				5	7				6		4	1	11
29	25	NORTHAMPTON T	2-1	Cook (p), Simpson	12631		9	3	10	8	2				5			7		6		4	1	11
30	Mar 3	Walsall	3-3	Mooney, Cook, James	6170		9	3	10	8	2				5			7		6		4	1	11
31	10	GILLINGHAM	0-0		7860		9	3	10	8	2				5			7		6		4	1	11
32	17	Coventry City	2-2	Hopkins, Little (p)	10695			3	10		2		6		5		9	7			8	4	1	11
33	24	MERTHYR TOWN	5-0	Thomson 2, Cook, Jenkins 2 (2p)	7663		9	3	10		2		6		5			7			8	4	1	11
34	31	Plymouth Argyle	0-2		6289		9	3	10	8	2		6		5			7				4	1	11
35	Apr 6	SOUTHEND UNITED	1-0	Simpson	11742		9	3	10		2				5			7		6	8	4	1	11
36	7	WATFORD	1-1	Hopkins	7969		9	3	10		2				5			7		6	8	4	1	11
37	9	Southend United	1-0	Hopkins	10407		9	3	10		2				5			7		6	8	4	1	11
38	14	Charlton Athletic	0-3		5930		9	3	10		2				5			7		6	8	4	1	11
39	21	BRISTOL ROVERS	5-0	Hopkins, Thomson, Cook 2, James	4118	3	9		10	7	2		6		5						8	4	1	11
40	23	Bristol Rovers	0-1		4155	3	9		10	7	2		6		5						8	4	1	11
41	28	Queen's Park Rangers	0-5		5394	3	9		10	7	2		6		5						8	4	1	11
42	May 5	SWINDON TOWN	4-2	Jennings 2, James 2	5757			3	10	8	2	9	6		5			7				4	1	11
					Apps	4	37	37	38	26	28	17	31	5	37	3	6	30	15	11	11	42	42	42
					Goals		25		13	8	3	8	1		3	1		6	1		5			7

F.A. Cup

	Date	Opponent	Score	Scorers	Att	Chamberlain HG	Cook TER	Curran JJ	Hopkins J	James D	Jenkins J	Jennings S	Little WJ	Mace RS	Mooney P	Oswald W	Readman JA	Simpson TM	Smith R	Sykes EAA	Thomson NS	Wilkinson RG	Williams RG	Wilson E
R1	Nov 30	Watford	2-1	James, Cook	6058		9	2	10	7	3	8	6		5							4	1	11
R2	Dec 10	Northampton Town	0-1		16092		9	3	10	7	2	8	6		5							4	1	11

Bristol City

12th in Division Two

No.	Date	Opponent	Score	Scorers	Att.	Blakemore C	Bourton CFT	Callaghan PJ	Cherrett PAM	Coggins WH	Dransfield W	Foster JTF	Garland GE	Geddes J	Gilhespy TWC	Glenn E	Hughes RG	Keating AE	Martin JC	Murray DJ	Neesam H	Newlands G	Paul JC	Pugsley J	Rankin A	Searle FB	Smailes A	Taylor JS	Torrance A	Wadsworth W	Walsh JJ	Walsh T	Williams B
1	Aug 27	Notts County	2-1	Blakemore, Gilhespy	15302	10				1					7	3			8		4				11		6			5	2	9	
2	31	PORT VALE	4-0	Martin 2, Gilhespy, T Walsh	20305	10				1					7	3			8		4				11		6			5	2	9	
3	Sep 3	OLDHAM ATHLETIC	2-1	Gilhespy, T Walsh	23694	10				1					7	3			8		4				11		6			5	2	9	
4	10	Grimsby Town	4-1	Gilhespy 2, Martin, T Walsh	13006	10				1					7	3			8		4				11		6			5	2	9	
5	17	READING	4-1	T Walsh 2, Gilhespy, Martin	22480	10				1					7	3			8		4				11		6			5	2	9	
6	19	Port Vale	1-5	Blakemore	11319	10				1					7	3			8		4				11		6			5	2	9	
7	24	Blackpool	2-6	Rankin, T Walsh	12507	10				1					7	3			8		4				11		6			5	2	9	
8	Oct 1	CHELSEA	1-1	Blakemore	24005	10			8	1					7	3							4	6	11					5	2	9	
9	8	Clapton Orient	2-4	Blakemore, Cherrett	21202	10		11	8	1					7	3							4	6						5	2	9	
10	15	WEST BROMWICH ALB.	0-1		24442	10		11	9	1					7	3			8				4	6						5	2		
11	22	FULHAM	3-0	Gilhespy, Martin, Wadsworth	7701				9	1					7	3		10	8				4		11		6			5	2		
12	29	Barnsley	3-2	Cherrett 2, Foster	10079			11	9	1		7				3		10	8				4				6			5	2		
13	Nov 5	WOLVERHAMPTON W.	4-1	Cherrett 2, Foster, Keating	14384			11	9	1		7				3		10	8				4				6			5	2		
14	12	Swansea Town	1-1	Callaghan	13600			11	9			7				3		10	8			1	4				6			5	2		
15	19	PRESTON NORTH END	1-3	Cherrett	9932			11	9	1		7				3		10	8				4	6						5	2		
16	26	Nottingham Forest	1-1	Cherrett	10040	10			9	1		7				3			8				4	6	11					5	2		
17	Dec 3	MANCHESTER CITY	2-0	Blakemore, Keating	23114	10			9	1					7	3		8					4	6	11					5	2		
18	10	Hull City	1-1	Paul	6716	10			9	1					7	3			8				4	6	11					5	2		
19	17	LEEDS UNITED	1-2	Blakemore	18326	10			9	1		7				3			8	5			4	6	11						2		
20	24	South Shields	3-1	Keating 2, Cherrett	4232				9	1		7				3		10		5			4	6	11						2		8
21	26	SOUTHAMPTON	3-0	Keating 2, Cherrett	17702			11	9	1		7				3		10		5			4	6							2		8
22	27	Southampton	2-3	Cherrett, Williams	10132			11	9	1		7				3		10		5			4	6							2		8
23	31	NOTTS COUNTY	1-2	Keating	6476	8		11	9	1		7				3	2	10		5	4			6									
24	Jan 7	Oldham Athletic	1-4	Geddes	12168			11		1		7		4		3		10		5				6							2	9	8
25	21	GRIMSBY TOWN	0-0		11690				9	1		7				3		10	8				4	6	11					5	2		
26	28	Leeds United	2-3	Blakemore (p), Cherrett	15534	10		11	9	1	8	7				3				5			4	6							2		
27	Feb 4	BLACKPOOL	2-2	Cherrett, Keating	11395			11	9	1	8	7				3		10		5			4	6							2		
28	11	Chelsea	2-5	Cherrett, Paul	31949	10			9	1		7	11			3					4		8						6	5	2		
29	15	Reading	2-3	Paul, Rankin	6287	10			9	1		7				3					4		8		11				6	5	2		
30	18	CLAPTON ORIENT	5-1	Keating 3, T Walsh 2 (1p)	15432					1		7				3		10		5	4		8		11				6		2	9	
31	25	West Bromwich Albion	0-0		23142					1		7				3		10		5	4		8		11				6		2	9	
32	Mar 3	Fulham	0-5		18524					1		7				3		10		5			8		11	4			6		2	9	
33	10	BARNSLEY	2-0	T Walsh, Williams	12662					1		7				3		10		5			4		11		6				2	9	8
34	17	Wolverhampton Wan.	2-5	Keating, Rankin	15492					1		7				3		10		5			4		11		6				2	9	8
35	24	SWANSEA TOWN	2-1	Cherrett, Williams	17123				9	1		7				3		10					4		11		6			5	2		8
36	31	Preston North End	1-5	Keating	14744				9	1		7				3		10					4		11		6			5	2		8
37	Apr 6	STOKE CITY	4-0	Keating 2, Cherrett, Foster	21503				9	1		7				3		10					4		11		6			5	2		8
38	7	NOTTM. FOREST	0-0		14575				9	1		7				3	2	10					4		11		6			5			8
39	9	Stoke City	0-1		13765	10	9			1		7		6			2			5			4		11			3					8
40	14	Manchester City	2-4	Bourton, Keating	31298		9			1		7				3		10		5			4		11		6	2					8
41	21	HULL CITY	0-1		10198		9			1		11			7	3		10					4				6			5	2		8
42	May 5	SOUTH SHIELDS	1-1	Williams	5607		9			1		7				3		10					4		11		6			5	2		8
					Apps	19	4	12	25	41	2	29	1	2	14	41	3	25	17	15	12	1	33	16	28	1	20	2	5	27	38	15	14
					Goals	7	1	1	15			3		1	7			16	5				3		3					1		9	4

F.A. Cup

Rd	Date	Opponent	Score	Scorers	Att.	Blakemore C	Bourton CFT	Callaghan PJ	Cherrett PAM	Coggins WH	Dransfield W	Foster JTF	Garland GE	Geddes J	Gilhespy TWC	Glenn E	Hughes RG	Keating AE	Martin JC	Murray DJ	Neesam H	Newlands G	Paul JC	Pugsley J	Rankin A	Searle FB	Smailes A	Taylor JS	Torrance A	Wadsworth W	Walsh JJ	Walsh T	Williams B
R3	Jan 14	TOTTENHAM HOTSPUR	1-2	Martin	36260				9	1					7	3		8	10				4	6	11					5	2		

Bristol Rovers

19th in Division Three (South)

	Date		Opponent	Score	Scorers	Att	Bennett F	Culley WN	Davies R	Densley AH	Dix RW	Douglas GH	Evans JH	Falconer F	Forbes J	Haydon JG	Homer S	King A	McKenna JG	Ormston A	Paterson J	Perry IL	Roberts T	Rotherham AE	Rowley J	Russell CJ	Smith L	Thom J	Trotman RW	Whatley JW	Whatmore EL	Williams TH
1	Aug	27	WALSALL	5-2	Douglas, Whatmore, Culley 3	12181	2	9				7	11		5	3									4		6			1	10	8
2		31	Plymouth Argyle	1-4	Whatmore	10084	2	9				7	11		5	3									4		6			1	10	8
3	Sep	3	Gillingham	1-3	Williams	6818	2	9				7	11		5	3									4		6			1	10	8
4		7	PLYMOUTH ARGYLE	3-1	Homer, Forbes, Russell	9013	2	9					11		5	3	7						6		4	10				1	8	
5		10	COVENTRY CITY	1-1	Homer	9688	2	9					11		5	3	7						6		4	10				1	8	
6		14	BRENTFORD	1-3	Whatmore	2578	2	9					11		5	3	7						6		4	10				1	8	
7		17	Newport County	1-3	Culley	7862	2	9					11		5	3	7						6		4	10				1	8	
8	Oct	1	Queen's Park Rangers	2-4	Douglas, Ormston	8448						7			5	3			2	9			6		4	11				1	10	8
9		8	WATFORD	3-1	Culley 2, Whatmore	7247		9				7	11		5	3			2				6		4	10				1		8
10		15	Charlton Athletic	1-2	Russell (p)	12461		9				7	11		5	3			2				6		4	10				1		8
11		22	Norwich City	2-4	Ormston, Forbes	6946	3					7	11		5				2	9			6		4	10				1		8
12		29	TORQUAY UNITED	5-1	Russell 2, Ormston 2, Williams	6824	3					7	11		5				2	9			6		4	10				1		8
13	Nov	5	Exeter City	1-4	Williams	6577	3					7	11		5				2	9			6		4			10		1		8
14		12	NORTHAMPTON T	2-2	Culley 2	7846		9				7	11		5	3			2						4	10	6			1		8
15		19	Southend United	1-2	Culley	4421		9				7	11			3			2			5	6		4	10				1	8	
16	Dec	3	Bournemouth	3-4	Evans, Culley 2	4414		9				7	11		5	3			2						4	10	6			1		8
17		17	Luton Town	0-2		5946	2	9				7	11			3						5	6	4						1	10	8
18		24	MILLWALL	1-6	Culley	7756	2	9					11			3	7					5	6	4						1	10	8
19		26	Merthyr Town	3-2	Forbes, Thom, Russell	1682	2					7	11		5	3				9						10	6	8		1		4
20		27	MERTHYR TOWN	2-1	Russell, Ormston	7797	2					7	11		5	3				9						10	6	8		1		4
21		31	Walsall	2-1	Ormston, Thom	2967	2					7	11		5	3				9						10	6	8		1		4
22	Jan	7	GILLINGHAM	2-4	Thom, Williams	5572	2					7	11		5	3				9						10	6	8		1		4
23		21	Coventry City	3-2	Williams, Ormston, Trotman	9521	2								5	3	7			9						11	6		8	1	10	4
24		28	NEWPORT COUNTY	2-1	Ormston, Forbes	4265	2								5	3	7			9						11	6		8	1	10	4
25	Feb	4	Swindon Town	1-2	Ormston	5403	2								5	3	7			9						11	6		8	1	10	4
26		11	QUEEN'S PARK RANGERS	0-4		6862	2								5	3	7			9	8				6	11				1	10	4
27		18	Watford	1-2	Ormston	7246	2						11			3	7			9		5		4		10	6			1		8
28		25	CHARLTON ATHLETIC	2-1	Ormston 2	7963	2				10		11			3	7			9		5		4			6			1		8
29	Mar	3	NORWICH CITY	3-0	Ormston, Dix, Williams	7031	2				10	11				3	7			9		5		4			6			1		8
30		10	Torquay United	0-0		4078	2				10	11				3	7			9		5		4			6			1		8
31		17	EXETER CITY	1-2	Williams (p)	9112	2				10					3	7	11		9		5	6	4						1		8
32		24	Northampton Town	0-2		9770	2								5	3	7			9			6		4	11				1	10	8
33		31	SOUTHEND UNITED	1-3	Culley	4764	2	9							5	3	7	11			8		6		4					1		10
34	Apr	6	Crystal Palace	2-3	Paterson, Culley	16126	2	9						6			7	11	4		8	5		3						1	10	
35		7	Brentford	1-5	Thom	7894	2	9						6			7	11			8	5		3				10		1		4
36		9	CRYSTAL PALACE	1-1	Whatmore	6275	2	9				7	11	6							8	5		3						1	10	4
37		14	BOURNEMOUTH	3-0	Homer 2, Roberts	5681	2		11	1				6	4		7			9	8	5	10	3								
38		18	SWINDON TOWN	1-0	Roberts	5445	2		11	1				6	4		7			9	8	5	10	3								
39		21	Brighton & Hove Albion	0-5		4118	2			1				6	4		7	11		9	8	5	10	3								
40		23	BRIGHTON & HOVE ALB	1-0	Ormston	4155				1				6	4	3	7	11		9	8	5	10	2								
41		28	LUTON TOWN	1-2	Ormston	5639				1				6	4	3	7	11		9	8	5	10	2								
42	May	5	Millwall	0-1		17747				1				6	4	3	7	11		9	8	5	10	2								

	Bennett F	Culley WN	Davies R	Densley AH	Dix RW	Douglas GH	Evans JH	Falconer F	Forbes J	Haydon JG	Homer S	King A	McKenna JG	Ormston A	Paterson J	Perry IL	Roberts T	Rotherham AE	Rowley J	Russell CJ	Smith L	Thom J	Trotman RW	Whatley JW	Whatmore EL	Williams TH
Apps	33	18	2	6	4	20	24	9	31	33	24	8	10	24	11	17	22	16	19	22	16	6	3	36	18	30
Goals		14			1	2	1		4		4			15	1		2			6		4	1		4	8

F.A. Cup

	Date		Opponent	Score	Scorers	Att	Bennett F	Culley WN	Davies R	Densley AH	Dix RW	Douglas GH	Evans JH	Falconer F	Forbes J	Haydon JG	Homer S	King A	McKenna JG	Ormston A	Paterson J	Perry IL	Roberts T	Rotherham AE	Rowley J	Russell CJ	Smith L	Thom J	Trotman RW	Whatley JW	Whatmore EL	Williams TH
R1	Nov	26	WALSALL	4-2	Williams 2, Douglas, Culley	6000		9				7	11			3			2			5			4		6			1	10	8
R2	Dec	10	Bournemouth	1-6	Evans	9098		9				7	11		5	3			2						4	10	6			1		8

Burnley

19th in Division One

	Date	Opponent	Score	Scorers	Att	Beel GW	Brown J	Bruton J	Burley GM	Cross B	Devine JC	Dougal PG	Dougall W	Down W	Forrest A	Freeman A	Haddow AS	Hargreaves H	Heslop AS	Hill JH	Knox W	Mantle J	McCluggage A	Page LA	Parkin G	Pollard W	Reid A	Richards P	Sommerville GDL	Steel J	Waterfield GS	Weston JM
1	Aug 27	Blackburn Rovers	1-2	Hargreaves	32441			7			8		6				9	10		5				11	4		2		1		3	
2	31	Arsenal	1-4	Bruton	19910			7			10		6							5				11	4	8	2	9	1		3	
3	Sep 3	BURY	2-3	Freeman, Bruton	22414	9		7			10		6			8				5	2			11	4				1		3	
4	5	ARSENAL	1-2	Beel	14668	9		7					6			8		10		5	2			11	4				1		3	
5	10	Sheffield United	2-5	Freeman, Beel	17479	9		7								8		10		5	2			11	4				1		3	6
6	17	ASTON VILLA	4-2	Beel 2, Hill, Page	19523	9		7			10		6			8				5	2			11	4				1		3	
7	24	Sunderland	3-2	Page 2, Hill	22420	9		7			10		6			8				5	2			11	4				1		3	
8	Oct 1	DERBY COUNTY	4-2	Freeman, Beel 3	11911	9		7			10		6			8				5	2			11	4				1		3	
9	8	West Ham United	0-2		27467	9	5	7			10		6			8					2			11	4				1		3	
10	15	PORTSMOUTH	2-0	Beel, Page	19492	9		7			10		6			8				5	2			11	4				1		3	
11	22	Middlesbrough	3-2	Beel 2, Weston	17803	9	5	7			10					8					2				6				1	4	3	11
12	29	SHEFFIELD WEDNESDAY	3-1	Page 2, Beel	16366	9	5	7			10				6	8							2	11	4				1		3	
13	Nov 5	Bolton Wanderers	1-7	Page	14340	9	6	7			10					8				5			2	11	4				1		3	
14	12	BIRMINGHAM	2-1	Beel, Freeman	14648	9	4	7			10			1		8				5			2	11	6						3	
15	19	Newcastle United	1-1	Beel	26991	9	4	7			10			1		8				5			2	11	6						3	
16	26	MANCHESTER UNITED	4-0	Devine, Beel 2, Hill	18509	9	4	7			10			1		8				5			2	11	6						3	
17	Dec 3	Tottenham Hotspur	0-5		20404	9	4	7			10			1		8				5			2	11	6						3	
18	10	HUDDERSFIELD T	0-1		19130	9		7			10			1		8				5			2	11	6					4	3	
19	17	Everton	1-4	Beel	30180	9		7					10	1						5			2	11	6	8				4	3	
20	24	CARDIFF CITY	2-1	W Dougall, Beel	13159	9		7					10	1		8				5			2	11	6					4	3	
21	26	Leicester City	0-5		20063	9		7					10	1		8				5			2	11	6					4	3	
22	27	LEICESTER CITY	5-1	Page 2, Beel 2, P Dougall	24824	9	5	7				10		1		8							2	11	6					4	3	
23	31	BLACKBURN ROVERS	3-1	Beel, Page, McCluggage	28351	9		7				10		1		8				5			2	11	6					4	3	
24	Jan 2	Liverpool	2-2	Page 2	26632	9		7				10		1		8				5			2	11	6					4	3	
25	7	Bury	0-2		13161	9		7	10					1		8				5			2	11	6					4	3	
26	21	SHEFFIELD UNITED	5-3	Bruton 2, Beel 3	12716	9		7						1		10				5			2	11	6	8				4	3	
27	Feb 4	SUNDERLAND	3-0	Beel, Page 2	11442	9		7						1		10				5	2			11	6	8				4	3	
28	8	Aston Villa	1-3	Mantle	18602		4		8					1		10			7	5		9	2	11	6						3	
29	11	Derby County	4-3	P Dougall, Beel, Page, Freeman	8503	9		7				10		1		8				5			2	11	6					4	3	
30	18	WEST HAM UNITED	0-0		14663	9		7				10		1		8				5			2	11	6					4	3	
31	25	Portsmouth	0-1		19666	9		7				10		1						5	2			11	6	8				4	3	
32	Mar 3	MIDDLESBROUGH	1-1	Beel	18209	9		7						1		10				5			2	11	6	8				4	3	
33	10	Sheffield Wednesday	0-5		12401	9	5	7						1		10							2	11	6	8				4	3	
34	17	BOLTON WANDERERS	2-2	Page, Beel	15865	9	4	7						1		10				5			2	11	6					8	3	
35	24	Birmingham	0-4		23689	9	4	7						1		10				5			2	11	6					8	3	
36	31	NEWCASTLE UNITED	5-1	Beel 2, Hill, Bruton, Page	12454	9		7						1		10				5			2	11	6	8				4	3	
37	Apr 6	LIVERPOOL	2-2	Pollard, Freeman	21824	9		7						1		10				5			2	11	6	8				4	3	
38	7	Manchester United	3-4	Beel 2, Bruton	28311	9		7			10			1		8				5			2	11	6					4	3	
39	14	TOTTENHAM HOTSPUR	2-2	Page 2	10906	9		7						1		10				5			2	11	6	8				4	3	
40	25	Huddersfield Town	2-1	Beel, Page	20643	9		7						1		10				5			2	11	6	8				4	3	
41	28	EVERTON	3-5	Page, Beel 2	24485	9	6	7						1		10				5			2	11		8				4	3	
42	May 5	Cardiff City	2-3	Beel, Page	8663	9		7		8				1		10				5			2	11	6					4	3	
					Apps	39	14	41	2	1	17	6	12	29	1	38	1	3	1	37	11	1	29	41	41	12	2	1	13	25	42	2
					Goals	35		6			1	2	1			6		1		4		1	1	22		1						1

F.A. Cup

	Date	Opponent	Score	Att	Beel GW	Brown J	Bruton J	Burley GM	Cross B	Devine JC	Dougal PG	Dougall W	Down W	Forrest A	Freeman A	Haddow AS	Hargreaves H	Heslop AS	Hill JH	Knox W	Mantle J	McCluggage A	Page LA	Parkin G	Pollard W	Reid A	Richards P	Sommerville GDL	Steel J	Waterfield GS	Weston JM
R3	Jan 14	ASTON VILLA	0-2	26150	9	10	7						1		8				5			2	11	6					4	3	

Bury

5th in Division One

No	Date	Opponent	Score	Scorers	Att	Adamson TK	Amos WR	Ball J	Bradshaw G	Bradshaw T	Bullock N	Chambers RJ	Crown L	Davin M	Dutton HR	Finney WA	Gale AR	Harrison W	Heap F	Massie AC	Matthews CHW	McLachlan F	Porter WJ	Pratt D	Richardson W	Robbie DM	Robinson A	Smith F	Smith JR	Stage W	Vernon JL
1	Aug 27	ARSENAL	5-1	Amos 2, Ball 2, Bullock	17614	3	11	10		5	9		2		6								4		1	7				8	
2	31	Liverpool	1-5	Amos	30047	3	11	10		5	9		2		6								4		1	7				8	
3	Sep 3	Burnley	3-2	Bullock 2, Ball	22414	3	11	10		5	9		2		6								4		1	7				8	
4	10	BOLTON WANDERERS	1-0	Ball	24593	3	11	10		5	9		2		6								4		1	7				8	
5	17	SHEFFIELD UNITED	1-0	Bradshaw T	14732	3	11	10		5	9		2		6								4		1	7				8	
6	19	LIVERPOOL	5-2	Ball 2, Bullock 2, Amos	10950	3	11	10		5	9		2		6								4		1	7				8	
7	24	Aston Villa	0-1		25538	3	11	10		5	9		2		6								4		1	7				8	
8	Oct 1	SUNDERLAND	5-3	Amos 2, Ball 2 (1p), Robbie	10233	3	11	10		5	9		2		6								4		1	7				8	
9	8	Derby County	2-5	Amos, Ball	15532	3	11	10		5	9		2		6								4		1	7				8	
10	15	WEST HAM UNITED	3-1	Ball, Bullock, Robbie	20110		11	10		5	9			8	6				2				4		1	7		3			
11	22	Birmingham	2-2	Bradshaw T, Davin	11925		11			5	9		3	8	6				2	10					1	7	4				
12	29	MIDDLESBROUGH	1-4	Bullock	18756		11	10		5	9		3	8	6				2		7		4		1						
13	Nov 5	Sheffield Wednesday	0-4		16808		11	10		5			3		6				2			4			1	7				8	9
14	12	NEWCASTLE UNITED	1-4	Amos	20844		11	10		5	9		3	8	6		7		2			4			1						
15	19	Huddersfield Town	0-3		12293		11	6		5	9		3	8			7		2	10			4		1						
16	26	EVERTON	2-3	Bradshaw T, Stage	24727	3	11	10		5	9					6			2				4		1	7				8	
17	Dec 3	Manchester United	1-0	Bullock	23581	3	11	10		5	9								2				4	6	1	7				8	
18	10	TOTTENHAM HOTSPUR	1-2	Ball	12204	3	11	10		5	9					4			2					6	1	7				8	
19	17	Cardiff City	1-0	Vernon	11961	3	11	10		5	8					4			2					6	1	7					9
20	24	BLACKBURN ROVERS	2-3	Ball, Vernon	12855	3	11	10		5						4			2					6	1	7				8	9
21	26	PORTSMOUTH	4-0	Vernon 3, Ball	17230	3	11	10		5	8		2			4								6	1	7					9
22	27	Portsmouth	0-1		15819	3	11	10		5			2			4								6	1	7				8	9
23	31	Arsenal	1-3	Vernon	17702	3	11	10		5			2			4					7			6	1					8	9
24	Jan 2	LEICESTER CITY	2-1	Ball, Chambers	15730	3	11	10	2	5		7				4								6	1					8	9
25	7	BURNLEY	2-0	Amos, Vernon	13161	3	11	10	2	5		7				4								6	1					8	9
26	21	Bolton Wanderers	1-2	Haworth (og)	32497	3	11		2	5		7				4				10				6	1					8	9
27	Feb 4	ASTON VILLA	0-0		9814		11	10	2	5	9			8			7		3				4	6	1						
28	11	Sunderland	0-1		13586		11	10	2	5	8			9					3		7		4	6	1						
29	18	DERBY COUNTY	3-0	Bullock 2, Matthews	11424		11	10	2	5	9								3		7		4	6	1					8	
30	25	West Ham United	2-1	Amos, Ball	19903		11	10	2	5	8								3		7		4	6	1						9
31	Mar 3	BIRMINGHAM	2-3	Bullock, Matthews (p)	13164		11		2	5	8	10							3		7		4	6	1						9
32	10	Middlesbrough	1-6	Bullock	13922		11	10	2	5	9								3		7		4	6	1					8	
33	12	Sheffield United	1-3	Bullock	6712		11		2		10					5	9	1	3		7		4	6						8	
34	17	SHEFFIELD WEDNESDAY	4-2	Smith JR 3 (1p), Amos	14185		11		2	5	8					6			3				4	10	1	7			9		
35	24	Newcastle United	3-2	Smith JR 2, Amos	28871		11		2	5	8								3	10			4	6	1	7			9		
36	31	HUDDERSFIELD T	2-3	Smith JR 2	14636		11		2		8					5			3	10			4	6	1	7			9		
37	Apr 7	Everton	1-1	Ball	37597	3	11	10	2	5	8												4	6	1	7			9		
38	9	Leicester City	2-2	Bradshaw T, Robbie	25446	3	11		2	5	8									10				6	1	7	4		9		
39	14	MANCHESTER UNITED	4-3	Ball, Bullock, Smith JR, Mann (og)	17440	3	11	10	2	5	8													6	1	7	4		9		
40	21	Tottenham Hotspur	4-1	Ball 2, Amos, Smith JR	15618	3	11	10	2	5														6	1	7	4		9		8
41	28	CARDIFF CITY	3-0	Amos, Bullock, Smith JR	13375	3	11	10	2	5	8													6	1	7	4		9		
42	May 5	Blackburn Rovers	1-0	Robbie	16836	3	11	10	2	5	8													6	1	7	4		9		
					Apps	26	42	34	19	40	34	4	17	7	14	13	4	1	21	6	8	2	25	26	41	28	6	1	9	22	12
					Goals		14	19		4	15	1		1							2					4			10	1	7

Two own goals

F.A. Cup

Rd	Date	Opponent	Score	Scorers	Att	Adamson TK	Amos WR	Ball J	Bradshaw G	Bradshaw T	Bullock N	Chambers RJ	Crown L	Davin M	Dutton HR	Finney WA	Gale AR	Harrison W	Heap F	Massie AC	Matthews CHW	McLachlan F	Porter WJ	Pratt D	Richardson W	Robbie DM	Robinson A	Smith F	Smith JR	Stage W	Vernon JL
R3	Jan 14	Charlton Athletic	1-1	Ball	18884	3	11	10	2	5		7				4								6	1					8	9
rep	18	CHARLTON ATHLETIC	4-3	Vernon 2, Amos, Ball (p)	15847	3	11	10	2	5		7				4									1					8	9
R4	28	MANCHESTER UNITED	1-1	Amos	22439	3	11	10	2	5	8												4	6	1	7					9
rep	Feb 1	Manchester United	0-1		48001		11	10	2	5	8	7							3				4	6	1						9

Played at 6 in Round 3 replay: L Curry

Cardiff City

6th in Division One

	Date		Opponent	Score	Scorers	Att	Baillie J	Blackburn GF	Castle FR	Curtis ER	Davies LS	Davies W	Farquharson TG	Ferguson H	Hardy W	Hillier EJG	Irving SJ	Jennings J	Keenor FC	Matson FR	McLachlan GH	Miles AE	Murphy J	Nelson J	Sloan TM	Smith TP	Thirlaway WJ	Wake HW	Warren FW	Watson T
1	Aug	27	BOLTON WANDERERS	2-1	McLachlan, L Davies	24107				10	8		1	9	6		4		5		11			2			7			3
2	Sep	3	Sheffield Wednesday	3-3	Ferguson, Curtis, Thirlaway	19218				10	8		1	9	6		4		5		11			2			7			3
3		5	Blackburn Rovers	0-0		14343				10	8		1	9	6		4		5		11			2			7			3
4		10	MIDDLESBROUGH	1-1	McLachlan	23033				10	8		1	9	6		4		5		11			2			7			3
5		12	BLACKBURN ROVERS	1-1	L Davies	15955				10	8		1	9	6		4		5		11			2			7			3
6		17	Birmingham	3-1	Thirlaway, Ferguson 2	23723				10	8		1	9	6		4		5		11			2			7			3
7		24	NEWCASTLE UNITED	3-1	Curtis, L Davies, Ferguson	30590				10	8		1	9	6		4		5		11			2			7			3
8	Oct	1	Huddersfield Town	2-8	Ferguson 2	12975				10	8		1	9	6		4		5		11			2			7			3
9		8	TOTTENHAM HOTSPUR	2-1	L Davies, Ferguson	21811				10	8		1	9	6		4		5		11			2			7			3
10		15	Manchester United	2-2	Thirlaway, Curtis	31090		6		10	8		1	9	3		4		5		11			2			7			
11		22	PORTSMOUTH	3-1	Thirlaway, Ferguson, McLachlan	9060		6		10	8		1	9	3				5		11			2			7	4		
12		29	Leicester City	1-4	Smith	25634							1	9	6		4			8	11			2	5	10	7			3
13	Nov	5	LIVERPOOL	1-1	Smith	12735					8		1	9	6		4		5		11			2		10	7			3
14		12	West Ham United	0-2		18189				10	8		1	9	6		4		5		11			2			7			3
15		19	DERBY COUNTY	4-4	L Davies 2, W Davies, Matson	6606					10	7	1	9	6		4		5	8	11			2						3
16		26	Sheffield United	4-3	McLachlan 2, L Davies, Ferguson	22999					10	8	1	9	6		4		5		11			2			7			3
17	Dec	3	ASTON VILLA	2-1	Ferguson 2	14264		4			10	8	1	9	6				5		11			2			7			3
18		10	Sunderland	2-0	Thirlaway, L Davies	16450					10	8	1	9	6		4		5		11			2			7			3
19		17	BURY	0-1		11961					10	8	1	9	6		4				11			2	5		7			3
20		24	Burnley	1-2	Thirlaway	13159				8	10		1	9	6		4		5		11			2			7			3
21		26	Everton	1-2	Wake	56305		6		8	10		1	9					5		11			2			7	4		3
22		27	EVERTON	2-0	L Davies, Wake	25387		4			10				6	1		3			11	9		2	5		7	8		
23		31	Bolton Wanderers	1-2	Miles	15745		4			10				6	1		3			11	9		2	5		7	8		
24	Jan	7	SHEFFIELD WEDNESDAY	1-1	Ferguson	9208		4			10		1	9	3				5		11			2	6		7	8		
25		21	Middlesbrough	2-1	Thirlaway, Ferguson	21728					10		1	9	6		8		5		11			2			7	4		3
26	Feb	4	Newcastle United	0-2		26439		6		8			1	9	5			3			11			2		10	7	4		
27		11	HUDDERSFIELD T	4-0	L Davies, Wadsworth (og), Thirlaway 2	21073				10	9		1		6		8	3	5		11			2			7	4		
28		22	BIRMINGHAM	2-1	Ferguson, McLachlan	10758		4		8	10		1	9	6			3	5		11			2			7			
29		25	MANCHESTER UNITED	2-0	L Davies, Ferguson	15579				8	10		1	9	6			3	5		11			2			7	4		
30	Mar	3	Portsmouth	0-3		25157				8	10		1	9	6			3	5		11			2			7	4		
31		5	Tottenham Hotspur	0-1		6250				10	9		1		6			3	5	8	11			2			7	4		
32		10	LEICESTER CITY	3-0	Ferguson 2, McLachlan	13178					10		1	9	6			3	5		11			2		8	7	4		
33		17	Liverpool	2-1	L Davies, Thirlaway	34532			9		10		1		6			3	5		11			2		8	7	4		
34		24	WEST HAM UNITED	1-5	Ferguson	14529	4				10		1	9	6			3	5		11			2		8	7			
35		31	Derby County	1-7	Thirlaway	15565		4			10		1	9	6			2	5		11					8	7			3
36	Apr	6	Arsenal	0-3		36828		4							6	1		3			11	9	10	2	5	8	7			
37		7	SHEFFIELD UNITED	2-2	McLachlan 2	11283								9	6	1		3	4		11			2	5	10	7	8		
38		9	ARSENAL	2-2	Smith, Wake	17699								9	6	1		3	4	7	11			2	5	10		8		
39		14	Aston Villa	1-3	McLachlan	22428					10		1		6			3	4		9			2	5		7	8	11	
40		21	SUNDERLAND	3-1	Warren, L Davies, McLachlan	10268					10		1		6			3	4		9			2	5		7	8	11	
41		28	Bury	0-3		13375					10		1		6			3	4		9			2	5	8	7		11	
42	May	5	BURNLEY	3-2	L Davies 2, Warren	8663					10		1		6			3	4		9			2	5	8	7		11	
						Apps	1	11	1	20	37	5	37	32	41	5	20	19	36	4	42	3	1	41	12	12	40	17	4	21
						Goals				3	15	1		18						1	11	1				3	11	3	2	

One own goal

F.A. Cup

	Date		Opponent	Score	Scorers	Att	Baillie J	Blackburn GF	Castle FR	Curtis ER	Davies LS	Davies W	Farquharson TG	Ferguson H	Hardy W	Hillier EJG	Irving SJ	Jennings J	Keenor FC	Matson FR	McLachlan GH	Miles AE	Murphy J	Nelson J	Sloan TM	Smith TP	Thirlaway WJ	Wake HW	Warren FW	Watson T
R3	Jan	14	SOUTHAMPTON	2-1	Ferguson, L Davies	23000		4			10		1	9	3				5		11			2	6		7	8		
R4		28	LIVERPOOL	2-1	McLachlan, Nelson	20000					10		1	9	6		8		5		11			2			7	4		3
R5	Feb	18	Nottingham Forest	1-2	Ferguson	30570					10		1	9	6		8	3	5		11			2			7	4		

Charlton Athletic

11th in Division Three (South)

	Date		Opponent	Score	Scorers	Att	Armitage GH	Astley DJ	Bethell R	Biswell GW	Borland JT	Codd H	Davies FP	Herod ER	Hird A	Horton JW	Lennox W	Lindon A	McGill T	McKenna T	McKinley CA	Paterson WF	Preedy CJ	Rankin JP	Sherlaw DD	Smith N	Welsh W	Whitlow FW	Wolfe TH
1	Aug	27	GILLINGHAM	1-0	Biswell	11752	5			8				3		11						4	1	10	7	2	9		6
2		29	Merthyr Town	0-0		4158				8				3	5	11						4	1		7	2	10	9	6
3	Sep	3	Coventry City	3-3	Biswell 2, Rankin	10958	5			8				3		11					7	4	1	10		2	9		6
4		10	NEWPORT COUNTY	3-2	Biswell, Horton, Welsh	7946	5			8				3	4	11							1	10	7	2	9		6
5		17	Swindon Town	2-2	Horton, Welsh (p)	8077	5			8				3	6	11				1		4		10	7	2	9		
6		19	MERTHYR TOWN	0-0		5383	5			8				3	6	11				1		4		10	7	2	9		
7		24	QUEEN'S PARK RANGERS	1-0	Welsh	12823	5			10				3	6	11			8	1	7	4				2	9		
8	Oct	1	Watford	2-1	Biswell, Sherlaw	5350	5			10				3	6	11			8	1	7	4			9	2			
9		8	MILLWALL	1-1	McKinley	27380	5			10				3	6	11			8	1	7	4			9	2			
10		15	BRISTOL ROVERS	2-1	Sherlaw 2	12461	5			10				3	6	11				1	7	4			8	2	9		
11		22	Torquay United	2-1	Sherlaw 2	4816	5			10				3	6	11			8	1	7	4			9	2			
12		29	EXETER CITY	0-0		13402	5			10				3	6	11			8	1	7	4			9	2			
13	Nov	5	Crystal Palace	0-5		16694	5			10				3	6	11	9			1	7	4			8	2			
14		12	NORWICH CITY	3-2	Horton, McKinley, Whitlow	10530				10			5	3	6	11				1	7	4			8	2		9	
15		19	Northampton Town	1-2	Sherlaw	10210				10			5	3	6	11					7	4	1		8	2		9	
16	Dec	3	Brighton & Hove Albion	2-2	Sherlaw 2	7992				8		4	5	3	6	11				1	7			10	9	2			
17		17	Brentford	1-1	McKinley	5245				8			5	3	6	11				1	7	4		10	9	2			
18		24	LUTON TOWN	4-3	Biswell 2, Rankin, Sherlaw	7265				8			5	3	6	11				1	7	4		10	9	2			
19		27	Walsall	0-1		6244				8			5	3	6	11				1	7	4		10	9	2			
20		31	Gillingham	1-1	Sherlaw	4134				8			5	3	6	11				1	7	4		10	9	2			
21	Jan	7	COVENTRY CITY	2-1	Borland, Hird	8866				8	11		5	3	6	7				1		4		10	9	2			
22		21	Newport County	3-4	Biswell 2, Rankin	3737				8	11	2	5		6	7				1		4		10		2	9		
23	Feb	4	Queen's Park Rangers	3-3	Sherlaw 2, Welsh	10830	5				11			3	6	7				1		4		10	9	2	8		
24		9	WALSALL	1-3	Welsh	4647							5	3	6	11				1	7	4		10	9	2	8		
25		11	WATFORD	0-2		5464					11		5	3	6	7						4	1	10	9	2	8		
26		18	Millwall	0-5		25498	5	8						3	6	11		1				4		10	7	2	9		
27		25	Bristol Rovers	1-2	Lennox	7963	5				11	4		3	6	7	9	1						10	8	2			
28	Mar	3	TORQUAY UNITED	1-0	Horton(pen	8290	5					4		3	6	11	9	1			7			10	8	2			
29		10	Exeter City	1-2	Lennox	5703	5		10			4		3	6	11	9	1						8	7	2			
30		17	CRYSTAL PALACE	0-4		11083	5		10			4		3	6	11		1			7			8	9	2			
31		24	Norwich City	0-0		7253	5					4		3	6	11	9				7		1	10	8	2			
32		26	SOUTHEND UNITED	1-2	Horton	2210						4	5	3	6	11	9						1	8	7	2	10		
33		31	NORTHAMPTON T	2-2	Rankin, Welsh	7121	5					4		3	6	11	9				7		1	8		2	10		
34	Apr	6	PLYMOUTH ARGYLE	2-0	Armitage, Rankin	9112	5					4		3	6	11	9				7		1	8		2	10		
35		7	Bournemouth	1-3	Horton	5764	5					4		3	6	11	9				7		1	8		2	10		
36		9	Plymouth Argyle	0-2		9686	5					4		3	6	11	9				7		1	8		2	10		
37		14	BRIGHTON & HOVE ALB	3-0	Horton, Lennox, Welsh	5930	5					4		3	6	11	9						1	8	7	2	10		
38		16	BOURNEMOUTH	1-1	Lennox	1227						4	5	3	6	11	9						1	8	7	2	10		
39		21	Southend United	2-1	Lennox, Rankin	4501	5					4		3	6	11	9						1	8	7	2	10		
40		28	BRENTFORD	3-2	Horton, Lennox, Rankin	7122	5					4		3	6	11	9						1	8	7	2	10		
41		30	SWINDON TOWN	3-1	Lennox 3	2900						4	5	3	6	11	9						1	8	7	2	10		
42	May	5	Luton Town	1-2	Sherlaw	5982	5					4		3	6	11	9						1	8	7	2	10		
						Apps	27	1	2	22	5	18	14	41	40	42	16	5	5	19	23	24	18	32	35	42	24	3	4
						Goals	1			9	1				1	8	9				3			7	13		7	1	

F.A. Cup

	Date		Opponent	Score	Scorers	Att	Armitage GH	Astley DJ	Bethell R	Biswell GW	Borland JT	Codd H	Davies FP	Herod ER	Hird A	Horton JW	Lennox W	Lindon A	McGill T	McKenna T	McKinley CA	Paterson WF	Preedy CJ	Rankin JP	Sherlaw DD	Smith N	Welsh W	Whitlow FW	Wolfe TH
R1	Nov	26	Merthyr Town	0-0		7000				8			5	3	6	11				1	7	4			9	2			10
rep		30	MERTHYR TOWN	2-1	Horton, Sherlaw	3875				8		4	5	3	6	11				1	7			10	9	2			
R2	Dec	10	Kettering Town	1-1	Horton	10954				10		4	5	3	6	11				1	7				8	2		9	
rep		15	KETTERING TOWN	2-1	Biswell 2	6000				8			5	3	6	11				1	7	4		10	9	2			
R3	Jan	14	BURY	1-1	Biswell	18884	5			8	11			3	6	7				1		4		10	9	2			
rep		18	Bury	3-4	Welsh 2, Biswell	15847	5			8	11			3	6	7				1		4		10		2	9		

Chelsea

3rd in Division Two

	Date	Opponent	Score	Scorers	Att.	Anderson GR	Biswell GW	Brown W	Crawford JF	Ferguson C	Ferguson W	Irving SJ	Jackson W	Law T	McKenna PJ	Miller HS	Millington S	Odell LF	Pearson GWM	Priestley J	Rodger GB	Russell W	Sales AA	Smith GW	Thain AE	Thompson JWJ	Townrow JE	Turnbull® RH	Wilding HTD	Williams WD	Wilson AN
1	Aug 27	Reading	2-1	Crawford, Thompson	24529				7		6			3			1		11					2	8	9	5		4		10
2	Sep 3	BLACKPOOL	3-0	Thompson, Wilding, Pearson	36529				7		6			3			1		11					2	8	9	5		4		10
3	7	NOTTS COUNTY	5-0	Thompson 2, Wilding, Thain, Wilson	18416				7		6			3			1		11					2	8	9	5		4		10
4	10	Fulham	1-1	Thain	39860				7		6			3			1		11					2	8	9	5		4		10
5	17	Clapton Orient	1-2	Wilson	34838				7		6			3			1		11					2	8	9	5		4		10
6	24	WEST BROMWICH ALB.	1-1	Thompson	44724				7		6			3	1				11					2	8	9	5		4		10
7	Oct 1	Bristol City	1-1	Wilson	24005				7		6			3	1				11					2	8	9	5		4		10
8	6	Notts County	1-0	Wilson	9127				7		6			3			1		11					2	8	9	5		4		10
9	8	STOKE CITY	1-0	Crawford (p)	41472				7		6			3			1		11					2	8	9	5		4		10
10	15	Southampton	4-2	Pearson 2, Thain, Thompson	14724				7		6			3			1		11	4				2	8	9	5				10
11	22	HULL CITY	2-0	Thompson, Wilson	15153				7		6			3			1		11	4				2	8	9	5				10
12	29	Preston North End	3-0	Thompson 2, Pearson	23107				7		6			3			1		11	4				2	8	9	5				10
13	Nov 5	SWANSEA TOWN	4-0	Crawford 2, Thain, Thompson	41220				7		6			3			1		11	4				2	8	9	5				10
14	12	Manchester City	1-0	Thompson	52830				7		6			3			1		11	4				2	8	9	5				10
15	19	NOTTM. FOREST	2-1	Thain, Thompson	28743				7		6			3			1		11	4				2	8	9	5				10
16	26	Port Vale	1-1	Crawford	14115			8	7		6			3			1		11	4				2		9			5		10
17	Dec 3	SOUTH SHIELDS	6-0	Thompson 4, Priestley, Miller	28719				7		6			3		8	1		11	4				2		9	5				10
18	10	Leeds United	0-5		22059				7					3		8	1		11	4			6	2		9	5				10
19	17	WOLVERHAMPTON W.	2-0	Turnbull(R), Wilson	24340				7		6			3		8	1		11	4				2			5	9			10
20	24	Barnsley	1-3	Priestley	5634				7		6			3		8	1		11	4				2			5	9			10
21	26	Grimsby Town	1-1	Turnbull(R)	18630				7		6			3			1		11	4				2			5	9		8	10
22	31	READING	0-0		26525				7		6			3			1		11	4				2		9	5			8	10
23	Jan 7	Blackpool	4-2	Wilding, Brown, Thompson, Wilson	8704			8	7		6			3			1		11					2		9	5		4		10
24	21	FULHAM	2-1	Thompson, Wilson	42297				7		6			3			1		11					2	8	9	5		4		10
25	28	CLAPTON ORIENT	1-0	Wilding	17875		7				6			3		9	1	2	11						8		5		4		10
26	Feb 4	West Bromwich Albion	0-3		23718	9	7				6			3			1	2	11	4							5		8		10
27	11	BRISTOL CITY	5-2	Priestley 2, Ferguson, Thain, Wilson	31949		9		7		6			3			1		11	4				2	8				5		10
28	20	Stoke City	0-1		15770	9			7		6			3			1		11	4				2	8				5		10
29	25	SOUTHAMPTON	0-2		46567		9		7		6			3			1		11	4				2	8				5		10
30	Mar 3	Hull City	2-0	Thompson 2	12679				7		6	4		3			1		11		5			2	8	9					10
31	10	PRESTON NORTH END	2-1	Thompson, Law (p)	49980				7		6	4		3			1		11		5			2	8	9					10
32	14	GRIMSBY TOWN	4-0	Thompson 3, Thain	14298				7		6	4		3			1		11		5			2	8	9					10
33	17	Swansea Town	0-0		15653	9			7		6	4		3			1		11		5			2	8						10
34	24	MANCHESTER CITY	0-1		51813				7		6	4		3			1		11		5			2	8	9					10
35	31	Nottingham Forest	2-2	Thompson, Jackson	10959				7		6	4	11			10	1	3			5			2	8	9					
36	Apr 6	OLDHAM ATHLETIC	2-1	Thain 2	53309				7		6	4	11	3		10	1				5			2	8	9					
37	7	PORT VALE	1-0	Crawford	29278				7		6	4	11	3			1				5			2	8	9					10
38	9	Oldham Athletic	1-2	Thain	18992	9			7		6		11	3		10	1				5	4		2	8						
39	14	South Shields	1-2	Irving	3395	9			7		6	4	11	3		10	1				5			2	8						
40	21	LEEDS UNITED	2-3	Rodger, Wilson	47562				7		6	4	11				1	3			5			2	8	9					10
41	28	Wolverhampton Wan.	2-1	Wilson, Jackson	16727				7	8	6	4	11			9	1	3			5			2							10
42	May 5	BARNSLEY	1-2	Biswell	13707		4				6		7			9	1	3	11		5	8		2							10
					Apps	5	5	2	39	1	41	11	8	38	2	11	40	6	35	17	13	2	1	40	31	29	25	3	17	2	38
					Goals		1	1	6		1	1	2	1		1			4	4	1				10	25		2	4		11

F.A. Cup

	Date	Opponent	Score	Scorers	Att.	Anderson GR	Biswell GW	Brown W	Crawford JF	Ferguson C	Ferguson W	Irving SJ	Jackson W	Law T	McKenna PJ	Miller HS	Millington S	Odell LF	Pearson GWM	Priestley J	Rodger GB	Russell W	Sales AA	Smith GW	Thain AE	Thompson JWJ	Townrow JE	Turnbull® RH	Wilding HTD	Williams WD	Wilson AN
R3	Jan 14	Wolverhampton Wan.	1-2	Brown	32134			8	7		6			3			1		11	4				2		9	5				10

Chesterfield

16th in Division Three (North)

						Abbott SW	Beeson GW	Betton A	Bilcliff B	Clayson WJ	Cousins H	Dennis W	Elwood JH	Hall JG	Hooper C	Matthews F	Nutter W	Oxley B	Price FT	Roberts, Harry	Roseboom E	Saxby A	Stevenson WW	Thompson O	Thomson JY	Tuckley WL	Turnbull WJ	Wass H	Whitworth E	Williams RS	Winfield W
1	Aug 27	WREXHAM	0-1		7164							3	5			10			11		8	2		6	1		7	4		9	
2	29	DURHAM CITY	4-2	Price 2, Clayson, Turnbull	3833					8		3	5						11	9	10	2		6	1		7	4			
3	Sep 3	Halifax Town	2-1	Turnbull 2	9464					8		3	5						11	9	10	2		6	1		7	4			
4	7	Durham City	0-2		1222					8		3	5						11	9	10	2		6	1		7	4			
5	10	Bradford Park Avenue	0-1		12816					8		3	5						11	9	10	2		6	1		7	4			
6	17	TRANMERE ROVERS	2-2	Clayson, Matthews	5681					9		3	5			8			11		10	2		6	1		7	4			
7	24	Stockport County	0-3		6252			3		9		2	5						11		8			6	1		7	4		10	
8	Oct 1	BARROW	6-0	Clayson 3, Williams 2, Price	2338			3		9		2	5					8	11					6	1		7	4		10	
9	8	Nelson	3-3	Clayson, Williams, Price	4659			3		9		2	5					8	11					6	1		7	4		10	
10	15	ROCHDALE	1-3	Oxley	5439			3		9		2	5					8	11					6	1		7	4		10	
11	22	DARLINGTON	1-3	Clayson	2899					8		3	5					7	11		10	2		6	1	9		4			
12	29	Ashington	0-0		2310	5				8		3	6					7	11			2		10	1	9		4			
13	Nov 5	CREWE ALEXANDRA	3-2	Roseboom, Elwood, Tuckley	3471	5				8		3	4					7	11		10	2		6	1	9					
14	12	Doncaster Rovers	0-4		8373	5				8		3	4					7	11		10	2		6	1	9					
15	19	WIGAN BOROUGH	0-0		2354	5	2			9		3						7	11		8			6	1			4		10	
16	Dec 3	HARTLEPOOLS UNITED	1-3	Roberts	2505	5	2			9		3		11				7		8	10			6	1			4			
17	10	Accrington Stanley	0-0		3771			3				2	8					7	11					6	1		9	4	5	10	
18	17	NEW BRIGHTON	2-3	Oxley, Elwood	1984			3				2	8	11				7						6	1		9	4	5	10	
19	24	Bradford City	3-3	Turnbull 2, Williams	7236			3			4	2	8					7	11						1		9	6	5	10	
20	26	Rotherham United	2-1	Price, Turnbull	6748			3			4	2	8					7	11						1		9	6	5	10	
21	27	ROTHERHAM UNITED	2-5	Turnbull, Oxley	5227			3			4	2	8					7	11						1		9	6	5	10	
22	31	Wrexham	2-1	Oxley, Williams	2399	2		3					8					7	11					6	1		9	4	5	10	
23	Jan 7	HALIFAX TOWN	3-0	Turnbull 2, Elwood	3437	2		3	1				8					7	11					6			9	4	5	10	
24	14	ACCRINGTON STANLEY	3-1	Williams, Price, Turnbull	3358			3	1			2	8					7	11					6			9	4	5	10	
25	21	BRADFORD PARK AVE.	0-0		6465	5		3	1			2	8				11	7						6			9	4		10	
26	28	Tranmere Rovers	3-6	Williams 2, Nutter	4162	5		3	1			2	8				11	7						6			9	4		10	
27	Feb 4	STOCKPORT COUNTY	1-1	Nutter	4768			3	1			2	8				11	7						6			9	4	5	10	
28	11	Barrow	0-2		3166			3	1			2	8				11	7						6			9	4	5	10	
29	18	NELSON	6-0	*See below	3804			3	1	9		2	8						11					6			7	4	5	10	
30	25	Rochdale	1-5	Williams	2602			3	1	9		2	8						11					6			7	4	5	10	
31	Mar 3	Darlington	2-4	Oxley, Nutter	6003		2	3	1				5				11	8						6			7	4	9	10	
32	10	ASHINGTON	3-0	Clayson, Oxley, Williams	2422		2	3	1	8	4		5				11	7									9	6		10	
33	17	Crewe Alexandra	1-4	Wass	4123		2	3	1		4		5		8		11	7									9	6		10	
34	24	DONCASTER ROVERS	1-0	Stevenson	4696		2		1			3	8				11	7					9	6				4	5	10	
35	31	Wigan Borough	2-3	Oxley, Williams	3299				1			3	8				11	7				2	9	6				4	5	10	
36	Apr 6	Southport	1-2	Williams	4369				1		6	3	5		8		11	7			10	2						4		9	
37	7	LINCOLN CITY	0-1		4770				1	8	6	3	5		10			7	11			2						4		9	
38	9	SOUTHPORT	5-2	Williams 2, Oxley 2, Clayson	3515		3		1	9	6		5				11	7			8	2						4		10	
39	11	Lincoln City	0-0		3650		3		1	9			5				11	7			8	2		6				4		10	
40	14	Hartlepools United	0-1		1314		3		1	9	4		5				11	7			8	2		6						10	
41	28	New Brighton	3-3	Turnbull, Nutter, Oxley	2702		2		1		4						11	7			8	3		6			9		5	10	
42	May 5	BRADFORD CITY	2-0	Roseboom 2	2152		2		1		4							7			8	3	10	6			9		5		11
					Apps	9	11	21	20	22	11	32	38	2	3	2	14	33	25	5	18	18	3	34	22	4	29	37	17	31	1
					Goals					11			4			1	4	10	6	1	3		1			1	11	3		15	

Scorers in game 29: Wass 2(1p), Clayson 2, Elwood, Williams

F.A. Cup

						Abbott SW	Beeson GW	Betton A	Bilcliff B	Clayson WJ	Cousins H	Dennis W	Elwood JH	Hall JG	Hooper C	Matthews F	Nutter W	Oxley B	Price FT	Roberts, Harry	Roseboom E	Saxby A	Stevenson WW	Thompson O	Thomson JY	Tuckley WL	Turnbull WJ	Wass H	Whitworth E	Williams RS	Winfield W
R1	Nov 26	Darlington	1-4	Roseboom	6916	5				10		3						7	11		8	2		6	1			4		9	

Clapton Orient

20th in Division Two

No	Month	Day	Opponent	Score	Scorers	Att	Ames LEG	Batten HG	Broadbent WH	Campbell A	Collins WE	Corkindale WJ	Dennison R	Duffy B	Evans TJ	Galbraith JMcD	Gardner JR	Holland J	Hope P	Jewhurst FH	Kerr RC	Lyons AT	MacDonald RJ	Sage W	Slater TA	Smith SC	Spence JFV	Streets SEE	Surtees AE	Turnbull RH	Whipp PL	Williams JT	Wood A	Woodward JH
1	Aug	27	Grimsby Town	2-2	Kerr, Dennison	15051			4	2	7	11	10	6	3	5					9										8		1	
2		29	SOUTHAMPTON	2-0	Dennison, Corkindale	13711			4	2	7	11	10	6					3		9						5				8		1	
3	Sep	3	READING	3-0	Duffy, Whipp, Kerr	18593			4	2	7	11	10	6	3						9			5							8		1	
4		5	Southampton	3-1	Kerr, Dennison, Whipp	7982			4	2	7	11	10	6	3						9						5				8		1	
5		10	Blackpool	1-0	Kerr	12337			4	2	7	11	10	6	3						9						5				8		1	
6		17	CHELSEA	2-1	Whipp, Kerr	34838			4		7	11	10	6	3				2		9						5				8		1	
7		24	Barnsley	2-4	Gardner 2	11951			4		7	11	10	6	3		9		2								5				8		1	
8	Oct	1	West Bromwich Albion	1-4	Corkindale	19994			4		7	11	10	6	3		9		2								5				8		1	
9		8	BRISTOL CITY	4-2	Dennison 3, Whipp	21202			4		7	11	10		3	5			2		9			6							8		1	
10		15	Stoke City	0-2		15009			4		7	11	10		3	5			2		9			6							8		1	
11		22	PRESTON NORTH END	1-1	Dennison	10533			4		7	11	10	6	3	5			2		9										8		1	
12		29	Swansea Town	0-5		12562			4		7	11	10	6		5			2		9	3						8					1	
13	Nov	5	FULHAM	3-2	Dennison, Gardner 2	15877			4		7	11	10	6		5	9		2				3								8		1	
14		12	Hull City	2-2	Smith, Gardner	6682			4		7		10	6		5	9		2				3			11					8			1
15		19	MANCHESTER CITY	0-2		14129					7	11	10			6	9		2	4			3				5				8		1	
16		26	South Shields	2-2	Whipp 2	5771			4		7		10	6		5	9		2				3			11					8		1	
17	Dec	3	LEEDS UNITED	2-1	Kerr 2	12838			4		7				3	5		10			9		2			11	6				8		1	
18		10	Nottingham Forest	3-4	Collins, Whipp 2	7802			4		7		10			5					9	3	2			11	6				8		1	
19		17	PORT VALE	0-1		9287			4		7		10			5			3		9		2			11	6				8		1	
20		24	Wolverhampton Wan.	3-5	MacDougall (og), Whipp, Holland	6023			4		7	11				5		10	3		9		2				6				8		1	
21		27	Oldham Athletic	0-5		23333			4		7	11				5	9		3		10		2				6				8		1	
22		31	GRIMSBY TOWN	1-2	Holland	8738	7		4	2		11	9	6		5		10					3								8		1	
23	Jan	7	Reading	0-4		10533	11		4	2	7			6		5		10			9	3									8		1	
24		21	BLACKPOOL	2-5	Gardner 2	11401			4			7				6	9					2	3				5		10		8	11	1	
25		28	Chelsea	0-1		17875			10	2	7			6		5					9		3	4							8	11	1	
26	Feb	4	BARNSLEY	2-0	Bradbent, Whipp	8985			10	2	7			6		5					9		3	4							8	11	1	
27		11	WEST BROMWICH ALB.	0-0		11443			10	2	7			6		5	9						3	4							8	11	1	
28		18	Bristol City	1-5	Streets	15432			10	2	7			6		5							3	4				9			8	11	1	
29		25	STOKE CITY	3-2	Turnbull, Whipp, Williams	20084		10		2	7			6		5							3	4						9	8	11	1	
30	Mar	3	Preston North End	0-0		18886		10	6	2	7					5							3	4						9	8	11	1	
31		10	SWANSEA TOWN	1-1	Turnbull	11508		10	6	2	7					5							3	4						9	8	11	1	
32		17	Fulham	0-2		21452		10	6	2	7					5							3	4						9	8	11	1	
33		24	HULL CITY	0-0		8869		10	4	2	7					5		6					3							9	8	11	1	
34		31	Manchester City	3-5	Turnbull 2, Batten	38272		10	4	2	7					5		6					3							9	8	11	1	
35	Apr	6	Notts County	0-3		13924		10	4	2	7			6		5							3							9	8	11	1	
36		7	SOUTH SHIELDS	2-2	Dennison, Turnbull	11019		5	4		7		10	6					2				3							9	8	11	1	
37		9	NOTTS COUNTY	0-1		10166		10	4		7		8	6		5			2				3		1					9		11		
38		14	Leeds United	0-4		22884	7		4				10	6					2		9	3		5	1	11					8			
39		16	OLDHAM ATHLETIC	2-0	Corkindale, Kerr	2929	7		4			11	10	6		5					9	3	2		1						8			
40		21	NOTTM. FOREST	2-2	Whipp, Kerr	9451	7		4			11	10	6		5					9	3	2								8		1	
41		28	Port Vale	0-0		5966	7		4			11	10	6		5					9	3	2								8		1	
42	May	5	WOLVERHAMPTON W.	0-0		12891		8	4			11	10	6		5					9	3	2		1							7		
						Apps	6	10	40	18	35	22	26	28	11	33	9	6	18	1	23	9	28	12	4	6	13	2	1	9	39	15	37	1
						Goals		1	1		1	3	10	1			7	2			8					1		1		5	12	1		

One own goal

F.A. Cup

No	Month	Day	Opponent	Score	Scorers	Att	Ames LEG	Batten HG	Broadbent WH	Campbell A	Collins WE	Corkindale WJ	Dennison R	Duffy B	Evans TJ	Galbraith JMcD	Gardner JR	Holland J	Hope P	Jewhurst FH	Kerr RC	Lyons AT	MacDonald RJ	Sage W	Slater TA	Smith SC	Spence JFV	Streets SEE	Surtees AE	Turnbull RH	Whipp PL	Williams JT	Wood A	Woodward JH
R3	Jan	14	Swindon Town	1-2	Whipp	19079			4		7					6	9		3				2			11	5		10		8		1	

Coventry City

20th in Division Three (South)

	Date		Opponent	Score	Scorers	Att	Bell WC	Bird W	Brown W	Clarke G	Crisp J	Dinsdale N	Fergus A	Galloway SR	Gardiner JG	Gay J	Heathcote I	Heigh R	Herbert F	Hickman W	Houldey CA	Hunter W	Johnson GH	Johnstone W	Lavender HA	McClure A	Newton J	Ramage J	Ramage PMF	Randle J	Raynor HA	Stanford H	Stoddart WNE	Tinning GE	Townsend JS	Ward D	Widdowson A
1	Aug	27	Watford	1-3	Stoddart	10151		6					2				8		10				7		11	5	1	4		3			9				
2		29	Swindon Town	0-6		8846		6					2					8	10				7		11		1	5		3			9				
3	Sep	3	CHARLTON ATHLETIC	3-3	Heathcote 2, Herbert	10958		6					2				8		10	5			7	9			1			3					11		
4		5	SWINDON TOWN	4-0	* See below	9553		4		6			2				8			5				9	7				10	3		1			11		
5		10	Bristol Rovers	1-1	Heathcote	9688		4		6			2				8			5				9	7				10	3		1			11		
6		17	PLYMOUTH ARGYLE	1-1	Heathcote	15249		4		6			2				8			5				9	7				10	3		1			11		
7		24	Merthyr Town	2-3	Hickman, Johnstone	3148		4		6			2				8			5				9			1		7	3					11		
8	Oct	1	WALSALL	0-1		13662		4		6			2				8		11	5				9					10	3		1					
9		8	Gillingham	2-1	Bird, Herbert	4667		4					2		6		8		11	5			7	99					10	3		1					
10		15	SOUTHEND UNITED	6-1	* See below	11059		4					2		6		8		11			5	7	9					10	3		1					
11		22	Brentford	1-4	Heathcote	4666		4					2		6		8		11			5	7	9					10	3		1					
12		29	BOURNEMOUTH	3-2	Heathcote 2, Johnstone	10933		4					2		6		8		11			5		9	7				10	3		1					
13	Nov	5	Brighton & Hove Albion	0-3		7153		4					2		6	3	8	7	11			5		9					10			1					
14		12	LUTON TOWN	4-2	Heathcote 2, Johnstone 2	10141		4							6	3	8		11	5		2	7	9					10			1					
15		19	Millwall	1-9	J Ramage	13695		6	4				2				8		11	5			7	9				3	10			1					
16	Dec	3	Exeter City	1-0	Heathcote	5716	11	7								3	8					6		9		5	1		10					2			
17		10	WATFORD	2-3	McClure, Heathcote	7448		7								3	8					6		9		5	1		10					2	11		
18		17	Norwich City	2-0	Bird 2	5358		7			10					3	8					6		9		5	1							2	11		
19		24	NORTHAMPTON T	2-4	Heathcote, Townsend	9250		7			10					3	8					6		9		5	1							2	11		
20		27	QUEEN'S PARK RANGERS	0-0		8975			4		10					3	8	7				6		9		5	1							2	11		
21	Jan	7	Charlton Athletic	1-2	Herbert	8866		7	4		8					3			10			6		9		5	1							2	11		
22		14	TORQUAY UNITED	5-1	Bird 2,Crisp,Galloway,Herbert	6878		7	4		8			9		3			10			6				5	1							2	11		
23		21	BRISTOL ROVERS	2-3	Herbert 2	9521		7	4		8			9		3			10			6				5	1							2	11		
24		28	Plymouth Argyle	0-4		4366		7	4		8			9		3			10			6				5	1							2	11		
25	Feb	4	MERTHYR TOWN	1-2	Herbert	6586			4		8		2		6	3			10				7	9		5	1								11		
26		11	Walsall	0-7		5878			4				2			3	9		10			6	7			5			8						11		
27		13	CRYSTAL PALACE	2-2	Herbert 2	2059			4				3		6				10			5		7					8				9	2			
28		18	GILLINGHAM	1-2	Hunter	8500			4				3		6				10			5		7					8					2		9	
29		25	Southend United	2-3	Bird, Herbert	5979	6	7	4										10		2	3				5	1		8							9	
30	Mar	3	BRENTFORD	0-0		8188	6	7	4										10		2	3				5	1		8							9	
31		10	Bournemouth	3-2	Johnson 2, Herbert	4493	6		4			5							10		2	3	7				1									9	8
32		17	BRIGHTON & HOVE ALB	2-2	Dinsdale, Widdowson	10695	6		4			5							10		2	3	7				1									9	8
33		24	Luton Town	1-3	Ward	8054			4			5			6						2	3	7				1		10							9	8
34		31	MILLWALL	0-3		11188			4			5			6						2	3	7				1		10							9	8
35	Apr	7	Torquay United	3-2	Herbert, Ward, Davies (og)	3275			4			5			6		8		11		2	3					1									9	10
36		9	Newport County	0-3		5170			4			5			6		8		11		2	3					1									9	10
37		10	NEWPORT COUNTY	0-2		10295						5			6		8		11		2	3					1				4					9	10
38		14	EXETER CITY	0-0		6905						5		9	6				11		2	3					1		10		4						8
39		21	Crystal Palace	0-1		5908	6		4			5							11		2	3		9			1		10								8
40		26	Queen's Park Rangers	5-1	Dinsdale 3, P Ramage 2	4095	6					9							11		2	3					1		10		4		5				8
41		28	NORWICH CITY	2-2	Herbert, Richmond (og)	9103	6					9							11		2	3					1		10		4		5				8
42	May	5	Northampton Town	1-2	Dinsdale	7583	6					9							11		2	3					1		10		4		5				8
						Apps	9	25	19	5	8	12	18	4	15	13	23	3	31	9	14	31	14	23	6	14	28	3	26	12	5	11	6	11	15	10	12
						Goals		6			1	5		1			15		13	2		1	2	7		1		1	5				1		1	2	1

Two own goals

Scorers in game 4: Hickman, Heathcote, Johnstone, P Ramage

Scorers in game 10: Heathcote 2, Johnstone 2, P Ramage 2

JY Thompson played in games 26 to 28 at 1

FD Reeve played in game 7 at 10 and game 8 at 7

HFJ Askew played in 6 games at 4; 2, 3 amd 16 to 19 inclusive

CG Ball played in 8 games at 7; 35 to 42 inclusive

JB Barnes played in 8 games at 11; 27 to 34 inclusive

F.A. Cup

	Date		Opponent	Score	Scorers	Att	Bell WC	Bird W	Brown W	Clarke G	Crisp J	Dinsdale N	Fergus A	Galloway SR	Gardiner JG	Gay J	Heathcote I	Heigh R	Herbert F	Hickman W	Houldey CA	Hunter W	Johnson GH	Johnstone W	Lavender HA	McClure A	Newton J	Ramage J	Ramage PMF	Randle J	Raynor HA	Stanford H	Stoddart WNE	Tinning GE	Townsend JS	Ward D	Widdowson A
R1	Nov	26	BOURNEMOUTH	2-2	Bird, P Ramage	13627	6	7					2			3	8		11			4		9			1	5	10								
rep		30	Bournemouth	0-2		5566	6	7								3	8		11			4		9		5	1		10					2			

Crewe Alexandra

17th in Division Three (North)

	Date	Opponent	Score	Scorers	Att	Alcock GL	Birtles F	Blake A	Boardman W	Brown J	Connell WC	Cooper A	Craig J	Davies B	Davies SH	Evans CH	Hindle F	Ireland W	Jones JW	Kay H	Morris Harry	Morris Harold	O'Connor JP	Owen J	Pringle RJ	Ralphs BVH	Sewell A	Shaw C	Shaw MV	Swindells H	Thomas LJ	Thornley T	Wareham J	Wootton H
1	Aug 27	HALIFAX TOWN	1-1	Kay	5174				11			9	8	1	3					4	5			10	2	7			6					
2	29	Ashington	2-0	Cooper, Owen	1825		8	5	11			9		1	3					4				10	2	7			6					
3	31	Wrexham	0-2		5259	10		5	11			9	8	1	3					4					2	7			6					
4	Sep 3	Bradford City	1-4	Kay	17491	10		8	11		1	9								4		5			2	7			6					3
5	5	WREXHAM	1-1	Craig	4158	10			11			9	8	1						4		5			2	7			6					3
6	10	NEW BRIGHTON	1-1	Owen	4656				11	9			8	1						4		5		10	2	7			6					3
7	17	Lincoln City	2-5	Kay, Owen	7175				11					1						9	4	5		10	2	7		8	6					3
8	24	HARTLEPOOLS UNITED	4-0	Boardman, Birtles, Owen, Kay	3016		9		11				8	1						4	5			10	2	7			6					3
9	Oct 1	Accrington Stanley	0-5		3675		9		11				8	1						4	5			10	2	7			6					3
10	8	WIGAN BOROUGH	1-2	Brown	4005		8		11	9				1						4	5			10	2	7			6					3
11	15	Doncaster Rovers	1-3	Cooper	6973				11	8		9		1						4	5			10	2	7			6					3
12	22	Tranmere Rovers	3-3	Cooper, Boardman, Owen	3817				11	8		9		1						5		4		10	2	7			6					3
13	29	BRADFORD PARK AVE.	1-3	Owen	5207				11	8		9		1						2	5	4		10		7			6					3
14	Nov 5	Chesterfield	2-3	Brown, Ralphs	3471					8		9		1						4	5			10	2	7			6				11	3
15	12	STOCKPORT COUNTY	3-0	Evans, Brown, Harry Morris	4185					9				1		8				4	5			10	2	7			6				11	3
16	19	Barrow	1-1	Brown	3869					9				1		8				4	5			10	2	7			6				11	3
17	Dec 3	Rochdale	0-4		3991		10			8				1				9		4	5					7			6		3	2	11	
18	17	Southport	2-3	Owen 2	3326					8				1				9		4	5			10	2	7			6				11	3
19	24	DURHAM CITY	5-2	M Shaw 3, Owen 2	2689		11			8				1						4	5			10	2	7	6		9					3
20	26	DARLINGTON	3-3	Kay, M Shaw 2	5326		11			8				1						4	5			10	2	7	6		9					3
21	31	Halifax Town	0-0		4266		11			8				1						4	5			10	2	7	6		9					3
22	Jan 2	NELSON	6-1	M Shaw 3, Owen 2, Birtles	2430		11			8				1						4	5			10	2	7	6		9					3
23	7	BRADFORD CITY	2-1	Owen, Pringle	5993		11			8				1						4	5			10	2	7	6		9					3
24	21	New Brighton	1-5	Owen	4039		11			8				1						4	5			10	2	7	6		9					3
25	Feb 4	Hartlepools United	3-4	Brown, M Shaw, Kay	3100		11	6		8				1		10				4	5				2	7			9					3
26	8	ROTHERHAM UNITED	3-2	Kay, Brown, Evans	2169		11	6		8	1					10				4	5				2	7			9					3
27	11	ACCRINGTON STANLEY	2-3	M Shaw 2	2576		11	6		8				1						4	5			10	2	7			9					3
28	18	Wigan Borough	1-2	Kay	3259		11							1		10				4	5			8	2	7	6		9					3
29	25	DONCASTER ROVERS	4-1	M Shaw, Owen, Kay, Evans	4861		11							1		8				4	5			10	2	7	6		9					3
30	Mar 3	TRANMERE ROVERS	2-3	Owen 2	5307									1		8				4	5		7	10	2	11	6		9					3
31	10	Bradford Park Avenue	0-2		9504		11							1		8			3	4	5			10	2	7	6		9					
32	17	CHESTERFIELD	4-1	Kay, O'Connor, Evans, Ralphs	4123		11							1		9			3	4	5		8	10	2	7	6							
33	21	LINCOLN CITY	0-0		1856		11							1		8			3	4	5			10	2	7	6		9					
34	24	Stockport County	0-1		9766									1		8		9	3	4	5			10	2	7	6						11	
35	31	BARROW	4-1	M Shaw 2, Evans, Owen	3536		11							1		8			3	4	5			10	2	7	6		9					
36	Apr 6	ASHINGTON	3-0	M Shaw 2, Owen	5874		11			8				1					3	4	5			10	2	7	6		9					
37	7	Rotherham United	0-2		3625		11			8				1					3	4	5			10	2	7	6		9					
38	9	Darlington	3-1	Brooks (og), M Shaw, Ralphs	4584		11			8				1					3	4		5		10	2	7	6		9					
39	14	ROCHDALE	1-1	Owen	2887		11							1					3	4	5			10	2	7	6		9	8				
40	21	Nelson	3-3	Birtles, Ralphs, Kay	2349		11							1			8		3	4	5			10	2	7	6		9					
41	28	SOUTHPORT	0-1		2552		11							1		8			3	4	5			10	2	7	6		9					
42	May 5	Durham City	1-5	M Shaw	851		11							1		8			3	4	5			10	2	7	6		9					
					Apps	3	27	6	13	22	2	9	6	40	3	14	1	3	12	42	35	7	2	36	40	42	21	1	40	1	1	1	6	26
					Goals		3		2	6		3	1			5				11	1		1	22	1	4			16					

One own goal

F.A. Cup

	Date	Opponent	Score	Scorers	Att	Alcock GL	Birtles F	Blake A	Boardman W	Brown J	Connell WC	Cooper A	Craig J	Davies B	Davies SH	Evans CH	Hindle F	Ireland W	Jones JW	Kay H	Morris Harry	Morris Harold	O'Connor JP	Owen J	Pringle RJ	Ralphs BVH	Sewell A	Shaw C	Shaw MV	Swindells H	Thomas LJ	Thornley T	Wareham J	Wootton H
R1	Nov 26	ASHINGTON	2-2	Owen, Wareham	4800					9				1		8				4	5			10	2	7			6				11	3
rep	30	Ashington	2-0	Ralphs, Ireland	3000									1		8		9		4	5			10	2	7			6				11	3
R2	Dec 10	STOCKPORT COUNTY	2-0	Kay, Owen	9064					8				1				9		4	5			10	2	7			6				11	3
R3	Jan 14	London Caledonians	3-2	M Shaw, Owen 2	26955		11			8				1						4	5			10	2	7	6		9					3
R4	28	Aston Villa	0-3		41000		11	6		8				1						4	5			10	2	7			9					3

R3 played at Stamford Bridge

Crystal Palace

5th in Division Three (South)

	Date		Opponent	Score	Scorers	Att	Barnes VHB	Brown J	Callender JW	Clarke GB	Cross CA	Flood JJ	Gallagher HS	Grant WA	Greener R	Hallam C	Hamilton J	Harry AE	Havelock PHW	Hilley C	Holmes E	Hopkins H	Hunt MH	Ivey LA	James WJH	Kelly J	Mulcahy PT	Orr R	Salt H	Smith LF	Tonner J	Turner W	Williamson WG
1	Aug	27	Norwich City	1-4	Hallam	13140			1	11	3	7	4			10	5			6								2			9		8
2		29	EXETER CITY	2-0	Hallam, Clark	11329			1	11	3	7	4			10	5			6								2			9		8
3	Sep	3	NORTHAMPTON T	1-0	Hilley	13771			1	11	3	7	4		6		5			10								2				8	9
4		7	Exeter City	2-2	Williamson, Hilley	5906				11	3	7	4				5			6						1		2			10	8	9
5		10	Southend United	1-6	Clarke	6808				11	3	7	4	9			5			6		2				1					10	8	
6		17	BRIGHTON & HOVE ALB	1-1	Hamilton	13557				11		7	4	9			5			6	3					1		2			10	8	
7		24	Bournemouth	2-2	Flood, Turner	5933				11		7	4				5			6	3					1		2			10	8	9
8	Oct	1	BRENTFORD	0-2		11552				11		7	4	9			5			6	3					1		2			10	8	
9		8	Luton Town	1-6	Clarke	8844				11		7			6		5				3					1		2		4	10	8	9
10		15	MILLWALL	0-4		18930	10			11					6		5	7			3		1					2		4	9	8	
11		22	QUEEN'S PARK RANGERS	1-1	Clarke	7115			1	11			4				5	7		6	3				9			2			10	8	
12		29	Watford	1-2	Turner	7346			1	11			4	10			5	7		6	3				9			2				8	
13	Nov	5	CHARLTON ATHLETIC	5-0	Turner, Havelock 2, Clarke 2	16694			1	11		7			6		4		9		3	10						2		5		8	
14		12	Swindon Town	3-3	Flood, Hopkins, Turner	7608				11	2	8	4		6			7			3	9				1				5		10	
15		19	NEWPORT COUNTY	2-0	Clarke 2	8683				11	2	7			6		4		9		3	10				1				5		8	
16	Dec	3	GILLINGHAM	2-2	Harry, Hopkins	9299				11	2	8			6		4	7			3	9				1				5		10	
17		17	MERTHYR TOWN	2-0	Harry, Barnes	6809	11	10			2				6		4	7			3	9				1				5		8	
18		24	Plymouth Argyle	1-5	Harry	11515	11	10			2				6		4	7			3	9				1				5	8		
19		27	Torquay United	2-0	Hopkins, Brown	3353		10		11	2				6		4	7			3	9		5		1					8		
20		31	NORWICH CITY	2-1	Clarke, Hopkins	7446		10		11	2				6		4	7			3	9				1				5	8		
21	Jan	7	Northampton Town	1-1	Greener	9860		10		11	2				6		4	7			3	9				1				5	8		
22		14	Walsall	1-1	Hopkins	4297		10		11	2				6		4	7			3	9				1				5	8		
23		21	SOUTHEND UNITED	4-1	Tonner 2, Brown, Clearke	10606		10		11	2				6		4	7				9				1		3	5		8		
24		28	Brighton & Hove Albion	2-4	Brown, Clarke	4494		10		11	2				6		4	7				9				1		3	5		8		
25	Feb	4	BOURNEMOUTH	6-1	Clarke 3, Hopkins, Tonner 2	10862				11	2				6		4	7				9				1		3	5		10	8	
26		11	Brentford	1-2	Turner	7580				11	2				6		4	7				9				1		3	5		10	8	
27		13	Coventry City	2-2	Hopkins 2	2059				11	2	8			6		4	7				9				1		3	5		10		
28		18	LUTON TOWN	3-2	Tonner 2, Salt	13370			1	11	2				6		4	7				9					8	3	5		10		
29		25	Millwall	1-1	Clarke	27736			1	11	2				6		4	7				9						3	5		10	8	
30	Mar	3	Queen's Park Rangers	0-2		16468			1	11	2				6			7				9						3	5	4	10	8	
31		10	WATFORD	2-1	Hopkins, Tonner	9851			1	11	2				6		4	7				9						3	5		10	8	
32		14	TORQUAY UNITED	3-2	Hopkins, Clarke, Turner	4842			1	11	2				6		4	7				9					10	3	5			8	
33		17	Charlton Athletic	4-0	Hopkins 2, Clarke, Harry	11083			1	11	2				6		4	7				9					10	3	5			8	
34		24	SWINDON TOWN	1-0	Harry	8373			1	11	2				6		4	7				9					10	3	5			8	
35	Apr	6	BRISTOL ROVERS	3-2	Clarke 2, Mulcahy	16126			1	11	2				6		4	7				9					10	3	5			8	
36		7	WALSALL	5-1	Hopkins, Clarke 2, Harry, Mulcahy	12530			1	11	2				6		4	7				9					10	3	5			8	
37		9	Bristol Rovers	1-1	Harry	6275				11	2				6		4	7				9				1	10	3	5			8	
38		14	Gillingham	1-3	Mulcahy	3623				11	2				6		4	7				9				1	10	3	5			8	
39		21	COVENTRY CITY	1-0	Mulcahy	5908			1	11	2				6		4	7				9					10	3	5			8	
40		26	Newport County	3-0	Clarke, Hopkins, Harry	2554			1	11	2				6		4	7				9					10	3	5			8	
41		28	Merthyr Town	2-2	Mulcahy, Turner	2169			1	11	2				6		4	7				9					10	3	5			8	
42	May	5	PLYMOUTH ARGYLE	0-2		12218			1	11	2				6		4	7				9					10	3	5			8	
						Apps	3	8	19	40	34	14	11	4	33	2	40	31	2	10	17	31	1	1	2	22	12	32	20	12	24	31	6
						Goals	1	2		22		2			1	2	1	8	2	2		14					5		1		8	7	1

F.A. Cup

	Date		Opponent	Score	Scorers	Att	Barnes VHB	Brown J	Callender JW	Clarke GB	Cross CA	Flood JJ	Gallagher HS	Grant WA	Greener R	Hallam C	Hamilton J	Harry AE	Havelock PHW	Hilley C	Holmes E	Hopkins H	Hunt MH	Ivey LA	James WJH	Kelly J	Mulcahy PT	Orr R	Salt H	Smith LF	Tonner J	Turner W	Williamson WG
R1	Nov	26	Dartford	3-1	Hopkins 2, Smith	6227				11	2	7			6		4		9		3	10				1				5		8	
R2	Dec	10	Swindon Town	0-0		16360	7		1	11	2	8			6		4				3	9								5		10	
rep		14	SWINDON TOWN	1-2	Hopkins	8500	7		1	11	2	8			6		4				3	9								5		10	

Darlington

7th in Division Three (North)

	Date	Opponent	Score	Scorers	Att.	Archibald J	Brooks J	Cassidy D	Childs JA	Cochrane AF	Deacon J	Dickson H	Fawcett DH	Gardner W	Gilfillan HM	Greaves T	Gregg RE	Harris J	Hutchinson R	Kelly J	Lees HH	McGiffen J	McKinnell JTB	Mellon JM	O'Donnell W	Penn T	Race W	Ruddy T	Scott J	Wallace FJ	Waugh J
1	Aug 27	NEW BRIGHTON	3-0	Ruddy, Dickson, Race	6961	1				10		4			11	2							6			3	7	9	8		5
2	31	Bradford City	1-0	Cochrane	15334	1	2			10		4			11								6			3	7		8		5
3	Sep 3	Lincoln City	0-1		7192	1	2		6	10		4			11		9									3	7		8		5
4	10	HARTLEPOOLS UNITED	5-0	Race, Gregg 3, Scott	6719	1	2			10		4			11		9						6			3	7		8		5
5	17	Accrington Stanley	0-0		7392	1	2			10		4			11		9						6			3	7		8		5
6	19	Halifax Town	1-2	Cochrane	4101	1	2			10		4			11		9						6			3	7				5
7	24	WIGAN BOROUGH	1-0	Harris	5921	1	2			10		4		8			9	11					6			3	7				5
8	Oct 1	Doncaster Rovers	0-5		5989	1	2			10		4		9	11	3							6				7		8		5
9	8	SOUTHPORT	3-1	Gregg, Cochrane, Cassidy	4789	1	2	7		10		4		9		3	8						6				11				5
10	15	ASHINGTON	5-1	Gregg 3, Dickson, Race	4902	1	2	7		10	8	4				3	9						6				11				5
11	22	Chesterfield	3-1	Dickson, Gregg, Childs	2899	1		7	9	10		4				2	8						6	3			11				5
12	29	WREXHAM	1-3	Dickson	6692	1		7		10		4				2	9				8		6	3			11				5
13	Nov 5	Durham City	3-3	Gregg, Cochrane, Lees	3274	1		7		10		4				2	9				8	11	6	3							5
14	12	BRADFORD PARK AVE.	1-3	Ruddy	7976	1		7				4					10				8	11	6	3		2		9			5
15	19	Tranmere Rovers	1-3	Lees	4099	1	2		5	10		4									8	11	6			3		9			
16	Dec 3	Barrow	0-2		4327	1	2			7		4					8				10	11	6			3		9			5
17	17	Rochdale	1-4	Cochrane	3912	1	2			7		4					8				10	11	6			3		9			5
18	24	ROTHERHAM UNITED	4-1	Lees, Gregg 2, Gardner	3409	1	2			7		4		8			9				10	11	6			3					5
19	26	Crewe Alexandra	3-3	Gregg, Lees, Gardner	5326	1	2			7		4		8			9				10	11	6	3							5
20	31	New Brighton	0-0		1829	1	2			7		4					8				10	11	6	3				9			5
21	Jan 2	BRADFORD CITY	1-2	Gregg	5248	1	2			7		4					8				10	11	6	3				9			5
22	7	LINCOLN CITY	9-2	*See below	8365	1	2			7							8			4	10	11	6	3				9			5
23	21	Hartlepools United	1-0	Cochrane	7485	1	2		5	7		4					8				10		6	3				9	11		
24	28	ACCRINGTON STANLEY	3-0	Ruddy, Lees, Gregg	3132	1	2			7		4					8				10		6	3				9			5
25	Feb 4	Wigan Borough	3-0	Gardner, Lees, Gregg	2000	1	2			7		4		9			8			11	10		6	3							5
26	11	DONCASTER ROVERS	3-0	Gardner 3	6714	1	2			7		4		9			8			11	10		6	3							5
27	18	Southport	0-2		4293	1	2	7		11		4		9			8			6	10			3							5
28	25	Ashington	3-2	Lees, Gardner 2	4232	1	2			7		4		9			8			11	10		6	3							5
29	Mar 3	CHESTERFIELD	4-2	Gardner 2, Lees, Gregg	6003	1	2			7		4		9			8		11		10		6	3							5
30	10	Wrexham	2-1	Cochrane, Gregg	3794	1	2			7		4		9			8		11		10		6	3							5
31	17	DURHAM CITY	5-0	Gregg 2, Gardner 2, Dickson	4668	1	2			7		4		9			8		11		10			3							5
32	24	Bradford Park Avenue	3-6	Gardner 2, Lees	16294	1	2			7		4		9			8			6	10			3				11			5
33	31	TRANMERE ROVERS	3-7	Gardner, Lees, Kelly	4989	1	2			7		4		9			8			11	10		6	3							5
34	Apr 6	HALIFAX TOWN	2-0	Gregg, Wheelhouse (og)	6187		2			7		4	1	9			8			11	10		6		3						5
35	7	Nelson	0-4		3816		2		5	7		4	1	8						6	10	11				3		9			
36	9	CREWE ALEXANDRA	1-3	Pringle (og)	4584		2	11		7		4	1	9			10			6	8					3					5
37	14	BARROW	1-1	McGiffen	1904		2			7		4	1	9			8				10	11	6		3						5
38	16	NELSON	4-1	Ruddy 2, McGiffen 2	1003			7				4	1				8					11	6	3	2			9		10	5
39	21	Stockport County	0-4		6921		2	7				4	1				8					11	6		3			9		10	5
40	23	STOCKPORT COUNTY	3-1	Lees 2, Waugh	1925		2			7		4	1				8				10	11	6	3				9			5
41	28	ROCHDALE	1-0	Gregg	2708		2			7	10	4	1				8					11	6	3				9			5
42	May 5	Rotherham United	1-3	Gardner	2058		2			11			1	7			8				10		6	3				9			5
					Apps	33	36	10	5	39	2	40	9	19	7	7	37	1	3	10	28	16	36	23	4	14	12	17	7	2	39
					Goals			1	1	8		5		16			21	1		1	16	4					3	8	1		1

Scorers in game 22: Lees 3, Ruddy 3, McGiffen, Gregg, Cochrane

Played in one game: J Armstrong (31, at 6), TO Carmedy (2,9), JG Dodsworth (42, 4), JP O'Connor (15,7), J Smith (24, 11), C Yorke (6, at 8).

Two own goals

F.A. Cup

	Date	Opponent	Score	Scorers	Att.	Archibald J	Brooks J	Cassidy D	Childs JA	Cochrane AF	Deacon J	Dickson H	Fawcett DH	Gardner W	Gilfillan HM	Greaves T	Gregg RE	Harris J	Hutchinson R	Kelly J	Lees HH	McGiffen J	McKinnell JTB	Mellon JM	O'Donnell W	Penn T	Race W	Ruddy T	Scott J	Wallace FJ	Waugh J
R1	Nov 26	CHESTERFIELD	4-1	Ruddy 3, Lees	6916	1	2			7		4					8				10	11	6			3		9			5
R2	Dec 10	ROCHDALE	2-1	Ruddy 2	7571	1	2			7		4					8				10	11	6			3		9			5
R3	Jan 14	Liverpool	0-1		28500	1	2			7		4					8				10	11	6	3				9			5

Derby County

4th in Division One

#	Date		Opponent	Res	Scorers	Att	Bacon A	Bedford H	Carr WP	Collin G	Cooper T	Crilly T	Crooks SD	Davison TR	Gill JJ	Hampton JW	Hope J	Malloch GC	McIntyre JMcM	McLaverty B	Mee GW	Murphy L	O'Brien MT	Olney BA	Robinson TC	Scott A	Stephenson GT	Storer H	Thoms H	Thornewell G	White A	Whitehouse JC	Wightman H	Wilkes HT
1	Aug	27	WEST HAM UNITED	2-3	Bedford, Whitehouse	18538		9			2	3			8				4	6		11	5	1						7		10		
2	Sep	3	Portsmouth	2-2	Bedford, Whitehouse	23489		9			2	3		5	8				4			11		1				6		7		10		
3		5	NEWCASTLE UNITED	1-1	Gill	20829		9			2	3			8				4	5		11		1				6		7		10		
4		10	LEICESTER CITY	2-1	Gill, Whitehouse	26008		9			2	3	7		8				4	5		11		1				6				10		
5		14	Newcastle United	3-4	Bedford 3	36965		9			2	3	7				8					11		1		4		6	5			10		
6		17	Liverpool	2-5	Bedford 2	34336		9			2	3	7		8				4			11		1				6	5			10		
7		24	ARSENAL	4-0	Gill, Whitehouse, Murphy, Crooks	16539		9			2	3	7		8				4			11						6	5			10		1
8	Oct	1	Burnley	2-4	Gill, Whitehouse	11911		9			2	3	7	5	8				4			11						6				10		1
9		8	BURY	5-2	Crooks 2, Murphy, Bedford, McIntyre	15532		9	3		2		7	5	8				4			11						6				10		1
10		15	Sheffield United	0-1		24862		9	3		2			5			8		4			11						6		7		10		1
11		22	Manchester United	0-5		18304	9		3					5			8	6	4			11								7		10	2	1
12		29	TOTTENHAM HOTSPUR	1-1	Hope	15963	9		3		2						8		4			11						6	5	7		10		1
13	Nov	5	Huddersfield Town	1-2	Bedford	7098		9	3		2		7				8		4		11							6	5			10		1
14		12	EVERTON	0-3		21590		9	3		2		7						4		11						10	6	5			8		1
15		19	Cardiff City	4-4	Stephenson, Crooks, Bedford	6606		9	2	3			7						4		11						10	6	5			8		1
16		26	SHEFFIELD WEDNESDAY	4-6	Whitehouse 2, Mee, Stephenson	16067		9	2	3			7						4		11						10	6	5			8		1
17	Dec	10	BLACKBURN ROVERS	6-0	* see below	10617		9	2	3			7	5							11					4	10	6				8		1
18		17	Middlesbrough	3-3	Whitehouse, Stephenson, Crooks	15235		9	2	3			7	5							11					4	10	6				8		1
19		24	BIRMINGHAM	4-1	Stephenson, Mee, Crooks, Bedford	8535		9	2	3			7	5							11					4	10	6				8		1
20		26	ASTON VILLA	5-0	Bedford 2,Whitehouse 2,Stephenson	23303		9	2	3			7	5							11				4		10	6				8		1
21		27	Aston Villa	1-0	McIntyre	43228	7	9	2	3									4		11		5				10	6				8		1
22		31	West Ham United	2-2	Bedford, Stephenson	17702		9	2	3			7	5							11				4		10	6				8		1
23	Jan	2	Bolton Wanderers	3-1	Whitehouse 2, Stephenson	23569		9	2	3			7	5							11				4		10	6				8		1
24		7	PORTSMOUTH	2-2	Stephenson	18611		9	2	3			7	5							11					4	10	6				8		1
25		21	Leicester City	0-4		36094			2	3			7	5							11					4	10	6			9	8		1
26	Feb	4	Arsenal	4-3	Gill 3, Crooks	21405		9	2	3			7	5	8						11					4	10	6						1
27		11	BURNLEY	3-4	Gill 2, Storer	8503		9	2	3			7	5	8						11					4	10	6						1
28		15	LIVERPOOL	2-3	Gill, Bedford	9021		9	2	3			7	5	8						11					4	10	6						1
29		18	Bury	0-3		11424		9	2	3			7	5	8	1			4		11						10	6						
30		25	SHEFFIELD UNITED	2-1	Bedford, Whitehouse	14257		9	2	3			7	5				6	4		11						10					8		1
31	Mar	10	Tottenham Hotspur	2-1	Bedford, Whitehouse	22458		9	2	3			7	5					4		11						10	6				8		1
32		17	HUDDERSFIELD T	0-0		24684		9	2	3			7	5					4		11						10	6				8		1
33		24	Everton	2-2	Bedford, Storer	28541		9	2	3			7	5					4		11						10	6				8		1
34		28	MANCHESTER UNITED	5-0	Bedford 2, Stephenson, Whitehouse	8323		9	2	3			7	5					4		11						10	6				8		1
35		31	CARDIFF CITY	7-1	Bedford 4, Whitehouse 2, Crooks	15565		9	2	3			7	5					4		11						10	6				8		1
36	Apr	6	Sunderland	1-0	Bedford	27431		9	2	3			7	5		1			4		11						10	6				8		
37		7	Sheffield Wednesday	2-2	McIntyre, Stephenson	28566		9	2	3					8	1			4		11						10	6	5					
38		9	SUNDERLAND	1-0	Stephenson	24226		9	2	3			7			1		6	4		11						10		5			8		
39		14	BOLTON WANDERERS	1-0	Whitehouse	12378		9	2	3			7			1		6	4		11						10		5			8		
40		26	Blackburn Rovers	2-3	Whitehouse, Crooks	21438		9	2	3			7	5		1			4		11						10	6				8		
41		28	MIDDLESBROUGH	2-1	Whitehouse, Bacon	12017	9		2	3			7	5		1		6	4		11							10				8		
42	May	5	Birmingham	1-2	Stephenson	16430		9	2	3			7	5		1		6	4		11						10					8		
						Apps	4	38	34	28	13	8	34	27	13	8	5	6	30	3	30	12	2	6	3	9	28	36	11	6	1	37	1	28
						Goals	1	27				10			10		1		3		2	2					17	2				21		

Scorers in game 17: Bedford 2 (1p), Stephenson, Crooks, Whitehouse

D Kelly played at 7 in game 37

F.A. Cup

Rd	Date		Opponent	Res	Scorers	Att	Bacon A	Bedford H	Carr WP	Collin G	Cooper T	Crilly T	Crooks SD	Davison TR	Gill JJ	Hampton JW	Hope J	Malloch GC	McIntyre JMcM	McLaverty B	Mee GW	Murphy L	O'Brien MT	Olney BA	Robinson TC	Scott A	Stephenson GT	Storer H	Thoms H	Thornewell G	White A	Whitehouse JC	Wightman H	Wilkes HT
R3	Jan	14	Millwall	2-1	Stephenson, Bedford	38850		9	2				7	5							11					4	10	6				8		1
R4		28	NOTTINGHAM FOREST	0-0		22594		9	2				7								11		5			4	10	6				8		1
rep	Feb	1	Nottingham Forest	0-2		35625		9	2				7								11		5			4	10	6				8		1

W Robson played at 3 in all three games

Doncaster Rovers

4th in Division Three (North)

	Date	Opponent	Score	Scorers	Att	Bott WE	Bowman J	Buckley JW	Emery FD	Farmery LIV	Fawcett G	Hall BAC	Keetley F	Keetley T	Longden E	Maughan J	McConnell P	McLean R	McNestry G	Milne AJ	Morgan J	Patterson MT	Phillipson MT	Tippett T	Underwood BR	Whitelaw R
1	Aug 27	LINCOLN CITY	3-0	T Keetley 2, Emery	8451			2	6				8	9		1	10		7	3	5		11		4	
2	31	New Brighton	1-3	T Keetley (p)	5715			2	6				8	9		1	10		7	3	5		11		4	
3	Sep 3	Hartlepools United	0-1		5314			2	6				8	9		1	10		7	3	5		11		4	
4	5	NEW BRIGHTON	5-1	T Keetley 2, Longden, McNestry, Phillipson	5435			2	6					9	8	1	10		7	3	5		11		4	
5	10	ACCRINGTON STANLEY	0-0		6143			2	6					9	8	1	10		7	3	5		11		4	
6	17	Wigan Borough	1-1	Phillipson	3325			2	6					9	8	1	10		7	3	5		11		4	
7	24	ROTHERHAM UNITED	2-0	T Keetley, Morgan	7764			2	6			9	8	7		1	10			3	5		11		4	
8	Oct 1	DARLINGTON	5-0	F Keetley 2, Hall 2, T Keetley	5989			2	6			9	8	7		1	10			3	5		11		4	
9	8	Ashington	2-1	F Keetley, Hall	2655			2	6			9	8	7		1	10			3	5		11		4	
10	15	CREWE ALEXANDRA	3-1	T Keetley 2 (1p), McConnell	6973			2	6			9	8	7		1	10			3	5		11		4	
11	22	Wrexham	2-1	Hall 2	3536		2		6			9	8	7		1	10			3	5		11		4	
12	29	DURHAM CITY	5-0	Hall 3, F Keetley, Emery	7176		2		6			9	8	7		1	10			3	5		11		4	
13	Nov 5	Southport	2-1	T Keetley 2	2840		2		6			9	8	7		1	10			3	5		11		4	
14	12	CHESTERFIELD	4-0	Hall 2, T Keetley, Underwood	8373		2		6			9	8	7		1	10			3	5		11		4	
15	19	Bradford Park Avenue	2-0	F Keetley, T Keetley	22202		2		6			9	8	7		1	10			3	5		11		4	
16	Dec 3	Stockport County	1-2	T Keetley	9760		2					9	8	7		1	10	4		3	5		11			6
17	17	Nelson	1-0	T Keetley	3410		3	2				9	8	7		1	10	4			5		11			6
18	24	ROCHDALE	5-2	T Keetley 2 (1p), Phillipson 2, Hall	5291		3	2	6			9	8	7		1	10	4			5		11			
19	26	HALIFAX TOWN	1-1	Hall	11380		3	2	6			9	8	7		1	10	4			5		11			
20	27	Halifax Town	1-0	Hall	12909		3	2	6			9	8	7		1	10				5		11			4
21	31	Lincoln City	0-2		8631		3	2	6			9	8	7		1	10	4			5		11			
22	Jan 7	HARTLEPOOLS UNITED	1-1	McConnell	7641		2		6			9	8	7		1	10	4		3	5		11			
23	14	BARROW	4-0	F Keetley 2, Bott, Hall	6120	11	2		6			9	8	7		1	10			3	5				4	
24	21	Accrington Stanley	3-1	Hall 2, T Keetley	4931	11	2		6			9	8	7		1	10			3	5				4	
25	28	WIGAN BOROUGH	4-1	T Keetley 2 (1p), Hall, Morgan	6264	11	2		6			9	8	7		1	10			3	5				4	
26	Feb 4	Rotherham United	1-2	T Keetley (p)	11530	11	2		6			9	8	7		1				3	5	10			4	
27	11	Darlington	0-3		6714		3	2	6			9	8	7		1					5	10	11		4	
28	18	ASHINGTON	3-2	Hall, Bott, Patterson	6553	11		2	6			9		7		1	10			3	5	8			4	
29	25	Crewe Alexandra	1-4	Patterson	4861	11	2		6			9	8	7		1				3	5	10			4	
30	Mar 3	WREXHAM	1-1	T Keetley	8519	11		2	6		5	9	8	7		1				3		10			4	
31	10	Durham City	3-1	T Keetley 2, F Keetley	1408	11		2	6				8	9		1	10			3	5			7	4	
32	17	SOUTHPORT	0-1		6622			2	6					9	8	1	10			3	5		11	7	4	
33	24	Chesterfield	0-1		4696	11		2	6				8	9		1	10			3	5			7	4	
34	31	BRADFORD PARK AVE	2-0	T Keetley 2	14176		3	2	6				8	9		1	10				5		11	7	4	
35	Apr 6	BRADFORD CITY	2-1	T Keetley 2	16134		3	2	6				8	9		1	10				5		11	7		4
36	7	Barrow	0-0		7989		3	2	6				8	9		1	10				5		11	7		4
37	9	Bradford City	0-1		13375	11	3	2	6				8	9		1	10				5			7		4
38	14	STOCKPORT COUNTY	0-2		5872		3	2	6				8	9	10	1					5		11	7		4
39	21	Tranmere Rovers	0-0		4072	11	3	2	6				8	9	10	1					5			7		4
40	28	NELSON	4-2	T Keetley 4	4117	11	3	2	6				8	9	10	1					5			7	4	
41	May 1	TRANMERE ROVERS	5-2	T Keetley 4, F Keetley	4056	11	3	2	6	1			8	9			10				5			7	4	
42	5	Rochdale	0-1		1768		3	2	6	1			8	9			10				5	11		7	4	
					Apps	13	27	30	40	2	1	24	37	42	7	40	35	6	6	27	41	6	28	12	30	8
					Goals	2			2			18	9	36	1		2		1		2	2	4		1	

FA Cup

	Date	Opponent	Score	Scorers	Att	Bott WE	Bowman J	Buckley JW	Emery FD	Farmery LIV	Fawcett G	Hall BAC	Keetley F	Keetley T	Longden E	Maughan J	McConnell P	McLean R	McNestry G	Milne AJ	Morgan J	Patterson MT	Phillipson MT	Tippett T	Underwood BR	Whitelaw R
R1	Nov 26	Carlisle United	1-2	McConnell	11128		2		6			9	8	7		1	10			3	5		11		4	

Durham City

21st in Division Three (North): Not re-elected

							Adey TW	Bell A	Butler E	Cooperthwaite J	Greenwell EE	Gurkin J	Harrison J	Hart G	Howlett CE	Joy F	Joyce M	Kirby W	Leedham TW	Lowson EB	Neilson GH	Nicholson F	Pearson R	Purdy A	Raine TA	Richardson W	Robson T	Scott D	Stephenson J	Stephenson JR	Stokoe JR
1	Aug	27	Bradford Park Avenue	0-4		14040		3	11		10	6							9	5		8		1	7				2	4	
2		29	Chesterfield	2-4	Leedham 2	3833		3	11		10	6							9	5		8		1	7				2	4	
3	Sep	3	TRANMERE ROVERS	1-3	Leedham	2842	6	3	11		10	5							9	4		8		1	7				2		
4		7	CHESTERFIELD	2-0	Leedham, JR Stephenson	1222	6	3			10	5				7			9	4				1			11		2	8	
5		10	Stockport County	1-2	Leedham	8690	6	3			10	5				7			9	4				1			11		2	8	
6		17	BARROW	4-1	Leedham 2, Greenwell 2	1895	6	3			10	5				7			9	4				1			11		2	8	
7		24	Nelson	1-2	McClure (og)	5495	6	3			10	5				7			9	4				1			11		2	8	
8	Oct	1	ROCHDALE	3-2	Robson 2 (1p), Leedham	2354	6	3			10	5				7			9	4				1			11		2	8	
9		8	Rotherham United	1-1	Robson (p)	4520	6	3			10	5								4				1	9		11		2	8	7
10		15	SOUTHPORT	0-0		2389	6	3			10	5				7			9	4				1			11		2	8	
11		22	WIGAN BOROUGH	3-0	Robson, JR Stephenson, Joy	789	6	3			10	5				7			9	4				1			11		2	8	
12		29	Doncaster Rovers	0-5		7176	6	3			10	5								4				1	9		11		2	8	7
13	Nov	5	DARLINGTON	3-3	Greenwell, Leedham, Joy	3274	6	3		2	10	5				7			9	4				1			11			8	
14		12	Accrington Stanley	0-2		4459	6	3			10	5				7				4				1			11	9	2	8	
15		19	HARTLEPOOLS UNITED	1-0	Robson	1580	6	3		2	10	5				7				4				1			11	9		8	
16	Dec	3	NEW BRIGHTON	2-1	Stokoe, Raine	1447		3			10	5				7				4	6			1	8		11		2		9
17		10	Hartlepools United	1-2	Raine	2497	6	3	11		10	5				7				4			9	1	8				2		
18		14	Lincoln City	1-2	Greenwell	1475	6	3	11		10	5				7				4			9	1	8				2		
19		17	HALIFAX TOWN	1-1	Cooperthwaite	1164	6			10		5				7				4		3	9	1	8		11		2		
20		24	Crewe Alexandra	2-5	Pearson, Greenwell	2689	6		11		10	5								4		3	9	1	8				2		7
21		31	BRADFORD PARK AVE.	0-1		2262				6	10	5		4		7			8	2		3	9	1			11				
22	Jan	2	Ashington	2-2	Joy 2	2099				6	10	5		4		7				2		3	9	1	8		11				
23		7	Tranmere Rovers	1-11	Raine	5205				2	10	5		6		7				4		3	9	1	8		11				
24		14	Bradford City	0-4		4422	6				10	5								2	4	3	9	1			11	8			7
25		21	STOCKPORT COUNTY	1-2	Adey (p)	1781	6			3	10	5								4			9	1		2	11			8	7
26		28	Barrow	2-1	Adey 2	3117	10		7	3		5		6						4			9	1		2	11	8			
27	Feb	4	NELSON	3-0	Pearson 2, Cooperthwaite	1537	10		7	8	11	5		6			3			4			9	1		2					
28		11	Rochdale	0-1		1458	10		7	8		5		6			3	1		4			9			2	11				
29		18	ROTHERHAM UNITED	1-4	Adey	2037	10		7			5		6			3	1		4			9			2	11			8	
30		25	Southport	1-3	Adey	3142	6		7		10	5					3	1		4			9			2	11			8	
31	Mar	3	Wigan Borough	0-3		4060	6		7		10	5					3	1	9	4						2	11			8	
32		10	DONCASTER ROVERS	1-3	Pearson	1408	6		7	10	8	5					3	1		4			9			2	11				
33		17	Darlington	0-5		4668	6		7		10	5		4	9			1		2						3	11			8	
34		24	ACCRINGTON STANLEY	2-1	Howlett 2	1343	6		7			5			9		3	1		4			10			2	11			8	
35	Apr	6	Wrexham	0-4		3767	6		7		11	5			9		3	1		4			10			2				8	
36		7	BRADFORD CITY	3-2	Howlett, Butler, Richardson	2135	6		7		11	5			9		3	1		4			10			2				8	
37		9	WREXHAM	1-1	Howlett	2399			7		11	5		6	9		3	1		4			10			2				8	
38		14	New Brighton	0-4		2710			7		11			6	9		3	1		5	4		10			2				8	
39		18	ASHINGTON	0-0		931			7		11	5	2	6	9		3	1		4			10							8	
40		21	LINCOLN CITY	0-4		1305	6		7		10	5	2				3	1		4							11			8	9
41		28	Halifax Town	1-3	Adey	2553	8		7			5	2	6	9		3	1		4			11				10				
42	May	5	CREWE ALEXANDRA	5-1	Cooperthwaite, Butler 2, JR Stephens	851			7	8	10	5	2	6			3	1		4							11			9	
						Apps	32	18	23	12	36	41	4	13	8	17	15	15	13	42	3	9	22	27	12	14	30	4	18	27	7
						Goals	6		3	3	5				4	4			9				4		3	1	5			4	1

One own goal

F.A. Cup

							Adey TW	Bell A	Butler E	Cooperthwaite J	Greenwell EE	Gurkin J	Harrison J	Hart G	Howlett CE	Joy F	Joyce M	Kirby W	Leedham TW	Lowson EB	Neilson GH	Nicholson F	Pearson R	Purdy A	Raine TA	Richardson W	Robson T	Scott D	Stephenson J	Stephenson JR	Stokoe JR
R1	Nov	26	WREXHAM	1-1	Stokoe	3690	6			3	10	5				7				4				1			11		2	8	9
rep		30	Wrexham	0-4		3804	6	3	11		10	5				7				4				1					2	8	9

Everton

Champions of Division One

No	Date	Opponent	Score	Scorers	Att	Bain D	Brown W	Cresswell W	Critchley E	Davies AL	Dean WR	Dominy AA	Easton WC	Forshaw R	Hardy HI	Hart H	Houghton H	Irvine RW	Kelly J	Martin GS	Meston SW	O'Donnell J	Raitt D	Rooney WF	Taylor EH	Troup A	Virr AE	Weldon A	White TA
1	Aug 27	SHEFFIELD WEDNESDAY	4-0	Dean, Forshaw, Troup, Welson	39485			2			9			8		5		7	4			3			1	11	6	10	
2	Sep 3	Middlesbrough	2-4	Critchley, Dean	30229			2	7		9			8		5			4			3			1	11	6	10	
3	5	Bolton Wanderers	1-1	Dean	18734				7		9			8		5			4			3	2		1	11	6	10	
4	10	BIRMINGHAM	5-2	Dean 2, Troup 2, Forshaw	37386				7		9			8		5			4			3	2		1	11	6	10	
5	14	BOLTON WANDERERS	2-2	Dean, Forshaw	22726			2	7		9			8		5			4			3			1	11	6	10	
6	17	Newcastle United	2-2	Dean 2	50359			2	7		9			8		5			4			3			1	11	6	10	
7	24	HUDDERSFIELD T	2-2	Dean 2	37269			2	7		9			8		5			4			3			1	11	6	10	
8	Oct 1	Tottenham Hotspur	3-1	Dean 2, Troup	7718			2	7		9			8		5			4			3			1	11	6	10	
9	8	MANCHESTER UNITED	5-2	Dean 5	40080			2	7		9			8		5			4			3			1	11	6	10	
10	15	LIVERPOOL	1-1	Troup	65729			2	7		9			8		5			4			3			1	11	6	10	
11	22	WEST HAM UNITED	7-0	* See below	20151			2	7					8		5			4			3			1	11	6	10	9
12	29	Portsmouth	3-1	Dean 3	23326			2	7		9			8		5			4			3			1	11	6	10	
13	Nov 5	LEICESTER CITY	7-1	Dean 3, Weldon 2, Critchley, Troup	30392		4	2	7		9			8		5						3			1	11	6	10	
14	12	Derby County	3-0	Dean 2, Weldon	21590			2	7	1	9			8		5			4			3				11	6	10	
15	19	SUNDERLAND	0-1		35993			2	7	1	9			8		5			4			3				11	6	10	
16	26	Bury	3-2	Dean 2, Critchley	24727			2	7		9			8		5		10	4			3			1	11	6		
17	Dec 3	SHEFFIELD UNITED	0-0		36141			2	7		9			8		5			4			3			1	11	6	10	
18	10	Aston Villa	3-2	Dean 3	40353			2	7		9			8		5			4			3		6	1	11		10	
19	17	BURNLEY	4-1	Critchley, Forshaw, Kelly, Troup	30180			2	7		9			8		5			4			3			1	11	6	10	
20	24	Arsenal	2-3	Dean, Troup	27995			2	7		9			8		5			4			3			1	11	6	10	
21	26	CARDIFF CITY	2-1	Dean 2	56305				7		9			8		5			4			3	2		1	11	6	10	
22	27	Cardiff City	0-2		25387				7		9							8	4			3	2	6	1	11	5	10	
23	31	Sheffield Wednesday	2-1	Dean 2	18354				7		9					5		8	4			3	2		1	11	6	10	
24	Jan 2	Blackburn Rovers	2-4	Dean 2	39300				7		9					5		8	4			3	2		1	11	6	10	
25	7	MIDDLESBROUGH	3-1	Dean 2, Irvine	46432			2	7		9					5		8	4			3		6	1	11		10	
26	21	Birmingham	2-2	Irvine 2	33675			2	7		9	10				5		8	4			3		6	1	11			
27	Feb 4	Huddersfield Town	1-4	Dean	50012			2	7		9					5		8	4			3			1	11	6	10	
28	11	TOTTENHAM HOTSPUR	2-5	Troup 2	27149		4	2	7		9					5		8				3			1	11	6	10	
29	25	Liverpool	3-3	Dean 3	55361			2	7		9			8	1	5			4			3				11	6	10	
30	Mar 3	West Ham United	0-0		31997			2	7		9			8	1	5			4			3				11	6	10	
31	10	PORTSMOUTH	0-0		29803			2	7				8		1	5	10		4			3				11	6	9	
32	14	Manchester United	0-1		25667			2	7		9		8		1	5			4			3				11	6	10	
33	17	Leicester City	0-1		26625			2	7		9				1	5			4	8		3				11	6	10	
34	24	DERBY COUNTY	2-2	Dean 2	28541	8		2	7	1	9					5			4	10		3				11	6		
35	31	Sunderland	2-0	Easton, Virr	15407	9		2	7	1			8			5			4	10		3				11	6		
36	Apr 6	BLACKBURN ROVERS	4-1	Dean 2, Hart, Martin	48521			2	7	1	9					5			4	8		3				11	6	10	
37	7	BURY	1-1	Dean	37597			2	7		9				1	5			4	8		3				11	6	10	
38	14	Sheffield United	3-1	Dean 2, Martin	26252			2		1	9					5			4	8	7	3				11	6	10	
39	18	NEWCASTLE UNITED	3-0	Critchley, Dean, Weldon	28266			2	7	1	9					5			4	8		3				11	6	10	
40	21	ASTON VILLA	3-2	Dean 2, Weldon	39825			2	7	1	9					5			4	8		3				11	6	10	
41	28	Burnley	5-3	Dean 4, Martin	24485			2	7	1	9					5			4	8		3				11	6	10	
42	May 5	ARSENAL	3-3	Dean 3	48715			2	7	1	9					5			4	8		3				11	6	10	

Scorers in game 11: White 2, Critchley, Forshaw, O'Donnell, Weldon, Henderson (og)

	Bain D	Brown W	Cresswell W	Critchley E	Davies AL	Dean WR	Dominy AA	Easton WC	Forshaw R	Hardy HI	Hart H	Houghton H	Irvine RW	Kelly J	Martin GS	Meston SW	O'Donnell J	Raitt D	Rooney WF	Taylor EH	Troup A	Virr AE	Weldon A	White TA
Apps	2	2	36	40	10	39	1	3	23	6	41	1	9	40	10	1	42	6	4	26	42	39	38	1
Goals				6		60		1	5		1		3	1	3		1				10	1	7	2

One own goal

F.A. Cup

Rd	Date	Opponent	Score	Scorers	Att	Bain D	Brown W	Cresswell W	Critchley E	Davies AL	Dean WR	Dominy AA	Easton WC	Forshaw R	Hardy HI	Hart H	Houghton H	Irvine RW	Kelly J	Martin GS	Meston SW	O'Donnell J	Raitt D	Rooney WF	Taylor EH	Troup A	Virr AE	Weldon A	White TA
R3	Jan 14	Preston North End	3-0	Dean, Irvine, Ward (og)	37788			2	7		9					5		8	4			3		6	1	11		10	
R4	28	Arsenal	3-4	Dean 2, Troup	44328			2	7		9					5		8	4			3			1	11	6	10	

Exeter City

8th in Division Three (South)

						Andrews H	Bastin CS	Chambers R	Charlton S	Clarke RL	Compton WA	Dent F	Ditchburn JH	Edwards TS	Gee H	Holland T	Jenkins TW	Kirk RH	Lievesley W	Lowton WG	Mason S	McDade P	McDevitt W	Miller C	Parkin T	Phoenix AE	Pollard R	Pool A	Purcell GW	Vaughan W	Wainwright TG	Warren H
1	Aug 27	Torquay United	1-1	Vaughan	10749				3				4					11	9	2			8					5	7	10	1	6
2	29	Crystal Palace	0-2		11329				3				4		6		7	11		2			8			9		5		10	1	
3	Sep 3	NORWICH CITY	2-2	Phoenix, McDevitt	7567				3		11	10	4		6			7		2			8			9		5			1	
4	7	CRYSTAL PALACE	2-2	Pool, Phoenix	5906				3				4		6			11	9	2			10			8		5	7		1	
5	10	Northampton Town	0-5		10249	9			3			10	4		6			11		2	5					8			7		1	
6	17	SOUTHEND UNITED	3-2	Dent 2, Purcell	6309				3		11	8	4			1				2				6		9		5	7	10		
7	24	Brighton & Hove Albion	2-0	Compton, Dent	10076						11	9			6	1							8	3		4	2	5	7	10		
8	Oct 1	BOURNEMOUTH	4-1	Compton 2, Dent, Purcell	6136						11	9			6	1							8	3		4	2	5	7	10		
9	8	Brentford	1-1	Dent	11326						11	9			6	1							8	3		4	2	5	7	10		
10	15	LUTON TOWN	3-2	Purcell 2, Dent	6827						11	9			6	1							8	3		4	2	5	7	10		
11	22	WATFORD	3-3	Purcell 2, Compton	5750						11	9			6	1							8	3		4	2	5	7	10		
12	29	Charlton Athletic	0-0		13402						11	9			6	1							8	3		4	2	5	7	10		
13	Nov 5	BRISTOL ROVERS	4-1	Dent 4	6577						11	9			6	1							8	3		4	2	5	7	10		
14	12	Queen's Park Rangers	1-0	Dent	8291						11	9			6	1							8	3		4	2	5	7	10		
15	19	SWINDON TOWN	0-0		6310				3		11	9			6	1							8			4	2	5	7	10		
16	Dec 3	COVENTRY CITY	0-1		5716				3		11	9			6	1							8			4	2	5	7	10		
17	17	WALSALL	3-0	Vaughan 2, Purcell	5206						11	9	4		6	1					5		8	3			2		7	10		
18	24	Merthyr Town	3-0	Compton, Dent 2	2000						11	9	4		6	1					5		8	3			2		7	10		
19	26	PLYMOUTH ARGYLE	2-0	Dent, Purcell	9580						11	9	4		6	1					5		8	3			2		7	10		
20	27	Plymouth Argyle	2-1	Compton, Russell (og)	14938						11	9	4		6	1					5		8	3			2		7	10		
21	31	TORQUAY UNITED	5-0	Compton, Dent 2, McDevitt, Vaughan	8224						11	9	4		6	1					5		8	3			2		7	10		
22	Jan 7	Norwich City	2-2	Dent 2, Purcell	6706						11	9	4		6	1					5		8	3			2		7	10		
23	21	NORTHAMPTON T	1-1	Vaughan	10231						11		4		6	1					5		8	3		9	2		7	10		
24	Feb 4	BRIGHTON & HOVE ALB	0-3		6916						11		4		6	1				9	5		8	3			2		7	10		
25	11	Bournemouth	0-2		5863						11	9	4		6	1					5		8	3			2		7	10		
26	15	Southend United	2-1	Mason, Gee (p)	2603						11		4		6	1					5	9	8	3			2		7	10		
27	18	BRENTFORD	0-1		7420						11		4	9	6	1					5	8		3			2		7	10		
28	25	Luton Town	1-2	Compton	8309						11		4	9	6	1					5		8	3	10		2		7			
29	Mar 3	Watford	2-3	Dent, Gee (p)	7951						11	10	4	9	6	1					5		8	3			2		7			
30	10	CHARLTON ATHLETIC	2-1	Vaughan, Purcell	5903						11	9	4		6	1					5		8	3			2		7	10		
31	17	Bristol Rovers	2-1	McDevitt, Dent	9112						11	9			6								8	3		4	2	5	7	10	1	
32	22	Newport County	0-1		2108					6	11	9											8	3		4	2	5	7	10	1	
33	24	QUEEN'S PARK RANGERS	4-0	Dent 2, Purcell, Vaughan	5657				3	6		9					7								11	4	2	5	8	10	1	
34	28	Gillingham	1-1	Vaughan	3138				3	6		9					7								11	4	2	5	8	10	1	
35	31	Swindon Town	0-3		2999				3	6	11	9									5		8			4	2		7	10	1	
36	Apr 6	Millwall	0-2		31654				3		11	9									6		8			4	2	5	7	10	1	
37	7	GILLINGHAM	2-2	Dent, Vaughan	6001				3		11	9									6		8			4	2	5	7	10	1	
38	9	MILLWALL	2-4	Purcell (p), Dent	12735				3	6	11	9					7									4	2	5	8	10	1	
39	14	Coventry City	0-0		6905		10		3	6		9				1		11					8			4	2	5	7			
40	21	NEWPORT COUNTY	5-1	Dent, Bastin 2, Purcell 2	4912		10		3	6		9				1		11			5		8			4	2		7			
41	28	Walsall	1-5	Bastin	5843		10	5	3	6		9				1		11					8			4	2		7			
42	May 5	MERTHYR TOWN	2-0	Compton, Dent	4506	9			3	6	11	10				1					5		8			4	2		7			

	Andrews H	Bastin CS	Chambers R	Charlton S	Clarke RL	Compton WA	Dent F	Ditchburn JH	Edwards TS	Gee H	Holland T	Jenkins TW	Kirk RH	Lievesley W	Lowton WG	Mason S	McDade P	McDevitt W	Miller C	Parkin T	Phoenix AE	Pollard R	Pool A	Purcell GW	Vaughan W	Wainwright TG	Warren H
Apps	2	3	1	18	9	33	34	20	3	29	29	4	8	2	7	20	2	36	25	3	28	36	23	40	33	13	1
Goals		3				9	26			2						1		3			2		1	13	9		

One own goal

F.A. Cup

						Andrews H	Bastin CS	Chambers R	Charlton S	Clarke RL	Compton WA	Dent F	Ditchburn JH	Edwards TS	Gee H	Holland T	Jenkins TW	Kirk RH	Lievesley W	Lowton WG	Mason S	McDade P	McDevitt W	Miller C	Parkin T	Phoenix AE	Pollard R	Pool A	Purcell GW	Vaughan W	Wainwright TG	Warren H
R1	Nov 26	ABERDARE ATHLETIC	9-1	Dent 4, Vaughan 2, Purcell 2, Compton	9378				3		11	9			6	1							8			4	2	5	7	10		
R2	Dec 10	ILFORD	5-3	Dent 2, Purcell 2, McDevitt	8501				3		11	9			6	1							8			4	2	5	7	10		
R3	Jan 14	Rotherham United	3-3	Vaughan, Mason, Jackson (og)	15500						11	9	4		6	1					5		8	3			2		7	10		
rep	18	ROTHERHAM UNITED	3-1	Vaughan 2, Purcell	11805						11	9	4		6	1					5		8	3			2		7	10		
R4	28	BLACKBURN ROVERS	2-2	Gee (p), Mason	17330						11	9	4		6	1					5		8	3			2		7	10		
rep	Feb 2	Blackburn Rovers	1-3	Compton	28348						11	9	4		6	1					5		8	3			2		7	10		

Fulham

21st in Division Two: Relegated

	Date	Opponent	Score	Scorers	Att	Avey FG	Barrett AF	Beecham EC	Craig EF	Devan CF	Dyer RE	Elliott SD	Ferguson RL	Gregory RJ	Harris GT	Hebden JT	Horler GH	Hoyland W	Johnson RJ	Lawson T	Lowe H	McKenna FC	McNab D	Oliver LF	Penn FJ	Smith JR	Sparke CF	Steele A	Temple JL	Walters C
1	Aug 27	PRESTON NORTH END	2-2	Elliott 2	25655		2	1	8			9			3			10					5	4	11			6	7	
2	29	Nottingham Forest	0-7		11430		2	1	8			9			3			10					5	4	11			6	7	
3	Sep 3	Swansea Town	1-2	Elliott	14617		3	1	8	11	2	9										10	5	4				6	7	
4	10	CHELSEA	1-1	McKenna	39860		3	1	10	7	2	9										8	5	4	11			6		
5	15	NOTTM. FOREST	2-0	McKenna, Elliott	9446		3	1	10	7	2	9										8	5	4	11			6		
6	17	BARNSLEY	3-1	Elliott, Craig, Devan	16924		3	1	10	7	2	9										8	5	4	11			6		
7	24	Wolverhampton Wan.	1-3	McKenna	11685		3	1	10	7	2	9										8	5	4	11			6		
8	Oct 1	PORT VALE	4-0	Hoyland, McKenna, Elliott, McNab	10560		3	1		7	2	9						10				8	5	4	11			6		
9	8	South Shields	1-2	Devan	6253		3	1		7	2	9						10			5	8		4	11			6		
10	15	LEEDS UNITED	1-1	Craig	16704		3	1	10		2	9									5	8		4	11			6	7	
11	22	Bristol City	0-3		7701		3	1	10		2	9										8	5	4	11			6	7	
12	29	WEST BROMWICH ALB.	3-1	Elliott 2, Temple	20577		3	1	10		2	9										8	5	4	11			6	7	
13	Nov 5	Clapton Orient	2-3	Elliott, Harris	15877		3	1	10			9			2			8	6				5	4	11				7	
14	12	STOKE CITY	1-5	Temple	10773		3	1	10		2	9							6			8	5	4	11				7	
15	19	Southampton	2-5	Elliott 2	4619		3	1	7			9		2				10				8	5	4	11			6		
16	26	GRIMSBY TOWN	2-2	McKenna, Elliott	6395		3	1	7		2	9						10				8	5	4	11			6		
17	Dec 3	Oldham Athletic	2-4	Elliott 2	10182		3	1	7		2	9						10				8	5	4	11			6		
18	10	NOTTS COUNTY	2-1	Elliott, Craig	11562			1	7		2	9		3				10				8	5	4	11			6		
19	17	Reading	1-2	McKenna	8472			1	7		2	9		3				10				8	5	4	11			6		
20	24	BLACKPOOL	2-2	Penn, Elliott	10853			1	7		2	9					3	10				8	5	4	11			6		
21	27	Hull City	2-3	McNab, McKenna	14050		6	1	7			9				2	3	10				8	5	4	11					
22	31	Preston North End	0-1		14816		6	1	7			9				2	3	10				8	5	4			11			
23	Jan 7	SWANSEA TOWN	3-2	Elliott, McKenna, Craig	15008		6	1	7			9				2	3	10				8	5	4	11					
24	21	Chelsea	1-2	Elliott	42297		6	1	7			9				2	3	10					5	4	11			8		
25	28	Barnsley	4-8	Craig, Elliott 2, Johnson	4563		6	1	7			9				2	3	10	4		5				11			8		
26	Feb 4	WOLVERHAMPTON W.	7-0	Elloitt 3, McKenna, Craig, Temple 2	12981		6	1	8			9		3		2						10	5	4	11				7	
27	11	Port Vale	1-4	Penn	7520		6	1	8			9		3		2							5	4	11	10			7	
28	18	SOUTH SHIELDS	2-0	Craig, Smith	15626		6	1	8			9		3		2		7					5	4	11	10				
29	25	Leeds United	1-2	Temple	17358		6	1	8			9		3		2							5	4	11			10	7	
30	Mar 3	BRISTOL CITY	5-0	Elloitt 3, Craig, Temple	18524		6	1	8			9		3		2						10	5	4	11				7	
31	10	West Bromwich Albion	0-4		17662		4	1	8			9		3		2							5	6	11		10		7	
32	17	CLAPTON ORIENT	2-0	McKenna, Penn	21452		6	1	8			9				2	3					10	5	4	11				7	
33	24	Stoke City	1-5	Craig	10120		6	1	8			9				2	3					10	5	4	11				7	
34	26	HULL CITY	0-2		7023		6	1	8			9		3		2						10	5	4	11				7	
35	31	SOUTHAMPTON	1-0	Smith	9316		3	1	8			10				2							5	4	11	9		6	7	
36	Apr 6	Manchester City	1-2	McNab	50660		3	1	8			10				2							5	4	11	9		6	7	
37	7	Grimsby Town	0-1		9005		3	1	8			10				2								4	11	9		6	7	5
38	9	MANCHESTER CITY	1-1	Temple	25997		3	1	8			10				2				6			5	4	11	9			7	
39	14	OLDHAM ATHLETIC	1-1	Ferguson	14394		3	1				9	11			2				6			5	4	10	8			7	
40	21	Notts County	1-0	Ferguson	7655		3	1	10			9	11			2							5	8	6			4	7	
41	28	READING	1-0	Craig	18918	8	3	1	10			9	11			2							5	4	6				7	
42	May 5	Blackpool	0-4		14466	8	3	1	10			9	11			2							5	4	6				7	
					Apps	2	39	42	39	7	16	42	4	10	3	22	8	17	3	2	3	25	38	41	40	7	2	25	24	1
					Goals				10	2		26	2		1			1	1			10	3		3	2			7	

F.A. Cup

	Date	Opponent	Score	Scorers	Att	Avey FG	Barrett AF	Beecham EC	Craig EF	Devan CF	Dyer RE	Elliott SD	Ferguson RL	Gregory RJ	Harris GT	Hebden JT	Horler GH	Hoyland W	Johnson RJ	Lawson T	Lowe H	McKenna FC	McNab D	Oliver LF	Penn FJ	Smith JR	Sparke CF	Steele A	Temple JL	Walters C
R3	Jan 14	Southport	0-3		8000		6	1	7			9				2	3	10				8	5	4	11					

Gillingham

16th in Division Three (South)

	Date	Opponent	Score	Scorers	Att	Amos ST	Arblaster WJ	Bartley JWE	Boswell W	Bradley PJ	Bromage E	Brown JT	Brown S	Crawford GW	Dee A	Dominy AA	Donaghy E	Dowell L	Ellis FC	Hebden GHR	Hillier S	Hodnett JE	Meston SW	Millington T	Nichol JB	Pickering WH	Poxton JH	Robertson JW	Rogers D	Sly H	Tyler S	Wilcox JC
1	Aug 27	Charlton Athletic	0-1		11752		10				11						6			1	8	5	7		4	3		2				9
2	Sep 1	Queen's Park Rangers	3-3	Wilcox, Hillier 2	9241		10				11									1	8	5	7		4	3		2	6			9
3	3	BRISTOL ROVERS	3-1	Wilcox, Arblaster, Hillier	6818		10				11									1	8	5	7		6	3			4		2	9
4	7	QUEEN'S PARK RANGERS	1-2	Hodnott	5499		10				11						6			1	8	5	7			3			4		2	9
5	10	Plymouth Argyle	2-2	Arblaster 2	10282		10				11									1	6	5	7			3			4	8	2	9
6	17	MERTHYR TOWN	1-1	Arblaster	5642		10				11									1	6	5	7		4	3				8	2	9
7	24	Walsall	4-7	Sly, Bromage, Wilcox 2	6923		10				11	7								1	6	5			4	3				8	2	9
8	Oct 1	NORTHAMPTON T	1-3	Arblaster	4226		10				11	7								1	6	5			4	3				8	2	9
9	8	COVENTRY CITY	1-2	Wilcox	4667	5	10			11										1	6		7		4	3				8	2	9
10	15	Newport County	1-1	Nichol	6589	4				11			1				10				6		7		5	3				8	2	9
11	22	Bournemouth	0-3		4119	4				11			1				10				6		7		5	3				8	2	9
12	29	BRIGHTON & HOVE ALB	0-1		4681					11	10		1						6			5	7		4	3				8	2	9
13	Nov 5	Southend United	2-1	Meston, Arblaster	6756	8	10	2		11			1	5					6				7		4	3						9
14	12	BRENTFORD	2-1	Wilcox 2	3293		10		8	11			1	5					6				7		4			2			3	9
15	19	Luton Town	1-6	Meston	4527		10		8	11			1	5					6			4	7					2			3	9
16	Dec 3	Crystal Palace	2-2	Wilcox, Arblaster	9299		10		8	11				5					6	1		4	7					2			3	9
17	17	Torquay United	1-1	Boswell	2992		10		8	11				5					6	1			7					2	4		3	9
18	24	NORWICH CITY	3-0	Boswell, Meston, Wilcox	4078		10		8		11			5					6	1			7					2	4		3	9
19	27	WATFORD	0-3		3310		10		8		11			5					6	1			7					2	4		3	9
20	31	CHARLTON ATHLETIC	1-1	Bromage	4134				8		11			5				10	6	1			7					2	4		3	9
21	Jan 7	Bristol Rovers	4-2	Wilcox 2, Meston, Boswell	5572				8		11			5				10	6	1			7					2	4		3	9
22	21	PLYMOUTH ARGYLE	3-1	Wilcox 2, Bromage	4473				8		11			5				10	6	1			7					2	4		3	9
23	Feb 4	WALSALL	2-0	Wilcox 2	4296						11			5				10	6	1	8		7					2	4		3	9
24	11	Northampton Town	0-1		9538				8		11			5				10	6	1			7					2	4		3	9
25	18	Coventry City	2-1	Boswell, Meston	8500				8		11			5				10	6	1			7					2	4		3	9
26	25	NEWPORT COUNTY	4-0	Bromage 2, Wilcox 2	5932				8		11			5				10	6	1			7					2	4		3	9
27	Mar 3	BOURNEMOUTH	2-1	Bromage, Wilcox	6817				8		11			5				10	6	1			7					2	4		3	9
28	10	Brighton & Hove Albion	0-0		7860						11			5		8		10	6	1				7				2	4		3	9
29	12	Merthyr Town	1-3	Robertson (p)	683						11			5		8		10	6	1				7				2	4		3	9
30	17	SOUTHEND UNITED	1-0	Wilcox	6240									5		8		10	6	1				7			11	2	4		3	9
31	24	Brentford	0-2		6107				8					5		10			6	1				7			11	2	4		3	9
32	28	EXETER CITY	1-1	Millington	3138				8					5		10			6	1				7			11	2	4		3	9
33	31	LUTON TOWN	0-4		4045									5	8	10			6	1				7			11	2	4		3	9
34	Apr 6	SWINDON TOWN	0-1		7930									5	6	8		10		1				7			11	2	4		3	9
35	7	Exeter City	2-2	Poxton, Pool (og)	6001				4							8		10	6	1		5		7			11	2			3	9
36	9	Swindon Town	1-6	Poxton	7901				4							8		10		1		5		7			11	2	6		3	9
37	14	CRYSTAL PALACE	3-1	Poxton 2, Wilcox	3623									5		8		10	6	1				7			11	2	4		3	9
38	21	Millwall	0-6		20744								1	5		8		10	6					7			11	2	4		3	9
39	25	MILLWALL	0-1		5794								1	5		8		10	6					7			11	2	4		3	9
40	28	TORQUAY UNITED	4-1	Wilcox 3, Dominy	3868			3								8		10	6	1		5		7			11	2	4			9
41	May 2	Watford	3-5	Wilcox, Dominy 2	3645			3							6	10				1		5		7			11	2	4	8		9
42	5	Norwich City	0-0		6556			2							6			10	3	1		5		7			11		4	8		9
																14		19														
					Apps	4	16	4	17	9	21	2	8	25	4	14	4	19	28	34	12	16	25	15	12	13	13	30	29	10	36	42
					Goals		6		4		6					3					3	1	5	1	1		4	1		1		25

One own goal

F.A. Cup

	Date	Opponent	Score	Scorers	Att	Amos ST	Arblaster WJ	Bartley JWE	Boswell W	Bradley PJ	Bromage E	Brown JT	Brown S	Crawford GW	Dee A	Dominy AA	Donaghy E	Dowell L	Ellis FC	Hebden GHR	Hillier S	Hodnett JE	Meston SW	Millington T	Nichol JB	Pickering WH	Poxton JH	Robertson JW	Rogers D	Sly H	Tyler S	Wilcox JC
R1	Nov 26	PLYMOUTH ARGYLE	2-1	Boswell, Meston	7900		10		8	11				5					6	1		4	7					2			3	9
R2	Dec 10	SOUTHEND UNITED	2-0	Wilcox 2	10215		10		8	11				5					6	1			7					2	4		3	9
R3	Jan 14	Stoke City	1-6	Wilcox	14855				8		11			5				10	6	1			7					2	4		3	9

Grimsby Town

11th in Division Two

	Date	Opponent	Score	Scorers	Att.	Bestall JG	Calderwood JC	Coglin S	Cooper J	Coupland CA	Cowell W	Cowper PP	Harris CV	Hunter W	Jacobson H	Marshall WE	Meikle A McL	Powell WM	Prior J	Read TA	Robson J	Twell B	Tyler W	Wilson CH	Wrack C	Wright N
1	Aug 27	CLAPTON ORIENT	2-2	Marshall, Robson	15051			10	8		1	4		5	3	11		6	7		9			2		
2	30	READING	3-3	Coglin 3	13431	8		10			1	4			3	11		6	7		9			2	5	
3	Sep 3	West Bromwich Albion	1-3	Prior	16521	8		10			1	4			3	11		6	7		9			2	5	
4	10	BRISTOL CITY	1-4	Robson	13006	8		10			1	4			3	11		6	7		9			2	5	
5	14	Reading	2-2	Prior 2	6295	8	3	10		4	1		2			11		6	7		9				5	
6	17	Stoke City	0-0		15216	8	3	10		4	1		2			11		6	7		9				5	
7	24	SOUTHAMPTON	2-2	Prior, Robson	11298	8	3	10		4	1		2			11		6	7		9				5	
8	Oct 1	Notts County	2-3	Robson 2	7174	8	3	10		4	1		2			11		6	7		9				5	
9	8	OLDHAM ATHLETIC	1-2	Bestall	10400	8	3	10		4	1		2			11	7	6			9				5	
10	15	Hull City	1-0	Bestall	18862	8	2	10		4	1				3	11	7	6			9				5	
11	22	LEEDS UNITED	3-2	Coglin, Meikle, Robson	11909	8		10		4	1				3	11	7	6			9			2	5	
12	29	Nottingham Forest	2-5	Coglin (p), Meikle	14546	8	6	10		4	1				3	11	7				9			2	5	
13	Nov 5	MANCHESTER CITY	4-1	Marshall, Robson 2, Bestall	12522	8	6	10		4	1		2		3	11	7				9				5	
14	12	South Shields	2-1	Coglin, Marshall	6430	8	6	10		4	1		2		3	11	7				9				5	
15	19	PORT VALE	3-0	Bestall, Marshall, Harris	10119	8	4	10			1		2		3	11	7	6			9				5	
16	26	Fulham	2-2	Robson, Coglin	6395	8	4	10			1		2		3	11	7	6			9				5	
17	Dec 3	BARNSLEY	3-1	Coglin, Robson, Marshall	10421	8	4	10			1		2		3	11	7	6			9				5	
18	10	Wolverhampton Wan.	1-0	Marshall	7431	8	4	10			1		2		3	11	7	6			9				5	
19	17	SWANSEA TOWN	1-2	Robson	9581	8	4	10			1		2		3	11	7	6			9				5	
20	24	Preston North End	0-3		12706	8	4	10			1		2		3	11	7	6			9				5	
21	26	CHELSEA	1-1	Coglin (p)	18630	8	4	10			1		2		3	11	7	6			9				5	
22	31	Clapton Orient	2-1	Coglin, Marshall	8738	8	2	10		4	1				3	11		6	7			9			5	
23	Jan 2	Blackpool	5-4	Bestall 4, Twell	10347	8	2	10		4	1				3	11		6	7			9			5	
24	7	WEST BROMWICH ALB.	0-6		12242	8	2	10		4	1				3	11		6	7			9			5	
25	21	Bristol City	0-0		11690	8			10				2		3	11		6	7	1	9			4	5	
26	Feb 4	Southampton	0-5		7180	8		11	10				2		3			6	7	1	9			4	5	
27	11	NOTTS COUNTY	1-0	Prior	7666	8	2	11	10						3			6	7	1	9			4	5	
28	18	Oldham Athletic	0-1		15701	8	2		10						3	11		6	7	1	9			4	5	
29	25	HULL CITY	1-1	Coglin	15986	8	2	10							3	11		6	7	1	9			4	5	
30	Mar 3	Leeds United	0-0		23567	8	2	10							3	11		6	7	1	9			4	5	
31	6	STOKE CITY	1-2	Wrack	8279	8	2	11	10						3			6	7	1	9		4		5	
32	10	NOTTM. FOREST	2-1	Robson 2	7466	8	4	10					2		3			6	7	1	9				5	11
33	14	Chelsea	0-4		14298	8	4	10					2		3			6	7	1	9				5	11
34	17	Manchester City	0-2		49185	8	4		10				2		3			6	7	1	9				5	11
35	24	SOUTH SHIELDS	4-1	Robson 2, Prior, Wright	7868	8	4		10				2		3			6	7	1	9				5	11
36	31	Port Vale	2-2	Robson, Bestall	9125	8	4		10				2		3			6	7	1	9				5	11
37	Apr 6	BLACKPOOL	3-3	Prior, Robson, Cooper	15097	8	4		10				2		3			6	7	1	9				5	11
38	7	FULHAM	1-0	Robson	9005	8	6		10				2		3	11			7	1	9			4	5	
39	14	Barnsley	4-1	Robson 3, Marshall	4516	8	6		10				2		3	11			7	1	9			4	5	
40	21	WOLVERHAMPTON W.	0-1		7248	8	6		10				2		3	11			7	1	9			4	5	
41	28	Swansea Town	2-3	Robson 2	9208	8	6	10	4				2		3	11			7	1	9				5	
42	May 5	PRESTON NORTH END	4-6	Robson 3, Bestall	8747	8			10				2		3	11		6	7	1	9			4	5	
					Apps.	41	34	32	15	13	24	4	27	1	37	33	13	35	29	18	39	3	1	16	41	6
					Goals	10		11	1				1			8	2		7		26	1			1	1

F.A. Cup

	Date	Opponent	Score	Scorers	Att.	Bestall JG	Calderwood JC	Coglin S	Cooper J	Coupland CA	Cowell W	Cowper PP	Harris CV	Hunter W	Jacobson H	Marshall WE	Meikle A McL	Powell WM	Prior J	Read TA	Robson J	Twell B	Tyler W	Wilson CH	Wrack C	Wright N
R3	Jan 14	Reading	0-4		19007	8		10			1		2		3	11	7	6			9			4	5	

Halifax Town

12th in Division Three (North)

	Date	Opponent	Score	Scorers	Att	Barber B	Bell T	Binns CH	Brannigan DM	Coleman E	Dark AJ	Dixon E	Duckett DT	Fox FS	Gadsden E	Groves A	Housley H	Hubbert H	Lees JW	Martin AF	Pennington J	Proctor N	Seabrook A	Smeaton AR	Swift W	Waites SH	Wheelhouse B
1	Aug 27	Crewe Alexandra	1-1	Martin	5174						5	9	4	1	3		10	6	2	11			8			7	
2	29	BARROW	5-2	Seabrook, Houseley 3, Hubbert	7769						5	9	4	1	3		10	6	2	11			8			7	
3	Sep 3	CHESTERFIELD	1-2	Martin	9464						5	9	4	1	3		10	6	2	11			8			7	
4	5	ASHINGTON	6-1	Seabrook 2, Proctor 2, Dixon 2	4944						5	9	4	1	3		10	6	2	11		8	7				
5	10	BRADFORD CITY	2-1	Seabrook, Dixon	19935						5	9	4	1	3		10	6	2	11		8	7				
6	12	Ashington	3-3	Dixon 2, Housley	1665						5	9	4	1	3		10	6	2	11		8	7				
7	17	New Brighton	1-3	Martin	5700						5	9	4	1	3		10	6	2	11		8	7				
8	19	DARLINGTON	2-1	Dixon, Martin	4101						5	9	4		3		8	6	2	11	1	10	7				
9	24	LINCOLN CITY	3-1	Dixon, Seabrook, Martin	9615						5	9	4		3		8	6	2	11	1	10	7				
10	Oct 1	Hartlepools United	1-0	Seabrook	4571						5	9	4		3		8	6	2	11	1	10	7				
11	8	ACCRINGTON STANLEY	3-1	Houseley, Martin (p), Dixon	7173						5	9	4		3		8	6	2	11	1	10	7				
12	15	Wigan Borough	3-1	Martin, Houseley, Dixon	4989						5	9	4		3		8	6	2	11	1	10	7				
13	22	Stockport County	0-3		9291						5	9	4		3		8	6	2	11	1	10	7				
14	29	TRANMERE ROVERS	2-2	Dixon, Seabrook	9503						5	9	4		3		8	6	2	11	1	10	7				
15	Nov 5	Bradford Park Avenue	2-3	Seabrook 2	15727		8				5	9	4		3			6	2	11	1	10	7				
16	19	Nelson	2-3	Bell, Hibbert	3862		8				5	9	4		3			6	2	11	1	10	7				
17	Dec 3	Rotherham United	0-0		4965				6		5	9			3		10		2	11	1	8	7				4
18	17	Durham City	1-1	Smeaton	1164		8			9	5					10			2	11	1		7	6	4		3
19	24	WREXHAM	4-1	Martin 2, Bell, Lees	3032		8			9	5					10		3	2	11	1			6	4	7	
20	26	Doncaster Rovers	1-1	Bell	11380		8			9	5					10		3	2	11	1			6	4	7	
21	27	DONCASTER ROVERS	0-1		12909		8			9	5					10		3	2	11	1			6	4	7	
22	31	CREWE ALEXANDRA	0-0		4266		8			9	5					10		3	2	11	1	4	7	6			
23	Jan 7	Chesterfield	0-3		3437		8		6		5	9				10		3	2	11	1		7	4			
24	14	NELSON	5-1	Martin 2, Dixon 2, Waites	3119		8		6		5	9		1		10		3	2	11				4		7	
25	21	Bradford City	0-0		18747		8				5	9		1		10		3	2	11				6	4	7	
26	Feb 4	Lincoln City	2-5	Dixon, Groves	5515		8				5	9		1		10		3	2	11				6	4	7	
27	11	HARTLEPOOLS UNITED	4-1	Smeaton, Dixon 2, Martin	2424		8		6		5	9		1		10			2	11				4		7	3
28	18	Accrington Stanley	2-3	Dixon, Groves	3241		8		6		5	9		1		10			2	11				4		7	3
29	25	WIGAN BOROUGH	2-2	Bell, Waites	2678		8		6		5	9		1		10		3		11				4		7	2
30	Mar 3	STOCKPORT COUNTY	1-3	Dixon	4770		10		6	8	5	9						3		11	1				4	7	2
31	10	Tranmere Rovers	2-2	Martin, Bell	5858		10		6		5	9						3		11	1		8		4	7	2
32	17	BRADFORD PARK AVE.	1-1	Seabrook	15842		10		6		5	9						3		11	1		8		4	7	2
33	24	Barrow	2-6	Dixon, Seabrook	4470		10		6		5	9						3		11	1		8		4	7	2
34	26	SOUTHPORT	1-0	Bell	1792		8					9						6	2	11	1	10		5	4	7	3
35	Apr 6	Darlington	0-2		6187		8		6	9	5					10			2	11	1				4	7	3
36	7	Southport	1-3	Groves	3524		8		6	9	5					10		2		11	1				4	7	3
37	10	ROCHDALE	1-1	Waites	3595		8		6	9	5					10		2		11	1	4				7	3
38	14	ROTHERHAM UNITED	0-0		3171	2	8			7		9				10				11	1	4		6	5		3
39	21	Rochdale	2-2	Coleman, Dixon	2099		8		6	7		9				10		2		11	1	4		5			3
40	23	NEW BRIGHTON	1-1	Martin	1761		8		6	9						10		2		11	1	4		5		7	3
41	28	DURHAM CITY	3-1	Coleman, Smeaton, Bell	2553		8			7		9				10		6	2	11	1	4		5			3
42	May 5	Wrexham	0-2		1726		8	1		7		9				10		6	2	11		4		5			3
					Apps	1	27	1	15	14	36	33	16	13	17	20	15	36	32	42	28	22	23	18	14	21	18
					Goals		7			2		19				3	6	2	1	14		2	11	3		3	

F.A. Cup

	Date	Opponent	Score	Scorers	Att	Barber B	Bell T	Binns CH	Brannigan DM	Coleman E	Dark AJ	Dixon E	Duckett DT	Fox FS	Gadsden E	Groves A	Housley H	Hubbert H	Lees JW	Martin AF	Pennington J	Proctor N	Seabrook A	Smeaton AR	Swift W	Waites SH	Wheelhouse B
R1	Nov 26	HARTLEPOOLS UNITED	3-0	Proctor, Seabrook, Coleman	10341					9	5				3		10	6	2	11	1	8	7	4			
R2	Dec 10	Tranmere Rovers	1-3	Seabrook	8554						5	9			3		8		4	11	1	10	7	6			2

Hartlepools United

15th in Division Three (North)

	Date	Opponent	Score	Scorers	Att	Boland GA	Brown, Jack	Carr T	Dobell D	Errington A	Hall B	Hardy C	Hardy S	Harris J (2)	Harrison H	Hickman J	Kell G	Liddle I	Mordue J	Mordue WM	Poyntz WI	Rayment J	Richardson GEH	Richardson GW	Robertson T	Robinson WA	Robson C	Williams JT	Young A	Young J
1	Aug 27	Wigan Borough	2-0	Dobell, W Mordue	6385			2	9	3	4		11		1					10	8		7	6					5	
2	Sep 3	DONCASTER ROVERS	1-0	Richardson	5314			2	9	3	4		11		1					10	8		7	6					5	
3	10	Darlington	0-5		6719			2	9	3	4		11		1					10	8		7	6					5	
4	14	Wrexham	2-3	Robinson 2	2927	11		2	9	3					1					8	5			6		10	7		4	
5	17	ASHINGTON	4-1	S Hardy 2, Robson, Robinson	4294			2	9	3			11		1					10	4			6		8	7		5	
6	24	Crewe Alexandra	0-4		3016			2	9	3	5		11		1					10	4			6		8	7			
7	27	Accrington Stanley	2-2	Liddle, W Mordue	6353			2			4		11		1			8		10	9			6	3		7	5		
8	Oct 1	HALIFAX TOWN	0-1		4571			2		3			11		1			8		10	9			6			7	5	4	
9	8	Bradford City	1-2	W Mordue	13762			2			4		11		1		3	8		10	6			9			7		5	
10	15	NEW BRIGHTON	3-3	S Hardy, Richardson, W Mordue	4243			2			4		11		1		3	8		10	6			9			7	5		
11	22	Rotherham United	0-5		2395				9		4			11	1		3	8		10				6	2		7		5	
12	29	ROCHDALE	0-2		4086	11		9			4				1		3	8		10				6	2		7		5	
13	Nov 5	Nelson	2-4	Robinson 2	2001	11		2			4				1		3	8		10	6					9	7		5	
14	12	SOUTHPORT	2-1	W Mordue 2	2429	11		2			4				1		3		8	10	6					9	7		5	
15	19	Durham City	0-1		1580	11		2			4					1				10	8			6	3	9	7		5	
16	Dec 3	Chesterfield	3-1	Robinson, W Mordue, Rayment	2505	11		2			4					1		8		10		7		6	3	9			5	
17	10	DURHAM CITY	2-1	Robinson 2	2497	11		2			4					1		8		10	6	7		5	3	9				
18	17	Tranmere Rovers	2-1	Robinson (p), W Mordue	4878	11		2			4					1		8		10	5	7		6	3	9				
19	24	STOCKPORT COUNTY	2-1	Robinson 2	2033	11		2			4				1			8		10	5	7		6	3	9				
20	26	LINCOLN CITY	1-2	Liddle	3961	11		2			4				1			8		10	5	7		6	3	9				
21	27	Lincoln City	5-1	Robinson 3, J Mordue, W Mordue	9277	11		2			4				1				8	10	5	7		6	3	9				
22	31	WIGAN BOROUGH	1-1	W Mordue	3546	11		2			4				1				8	10	5	7		6	3	9				
23	Jan 2	BARROW	6-2	Robson 2, Robinson 2, J Mordue 2	3377	11		2			4				1				8	10	5				3	9	7		6	
24	7	Doncaster Rovers	1-1	Boland	7641	11		2			4				1				8	10	5	7		6	3	9				
25	14	BRADFORD PARK AVE.	1-1	Robinson (p)	5023	11		2			4				1				8	10	5	7		6	3	9				
26	21	DARLINGTON	0-1		7485	11		2							1				8	10	5	7		6	3	9			4	
27	28	Ashington	1-3	W Mordue	1407	11		2							1					10	5			6	3	9	7		4	8
28	Feb 4	CREWE ALEXANDRA	4-3	Boland, W Mordue, J Young, Robinson	3100	11		2			4				1					10	5				3	9	7		6	8
29	11	Halifax Town	1-4	W Mordue	2424	11					4				1		2		8	10	5				3	9	7		6	
30	18	BRADFORD CITY	2-3	Rayment, Robinson (p)	4475	11				3	4				1		2		8	10	5	7				9			6	
31	25	New Brighton	1-2	Robinson	2861	11					4				1				8	10	5	7		6	2	9		3		
32	Mar 3	ROTHERHAM UNITED	1-3	W Mordue	4190	11					4				1		2		8	10	5	7		6		9		3		
33	10	Rochdale	1-0	Robinson	2582	11	1				4									10	5	7		6	2	9		3		8
34	17	NELSON	4-5	Rigg (og), Robinson 3	2972	11	1				4									10	5	7		6	2	9		3		8
35	24	Southport	2-0	Boland, Dobell	2518	11			9		4				1							7		6	2	10		3	5	8
36	Apr 6	Barrow	0-2		7059	11	1				4									10		7		6	2	9		3	5	8
37	7	Bradford Park Avenue	0-3		12715	11	1	2			4											7		10	3	9		5	6	8
38	9	ACCRINGTON STANLEY	0-2		2245	11	1	2			4	10										7		8	3	9		5	6	
39	14	CHESTERFIELD	1-0	Robinson	1314	11		2			4				1					10				6		9	7	3	5	8
40	21	WREXHAM	4-2	Robinson, Robson, J Young, W Mordue	1542	11		2			4				1					10				6		9	7	3	5	8
41	28	TRANMERE ROVERS	2-0	W Mordue, Robinson	2132	11		2			4				1					10				6		9	7	3	5	8
42	May 5	Stockport County	2-2	Robinson, Robson	4991	11		2			4				1					10				6		9	7	3	5	8
					Apps	32	5	33	8	8	37	1	9	1	33	4	9	12	11	39	31	19	3	36	25	33	20	15	27	11
					Goals	3			2				3					2	3	16		2		2		28	5			2

One own goal

F.A. Cup

	Date	Opponent	Score	Scorers	Att	Boland GA	Brown, Jack	Carr T	Dobell D	Errington A	Hall B	Hardy C	Hardy S	Harris J (2)	Harrison H	Hickman J	Kell G	Liddle I	Mordue J	Mordue WM	Poyntz WI	Rayment J	Richardson GEH	Richardson GW	Robertson T	Robinson WA	Robson C	Williams JT	Young A	Young J
R1	Nov 26	Halifax Town	0-3		10341	11		2			4				1					10	8	7		9	3			6	5	

Huddersfield Town

2nd in Division One

	Date	Opponent	Score	Scorers	Att	Barkas E	Brown G	Campbell WR	Carr WE	Cumming L	Dent JG	Goodall FR	Jackson AS	Kelly RF	Meads T	Mercer WH	Pickering WH	Raw H	Redfern L	Smailes J	Smith N	Smith WH	Spence MB	Steele DM	Stephenson C	Turner H	Wadsworth SJ	Wilson GMcI	Wilson T
1	Aug 27	NEWCASTLE UNITED	1-3	Brown	24465		9					2	7	10	6			8				11		4		1	3		5
2	29	Birmingham	1-3	Brown	16432	2	9		6					7	8							11		4	10	1	3		5
3	Sep 3	West Ham United	2-4	Brown, Jackson	23925	2	8				9		7	10	6							11		4		1	3		5
4	10	Tottenham Hotspur	2-2	Dent, Brown	27983	3	8				9	2	7	10	6							11		4		1			5
5	17	MANCHESTER UNITED	4-2	Brown 3, Dent	17307	3	8				9	2	7	10	6							11		4		1			5
6	24	Everton	2-2	WH Smith, Jackson	37269	3					9	2	7	8	6							11		4	10	1			5
7	Oct 1	CARDIFF CITY	8-2	Kelly 3, Jackson, Dent 2, Goodall (p), WH Smith	12975	3					9	2	7	8	6							11		4	10	1			5
8	8	Blackburn Rovers	1-1	Jackson	28032	3					9	2	7	8	6							11		4	10	1			5
9	15	BOLTON WANDERERS	1-0	Jackson (p)	19818	3					9		7	8	2						6	11		4	10	1			5
10	22	ASTON VILLA	1-1	Jackson	14679	3					9		7	8	2						6	11		4	10	1			5
11	29	Sunderland	0-3		22070	3	8				9	2		7	6							11		4	10	1			5
12	Nov 5	DERBY COUNTY	2-1	WH Smith, Goodall (p)	7098	3	9					2	7	8	6	1						11		4	10				5
13	12	Sheffield United	7-1	Meads, WH Smith 2, Brown 2, Jackson 2	22163	3	9					2	7	8	6	1					4	11			10				5
14	19	BURY	3-0	Brown 2, WH Smith	12293	3	9					2	7	8	6	1					4	11			10				5
15	26	Liverpool	2-4	WH Smith, Goodall (p)	34128	3	9					2	7	8	6	1					4	11			10				5
16	Dec 3	ARSENAL	2-1	WH Smith 2	15140	3	9					2	7	8	6	1					4	11			10				5
17	10	Burnley	1-0	Brown	19130	3	9					2	7	8	6	1						11		4	10				5
18	17	LEICESTER CITY	3-1	Brown 2, Kelly	13717	3	9						7	8	6	1			4			11			10		2		5
19	24	Portsmouth	1-2	Brown	21785	3	9					2	7	8		1			4			11			10		6		5
20	26	SHEFFIELD WEDNESDAY	1-0	Jackson	21336	3	9						7		10	1		8	4			11		6			2		5
21	27	Sheffield Wednesday	5-0	Barkas (p), WH Smith, Brown 3	41824	3	9						7		6	1		8	4			11			10		2		5
22	31	Newcastle United	3-2	Brown, Jackson, Barkas (p)	33640	3	9						7		6	1		8	4			11			10		2		5
23	Jan 2	Middlesbrough	1-3	Brown	26032	3	9						7		6	1		8	4			11			10		2		5
24	7	WEST HAM UNITED	5-2	Jackson 2, Brown 3	10972		9					2	7	8					4			11		6	10	1	3		5
25	21	TOTTENHAM HOTSPUR	4-2	Brown, WH Smith 2, Jackson	17892		9					2	7	8					4			11		6	10	1	3		5
26	Feb 4	EVERTON	4-1	Dent, WH Smith 3	50012		10				9	2	7	8		1			4			11		6			3		5
27	11	Cardiff City	0-4		21073		10				9	2	7	8		1			4			11		6			3		5
28	25	Bolton Wanderers	1-0	WH Smith	44082	3	9					2	7	8		1			4			11		6	10				5
29	Mar 7	Manchester United	0-0		35413	3	9					2	7	8		1			4			11		6	10				5
30	10	SUNDERLAND	4-2	Stephenson, Jackson, Kelly, Brown	17497	3	9						7	8		1			4	11				6	10		2		5
31	14	BLACKBURN ROVERS	3-1	Goodall (p), Jackson, Brown	10890	3	9					2	7	8	6	1			4			11			10				5
32	17	Derby County	0-0		24684		9					2	7	8	6	1			4			11			10		3		5
33	31	Bury	3-2	G Wilson, Dent, Raw	14636	3		4		10	9				6	1	2	8		11			5					7	
34	Apr 7	LIVERPOOL	2-4	Jackson 2	27290	3	9					2	7	11		1		8	4					6	10				5
35	9	BIRMINGHAM	2-0	Dent 2	28779	3					9	2	7	8					4			11		6	10	1			5
36	10	MIDDLESBROUGH	2-4	Stephenson, Goodall (p)	29034	3					9	2	7	8	6				4			11			10	1			5
37	14	Arsenal	0-0		38707	3	9					2	7	8		1			4			11	6		10				5
38	25	BURNLEY	1-2	Brown	20643	3	10				9	2	7	8		1			4	11			6						5
39	28	Leicester City	2-1	Raw, Barkas (p)	29191	2					9		7					8	4			11		6	10	1	3		5
40	30	SHEFFIELD UNITED	0-1		22380	2	10				9	3	7					8	4			11	6			1			5
41	May 2	Aston Villa	0-3		30173	2	9	4				3	7	8	6							11			10	1			5
42	5	PORTSMOUTH	4-1	Jackson 2, WH Smith, Barkas	11206	2					9		7	8				10	4			11	6			1	3		5
					Apps	36	32	2	1	1	18	29	39	35	27	23	1	10	23	3	6	38	5	24	31	19	17	1	41
					Goals	4	27				8	5	19	5	1			2				17			2			1	

F.A. Cup

	Date	Opponent	Score	Scorers	Att	Barkas E	Brown G	Campbell WR	Carr WE	Cumming L	Dent JG	Goodall FR	Jackson AS	Kelly RF	Meads T	Mercer WH	Pickering WH	Raw H	Redfern L	Smailes J	Smith N	Smith WH	Spence MB	Steele DM	Stephenson C	Turner H	Wadsworth SJ	Wilson GMcI	Wilson T
R3	Jan 14	LINCOLN CITY	4-2	Brown, WH Smith, Goodall (p), Steele	19229		9					2	7	8					4			11		6	10	1	3		5
R4	28	WEST HAM UNITED	2-1	Brown, Jackson	27525		9					2	7	8		1			4			11		6	10		3		5
R5	Feb 18	MIDDLESBROUGH	4-0	Steele, Brown, Jackson, WH Smith	55200	3	9					2	7	8		1			4			11		6	10				5
R6	Mar 3	TOTTENHAM HOTSPUR	6-1	WH Smith 2, Brown 4	52390	3	9					2	7	8		1			4			11		6	10				5
SF	24	Sheffield United	2-2	Jackson, Brown	69260		9					2	7	8	6	1			4			11			10		3		5
rep	26	Sheffield United	0-0	(aet)	53749						9	2	7	8	6	1						11	4		10		3		5
rep2	Apr 2	Sheffield United	1-0	Jackson	69360	3					9	2	7	8		1			4			11		6	10				5
F	21	Blackburn Rovers	1-3	Jackson	92041	3	9					2	7	8		1			4			11		6	10				5

SF at Old Trafford, replay at Goodison Park, second replay at Maine Road. Final at Wembley Stadium.

Hull City

14th in Division Two

	Date	Opponent	Score	Scorers	Att.	Alexander S	Barraclough W	Bell M	Bleakley T	Crozier J	Dixon S	Gibson F	Gibson J	Guyan G	Howieson J	Maddison G	Martin G	Mooney P	Nelson A	Scott H	Starling R	Sullivan N	Swan C	Taylor W	Watson J	Whitworth G	Wilson G	Wyper T
1	Aug 27	Barnsley	1-1	Guyan	10830			3			5		2	9		1	10	4		8		6		11				7
2	29	Preston North End	2-4	Scott 2	21811			3			5		2	9		1	10	4		8		6		11				7
3	Sep 3	WOLVERHAMPTON W.	2-0	Scott, Taylor	11050						5		2	9		1	10	4		8		6		11			3	7
4	5	PRESTON NORTH END	0-0		8915			3			5		2			1	10	4		8	9	6		11				7
5	10	Port Vale	2-1	Scott 2	12169			3			5		2			1	10	4		8		6		11		9		7
6	17	SOUTH SHIELDS	1-0	Martin	10252			3			5		2			1	10	4		8		6		11		9		7
7	24	Leeds United	0-2		21943			3			5		2	9		1	7	4		8		6		11		10		
8	Oct 1	NOTTM. FOREST	2-0	Martin 2	8274			3	6		5		2		10	1	9	4		8				11				7
9	8	Manchester City	1-2	Scott	42038			3	6		5		2		10	1	9	4		8				11				7
10	15	GRIMSBY TOWN	0-1		18862			3	6		5		2		10	1	9			8			4	11				7
11	22	Chelsea	0-2		15153			2		11	5				10	1	8	4	9			6	7				3	
12	29	BLACKPOOL	2-2	Nelson, Howieson	9067			3		11	5		2		10	1	8	4	9			6	7					
13	Nov 5	Reading	0-3		9935			3	6		5		2		10	1	8					4	7	11		9		
14	12	CLAPTON ORIENT	2-2	Martin 2	6682			3	6		8		2		10	1	9					4	7	11	5			
15	19	West Bromwich Albion	1-1	Sullivan	8857			3	6		8		2		10	1	9					4	7	11	5			
16	26	SOUTHAMPTON	1-0	Keeping (og)	8081			3	6		8		2		10	1	9						4	11	5			7
17	Dec 3	Stoke City	1-3	Howieson	9638			3	6			1	2		10		9				8		4	11	5			7
18	10	BRISTOL CITY	1-1	Martin	6716			3	6		8	1	2		10		9						4	11	5			7
19	17	Notts County	1-1	Taylor	8758	8		3	6		4	1	2		10		7		9					11	5			
20	24	OLDHAM ATHLETIC	2-2	Nelson, Alexander	6662	8		3	6		4	1	2		10		7		9					11	5			
21	27	FULHAM	3-2	Nelson 3	14050	8		3	6		4	1	2		10		7		9					11	5			
22	31	BARNSLEY	2-1	Alexander, Scott	9569	10		3	6		4	1	2				7		9	8				11	5			
23	Jan 7	Wolverhampton Wan.	1-1	Nelson	12106	10		3	6		4		2			1	7		9	8				11	5			
24	21	PORT VALE	1-0	Nelson	7106	8	11	3	6		4		2			1	7		9		10				5			
25	Feb 4	LEEDS UNITED	3-1	Martin 2, Wyper	12520		11	3	6		5		2			1	10		9			4	8					7
26	11	Nottingham Forest	1-1	Swan	6617		11	3	6		5		2			1	10		9			4	8					7
27	22	South Shields	0-1		4322		11	3	6		5		2			1	10		9			4	8					7
28	25	Grimsby Town	1-1	Guyan	15986		11	3	6		5		2	9		1	10			8		4						7
29	Mar 3	CHELSEA	0-2		12679			3	6		5		2	9		1	10			8		4		11				7
30	10	Blackpool	1-2	Sullivan	9988			3	6		5		2		10	1	8		9			4	7	11				
31	17	READING	0-1		6493			3	6		5		2	9	10	1					8	4	7	11				
32	24	Clapton Orient	0-0		8869			3	6		5		2		10	1			9		8	4		11				7
33	26	Fulham	2-0	Nelson, Taylor	7023			3	6		5		2		10	1			9		8	4		11				7
34	31	WEST BROMWICH ALB.	1-1	Howieson	7964			3	6		5		2		10	1			9		8	4		11				7
35	Apr 6	SWANSEA TOWN	0-2		8877			3	6		5		2		10	1			9		8	4		11				7
36	7	Southampton	0-2		11955			3	6		5		2		10	1			9		8	4		11				7
37	9	Swansea Town	0-2		15732			3	6				2		10	1					8	4		11	5	9		7
38	14	STOKE CITY	1-0	Howieson	4848		11	3	6				2		10	1			9		8	4	7		5			
39	16	MANCHESTER CITY	0-0		6088		11		6		5		2		10	1					8	4		7		9	3	
40	21	Bristol City	1-0	Whitworth	10198		11		6		5		2		10	1					8	4		7		9	3	
41	28	NOTTS COUNTY	1-1	Whitworth	5284				6	11	5		2		10	1					8	4		7		9	3	
42	May 5	Oldham Athletic	0-5		4936		11		6		5		2		10	1					8	4		7		9	3	
					Apps	6	9	37	33	3	39	6	41	7	27	36	30	11	18	14	15	30	15	34	13	9	6	23
					Goals	2								2	4		8		8	7		2	1	3		2		1

One own goal

F.A. Cup

	Date	Opponent	Score	Scorers	Att.	Alexander S	Barraclough W	Bell M	Bleakley T	Crozier J	Dixon S	Gibson F	Gibson J	Guyan G	Howieson J	Maddison G	Martin G	Mooney P	Nelson A	Scott H	Starling R	Sullivan N	Swan C	Taylor W	Watson J	Whitworth G	Wilson G	Wyper T
R3	Jan 14	LEICESTER CITY	0-1		23141	8		3	6		4		2		10	1	7		9					11	5			

Leeds United

Second in Division Two: Promoted

	Date	Opponent	Score	Scorers	Att.	Allan J	Armand JE	Atkinson JW	Baker A	Coutts T	Edwards W	Hart EA	Jennings THO	Johnson W	Keetley CF	Menzies WJ	Mitchell TM	Potts JF	Reed G	Roberts HB	Robinson D	Sissons AE	Stacey A	Townsley T	Turnbull RJ	Wainscoat WR	White J
1	Aug 27	South Shields	5-1	White 2, Jennings, Mitchell, Wainscoat	9826						4		9			3	11	1	6	2				5	7	10	8
2	29	BARNSLEY	2-2	Jennings, White	21219						4		9			3	11	1	6	2				5	7	10	8
3	Sep 3	SOUTHAMPTON	2-0	Wainscoat 2	19479						4	5	9			3	11	1	6					2	7	10	8
4	10	NOTTM. FOREST	4-0	Jennings, Mitchell, Turnbull, Wainscoat	19478						4	5	9			3	11	1	6					2	7	10	8
5	17	Manchester City	1-2	Jennings	40931						4	5	9			3	11	1	6					2	7	10	8
6	24	HULL CITY	2-0	Jennings, Wainscoat	21943						4	5	9			3	11	1	6			7		2		10	8
7	26	Barnsley	1-2	Mitchell	13038						4		9			3	11	1	6	2				5	7	10	8
8	Oct 1	Preston North End	1-5	White	16966	3					4		9				11	1	6	2				5	7	10	8
9	8	SWANSEA TOWN	5-0	White 2, Jennings 2 (1p), Turnbull	18097	3			4				9				11	1	6	2				5	7	10	8
10	15	Fulham	1-1	White	16704	3			4				9				11	1	6	2				5	7	10	8
11	22	Grimsby Town	2-3	Jennings, Wainscoat	11909	3				4			9				11	1	6	2				5	7	10	8
12	29	OLDHAM ATHLETIC	1-0	Mitchell	17615	2		4					9			3	11	1	6					5	7	10	8
13	Nov 5	Notts County	2-2	Jennings 2	9866	2		4					9			3	11	1	6					5	7	10	8
14	12	READING	6-2	Turnbull 2, White 2, Jennings, Wainscoat	17257	2		4					9			3	11	1	6					5	7	10	8
15	19	Blackpool	2-0	Mitchell 2	9008	2		4					9			3	11	1	6					5	7	10	8
16	26	WEST BROMWICH ALB.	1-2	Townsley	23690	2		4					9			3	11	1	6					5	7	10	8
17	Dec 3	Clapton Orient	1-2	Mitchell	12838	3					4	5	9				11	1	6					2	7	10	8
18	10	CHELSEA	5-0	Jennings 4, White	22059	3					4	5	9				11	1	6					2	7	10	8
19	17	Bristol City	2-1	Wainscoat, White	18326	3					4	5	9				11	1	6					2	7	10	8
20	24	STOKE CITY	5-1	Jennings 2, Hart, Turnbull, White	12889						4	5	9			3	11	1	6					2	7	10	8
21	26	Port Vale	2-1	Wainscoat, White	18869						4	5	9			3	11	1	6					2	7	10	8
22	27	PORT VALE	3-0	Jennings 2, Wainscoat	32295						4	5	9			3	11	1	6					2	7	10	8
23	31	SOUTH SHIELDS	3-0	Keetley, Turnbull, Wainscoat	12952						4	5			9	3	11	1	6					2	7	10	8
24	Jan 7	Southampton	4-1	White 2, Keetley, Wainscoat	13966						4	5			9	3	11	1	6			7		2		10	8
25	21	Nottingham Forest	2-2	Keetley, White	13133						4	5			9	3	11	1	6			7		2		10	8
26	28	BRISTOL CITY	3-2	Keetley 3	15534						4	5			9		11	1	6		3			2	7	10	8
27	Feb 4	Hull City	1-3	Jennings	12520	3					4	5	9				11	1	6			7		2		10	8
28	11	PRESTON NORTH END	2-4	Wainscoat 2	24216						4	5		1	9	3	11		6			7		2		10	8
29	18	Swansea Town	1-1	Jennings	13444						4	5	9	1		3	11		6			7		2		10	8
30	25	FULHAM	2-1	Wainscoat, White	17358						4	5	9	1		3	11		6			7		2		10	8
31	Mar 3	GRIMSBY TOWN	0-0		23567						4	5	9	1		3	11		6			7		2		10	8
32	10	Oldham Athletic	1-0	Keetley	22029							5			9	3	11	1	6				4	2	7	10	8
33	17	NOTTS COUNTY	6-0	Keetley 3, Armand, Turnbull, White	17643		10				4	5			9	3	11	1	6					2	7		8
34	24	Reading	1-0	Keetley	13098						4	5			9	3	11	1	6					2	7	10	8
35	31	BLACKPOOL	4-0	Wainscoat 2, Armand, Mitchell	19630		8					5			9	3	11	1	6				4	2	7	10	
36	Apr 7	West Bromwich Albion	1-0	Turnbull	23644						4	5			9	3	11	1	6					2	7	10	8
37	9	Wolverhampton Wan.	0-0		25251						4	5			9	3	11	1	6					2	7	10	8
38	10	WOLVERHAMPTON W.	3-0	Keetley 2, White	29821						4	5			9	3	11	1	6					2	7	10	8
39	14	CLAPTON ORIENT	4-0	Keetley 3, White	22884						4	5			9	3	11	1	6					2	7	10	8
40	21	Chelsea	3-2	Keetley 2, White	47562						4	5			9	3	11	1	6					2	7	10	8
41	25	MANCHESTER CITY	0-1		48780						4	5			9	3	11	1	6					2	7	10	8
42	May 5	Stoke City	1-5	Wainscoat	12401						4	5			9	3	11	1	6					2	7	10	8
					Apps	13	2	5	2	1	32	30	26	4	16	33	42	38	42	7	1	8	2	42	34	41	41
					Goals		2					1	21		18		8							1	8	18	21

F.A. Cup

	Date	Opponent	Score	Scorers	Att.	Allan J	Armand JE	Atkinson JW	Baker A	Coutts T	Edwards W	Hart EA	Jennings THO	Johnson W	Keetley CF	Menzies WJ	Mitchell TM	Potts JF	Reed G	Roberts HB	Robinson D	Sissons AE	Stacey A	Townsley T	Turnbull RJ	Wainscoat WR	White J
R3	Jan 14	Manchester City	0-1		50473						4	5	9			3	11	1	6					2	7	10	8

Leicester City

3rd in Division One

No	Date	Opponent	Score	Scorers	Att	Adcock H	Barry LJ	Baxter J	Bell WJ	Bishop SM	Black AH	Brown JT	Callachan H	Campbell K	Carr G	Carrigan P	Chandler ACH	Duncan J	Findlay W	Gibson T	Hine EW	Lane WHC	Lochhead AW	McLaren J	Osborne R	Russell A	Watson N
1	Aug 27	Aston Villa	3-0	Adcock, Bell, Bishop	47288	7			11	6		2				5	9	4			8		10	1	3		
2	29	SHEFFIELD UNITED	3-1	Adcock, Duncan, Hine	27117	7			11	6	2					5	9	4			8		10	1	3		
3	Sep 3	SUNDERLAND	3-3	Lochhead 2, Chandler	28977	7			11	6	2					5	9	4			8		10	1	3		
4	5	Sheffield United	1-1	Chandler	13096	7			11	6	2					5	9	4			8		10	1	3		
5	10	Derby County	1-2	Chandler	26008	7			11		2					5	9	4	6		8		10	1	3		
6	17	WEST HAM UNITED	2-3	Adcock, Chandler	25482	7			11	6	2						9	4			8		10	1	3		5
7	22	Tottenham Hotspur	1-2	Hine	9436	7			11	6	2						9		4		8		10	1	3		5
8	24	Portsmouth	0-2		20959	7				6	2				11		9	4			8		10	1	3		5
9	Oct 1	MANCHESTER UNITED	1-0	Adcock	22385	7	11				2				6		9		4		8		10	1	3		5
10	8	LIVERPOOL	1-1	Hine	25312	7	11				2				6		9		4		8		10	1	3		5
11	15	Arsenal	2-2	Adcock, Hine	36640	7	11				2				6		9		4		8		10	1	3		5
12	22	Blackburn Rovers	0-0		11115	7	11				2				6		9		4		8		10	1	3		5
13	29	CARDIFF CITY	4-1	Hine 2, Chandler, Lochhead	25634	7	11				2				6		9		4		8		10	1	3		5
14	Nov 5	Everton	1-7	Chandler	30392	7	11				2				6	5	9		4		8		10	1	3		
15	12	BOLTON WANDERERS	4-2	Lochhead 2, Chandler, Hine	21249	7	11			6	2				5		9		4		8		10	1	3		
16	19	Sheffield Wednesday	2-1	Chandler, Hine	15969	7	11				2				5		9		4		8		10	1	3		6
17	26	NEWCASTLE UNITED	3-0	Chandler 2, Lochhead	33375	7	11				2				5		9		4		8		10	1	3		6
18	Dec 3	Birmingham	2-0	Hine, Lochhead	24272	7	11	6			2				5		9		4		8		10	1	3		
19	10	MIDDLESBROUGH	3-3	Chandler 2, Lochhead	26812	7	11	6			2				5		9		4		8		10	1	3		
20	17	Huddersfield Town	1-3	Chandler	13717	7	11	6			2				5		9		4		8		10	1	3		
21	24	TOTTENHAM HOTSPUR	6-1	Chandler 3, Adcock, Bishop, Lochhead	19987	7	11			6	2				5		9		4		8		10	1	3		
22	26	BURNLEY	5-0	Lochhead 2, Adcock, Bishop, Hine	20063	7	11			6	2				5		9		4		8		10	1	3		
23	27	Burnley	1-5	McCluggage (og)	24824	7	11			6	2				5		9		4		8		10	1	3		
24	31	ASTON VILLA	3-0	Hine 2, Chandler	25233	7	11			6	2				5		9		4		8		10	1	3		
25	Jan 2	Bury	1-2	Chandler	15730	7	11			6	2	3			5		9		4		8		10	1			
26	7	Sunderland	2-2	Barry, Lochhead	20770	7	11			6	2				5		9		4		8		10	1	3		
27	21	DERBY COUNTY	4-0	Chandler 2, Adcock, Lochhead	36094	7	11			6	2				5		9	4			8		10	1	3		
28	Feb 4	PORTSMOUTH	6-2	Chandler 2, Lochhead 2, Barry, Hine	23987	7	11			6	2				5		9	4			8		10	1	3		
29	11	Manchester United	2-5	Chandler, Duncan	16640	7	11				2				5		9	4	6		8		10	1	3		
30	25	ARSENAL	3-2	Adcock, Bishop, Duncan	25835	7	11			6	2				5		9	4			8		10	1	3		
31	Mar 10	Cardiff City	0-3		13178	7	11				2	3			5			6	4		8	9	10	1			
32	12	West Ham United	0-4		6211	7	11			6	2	3			5		9		4	10	8			1			
33	17	EVERTON	1-0	Adcock	26625	7	11			6	2	3			5		9	4			8		10	1			
34	24	Bolton Wanderers	3-3	Hine 2, Chandler	18142	7	11			6	2	3			5		9	4			8		10	1			
35	31	SHEFFIELD WEDNESDAY	2-2	Chandler, Hine	18634	7	11				2	3			5		9	6	4		8		10	1			
36	Apr 7	Newcastle United	5-1	Chandler 4, Hine	32492	7	11				2		3	1	5		9	6	4		8		10				
37	9	BURY	2-2	Hine, Lochhead	25446	7	11				2		3	1	5		9	6	4		8		10				
38	14	BIRMINGHAM	3-0	Barry, Chandler, Hine	17558	7	11				2		3	1	5		9	6			8		10			4	
39	21	Middlesbrough	1-1	Carr	18854	7	11				2	3		1	5		9	6	4		8		10				
40	25	Liverpool	1-1	Chandler	23657	7	11			6	2			1	5		9	4		8			10		3		
41	28	HUDDERSFIELD T	1-2	Carr	29191	7	11			6	2			1	5		9	4			8		10		3		
42	30	BLACKBURN ROVERS	6-0	Chandler 3, Barry, Hine, Lochhead	14914	7	11			6	2				5		9		4		8		10	1	3		
					Apps	42	34	3	7	23	41	8	3	6	35	6	41	21	28	2	41	1	41	36	32	1	10
					Goals	10	4		1	4					2		34	3			20		17				

One own goal

F.A. Cup

Rd	Date	Opponent	Score	Scorers	Att	Adcock H	Barry LJ	Baxter J	Bell WJ	Bishop SM	Black AH	Brown JT	Callachan H	Campbell K	Carr G	Carrigan P	Chandler ACH	Duncan J	Findlay W	Gibson T	Hine EW	Lane WHC	Lochhead AW	McLaren J	Osborne R	Russell A	Watson N
R3	Jan 14	Hull City	1-0	Barry	23141	7	11			6	2				5		9	4			8		10	1	3		
R4	28	Reading	1-0	Adcock	27243	7	11			6	2				5		9	4			8		10	1	3		
R5	Feb 18	TOTTENHAM HOTSPUR	0-3		47296	7	11			6	2				5		9	4			8		10	1	3		

Lincoln City

Second in Division Three (North)

	Date	Opponent	Score	Scorers	Att	Andrews H	Bassnett A	Bissett JT	Bosbury CE	Campbell A	Dinsdale WA	Foulkes CE	Freeman JA	Gillott E	Hale A	Hill LG	Keating RE	Maidment T	McConville P	Pegg FE	Pringle H	Robson JW	Worthy A	Yorke AE
1	Aug 27	Doncaster Rovers	0-3		8451	10	4	2	7		9				6	1				11	8	5		3
2	29	WIGAN BOROUGH	4-1	Dinsdale, Pegg 2, Bosbury	5518	10	4		7		9	5			6	1				11	8		2	3
3	Sep 3	DARLINGTON	1-0	Dinsdale	7192	10	4		7		9	5			6	1				11	8		2	3
4	7	Wigan Borough	3-1	Dinsdale, Pegg 2	4260	10	4		7		9	5			6	1				11	8		2	3
5	10	Ashington	5-4	Bosbury, Pegg, Dinsdale, Pringle 2	3066	10	4		7		9	5			6	1				11	8		2	3
6	17	CREWE ALEXANDRA	5-2	Dinsdale 2, Hale, Bosbury, Andrews	7175	10	4		7		9	5			6	1				11	8		2	3
7	24	Halifax Town	1-3	Dinsdale	9615	10	4		7		9	5			6	1				11	8		2	3
8	Oct 1	BRADFORD CITY	2-2	Dinsdale, Bosbury	6049	10	4		7		9	5			6	1				11	8		2	3
9	8	New Brighton	3-2	Dinsdale, Bassnett, Pringle	4667	10	4		7		9	5				1				11	8	6	2	3
10	15	STOCKPORT COUNTY	2-0	Andrews, Dinsdale	7468	10	4		7		9	5				1				11	8	6	2	3
11	22	Rochdale	3-0	Bassnett, Dinsdale, Pegg	5229	10	4		7		9	5			6	1				11	8		2	3
12	29	NELSON	0-0		7956	10	4		7		9	5			6	1				11	8		2	3
13	Nov 5	Barrow	3-3	Dinsdale 2, Foulkes	5131	10	4		7		9	5			6	1				11	8		2	3
14	12	ROTHERHAM UNITED	4-1	Pegg 2, Bosbury 2	5819	10	4		7		9	5			6	1				11	8		2	3
15	19	Southport	1-3	Dinsdale	3113	10	4		7		9	5			6	1				11	8		2	3
16	Dec 3	Wrexham	0-1		4400	10			7		9	5	4		6	1				11	8		2	3
17	14	DURHAM CITY	2-1	Bassnett, Campbell	1475	11	4		7	10	9	5			6	1					8		2	3
18	17	Bradford Park Avenue	0-3		10977	10	4		7		9	5			6	1				11	8		2	3
19	24	TRANMERE ROVERS	1-1	Campbell	5363		4		7	10	9	5				1				11	8	6	2	3
20	26	Hartlepools United	2-1	Pringle, Pegg	3961		4		7	10	9	5			6	1				11	8		2	3
21	27	HARTLEPOOLS UNITED	1-5	Bassnett	9277		4		7	10	9	5			6	1				11	8		2	3
22	31	DONCASTER ROVERS	2-0	Andrews, Pegg	8631	10	4		7					5	6	1	9		3	11	8		2	
23	Jan 2	Accrington Stanley	0-1		5682	10	4		7					5	6	1	9		3	11	8		2	
24	7	Darlington	2-9	Dinsdale, Andrews	8365	10	4		7		9			5	6	1			3	11	8		2	
25	21	ASHINGTON	3-1	Yorke, Hale, Bassnett	5768	10	4		7		9	5			6	1				11	8		2	3
26	28	Stockport County	0-2		7478	10	4		7		9	5			6	1				11	8		2	3
27	Feb 4	HALIFAX TOWN	5-2	Andrews 3, Bosbury 2	5515	10	4		7		9	5			6	1		8		11			2	3
28	11	Bradford City	1-3	Pegg	7229	10	4		7		9	5			6	1		8		11			2	3
29	18	NEW BRIGHTON	1-2	Pegg	5375	10	4		7		9	5	6			1				11	8		2	3
30	Mar 3	ROCHDALE	3-1	Dinsdale 2, Pringle	5760	10	4		7		9	5			6	1				11	8		2	3
31	10	Nelson	3-1	Maidment, Pringle, Bosbury	3422		4		7		9	5			6	1		8		11	10		2	3
32	17	BARROW	5-0	Campbell 2, Dinsdale 2, Maidment	5202		4		7	10	9	5			6	1		8		11			2	3
33	21	Crewe Alexandra	0-0		1856		4		7		9	5			6	1		8		11	10		2	3
34	24	Rotherham United	4-2	Maidment 2, Dinsdale, Bosbury	4339		4		7		9	5			6	1		8		11	10		2	3
35	31	SOUTHPORT	2-0	Yorke, Pegg	4427		4		7		9	5			6	1		8		11	10		2	3
36	Apr 6	ACCRINGTON STANLEY	3-1	Bosbury 2, Pegg	8810		4		7		9	5			6	1		8		11	10		2	3
37	7	Chesterfield	1-0	Dinsdale	4770		4		7		9	5			6	1		8		11	10		2	3
38	11	CHESTERFIELD	0-0		3650		4		7		9	5			6	1		8		11	10		2	3
39	14	WREXHAM	5-0	Dinsdale 2, Maidment 2, Bosbury	4005		4		7		9	5			6	1		8		11	10		2	3
40	21	Durham City	4-0	Bosbury 2, Pringle, Dinsdale	1305		4		7		9	5			6	1		8		11	10		2	3
41	28	BRADFORD PARK AVE.	2-0	Dinsdale, Maidment	9785		4		7		9	5			6	1		8		11	10		2	3
42	May 5	Tranmere Rovers	2-2	Pringle, Dinsdale	4029		4		7		9	5			6	1		8		11	10		2	3
					Apps	27	41	1	42	5	40	38	2	3	38	42	2	14	3	41	39	4	41	39
					Goals	7	5		15	4	26	1			2			7		14	8			2

F.A. Cup

	Date	Opponent	Score	Scorers	Att	Andrews H	Bassnett A	Bissett JT	Bosbury CE	Campbell A	Dinsdale WA	Foulkes CE	Freeman JA	Gillott E	Hale A	Hill LG	Keating RE	Maidment T	McConville P	Pegg FE	Pringle H	Robson JW	Worthy A	Yorke AE
R1	Nov 26	Accrington Stanley	5-2	Dinsdale 2, Pringle, Andrews, Bosbury	7245	10	4		7		9	5			6	1				11	8		2	3
R2	Dec 10	Gainsborough Trinity	2-0	Bosbury 2	7591	10	4		7		9	5			6	1				11	8		2	3
R3	Jan 14	Huddersfield Town	2-4	Pringle, Dinsdale	19229	10	4		7		9	5	6			1					8		2	3

W Hamilton played at 11 in R3

Liverpool

16th in Division One

	Date	Opponent	Score	Scorers	Att	Bromilow TG	Chambers H	Clark JR	Devlin WA	Done R	Edmed RA	Hodgson G	Hopkin F	Jackson J	Longworth E	Lucas T	McBain N	McKinlay D	McMullan D	McNab JS	Morrison TK	Murray WT	Pither GB	Race H	Reid TI	Riley AJ	Scott E	Scott T	Shears AE	Walsh JA
1	Aug 27	Sheffield United	1-1	Devlin	21667	6	10		9		7	8	11	5		2		3		4							1			
2	31	BURY	5-1	Devlin 4, Hodgson	30047	6	10		9		7	8	11	5		2		3		4							1			
3	Sep 3	ASTON VILLA	0-0		42196	6	10		9		7	8	11	5		2		3		4							1			
4	10	Sunderland	1-2	Hodgson	29479	6	10		9		7	8	11	5		2		3		4							1			
5	17	DERBY COUNTY	5-2	Devlin 2, McNab, Hodgson, Edmed	34336	6	10		9		7	8	11	5		2		3		4							1			
6	19	Bury	2-5	Devlin, Crown (og)	10950	6	10		9		7	8	11	5		2		3		4							1			
7	24	West Ham United	1-3	Edmed	26876	6	10		9		7	8		5		2		3	4				11				1			
8	Oct 1	PORTSMOUTH	8-2	Devlin 4, Hodgson 3, Pither	25252	6			9		7	8		5		2		3	4				11		10		1			
9	8	Leicester City	1-1	Hodgson	25312	6			9		7	8		5		2		3	4				11		10	1				
10	15	Everton	1-1	Edmed	65729	6			9		7	8		5		2		3	4				11		10	1				
11	22	Bolton Wanderers	1-2	Edmed	12024	6			9		7	8		5		2		3		4			11		10	1				
12	29	BLACKBURN ROVERS	4-2	Reid 2, Devlin, Hodgson	28489	6			9		7	8	11	5		2		3							10	1			4	
13	Nov 5	Cardiff City	1-1	Devlin	12735	6			9	3	7	8	11	5		2			4						10	1				
14	12	SHEFFIELD WEDNESDAY	5-2	Reid 3, Hodgson 2	24253	6			9		7	8	11	5		2		3	4						10	1				
15	19	Middlesbrough	1-1	Chambers	18741	6	10		9		7	8	11	5		2		3	4							1				
16	26	HUDDERSFIELD T	4-2	Hodgson 2, Bromilow, Edmed	34128	6	10				7	8	11	5		2		3	4						9	1				
17	Dec 3	Newcastle United	1-1	Hodgson	26534	6	10				7	8	11	5		2		3	4						9	1				
18	10	BIRMINGHAM	2-3	Hodgson 2	24255	6	10				7	8	11	5		2		3	4						9	1				
19	17	Tottenham Hotspur	1-3	Jackson	21234	6	10		9	2	7		11	5				3	4							1		8		
20	24	MANCHESTER UNITED	2-0	T Scott , Chambers	14971	6	10		9		7		11	5		2		3	4							1		8		
21	27	ARSENAL	0-2		41024	6	10		9		7		11	5		2		3	4							1		8		
22	31	SHEFFIELD UNITED	2-1	Chambers, Reid	13797	6	10				7		11	5		2		3	4						9	1				8
23	Jan 2	BURNLEY	2-2	Edmed, Reid	26632	6	10				7		11	5		2		3	4						9	1				8
24	7	Aston Villa	4-3	Edmed 2, Reid, Hopkin	29505	6	10				7		11	5		2		3	4						9	1				8
25	21	SUNDERLAND	2-5	Hopkin, Reid	28243	6	10				7		11	5		2		3	4						9	1				8
26	Feb 4	WEST HAM UNITED	1-3	Edmed (p)	23897	6	10	8			7		11	5		2		3	4						9	1				
27	11	Portsmouth	0-1		17141	6	10	9			7		11	5		2		3			4					1				8
28	15	Derby County	3-2	Edmed 2, Race	9021	6	10				7		11	5		2		3			4			9		1			8	
29	25	EVERTON	3-3	Hopkin, Bromilow, Hodgson	55361	6	10				7	8	11	5		2		3			4			9		1				
30	Mar 3	BOLTON WANDERERS	4-2	Reid 2, Edmed, Hodgson	37115	6	10			2	7	8	11					3			4			5	9	1				
31	7	Arsenal	3-6	Hodgson 2, Race	14037	6	10			2	7	8	11					3			4			5	9	1				
32	10	Blackburn Rovers	1-2	Edmed (p)	16249	6					7	8	11	5			2	3			4			10	9		1			
33	17	CARDIFF CITY	1-2	Reid	34532	6					7	8	11	5			2	3			4			10	9		1			
34	24	Sheffield Wednesday	0-4		12255	6					7	8	11	5			2	3			4			9			1		10	
35	31	MIDDLESBROUGH	1-1	Hodgson	26840	6					7	8	11	5			2	3			4			10	9		1			
36	Apr 6	Burnley	2-2	Walsh, Reid	21824	6					7	8	11	5			2	3			4				9		1			10
37	7	Huddersfield Town	4-2	Reid, Hodgson, Edmed, Walsh	27290	6					7	8	11	5			2	3			4				9		1			10
38	14	NEWCASTLE UNITED	0-0		28669	6					7	8	11	5			2	3			4				9		1			10
39	21	Birmingham	0-2		16063	6					7	8	11	5	3						4				9		1		2	10
40	25	LEICESTER CITY	1-1	Reid	23657	6					7	8		5			2	3			4		11	10	9		1			
41	28	TOTTENHAM HOTSPUR	2-0	Bromilow, Hodgson	31780	6					7	8	11	5			2	3			4	9		10		1				
42	May 5	Manchester United	1-6	Hodgson	30625	6					7	8	11	5			2	3	4			9		10		1				
					Apps	42	24	2	18	4	42	32	36	40	1	28	10	40	19	7	15	2	6	11	25	25	17	3	4	9
					Goals	3	3		14		14	23	3	1						1			1	2	15			1		2

One own goal

F.A. Cup

	Date	Opponent	Score	Scorers	Att	Bromilow TG	Chambers H	Clark JR	Devlin WA	Done R	Edmed RA	Hodgson G	Hopkin F	Jackson J	Longworth E	Lucas T	McBain N	McKinlay D	McMullan D	McNab JS	Morrison TK	Murray WT	Pither GB	Race H	Reid TI	Riley AJ	Scott E	Scott T	Shears AE	Walsh JA
R3	Jan 14	DARLINGTON	1-0	Chambers	28500	6	10				7		11	5		2		3	4						9	1				8
R4	28	Cardiff City	1-2	Edmed	20000	6	10				7		11	5		2		3		4					9	1				8

Luton Town

13th in Division Three (South)

	Date		Opponents	Score	Scorers	Att	Abbott H	Banks JA	Black JR	Davies AS	Dennis GT	Fraser CR	Fulton JJ	Galloway SR	Gordon J	Graham RC	Harkins J	Kingham HR	Millar RM	Muir J	Nunn AS	Panther FG	Pointon J	Ramage J	Reid S	Rennie A	Reynolds JW	Richards D	Till J	Woods H	Yardley J
1	Aug	27	Southend United	0-1		11186	1		4		11			9					6				7		8	5		2	3	10	
2		29	NORWICH CITY	1-3	Rennie	9157	1		4		11								6			9	7		8	5		2	3	10	
3	Sep	3	BRIGHTON & HOVE ALB	2-5	Panther, Banks	9468	1	10	4	11						2			6			9	7		8	5			3		
4		5	Norwich City	0-3		13640		10		11		6	5		4	3		2		1		9	7								8
5		10	Bournemouth	2-2	Yardley, Galloway	6040		10		11		6	5	9	4	3		2		1			7								8
6		17	BRENTFORD	5-2	Yardley 3, Reid, Pointon	9182			4		10	6	5			3		2		1	11		7		9						8
7		24	Watford	0-1		12903	1		4		10	6	5			3		2			11		7		9						8
8	Oct	1	Millwall	2-3	Rennie, Harkins	7645			4			6	5			3	10	2		1	11		7			9					8
9		8	CRYSTAL PALACE	6-1	Black,Rennie 2,Harkins,Pointon,Yardley	8844			4			6	5			3	10	2		1	11		7			9					8
10		15	Exeter City	2-3	Rennie, Nunn	6827			4			6	5			3	10	2		1	11		7			9					8
11		22	NEWPORT COUNTY	1-1	Harkins	5192				11		6	5			3	10	2	4	1			7			9					8
12		29	Swindon Town	2-4	Pointon, Rennie	7580						6	5		4	3		2		1			7			9				10	8
13	Nov	5	QUEEN'S PARK RANGERS	0-1		7695		10				6	5		4	3		2		1			7			9					8
14		12	Coventry City	2-4	Reid, Yardley	10141			4		11	6				3		2		1			7		9	5				10	8
15		19	GILLINGHAM	6-1	Dennis (p),Woods,Reid,Rennie,Pointon,Yardley	4527	1		4		11	6				3		2					7		9	5				10	8
16	Dec	3	MERTHYR TOWN	5-1	Reid 4, Dennis	5040	1		4		11	6				3		2					7		9	5				10	8
17		17	BRISTOL ROVERS	2-0	Pointon, Woods	5946	1		4		11	6				3		2					7		9	5				10	8
18		24	Charlton Athletic	3-4	Yardley, Pointon, Rennie	7265	1		4		11	6				3		2					7		8	5				10	9
19		26	Northampton Town	5-6	Yardley, Reid 4	10153	1		4		11	6				3		2					7		9	5				10	8
20		31	SOUTHEND UNITED	0-0		5402	1		4		11	6				3		2					7		9	5				10	8
21	Jan	7	Brighton & Hove Albion	1-3	Pointon	5707	1	9	4		11	6				3		2					7			5				10	8
22		21	BOURNEMOUTH	3-3	Yardley, Woods, Fraser	6453	1		4		11	6						2					7		9	5		3		10	8
23		28	Brentford	2-4	Yardley 2	3291	1		4		11	6				3		2					7	5		9				10	8
24	Feb	4	WATFORD	3-2	Rennie, Yardley, Woods	8012	1		4		11	6				2							7	5		9			3	10	8
25		11	MILLWALL	1-1	Yardley	8738	1		4			6									11		7	5		9		2	3	10	8
26		18	Crystal Palace	2-3	Rennie 2	13370	1		4		11	6											7	5		9		2	3	10	8
27		25	EXETER CITY	2-1	Rennie, Nunn	8309	1		4			6									11		7	5		9		2	3	10	8
28	Mar	3	Newport County	2-7	Rennie, Woods	3995	1		4			6									11		7	5		9		2	3	10	8
29		10	SWINDON TOWN	2-1	Yardley, Woods	6973	1				11							2	6				7	5		9	4	3		10	8
30		17	Queen's Park Rangers	2-3	Yardley, Dennis	11217	1				11							2	6				7	5		9	4	3		10	8
31		19	NORTHAMPTON T	2-0	Yardley, Woods	8194	1	7	4		6		5			2					11					9		3		10	8
32		24	COVENTRY CITY	3-1	Rennie, Yardley, Nunn	8054	1	7	4		6		5			2					11					9		3		10	8
33		31	Gillingham	4-0	Dennis 2, Rennie 2	4045	1	7	4		11		5			2			6							9		3		10	8
34	Apr	6	TORQUAY UNITED	5-0	Rennie 3, Woods, Dennis	10397	1	7	4		11		5			2			6							9		3		10	8
35		7	PLYMOUTH ARGYLE	1-1	Banks	10451	1	9	4		11		5			2			6				7					3		10	8
36		9	Torquay United	4-0	Yardley 2, Pointon, Dennis	2994	1		4		11		5			2			6		7		8					3		10	9
37		14	Merthyr Town	0-0		2089	1	7	4		11		5			2			6							9		3		10	8
38		21	WALSALL	4-1	Rennie 2, Yardley, Dennis	6118	1	7	4		11		5			2			6							9		3		10	8
39		23	Walsall	1-4	Rennie	3666	1	7	4		11					2			6					5		9		3		10	8
40		28	Bristol Rovers	2-1	Woods, Yardley	5639	1		4		11		5			2			6		7					9		3		10	8
41	May	2	Plymouth Argyle	0-4		4719	1				11		5			2			6		7					9		3		10	8
42		5	CHARLTON ATHLETIC	2-1	Rennie, Yardley	5982	1		4		11		5			2			6		7					9		3		10	8
						Apps	32	13	34	4	30	25	21	2	4	33	4	22	16	10	14	3	32	9	13	36	2	21	8	32	39
						Goals		2	1		8	1		1			3				3	1	8		11	23				9	23

Played at 4 in game 41: R Lumsden

Played at 11 in games 12 and 13: H Briggs

F.A. Cup

	Date		Opponents	Score	Scorers	Att	Abbott H	Banks JA	Black JR	Davies AS	Dennis GT	Fraser CR	Fulton JJ	Galloway SR	Gordon J	Graham RC	Harkins J	Kingham HR	Millar RM	Muir J	Nunn AS	Panther FG	Pointon J	Ramage J	Reid S	Rennie A	Reynolds JW	Richards D	Till J	Woods H	Yardley J
R1	Nov	30	CLAPTON	9-0	Dennis 2, Woods, Yardley 4, Reid 2	9639	1		4		11	6				3		2					7		9	5				10	8
R2	Dec	10	NORWICH CITY	6-0	Reid 3, Woods, Yardley, Dennis	10750	1		4		11	6				3		2					7		9	5				10	8
R3	Jan	14	Bolton Wanderers	1-2	Reid	20266	1		4		11	6				3		2					7		9	5				10	8

First game with Clapton on Nov 26th abandoned with Luton leading 5-0 (same 11 players, goals from Yardley, Dennis, Reid 2 and Woods)

Manchester City

Champions of Division Two: Promoted

#	Month	Day	Opponent	Score	Scorers	Att	Allan J	Appleton F	Austin SW	Barber LF	Barrass MW	Bell PN	Bennett ET	Broadhurst C	Brook EF	Cookson S	Cowan S	Foster CL	Gibbons S	Gorringe FC	Gray A	Hicks GW	Horne A	Johnson TCF	Marshall RS	McCloy P	McMullan J	Pringle CR	Ridley JG	Roberts F	Robertson G	Sharp S	Smelt T	Tait T	Tilson SF
1	Aug	27	Wolverhampton Wan.	2-2	Hicks, McMullan	22600						7		9		2	5				1	11		10		3	6	4		8					
2		29	SWANSEA TOWN	7-4	* see below	34316						7		9		2	5				1	11		10		3	6	4		8					
3	Sep	3	PORT VALE	1-0	Johnson	37583						7		9		2	5				1	11		10		3	6	4		8					
4		5	Swansea Town	3-5	Bell, Hicks, Johnson	17554					8	7		9		2	5				1	11		10		3	6	4							
5		10	South Shields	1-0	McMullan	7623					8	7		9			5				1	11		10		3	6	4	2						
6		17	LEEDS UNITED	2-1	Johnson 2	40931					8	7		9			5				1	11		10		3	6	4	2						
7		24	Nottingham Forest	5-4	Hicks 2, Johnson 2, Broadhurst	12893					8	7		9			5				1	11		10		3	6	4	2						
8	Oct	1	OLDHAM ATHLETIC	3-1	Broadhurst 2, Johnson	25216					8	7		9					5		1	11		10		3	6	4	2						
9		8	HULL CITY	2-1	Barrass 2	42038					8	7		9					5		1	11		10		3	6	4	2						
10		15	Preston North End	0-1		30590	10				8	7		9			5				1	11				3		4	2		6				
11		22	Blackpool	2-2	Hicks, Roberts	17013						7		9			5				1	11		10		3	6	4	2	8					
12		29	READING	4-1	Austin 2, Johnson, Roberts	33717		2	7	1	6	11					5							10		3		4		9			8		
13	Nov	5	Grimsby Town	1-4	Smelt	12522			7			11					5				1			10		3	6		2	9	4		8		
14		12	CHELSEA	0-1		52830			7		8						5				1	11		10		3	6	4	2	9					
15		19	Clapton Orient	2-0	Austin, Roberts	14129	8		7							2	5				1	11		10		3	6	4		9					
16		26	STOKE CITY	4-0	Allan, Austin, Johnson, Roberts	36456	8		7			11				2	5				1			10		3	6	4		9					
17	Dec	3	Bristol City	0-2		23114	8		7			11				2	5				1			10		3	6	4		9					
18		10	WEST BROMWICH ALB.	3-1	Austin, Broadhurst, Johnson	29747	8		7					9		2	5				1	11		10		3	6	4							
19		17	Southampton	1-1	Broadhurst	10013	8		7		5			9		2					1	11		10		3	6	4							
20		24	NOTTS COUNTY	3-1	Broadhurst 2, Hicks	18362			7					9		2	5				1	11		10		3	6	4		8					
21		26	Barnsley	3-0	Broadhurst 2, Roberts	17252			7		4			9		2	5	11			1			10		3	6			8					
22		31	WOLVERHAMPTON W.	3-0	Johnson 2, Broadhurst	25991			7		4			9			5	11			1			10		3	6		2	8					
23	Jan	2	BARNSLEY	7-3	* see below	38226			7		4						5	11		9	1			10		3	6		2	8					
24		7	Port Vale	2-1	Hicks, Roberts	14310			7		5			9							1	11		10		3	6	4	2	8					
25		21	SOUTH SHIELDS	3-0	Austin, Broadhurst, Johnson	29200			7	1	4			9			5					11		10		3	6		2	8					
26	Feb	4	NOTTM. FOREST	3-3	Austin, Broadhurst, Hicks	30037			7	1	4			9			5					11		10		3	6		2	8					
27		11	Oldham Athletic	2-3	Bell, Broadhurst	25426					4	7		9			5				1	11		10		3	6		2	8					
28		25	PRESTON NORTH END	2-2	Roberts 2	59500			7				4	9			5				1	11		10		3	6		2	8					
29	Mar	3	BLACKPOOL	4-1	Roberts 4	40906			7												1	11		10	8	3	6	5	2	9		4			
30		10	Reading	1-1	Marshall	13313			7								5				1	11		10	8	3	6		2	9		4			
31		17	GRIMSBY TOWN	2-0	McMullan, Roberts	49185									11		5				1		7		8	3	6		2	9		4			10
32		24	Chelsea	1-0	Roberts	51813					5				11						1		7		8	3	6		2	9		4			10
33		31	CLAPTON ORIENT	5-3	Roberts 3, Brook, Horne	38272					5				11						1		7		8	3		6	2	9		4			10
34	Apr	6	FULHAM	2-1	Marshall, Roberts	50660					5				11						1		7		8	3	6		2	9		4			10
35		7	Stoke City	0-2		29455					5		3		11						1		7		8		6		2	9		4			10
36		9	Fulham	1-1	Tait	25997				1	4		3		11		5					7			8		6		2					9	10
37		14	BRISTOL CITY	4-2	Hicks, Johnson, Marshall, Tait	31298				1	6		3		11		5					7		10	8				2			4		9	
38		16	Hull City	0-0		6088				1	5		3		11							7		10	8		6		2			4		9	
39		21	West Bromwich Albion	1-1	Brook	15409				1	5				11							7		10	8	3	6		2			4		9	
40		25	Leeds United	1-0	Tait	48780				1	5				11							7		10	8	3	6		2			4		9	
41		28	SOUTHAMPTON	6-1	Marshall 3, Horne, Johnson, Tait	42361				1	5				11				4				7	10	8	3	6		2					9	
42	May	5	Notts County	1-2	Marshall	9907				1	5				11				4				7	10	8	3	6		2					9	
						Apps	6	1	18	10	28	16	5	21	12	11	28	3	4	1	32	28	7	35	14	38	38	22	30	26	2	11	2	7	6
						Goals	1		9		2	3		14	2					2		10	2	19	7		4			20			1	4	

Scorers in game 2: Johnson3, Bell, Broadhurst, Hicks, Roberts

Scorers in game 23: Austin 2, Gorringe 2, Johnson, McMullan, Roberts

F.A. Cup

Rd	Month	Day	Opponent	Score	Scorers	Att	Allan J	Appleton F	Austin SW	Barber LF	Barrass MW	Bell PN	Bennett ET	Broadhurst C	Brook EF	Cookson S	Cowan S	Foster CL	Gibbons S	Gorringe FC	Gray A	Hicks GW	Horne A	Johnson TCF	Marshall RS	McCloy P	McMullan J	Pringle CR	Ridley JG	Roberts F	Robertson G	Sharp S	Smelt T	Tait T	Tilson SF
R3	Jan	14	LEEDS UNITED	1-0	Johnson	50473			7		4			9			5				1	11		10		3	6		2	8					
R5		28	Sunderland	2-1	Broadhurst, Hicks	38658			7	1	4			9			5					11		10		3	6		2	8					
R5	Feb	18	STOKE CITY	0-1		73668	7							9					5		1	11		10		3	6	4	2	8					

Manchester United

18th in Division One

No	Date	Opponent	Score	Scorers	Att	Bain J	Barson F	Bennion SR	Chapman W	Ferguson AD	Hanson J	Haslam G	Hilditch CG	Johnston WG	Jones T	Mann FD	McLenahan H	McPherson FC	Moore CW	Nicol G	Partridge E	Ramsden CW	Rawlings WE	Richardson LH	Silcock J	Spence JW	Steward A	Sweeney EE	Taylor C	Thomas H	Williams DR	Wilson JT
1	Aug 27	MIDDLESBROUGH	3-0	Spence 2, Hanson	44957		5	4	7		8							11	2		10				3	9	1					6
2	29	Sheffield Wednesday	2-0	Hanson, Partridge	17944			4	7		8		5					11	2		10				3	9	1					6
3	Sep 3	Birmingham	0-0		25863		5	4	7		8				2			11			10				3	9	1					6
4	7	SHEFFIELD WEDNESDAY	1-1	McPherson	18759		5	4	7		8				2			11			10				3	9	1					6
5	10	NEWCASTLE UNITED	1-7	Spence	50217			4	7		8		5						2		10				3	9	1			11		6
6	17	Huddersfield Town	2-4	Spence 2	17307			4	7		8	5	6						2		10				3	9	1			11		
7	19	Blackburn Rovers	0-3		18243	6		4	7		8	5							2		10				3	9	1			11		
8	24	TOTTENHAM HOTSPUR	3-0	Hanson 2, Spence	13952			4			8	5				6		11	2		10	7		1	3	9						
9	Oct 1	Leicester City	0-1		22385			4								5		11	2		10	7		1	3	9		8				6
10	8	Everton	2-5	Bennion, Spence	40080			4			8		5					11	2		10			1	3	9					7	6
11	15	CARDIFF CITY	2-2	Spence, Sweeney	31090		5	4						10				11	2					1	3	9		8			7	6
12	22	DERBY COUNTY	5-0	Spence 3, Johnston, McPherson	18304		5	4						10	2			11						1	3	9		8			7	6
13	29	West Ham United	2-1	McPherson, Barrett (og)	21972		5				8			10	2	4		11						1	3	9					7	6
14	Nov 5	PORTSMOUTH	2-0	McPherson, og	13119		5	4			8			10	2			11						1	3	9					7	6
15	12	Sunderland	1-4	Spence	13319		5	4			8			10	2			11						1	3	9					7	6
16	19	ASTON VILLA	5-1	Partridge 2,Johnston,McPherson,Spence	25991		5	4						10	3			11	2		8			1		9					7	6
17	26	Burnley	0-4		18509		5	4						10	3			11	2		8			1		9					7	6
18	Dec 3	BURY	0-1		23581			4					5	10	2			11			8			1	3	9					7	6
19	10	Sheffield United	1-2	Spence	11984			4						10	3	5			2		8			1		9				11	7	6
20	17	ARSENAL	4-1	Hanson, McPherson, Partridge, Spence	18120			4			9			10	3	5		11	2		8			1		7						6
21	24	Liverpool	0-2		14971			4			9			10	3	5		11	2		8			1		7						6
22	26	BLACKBURN ROVERS	1-1	Spence	31131			4			9			10	3	5		11	2		8			1		7						6
23	31	Middlesbrough	2-1	Hanson, Johnston	19652			4			9			10	3	5			2		11			1		7			8			6
24	Jan 7	BIRMINGHAM	1-1	Hanson	16853			4			9			10	3	5		11	2					1		7			8			6
25	21	Newcastle United	1-4	Partridge	25912			4			9			10	2	5		11			8			1	3	7						6
26	Feb 4	Tottenham Hotspur	1-4	Johnston	23545				7		8			10	2	5	4	11						1	3	9						6
27	11	LEICESTER CITY	5-2	Nicol 2, Spence 2, Hanson	16640			4			8				3	5			2	9	11			1		7		10				6
28	25	Cardiff City	0-2		15579			4			8			10	2	5				9	11			1	3	7						6
29	Mar 7	HUDDERSFIELD T	0-0		35413			4			9			10	2	5		11			8			1	3	7						6
30	10	WEST HAM UNITED	1-1	Johnston	21577			4	7		9			10	3	5		11	2		8			1								6
31	14	EVERTON	1-0	Rawlings	25667			4			8			10	3	5		11	2				9	1		7						6
32	17	Portsmouth	0-1		25400		5	4			8			10	3				2				9	1		7				11		6
33	28	Derby County	0-5		8323			4			8			10	2	5							9	1	3	7				11		6
34	31	Aston Villa	1-3	Rawlings	24691			4						10	3	5	6	11	2	9			9	1		7						
35	Apr 6	Bolton Wanderers	2-3	Spence, Thomas	23795			4						10	3	5	6		2	9			9	1		7				11		
36	7	BURNLEY	4-3	Rawlings 3, Williams	28311			4		8				10	2	5	6						9	1	3					11	7	
37	9	BOLTON WANDERERS	2-1	Johnston, Rawlings	28590					8	4			10	2	5	6						9	1	3					11	7	
38	14	Bury	3-4	Johnston, McLenahan, Williams	17440			4		8				10	2	5	6	11					9	1	3						7	
39	21	SHEFFIELD UNITED	2-3	Rawlings, Thomas	27137			4		8				10	2	5	6						9	1	3	7				11		
40	25	SUNDERLAND	2-1	Hanson, Johnston	9545						8			10	2	5	4						9		3	7	1			11		6
41	28	Arsenal	1-0	Rawlings	22452						8			10	3	5	4		2				9			7	1			11		6
42	May 5	LIVERPOOL	6-1	Spence 3, Rawlings 2, Hanson	30625						8			10	3	5	4		2				9			7	1			11		6
						1	11	36	9	4	30	3	5	31	33	26	10	26	25	4	23	2	12	32	26	38	10	4	2	13	13	33
								1			10			8			1	6		2	5		10			22		1		2	2	

Two own goals

F.A. Cup

Rd	Date	Opponent	Score	Scorers	Att	Bain J	Barson F	Bennion SR	Chapman W	Ferguson AD	Hanson J	Haslam G	Hilditch CG	Johnston WG	Jones T	Mann FD	McLenahan H	McPherson FC	Moore CW	Nicol G	Partridge E	Ramsden CW	Rawlings WE	Richardson LH	Silcock J	Spence JW	Steward A	Sweeney EE	Taylor C	Thomas H	Williams DR	Wilson JT
R3	Jan 14	BRENTFORD	7-1	Hanson 4, Spence, McPherson, Johnston	18538			4			8			10	2	5		9			11			1	3	7						6
R4	28	Bury	1-1	Johnston	22439			4			8			10	2	5		9						1	3	7					11	6
rep	Feb 1	BURY	1-0	Spence	48001			4			8			10	2	5		9						1	3	7					11	6
R5	18	BIRMINGHAM	1-0	Johnston	52568			4			8			10	2	5				9	11			1	3	7						6
R6	Mar 3	Blackburn Rovers	0-2		42312			4			8			10	3	5			2		11			1		9					7	6

Merthyr Town

21st in Division Three (South)

	Date	Opponent	Score	Scorers	Att	Astley DJ	Bishop GA	Crewe W	Davies B	Evans DR	Evans SIVL	Ford E	Jones E	Jones EL	Lawley GH	Lewis B	Lewis TJ	Lindon AE	Livingstone AMcK	Mason FO	Mays AW	McLachlan A	McWhirr J	Morgan A	Page J	Pedlar P	Powell EF	Richards D	Smith AJ	Trigg C
1	Aug 27	Plymouth Argyle	0-5		11455		5	6			1	11					4		10		9		7		2	3	8			
2	29	CHARLTON ATHLETIC	0-0		4158		5	6			1	11					4		10		9		7		2	3	8			
3	Sep 3	TORQUAY UNITED	1-3	Powell	4644		5	6			1	11					4		10		9		7		2	3	8			
4	10	WALSALL	3-2	Mays 2, McWhirr	3066		5	4			1	11	8								9	6	7		2	3	10			
5	17	Gillingham	1-1	McWhirr	5642		5	4			1	11	8								9	6	7		2	3	10			
6	19	Charlton Athletic	0-0		5883		5	4				11	8					1			9	6	7		2	3	10			
7	24	COVENTRY CITY	3-2	Pedler, Mays, McLachlan	3148		5	4				11	8					1			9	6	7		2	3	10			
8	Oct 1	Newport County	1-1	McWhirr	3147		5	4				11	8		7			1			9	6	10		2	3				
9	3	MILLWALL	0-0		3210		5	4				11	8		7			1			9	6	10		2	3				
10	8	SWINDON TOWN	8-2	Mays 2, McWhirr 2, :Lawley 2, Ford 2	5418		5	4				11	8		7			1			9	6	10		2	3				
11	15	Queen's Park Rangers	0-0		11406		5	4				11	8		7			1			9	6	10		2	3				
12	22	Southend United	1-2	Pedler	3774		5	4				11	8		7			1			9	6	10		2	3				
13	29	NORTHAMPTON T	1-3	E Jones	5000		5	4				11	8		7			1			9	6	10		2	3				
14	Nov 5	Norwich City	0-4		7967		5	4		3		11	8		7		6	1					10		2	9				
15	12	BRIGHTON & HOVE ALB	4-2	E Jones, McWhirr, Powell 2	3111		5	4					8		11		6	1			9		7		2	3	10			
16	19	Bournemouth	1-2	McWhirr	2077	8	5	4							11		6	1			9		7		3	2	10			
17	Dec 3	Luton Town	1-5	Ford	5040	9	5	4				11	8		7		6	1	10						2	3				
18	10	BRENTFORD	3-1	Astley	2465	9	5	4				11	8		7		6	1	10						2	3				
19	17	Crystal Palace	0-2		6809	9	5	4				11	8		7		6	1	10	2						3				
20	24	EXETER CITY	0-3		2000	9	5	4				11	8		7		6	1	10						2	3				
21	26	BRISTOL ROVERS	2-3	Mays 2	1682		6	5				7	10		11			1	8	4	9					2		3		
22	27	Bristol Rovers	1-2	Mays	7797		4	5				7	6		11			1	8		9					2		3		10
23	Jan 7	Torquay United	2-2	Mays, Smith	3234		4	6				11	8		7			1	10		9				2	3			5	
24	14	PLYMOUTH ARGYLE	1-4	Mays	1463		4					11	8		7		6	1			9				2	3			5	10
25	21	Walsall	2-2	E Jones, Livingstone	4747		5	6				11	8		7			1	10		9				2	3			4	
26	Feb 4	Coventry City	2-1	Morgan 2	6586		5	4				11				1	6		10		9			7	2	3	8			
27	11	NEWPORT COUNTY	0-2		2229			4				11				1	6		10		9			7	2	3	8		5	
28	18	Swindon Town	2-1	Smith 2	6464			4				11				1	6		10			5		7	2	3	8		9	
29	25	QUEEN'S PARK RANGERS	0-4		2869			4		2		10				1	6		11		9	5		7		3	8			
30	Mar 3	SOUTHEND UNITED	2-3	Smith, Davies	2289			4	10			11				1	6				7	5			2	3	8		9	
31	10	Northampton Town	0-6		8549		5	4	8			11				1			10			6			2	3	7		9	
32	12	GILLINGHAM	3-1	Mays, Ford, Livingstone	683		5	4	8	2		11				1			10		9	6		7		3				
33	17	NORWICH CITY	1-1	Mays	2317		5	4	8			11				1			10		9	6		7	2	3				
34	24	Brighton & Hove Albion	0-5		7663		5	4	8	3		11				1	6		10		9				2		7			
35	31	BOURNEMOUTH	1-1	Livingstone	1039		5	4	8	3		11				1			10		9	6			2		7			
36	Apr 7	Millwall	0-3		19969		5		8	3		11				1			10		9	6			2		7		4	
37	9	Watford	1-1	Mays	8360		5	9								1			11	3	8	6		7	2		10		4	
38	10	WATFORD	3-1	Crewe, Mays, Powell	2590		5	9						7		1			11	3	8	6			2		10	4		
39	14	LUTON TOWN	0-0		2089		5	9						7		1	6		11	2	8					3	10	4		
40	21	Brentford	0-4		4583		5	9						7		1			11	3	8	6			2		10		4	
41	28	CRYSTAL PALACE	2-2	Crewe 2	2169		5	9						7		1			10	3	8	6			2		11		4	
42	May 5	Exeter City	0-2		4506		5	9				11		7		1	4		10		8	6			2	3				
					Apps	5	38	40	7	6	5	35	21	5	18	17	19	20	27	7	35	23	16	7	36	35	23	4	11	2
					Goals	3		3	1			4	3		2				3		14	1	7	2		2	4		4	

F.A. Cup

	Date	Opponent	Score	Scorers	Att	Astley DJ	Bishop GA	Crewe W	Davies B	Evans DR	Evans SIVL	Ford E	Jones E	Jones EL	Lawley GH	Lewis B	Lewis TJ	Lindon AE	Livingstone AMcK	Mason FO	Mays AW	McLachlan A	McWhirr J	Morgan A	Page J	Pedlar P	Powell EF	Richards D	Smith AJ	Trigg C
R1	Nov 26	CHARLTON ATHLETIC	0-0		7000		5	4					8		11		6	1			9		7		2	3	10			
rep	30	Charlton Athletic	1-2	E Jones	3875	10	5	4					8		11		6	1			9		7		2	3				

Middlesbrough

22nd in Division One: Relegated

	Date	Opponents	Score	Scorers	Att	Ashman D	Birrell W	Bruce RF	Camsell GH	Carr J	Ferguson RG	Freeman RV	Hall BAC	Jarvis S	Kennedy F	Mathieson JA	McClelland J	McKay JR	Millar WM	Miller J	Peacock J	Pease WH	Smith J	Twine FW	Webster M	Williams O
1	Aug 27	Manchester United	0-3		44957	6	8		9	10	5					1				4		7	3	2		11
2	31	TOTTENHAM HOTSPUR	3-1	Camsell, McKay, Williams	29113	6			9	10	5					1		8		4		7	3	2		11
3	Sep 3	EVERTON	4-2	Camsell 4	30299	6			9	10	5					1		8		4		7	3	2		11
4	10	Cardiff City	1-1	Pease	23033	6			9	10	5					1		8		4		7	3	2		11
5	12	Tottenham Hotspur	2-4	Camsell, Carr	19219	6			9	10	5					1		8		4		7	3	2		11
6	17	BLACKBURN ROVERS	2-0	Ashman, Camsell	28300	6	8		9	10	5				11	1				4		7	3	2		
7	24	Bolton Wanderers	0-0		21720	6	8		9						11	1		10		4		7	3	2	5	
8	Oct 1	SHEFFIELD WEDNESDAY	3-3	Camsell 2, McKay	22230	6	8		9		5				11	1		10		4		7	3	2		
9	8	Aston Villa	1-5	Birrell	38180	6	8		9	10	5					1				4		7	3	2		11
10	15	Birmingham	2-3	Camsell, Pease	17143		8		9	10	5					1				4	6	7	3	2		11
11	22	BURNLEY	2-3	Pease 2	17803		10		9		5	3				1	8			4	6	7	3			11
12	29	Bury	4-1	Pease 3, Carr	18756				9	10						1	8			4	6	7	3	2	5	11
13	Nov 5	SHEFFIELD UNITED	3-0	Camsell 2, McClelland	22061				9	10						1	8			4	6	7	3	2	5	11
14	12	Arsenal	1-3	Camsell	25921				9	10	5					1	8			4	6	7	3	2		11
15	19	LIVERPOOL	1-1	Pease	18741				9	10	5					1	8			4	6	7	3	2		11
16	26	West Ham United	5-4	Camsell 2, Williams 2, Pease	14666				9	10	5					1	8			4	6	7	3	2		11
17	Dec 3	PORTSMOUTH	5-1	Camsell 2, Carr, McClelland, Williams	18163				9	10	5					1	8			4	6	7	3	2		11
18	10	Leicester City	3-3	Camsell 2, Pease	26815				9	10	5					1	8			4	6	7	3	2		11
19	17	DERBY COUNTY	3-3	Camsell, Ferguson, McClelland	15235				9		5	3			10	1	8		11	4	6	7		2		
20	24	Sunderland	0-1		23633				9	10	5					1	8			4	6	7	3	2		11
21	26	NEWCASTLE UNITED	1-1	Pease	37478				9	10	5					1	8			4	6	7	3	2		11
22	27	Newcastle United	3-3	Pease 2, Camsell	40208				9		5	2			10	1	8			4	6	7	3			11
23	31	MANCHESTER UNITED	1-2	McClelland	19652				9		5	2			10	1	8			4	6	7	3			11
24	Jan 2	HUDDERSFIELD T	3-1	Camsell 2, Pease	26032	6			9		5				10	1	8				4	7	3	2		11
25	7	Everton	1-3	Peacock	46432	6			9		5				10	1	8				4	7	3	2		11
26	21	CARDIFF CITY	1-2	Camsell	21728	6			9	10	5					1				4	8	7	3	2		11
27	Feb 4	BOLTON WANDERERS	2-5	Camsell 2	21109	6		8	9	10	5					1				4		7	3	2		11
28	11	Sheffield Wednesday	3-2	Bruce, Camsell, Carr	15631			8	9	10	5					1				4	6	7	3	2		11
29	23	Blackburn Rovers	0-3		12855	5			9							1	8	10		4	6	7	3	2		11
30	25	BIRMINGHAM	1-1	McClelland	18329	5			9	10						1	8			4	6	7	3	2		11
31	Mar 3	Burnley	1-1	Camsell	18209				9	10	5					1	8			4	6	7	3	2		11
32	10	BURY	6-1	Camsell 4, Pease 2	13922				9	10						1	8			4	6	7	3	2	5	11
33	17	Sheffield United	1-4	Pease	26328			10	9							1		8		4	6	7	3	2	5	11
34	21	ASTON VILLA	0-0		15698			10	9	7	5					1		8		4	6		3	2		11
35	31	Liverpool	1-1	Millar	26840			10	9	8	5					1			11	4	6	7	3	2		
36	Apr 7	WEST HAM UNITED	2-2	Carr, Ferguson	21860			10	9	8	5					1			11	4	6	7	3	2		
37	10	Huddersfield Town	4-2	Bruce, Hall, Millar, Pease	29034			10		8	5		9	2		1			11	4	6	7	3			
38	14	Portsmouth	1-4	Bruce (p)	23897			10		8	5		9	2		1			11	4	6	7	3			
39	18	ARSENAL	2-2	Bruce, Camsell	16731			10	9	8	5					1			11	4	6	7	3	2		
40	21	LEICESTER CITY	1-1	Pease	18854			10	9	8	5			2		1			11	4	6	7	3			
41	28	Derby County	1-2	Carr	12017			10	9	8	5			2		1			11	4	6	7	3			
42	May 5	SUNDERLAND	0-3		41997			10	9	8	5			2		1				4	6	7	3			11
					Apps	15	7	12	40	32	35	4	2	5	8	42	19	9	8	40	32	41	41	34	5	31
					Goals	1	1	4	33	6	2		1				5	2	2		1	19				4

F.A. Cup

	Date	Opponents	Score	Scorers	Att	Ashman D	Birrell W	Bruce RF	Camsell GH	Carr J	Ferguson RG	Freeman RV	Hall BAC	Jarvis S	Kennedy F	Mathieson JA	McClelland J	McKay JR	Millar WM	Miller J	Peacock J	Pease WH	Smith J	Twine FW	Webster M	Williams O
R3	Jan 14	South Shields	3-0	Peacock 2, Camsell	25682	6			9	10	5					1	7			4	8		3	2		11
R4	28	Southport	3-0	Camsell 3	11000	6			9	10	5					1				4	8	7	3	2		11
R5	Feb 18	Huddersfield Town	0-4		55200				9	10	5					1	8			4	6	7	3	2		11

Millwall

Champions of Division Three (South): Promoted

	Date	Opponent	Score	Scorers	Att	Amos AH	Battiste W	Black AJ	Bryant WI	Chance GH	Cock JG	Collins AJ	Fort J	Gomm AF	Graham L	Gregory FI	Harford GB	Harris CH	Hawkins JFV	Hill RH	Jones VW	Keen WJ	Landells J	Lansdale J	Lincoln A	Noble AH	Page JE	Parker RR	Phillips WJ	Pipe JJ	Tilling HW
1	Aug 27	Northampton Town	2-5	Landells, Hawkins	12188	4		11	5	7					6	2			8	3			9	1					10		
2	29	TORQUAY UNITED	9-1	Hawkins 3, Landells, Bryant 3, Phillips 2	6204	4		11	5	7					6				8	3			9	1					10		2
3	Sep 3	SOUTHEND UNITED	5-1	Landells 3, Phillips, Hawkins	15690	4		11	5	7					6				8	3			9	1					10		2
4	7	Torquay United	1-0	Chance	5413	4		11		7				5	6				8	3			9	1					10		2
5	10	Brighton & Hove Albion	1-3	Landells	12984	4		11	5	7									8	3			9	1		6			10		2
6	17	BOURNEMOUTH	2-0	Landells, Amos	14371	4		11	5	7									8	3			9	1		6			10		2
7	24	Brentford	1-6	Hawkins	12513	4		11	5	7									8	3			9	1		6			10		2
8	Oct 1	LUTON TOWN	3-2	Hawkins, Landells 2	7645	4		11	5	7							1		8	3			9		10	6					2
9	3	Merthyr Town	0-0		3210	4		11		7		5	2				1		8	3	6		9		10						
10	8	Charlton Athletic	1-1	Bryant	27380	4		11	5	7			2				1		8	3	6		9		10						
11	15	Crystal Palace	4-0	Parker 3, Phillips	18930	4		11	5	7			2		6		1			3							8	9	10		
12	22	SWINDON TOWN	3-3	Bryant 2, Parker	8338	4		11	5	7			2		6		1		8	3								9	10		
13	29	Queen's Park Rangers	1-0	Bryant	16960	4		11	9	7		5	2		6		1			3							8		10		
14	Nov 5	WATFORD	4-2	Amos (p), Page, Phillips, Bryant	13302	4		11	9	7		5	2		6		1			3							8		10		
15	12	Newport County	3-1	Chance, Collins, Landells	5727	4		11		7		5	2		6		1			3			9				8		10		
16	19	COVENTRY CITY	9-1	Landells 4, Cock 2, Collins, Phillips 2	13695	4		11		7	9	5	2		6					3			8	1					10		
17	Dec 3	WALSALL	7-1	Landells 2, Phillips 3, Cock 2	15338	4		11	5	7	9		2		6		1			3			8						10		
18	10	Plymouth Argyle	2-3	Landells, Cock	16557	4		11		7	9	5	2		6		1			3			8						10		
19	17	PLYMOUTH ARGYLE	2-0	Cock, Landells	18567	4		11	5	7	9		2		6		1			3			8						10		
20	24	Bristol Rovers	6-1	Cock 2, Black 2, Phillips, Perry (og)	7756	4		11	5	7	9		2		6		1			3			8						10		
21	27	NORWICH CITY	2-1	Landells 2	16550	4		11	5	7	9		2		6		1			3			8						10		
22	31	NORTHAMPTON T	3-0	Black, Landells, Phillips	26334	4		11	5	7	9		2		6		1			3			8						10		
23	Jan 7	Southend United	1-0	Cock	9767	4		11	5	7	9		2		6		1			3			8						10		
24	21	BRIGHTON & HOVE ALB	6-0	Landells 2, Phillips 3 (1p), Cock	20696	4		11	5	7	9		2		6		1			3			8						10		
25	28	Bournemouth	0-5		4695	4		11	5	7	9		2		6		1			3			8						10		
26	Feb 4	BRENTFORD	3-0	Cock, Phillips, Chance	16885	4		11		7	9				6	2	1					5	8						10	3	
27	11	Luton Town	1-1	Cock	8738	4			5	7	9				6	2	1	11					8						10	3	
28	18	CHARLTON ATHLETIC	5-0	Chance, Phillips 2, Black, Landells	25498	4		11	5	7	9		2		6		1			3			8						10		
29	25	CRYSTAL PALACE	1-1	Landells	27736	4		11	5	7	9		2		6		1			3			8						10		
30	Mar 3	Swindon Town	0-3		11716	4		11	5	7	9		2		6		1			3			8						10		
31	10	QUEEN'S PARK RANGERS	6-1	Phillips 2, Landells, Bryant, Cock 2	18689	4		11	5	7	9		2		6		1						8						10	3	
32	17	Watford	3-0	Cock, Phillips 2	13727	4		11	5	7	9				6		1			2			8						10	3	
33	24	NEWPORT COUNTY	5-1	Cock 4, Phillips	15558	4		11	5	7	9				6		1			2			8						10	3	
34	31	Coventry City	3-0	Chance, Black, Bryant	11188	4		11	5	7	9				6		1			2			8						10	3	
35	Apr 6	EXETER CITY	2-0	Black, Phillips	31654	4		11	5	7	9				6		1			2			8						10	3	
36	7	MERTHYR TOWN	3-0	Landells 2, Cock	19969	4		11	5	7	9		2		6		1			3			8						10		
37	9	Exeter City	4-2	Landells, Black, Chance, Bryant	12735	4		11	5	7	9				6		1			2			8						10	3	
38	14	Walsall	5-2	Landells 3, Black, Cock	6302	4		11	5	7	9		2		6		1			3			8						10		
39	21	GILLINGHAM	6-0	Phillips 2, Cock 3, Bryant	20744	4		11	5	7	9		2				1			3	6		8						10		
40	25	Gillingham	1-0	Cock	5794	4		11		7	9		2	5			1			3	6		8						10		
41	30	Norwich City	0-2		8979	4	7	11			9			5	6		1			2			8						10	3	
42	May 5	BRISTOL ROVERS	1-0	Landells	17747	4		11	5	7	9		2		6		1			3			8						10		
					Apps	42	1	41	34	41	27	6	26	3	34	3	34	1	11	39	4	1	38	8	3	4	4	2	39	9	7
					Goals	2		7	12	6	25	2							7				33				1	4	27		

One own goal

F.A. Cup

	Date	Opponent	Score	Scorers	Att	Amos AH	Battiste W	Black AJ	Bryant WI	Chance GH	Cock JG	Collins AJ	Fort J	Gomm AF	Graham L	Gregory FI	Harford GB	Harris CH	Hawkins JFV	Hill RH	Jones VW	Keen WJ	Landells J	Lansdale J	Lincoln A	Noble AH	Page JE	Parker RR	Phillips WJ	Pipe JJ	Tilling HW
R3	Jan 14	DERBY COUNTY	1-2	Cock	38850	4		11		7	9	5	2		6		1			3			8						10		

Nelson

22nd in Division Three (North)

	Date	Opponent	Score	Scorers	Att	Bedford L	Bossons WH	Bottrill WG	Brown A	Cochrane DS	Dargon J	Fletcher J	Gaskell RH	Halliwell JA	Hampson J	Harris A	Hayes GT	Hepworth A	Jones JW	McClure D	McGuire J	Pearson JS	Radford B	Ridge D	Rigg C	Ruffell WG	Sharp B	Simpson E	Slack WB	Spence GB	Stoneham I	Taylor H	Warhurst SL	White HA	Wilson G
1	Aug 27	ACCRINGTON STANLEY	1-4	Sharp	8007	11		7						4	9				3						2		10	6			1			8	5
2	Sep 3	Rochdale	0-1		9869	11		7						4	9				3						2		10	6			1			8	5
3	10	ROTHERHAM UNITED	6-1	Hampson 2,Bottrill,White 2,Sharp	4881	11		7						4	9				3						2		10	6			1			8	5
4	12	BARROW	4-0	Bedford, White 2, Bottrill	4928	11		7						4	9				3						2		10	6			1			8	5
5	17	Southport	2-1	Hampson, Bedford	5406	11		7						5	9	4			3						2	8	10	6			1				
6	24	DURHAM CITY	2-1	Hampson 2	5495	11		7	6					4	9					3					2	10	8						1		5
7	29	Barrow	1-3	Bedford	4306	11		7	6					4	9					3					2		10						1	8	5
8	Oct 1	Wrexham	2-5	White 2	4828	11								4	9	6				3					2	7	10						1	8	5
9	8	CHESTERFIELD	3-3	Hampson, White (p), Sharp	4659	11	1							4	9	6				3					2		10			7				8	5
10	15	Bradford Park Avenue	2-3	Sharp, Bottrill	14833	11		8						2		4									3		10			7			1	9	6
11	22	NEW BRIGHTON	0-3		2698	11		8						4					3						2	10		6		7			1	9	5
12	29	Lincoln City	0-0		7956	11		8				9		4					3	2							10	6		7			1		5
13	Nov 5	HARTLEPOOLS UNITED	4-2	Sharp 3, Spence	2001	11		8						4						3					2	10	9	6		7			1		5
14	12	Bradford City	1-9	Cochrane	15638	11		8		9				4					3						2		10	6		7	1				5
15	19	HALIFAX TOWN	3-2	Bottrill, Cochrane, Sharp	3862		1	8		9		11		4					3			2					10	6		7					5
16	Dec 3	ASHINGTON	1-5	Spence	2936		1	8				11		10					3		9	2		4				6		7					5
17	10	Wigan Borough	2-4	Ruffell, McGuire	2736		1	8						4					3	2	9					7	10	6				11			5
18	17	DONCASTER ROVERS	0-1		3410	11		8						4						2	9		10		3	7	6						1		5
19	27	Tranmere Rovers	1-1	Bedford	8946	11		7						4						2	9		10		3	8	6						1		5
20	31	Accrington Stanley	1-7	Ruffell	4207	11		7						4						2	9		10		3	8	6						1		5
21	Jan 2	Crewe Alexandra	1-6	Wilson (p)	2430	11		7						4		6			3		9				2	8						10	1		5
22	7	ROCHDALE	6-3	Radford 3,Taylor,McClure,McGuire	2539			8						4						2	10		9	6	3					7		11	1		5
23	14	Halifax Town	1-5	Radford	3119			7						4						2			9	6	3	10				8		11	1		5
24	21	Rotherham United	3-4	Sharp, Taylor 2	4505			7			8			4						2	10	3	9				6					11	1		5
25	Feb 4	Durham City	0-3		1537			7					8	4						2	10		9				6					11	1		5
26	11	WREXHAM	4-0	Radford 4 (1p)	2721			7					8	4						2	10		9		3		6					11	1		5
27	18	Chesterfield	0-6		3804			7						4						2	10		9		3		8	6				11	1		5
28	25	BRADFORD PARK AVE.	1-2	Wilson (p)	8096			7						4		6				2	10		9		3		8					11	1		5
29	Mar 3	New Brighton	0-4		4290			7					8	4						2	6		9		3		10					11	1		5
30	10	LINCOLN CITY	1-3	Bottrill	3422			8				11		4		6				2			9		3	7	10						1		5
31	17	Hartlepools United	5-4	Sharp, Slack, Radford 2, Bottrill	2972			7						4			8	6		2			9		3		10		11						5
32	20	SOUTHPORT	1-1	Bottrill	3583			7						4			10	6		2			9		3		8		11				1		5
33	24	BRADFORD CITY	0-3		5085			7						4			10	6		2		3	9				8		11				1		5
34	Apr 6	Stockport County	0-8		8430			7						4				6		2	8	3	9				10		11				1		5
35	7	DARLINGTON	4-0	Sharp, Taylor, Hayes 2 (1p)	3816									4			9	6		2	8	3					10			7		11	1		5
36	9	STOCKPORT COUNTY	0-4		5441									4			9	6		2	8	3					10			7		11	1		5
37	14	Ashington	1-5	Slack	1410									2			9	6						4	3		8	10	11	7			1		5
38	16	Darlington	1-4	Hayes	1003			7						2		4	8	6						5	3		10	9	11				1		
39	21	CREWE ALEXANDRA	3-3	Slack, Radford, Sharp	2349						8			4				6		2	7		9	5	3		10		11				1		
40	24	TRANMERE ROVERS	3-5	Hayes, Radford 2	1126									6			8			2	7		9	4	3		10		11				1		5
41	28	Doncaster Rovers	2-4	Radford, Hayes	4117			7						4			9				8		10	5	2		6		11				1		3
42	May 5	WIGAN BOROUGH	3-3	Radford 2, Wilson	2183			7						4				6		2	8		9		3		10		11				1		5
					Apps	18	4	35	2	2	2	4	3	42	9	8	9	10	12	28	20	7	20	8	32	12	37	15	10	13	6	12	31	9	39
					Goals	3		7		2					6		5			1	2		17			3	11		3	2		4		7	3

Played in one game: JE Broadhurst (10, at 5), A Jones (25, 3), J Mangham (31, 1)

F.A. Cup

	Date	Opponent	Score	Scorers	Att	Bedford L	Bossons WH	Bottrill WG	Brown A	Cochrane DS	Dargon J	Fletcher J	Gaskell RH	Halliwell JA	Hampson J	Harris A	Hayes GT	Hepworth A	Jones JW	McClure D	McGuire J	Pearson JS	Radford B	Ridge D	Rigg C	Ruffell WG	Sharp B	Simpson E	Slack WB	Spence GB	Stoneham I	Taylor H	Warhurst SL	White HA	Wilson G
R1	Nov 26	BRADFORD PARK AVE.	0-3		9000		1	8		9		11		4					3			2					10			7	6				5

New Brighton

10th in Division Three (North)

						Beattie D	Carr LW	Dickie GJ	Flood LTB	Harley AJ	Hoddinott FT	Howson GS	Laycock FW	Lewis TH	Lightbody JW	McDonald J	McKenna J	Mehaffy JAC	Morrison R	Reid JW	Roberts WD	Sanderson FC	Smedley JH	Wade E	Whitter E	Williams H
1	Aug 27	Darlington	0-3		6961		2	11			10	3	8				6	1		5		4			7	9
2	31	DONCASTER ROVERS	3-1	Hoddinott, Laycock, Reid	5715		2	11			10		8			3	6	1		5		4			7	9
3	Sep 3	ASHINGTON	6-0	Laycock 2, Williams 3, Whitter	5489		3	11			10		8			2	6	1		5		4			7	9
4	5	Doncaster Rovers	1-5	Williams	5435	4	3	11			10		8			2	6	1		5					7	9
5	10	Crewe Alexandra	1-1	Laycock	4656	4	3	11			10		8			2		1		5			6		7	9
6	17	HALIFAX TOWN	3-1	Hoddinott, Dickie, Harley	5700	4	3	11		9	10		8			2		1	6	5					7	
7	24	Bradford City	1-3	Laycock	11701	4	3	11		9	10		8			2		1	6	5					7	
8	Oct 1	TRANMERE ROVERS	0-1		9228		3	11		9	10		8	4		2		1	6	5					7	
9	8	LINCOLN CITY	2-3	Hoddinott 2 (1p)	4667		3	11		9	10	2		4				1	6	5		8			7	
10	15	Hartlepools United	3-3	Harley 2, Hoddinott	4243		3	11		9	10			4		2		1		5			6	8	7	
11	22	Nelson	3-0	Harley, Dickie, Wade	2698		3	11		9	10			4		2		1		5			6	8	7	
12	Nov 5	Stockport County	0-0		6382		3	11		9	10			4		2		1		5			6	8	7	
13	12	ROCHDALE	2-1	Harley 2	4409		3	11		9	10			4		2		1	6	5				8	7	
14	19	Rotherham United	0-0		4135		3	11		9	10	2		4				1	6	5				8	7	
15	Dec 3	Durham City	1-2	Dickie	1447		3	11		9	10			4		2		1	6	5				8	7	
16	17	Chesterfield	3-2	Harley, Whitter, Wade	1984		3	11		9	10					2		1	4	5			6	8	7	
17	24	BRADFORD PARK AVE.	1-2	Harley	2589		3	11		9	10		8			2		1	4	5			6		7	
18	26	Accrington Stanley	1-2	Harley	5644		3	11		9			10			2		1	4	5		8	6		7	
19	27	ACCRINGTON STANLEY	3-1	Laycock 2, Whitter	5384		3	11		9			10			2		1	4	5		8	6		7	
20	31	DARLINGTON	0-0		1829		3	11		9			10			2		1	4	5		8	6		7	
21	Jan 7	Ashington	2-3	Dickie, Whitter	1619		3	11		9	8		10	4		2		1	6	5					7	
22	21	CREWE ALEXANDRA	5-1	Laycock 2, Hoddinott, Harley 2	4039		3	11		9	8		10	4		2		1	6	5					7	
23	Feb 4	BRADFORD CITY	1-1	Whitter	2939		3	11			10		9			2		1	4	5		8	6		7	
24	11	Tranmere Rovers	0-4		6664		3	11	1		10		9	4		2			6	5		8			7	
25	15	SOUTHPORT	0-1		2871		3	11		9	10		8	4		2		1	6	5					7	
26	18	Lincoln City	2-1	Laycock, Lightbody	5375		3	11					8	4	9	2		1	6	5				10	7	
27	25	HARTLEPOOLS UNITED	2-1	Laycock, Roberts	2861		3	11					10	4		2		1	6	5	9			8	7	
28	Mar 3	NELSON	4-0	Roberts 2, Laycock, Dickie	4290		3	11					10	4		2		1	6	5	9			8	7	
29	7	WREXHAM	0-0		3020		3	11					10	4		2		1	6	5	9			8	7	
30	10	Barrow	1-2	Dickie	6232			11				3	10	4		2		1	6	5	9			8	7	
31	17	STOCKPORT COUNTY	0-0		4876	4		11			10	2		5		3		1	6		9			8	7	
32	24	Rochdale	0-0		2404	4		11				2	10	5		3		1	6		9			8	7	
33	31	ROTHERHAM UNITED	1-1	Sanderson	3240	4		11				2	10	5		3		1	6		9	8			7	
34	Apr 6	Wigan Borough	2-2	Whitter 2	4858	4		11		10		2		5		3		1	6		9	8			7	
35	7	Wrexham	2-0	Harley, Roberts	4296	4	2	11		10						3		1	6	5	9			8	7	
36	9	WIGAN BOROUGH	2-1	Harley, Dickie	4128	4	3	11		10						2		1	6	5	9			8	7	
37	14	DURHAM CITY	4-0	Dickie, Roberts 3	2710	5		11		10		2				3		1	4		9		6	8	7	
38	18	BARROW	3-3	Roberts, Wade, Dickie	1575	5		11		10		2				3		1	4		9		6	8	7	
39	21	Southport	2-4	Roberts, Dickie	2139	5		11	1	10		2	8			3			4		9		6		7	
40	23	Halifax Town	1-1	Laycock	1761	5	3	11		10			8			2		1	4		9		6		7	
41	28	CHESTERFIELD	3-3	Harley, Dickie (p), Roberts	2702	5	3	11		10			8			2		1	4		9		6		7	
42	May 5	Bradford Park Avenue	1-2	Laycock	9538		3	11		10			8	5		2		1	4		9		6		7	
					Apps	15	34	42	2	27	23	11	28	22	1	39	4	40	34	32	16	11	16	18	42	5
					Goals			11		14	6		14		1					1	10	1		3	7	4

F.A. Cup

						Beattie D	Carr LW	Dickie GJ	Flood LTB	Harley AJ	Hoddinott FT	Howson GS	Laycock FW	Lewis TH	Lightbody JW	McDonald J	McKenna J	Mehaffy JAC	Morrison R	Reid JW	Roberts WD	Sanderson FC	Smedley JH	Wade E	Whitter E	Williams H
R1	Nov 26	Shildon	3-1	Whitter, Harley 2	4539		3	11		9	10			4		2		1		5			6	8	7	
R2	Dec 10	RHYL ATHLETIC	7-2	Lewis, Dixon (og), Reid, Harley 4	8227		3	11		9	10			4		2		1	6	5				8	7	
R3	Jan 14	CORINTHIANS	2-1	Whitter 2	9256		3	11		9	8		10	4		2		1	6	5					7	
R4	28	Port Vale	0-3		10867		3	11		9	8		10	4		2		1	6	5					7	

Newcastle United

9th in Division One

	Date	Opponent	Score	Scorers	Att	Barber S	Boyd JM	Bradley R	Burns MT	Carlton W	Chalmers W	Clark JR	Curry T	Evans TJ	Gallacher HR	Gibson WM	Gillespie WF	Harris J	Hudspeth FC	Lang T	Little J	Low J	Maitland AE	McCurley J	McDonald TH	McKay R	McKenzie RR	Park O	Seymour GS	Spencer CW	Urwin T	Wilkinson J	Wilson W
1	Aug 27	Huddersfield Town	3-1	Gallacher 3	24465										9			6	3				2		10	8	4		11	5	7		1
2	Sep 3	TOTTENHAM HOTSPUR	4-1	Seymour 2, Gallacher, McDonald (p)	41038										9			6	3				2		10	8	4		11	5	7		1
3	5	Derby County	1-1	Seymour	20829										9			6	3				2		10	8	4		11	5	7		1
4	10	Manchester United	7-1	* see below	50217										9			6	3				2		10	8	4		11	5	7		1
5	14	DERBY COUNTY	4-3	McKay 3, Gallacher	36965										9			6	3				2		10	8	4		11	5	7		1
6	17	EVERTON	2-2	McDonald, McKay	50359										9			6	3				2		10	8	4		11	5	7		1
7	24	Cardiff City	1-3	Gallacher	30590										9			6	3	11	2				10	8	4			5	7		1
8	Oct 1	BLACKBURN ROVERS	0-1		30869				1						9			6	3		2				10	8	4		11	5	7		
9	8	Bolton Wanderers	2-1	Gallacher, McKay	30676								4		9			6	3			7	2		10	8				5	11		1
10	15	SHEFFIELD WEDNESDAY	4-3	Gallacher 2, McDonald 2(	29886								4		9			6	3			7	2		10	8				5	11		1
11	22	SHEFFIELD UNITED	1-0	Gallacher	12376										9			6	3			7	2		10	8	4	5			11		1
12	29	Aston Villa	0-3		50797							8						6	3			7	2		10			4		5	11	9	1
13	Nov 5	SUNDERLAND	3-1	McDonald, McKay, Seymour	44780								4		9			6	3				2		10	8			11	5	7		1
14	12	Bury	4-1	* see below	20844								4		9			6	3				2		10	8			11	5	7		1
15	19	BURNLEY	1-1	Gallacher	26991		7						4		9			6	3				2		10	8			11	5			1
16	26	Leicester City	0-3		33375								4		9			6	3				2			8			11	5	7		1
17	Dec 3	LIVERPOOL	1-1	McKay	26534					4					9			6	3				2		10	8			11	5	7		1
18	10	Arsenal	1-4	Seymour	42630									3	9			6					2		10	8	4		11	5	7		1
19	17	PORTSMOUTH	1-3	McDonald	19582		7			4				3	9			6					2		10	8			11	5			1
20	24	West Ham United	2-5	Boyd, Evans	19296		7						4	3				6					2		10	8				5	11	9	1
21	26	Middlesbrough	1-1	Gallacher	37478		7					8			9			4	3				2		6	10				5	11		1
22	27	MIDDLESBROUGH	3-3	Boyd, Gallacher, McDonald	40208		7					8			9			4	3				2		6	10				5	11		1
23	31	HUDDERSFIELD T	2-3	Gallacher 2	33640		7					8			9			4	3				2		6	10				5	11		1
24	Jan 2	BIRMINGHAM	1-1	Gallacher	34434		7					8		2	9			4	3						6	10		5			11		1
25	7	Tottenham Hotspur	2-5	McKay, Hudspeth (p)	34731		7							2	9	6		4	3						10	8				5	11		1
26	21	MANCHESTER UNITED	4-1	Wilkinson 2, McKay, Seymour	25912											6	3	4					2		10	8		5	11		7	9	1
27	Feb 4	CARDIFF CITY	2-0	McKay, Wilkinson	26439		7									6	3	4					2		10	8		5	11			9	1
28	11	Blackburn Rovers	0-1		12504									3		6		4					2		10	8		5	11		7	9	1
29	18	BOLTON WANDERERS	2-2	McCurley, Urwin	28932											6		4	3				2	8	10			5	11		7	9	1
30	25	Sheffield Wednesday	0-0		25462					4				3		6							2	8	10			5	11		7	9	1
31	Mar 10	ASTON VILLA	7-5	* see below	23053									3		6		4					2	8	10			5	11		7	9	1
32	17	Sunderland	1-1	McDonald	40071									3		6		4					2		10	8		5	11		7	9	1
33	24	BURY	2-3	Gallacher, McDonald	28871				1					3	9	6		4					2	11	10	8		5			7		
34	31	Burnley	1-5	Wilkinson	12454	6												4			3		2		10	8		5	11		7	9	1
35	Apr 7	LEICESTER CITY	1-5	Chalmers	32492			2	1		11				9	6		4					3		10	8		5			7		
36	10	Birmingham	2-0	Wilkinson 2	23436				1				6	3	8			4					2		10			5	11		7	9	
37	14	Liverpool	0-0		28669				1				6	3	8			4					2		10			5	11		7	9	
38	18	Everton	0-3		28266				1				6		8		3	4					2		10			5	11		7	9	
39	21	ARSENAL	1-1	Seymour	22819				1				6		8		3	4					2		10			5	11		7	9	
40	23	Sheffield United	1-1	Gallacher	16895				1				6		8		3	4					2		10			5	11		7	9	
41	28	Portsmouth	1-0	Seymour	28364				1				6		8		3	4					2		10			5	11		7	9	
42	May 5	WEST HAM UNITED	3-1	Gallacher, Boyd, McDonald (p)	17909		7		1				6		9		3	4					2		10	8		5	11				
					Apps	1	10	1	10	3	1	5	14	12	32	10	7	41	23	1	3	4	38	4	41	32	10	20	29	23	38	16	32
					Goals		3				1			1	21			1	1					3	13	12			12		2	9	

Scorers in game 4: Seymour 2, McDonald, Gallacher, Urwin, Harris, McKay

Scorers in game 14: Seymour, Gallacher, McKay, McDonald (p)

Scorers in game 31: Wilkinson 3, McCurley 2, McDonald, Seymour

W Halliday played at 10 in game 16

F.A. Cup

	Date	Opponent	Score	Scorers	Att	Barber S	Boyd JM	Bradley R	Burns MT	Carlton W	Chalmers W	Clark JR	Curry T	Evans TJ	Gallacher HR	Gibson WM	Gillespie WF	Harris J	Hudspeth FC	Lang T	Little J	Low J	Maitland AE	McCurley J	McDonald TH	McKay R	McKenzie RR	Park O	Seymour GS	Spencer CW	Urwin T	Wilkinson J	Wilson W
R3	Jan 14	Blackburn Rovers	1-4	Seymour	27652										9	6		4	3				2	10		8			11	5	7		1

Newport County

9th in Division Three (South)

						Anderson R	Barratt P	Blakemore L	Bowsher SJ	Brittan CH	Clifford JCT	Gittins J	Harper T	Hinton IF	Maidment JHC	Nairn WJ	Pick WE	Pritchard TF	Pugh RAL	Richardson S	Sims S	Taylor D	Thomas WR	Walker F	Wardell A	Waterston AR	Weaver RW	Wetherby T	Williams W	Young H
1	Aug 27	Queen's Park Rangers	2-4	Gittins, Barrett	15489	2	10		6			8	7	3	1	4		5								9				11
2	Sep 1	BRIGHTON & HOVE ALB	3-1	Waterston, Weaver 2	6146	2			6	7		10		3	1			5		4						9	8			11
3	3	WATFORD	3-2	Waterston, Gittens 2	7362	2			6	7		10		3	1			5		4						9	8			11
4	10	Charlton Athletic	2-3	Weaver, Pritchard	7946	2			6	7		10		3	1			5		4						9	8			11
5	14	Brighton & Hove Albion	4-1	Weaver 3, Pick	3700	2				7		8		3	1		10	5		4							9		6	11
6	17	BRISTOL ROVERS	3-1	Weaver, Brittain, Gittens	7862	2				7		8		3	1		10	5		4							9		6	11
7	24	Plymouth Argyle	0-2		10011	2				7		8		3	1		10			4	5						9		6	11
8	Oct 1	MERTHYR TOWN	1-1	Brittain	3147	2				7		8		3	1		10			4	5						9		6	11
9	8	Walsall	3-0	Pick 2, Weaver	11738	2	10		5			8		3	1		7			4							9		6	11
10	15	GILLINGHAM	1-1	Barrett	6589	2	10		5			8		3	1		7			4							9		6	11
11	22	Luton Town	1-1	Maidment (p)	5192	2	8		5					3	1					4			10	6	7		9			11
12	29	BRENTFORD	3-0	Maidment (p), Barratt, Weaver	5790	2	8		5	7				3	1					4			10	6			9			11
13	Nov 5	Bournemouth	0-0		5324	2	8		5	7				3	1					4			10	6			9			11
14	12	MILLWALL	1-3	Waterston	5727	2	8		5					3	1	6	11			4			10			9				7
15	19	Crystal Palace	0-2		8683	2		1	5	7		8		3					6	4		10				9				11
16	Dec 3	Torquay United	1-1	Waterston	3489	2			5	7		8		3	1				6	4			10			9				11
17	17	Northampton Town	2-1	Waterston, Gittens	8945	2			5	7		8		3	1				6	4			10			9				11
18	24	SOUTHEND UNITED	3-2	Gittens 2, Waterston	3837	2			5	7		8		3	1				6	4			10			9				11
19	26	SWINDON TOWN	1-3	Young	3610	2			5	7		8		3	1				6	4			10			9				11
20	27	Swindon Town	1-4	Waterston	9715	2						8		6	1				10	4	5				7	9		3		11
21	Jan 7	Watford	3-2	Young, Harper, Waterston	5972	2	10		5			8	7	3	1				6	4						9				11
22	14	NORWICH CITY	2-2	Waterston 2	2875	2	10					8	7	3	1				6	4	5					9				11
23	21	CHARLTON ATHLETIC	4-3	Waterston 4	3737	2	10					8	7	3	1	4			6	5						9				11
24	28	Bristol Rovers	1-2	Gittens	4265	2	10				5	8	7	3	1				6	4						9				11
25	Feb 4	PLYMOUTH ARGYLE	1-1	Harper	3502	2	10		5			8	7	3	1				6	4						9				11
26	11	Merthyr Town	2-0	Gittens 2	2229	2	10		5	9		8	7	3	1				6	4										11
27	18	WALSALL	4-1	Brittain 3, Gittens	5561	2			5	9		8	7	3	1		11		6	4			10							
28	25	Gillingham	0-4		5932	2			5	9		8	7	3	1		11		6	4			10							
29	Mar 3	LUTON TOWN	7-2	Gittens 2, Pick, Waterston 3, Harper	3995	2			5			8	7	3	1		11		6	4			10			9				
30	10	Brentford	1-3	Waterston	5759	2			5			8	7	3	1		11		6	4			10			9				
31	17	BOURNEMOUTH	4-3	Brittain, Gittens 2, Waterston	3754	2			5	7		8		3	1				6	4			10			9				11
32	22	EXETER CITY	1-0	Gittens	2108	2			5			8	7	3	1				6	4			10			9				11
33	24	Millwall	1-5	Richardson	15558	2	8		5				7	3	1				6	4			10			9				11
34	Apr 6	QUEEN'S PARK RANGERS	1-6	Thomas	5918	2			5			8	7	3	1				6	4			10			9				11
35	7	Norwich City	1-1	Thomas	7641	2					5	8	7	3	1				6	4			10			9				11
36	9	COVENTRY CITY	3-0	Waterston 3	5170	2		1			5		7	3					6	4		8	10			9				11
37	10	Coventry City	2-0	Young, Waterton	10295	2		1	5					3					6	4		8	10		7	9				11
38	14	TORQUAY UNITED	2-2	Barrett, Waterston	3199	2	10	1	5					3			7		6	4		8				9				11
39	21	Exeter City	1-5	Gittens	4912	2			5			8		3	1		7		6	4			10			9				11
40	26	CRYSTAL PALACE	0-3		2554	2			5			8	7	3	1		11		6	4			10			9				
41	28	NORTHAMPTON T	4-1	Gittens, Waterston 2, Harper	2753	2	10		5			8	7	3	1		11		6	4						9				
42	May 5	Southend United	1-5	Waterston	4796	2	10		5			8	7	3	1		11		6	4						9				
					Apps	42	17	4	32	18	3	34	19	42	38	3	16	6	28	41	4	4	21	3	3	30	12	1	6	35
					Goals		4			6		18	4		2		4	1		1			2			27	9			3

F.A. Cup

						Anderson R	Barratt P	Blakemore L	Bowsher SJ	Brittan CH	Clifford JCT	Gittins J	Harper T	Hinton IF	Maidment JHC	Nairn WJ	Pick WE	Pritchard TF	Pugh RAL	Richardson S	Sims S	Taylor D	Thomas WR	Walker F	Wardell A	Waterston AR	Weaver RW	Wetherby T	Williams W	Young H
R1	Nov 26	SWINDON TOWN	0-1		9600	2	10		5	7		8		3	1				6	4						9				11

Northampton Town

2nd in Division Three (South)

	Date	Opponent	Score	Scorers	Att.	Aitkin JG	Allon TG	Bowen EC	Brett FB	Cave W	Cockle ES	Daley J	Fraser WC	George HS	Hammond L	Hoten RV	Jeffs TE	Loasby H	Maloney RJH	Odell GW	Price E	Russell GH	Shaw WH	Smith TG	Watson WJ	Wells TC	Wilson JR
1	Aug 27	MILLWALL	5-2	Aitken, Hoten, Loasby 2, Smith	12188	11	4					7			1	10	3	9	5	6				8	2		
2	29	Brentford	0-3		7220	11	4					7			1		3	9	5	6	10			8	2		
3	Sep 3	Crystal Palace	0-1		13771	11	4					7			1	10	3	9	5	6				8	2		
4	5	BRENTFORD	3-2	Aitken, Loasby, Smith	7220	11	4					7			1	10	3	9	5	6		2		8			
5	10	EXETER CITY	5-0	Daley, Hoten, Loasby, Smith, Wilson	10249		4		2			7			1	10	3	9	5					8		11	6
6	17	Torquay United	5-1	Loasby 2, Wells 2, Gough (og)	4625		4		2			7			1	10	3	9	5					8		11	6
7	24	NORWICH CITY	4-2	Loasby 2, Wells 2	13921		4		2			7			1	10	3	9	5					8		11	6
8	Oct 1	Gillingham	3-1	Loasby 2, Smith	4226		4		2			7			1	10	3	9	5					8		11	6
9	8	Southend United	0-2		8768		4		2			7			1	10	3	9	5					8		11	6
10	15	BRIGHTON & HOVE ALB	1-0	Curran (og)	13214	11	4		2			7			1	10	3	9	5	6				8			
11	22	PLYMOUTH ARGYLE	2-1	Hoten, Maloney	9434		4		2			7			1	10	3	9	5	6				8		11	
12	29	Merthyr Town	3-1	Allon, Loasby 2	5000		4		2			7			1	10	3	9	5	6				8		11	
13	Nov 5	WALSALL	10-0	*see below	11340		4		5			7			1	10	3	9		6				8	2	11	
14	12	Bristol Rovers	2-2	Loasby, Smith	7846		4		5			7			1	10	3	9		6				8	2	11	
15	19	CHARLTON ATHLETIC	2-1	Loasby, O'Dell	10210		4		5			7			1	10	3	9		6				8	2	11	
16	Dec 3	QUEEN'S PARK RANGERS	1-0	Loasby	9737		4		5			7			1	10	3	9		6				8	2	11	
17	17	NEWPORT COUNTY	1-2	Maloney	8945		4		3		9	7			1	10			5	6				8	2	11	
18	24	Coventry City	4-2	O'Dell 2, Daley, Smith	9250		4		3			7			1	10			5	9				8	2	11	6
19	26	LUTON TOWN	6-5	Allon, Daley, Hoten, Maloney, Smith 2	10153		4		3			7			1	10			5	9				8	2	11	6
20	31	Millwall	0-3		26334		4		3			7			1	10			5	9				8	2	11	6
21	Jan 7	CRYSTAL PALACE	1-1	O'Dell	9860	11	4					7			1	10			5	9		3		8	2		6
22	21	Exeter City	1-1	Wells	10231							7			1		3		5	6	9		10	8	2	11	4
23	28	TORQUAY UNITED	4-4	Allon, Price 2, Wells	4832		4							7	1		3		5	6	9		10	8	2	11	
24	Feb 4	Norwich City	4-3	Bowen 3, Wells	6760		4	9					7		1		3		5		10			8	2	11	6
25	11	GILLINGHAM	1-0	Shaw	9538		4	9				7			1		3		5				10	8	2	11	6
26	18	SOUTHEND UNITED	2-1	Allon, Wells	13133		4	9		1			7			10			5	6		3		8	2	11	
27	25	Brighton & Hove Albion	1-2	Wells	12631		7	9	3						1	10			5	6				8	2	11	4
28	Mar 3	Plymouth Argyle	3-3	Bowen 2, Fraser	13942		4	9	3				7		1	10			5	6				8	2	11	
29	10	MERTHYR TOWN	6-0	Aitken 2, Bowen, Fraser, O'Dell	8549	11	4	9	3				7		1				5	6			10	8	2		
30	17	Walsall	1-1	Fraser	7800		4	9	3				7		1				5	6			10	8	2	11	
31	19	Luton Town	0-2		8194	11	4	9	3				7		1				5	6			10	8	2		
32	24	BRISTOL ROVERS	2-0	Bowen, Fraser	9770		4	9	3				7	11	1	10			5	6				8	2		
33	31	Charlton Athletic	2-2	Bowen, Wells	7121		4	9				7			1	10			5	6		3		8	2	11	
34	Apr 7	SWINDON TOWN	3-0	Bowen 2, Hoten	14174		4	9				7			1	10			5	6		3		8	2	11	
35	9	Bournemouth	1-1	Bowen	9099	11	4	9				7			1	10			5	6		3		8	2		
36	10	BOURNEMOUTH	1-1	Aitken	11693	11	4	9				7			1	10			5	6		3		8	2		
37	14	Queen's Park Rangers	4-0	Bowen, Hoten 2, O'Dell	8399		4	9				7			1	11			5	10		3		8	2		6
38	18	Watford	0-2		4221		4	9				7			1	11			5	10		3		8	2		6
39	21	WATFORD	5-0	Allon, Bowen, Hoten 2, Smith	6255		4	9				7			1	10			5	6		3		8	2	11	
40	25	Swindon Town	0-4		5289		4	9				7			1	10			5	6		3		8	2	11	
41	28	Newport County	1-4	Bowen	2753		4	9				7			1	10			5	6		3		8	2	11	
42	May 5	COVENTRY CITY	2-1	Bowen, Daley	7583		4	9				7			1	10			5	6		3		8	2	11	

Scorers in game 13: Loasby 3, Smith 3, Wells 3, Hoten

	Aitkin JG	Allon TG	Bowen EC	Brett FB	Cave W	Cockle ES	Daley J	Fraser WC	George HS	Hammond L	Hoten RV	Jeffs TE	Loasby H	Maloney RJH	Odell GW	Price E	Russell GH	Shaw WH	Smith TG	Watson WJ	Wells TC	Wilson JR
Apps	10	41	19	22	1	1	33	7	2	41	34	20	16	38	35	4	13	6	42	33	29	15
Goals	5	5	15				4	4			10		18	3	6	2		2	12		13	1

Two own goals

F.A. Cup

	Date	Opponent	Score	Scorers	Att.	Aitkin JG	Allon TG	Bowen EC	Brett FB	Cave W	Cockle ES	Daley J	Fraser WC	George HS	Hammond L	Hoten RV	Jeffs TE	Loasby H	Maloney RJH	Odell GW	Price E	Russell GH	Shaw WH	Smith TG	Watson WJ	Wells TC	Wilson JR
R1	Nov 26	LEYTON	8-0	*See below	12043		4		5			7			1	10	3	9		6				8	2	11	
R2	Dec 10	BRIGHTON & HOVE ALB.	1-0	Daley	16092		4		3			7			1	10		9	5	6				8	2	11	
R3	Jan 14	Sunderland	3-3	Cowen, Daley, Wells	25484		4					7			1	10	3		5	6				8	2	11	
rep	19	SUNDERLAND	0-3		21148		4					7	9		1	10	3		5	6				8	2	11	

Scorers in R1: Daley, Hoten 3, Loasby 3, Wells

Played in R3: JE Cowen (at 9)

Norwich City

17th in Division Three (South)

	Date		Opponent	Score	Scorers	Att	Allman L	Bradley CM	Campbell AMacE	Cousins WA	Crockford HA	Cropper A	Cropper RW	Dennington C	Ferrari FW	Hannah JH	Hetherington J	Jackson JH	Lamb J	Mason A	McGrae JR	McLaverty B	Moule AS	Pembleton A	Porter EW	Richmond J	Robinson LStJ	Rowe GW	Slicer J	Varco PS
1	Aug	27	CRYSTAL PALACE	4-1	Varco, Moule, Slicer, Hannah (p)	13140			3					1		2					6		10	4	7	5	8		11	9
2		29	Luton Town	3-1	Varco 2, Moule	9157			3					1		2			4		6		10	5	7		8		11	9
3	Sep	3	Exeter City	2-2	Varco, Charlton (og)	7567			3					1		2			4		6		10	5	7		8		11	9
4		5	LUTON TOWN	3-0	Robinson, Varco, Moule	13640			3					1		2			4		6		10	5	7		8		11	9
5		10	TORQUAY UNITED	4-0	Varco 2, Robinson, Moule	12887			3					1		2			4		6		10	5	7		8		11	9
6		17	Walsall	1-1	Moule	9885			3		10			1		2			4		6		9	5	7		8		11	
7		24	Northampton Town	2-4	Varco 2	13921			3					1		2			4		6		10	5	7		8		11	9
8	Oct	1	SOUTHEND UNITED	2-1	Varco, Porter	9079			3					1		2			4		6		10	5	7		8		11	9
9		8	Brighton & Hove Albion	0-1		9286			3					1		2			4		6		10	5	7		8		11	9
10		15	BOURNEMOUTH	3-3	Moule 2, Cropper	9675			3				10	1		2					6		8	4	7	5			11	9
11		22	BRISTOL ROVERS	4-2	Porter, Varco, Moule, Cropper	6946							10	1		2			4		6		8	5	7			3	11	9
12		29	Plymouth Argyle	2-4	Varco 2	10912							10	1		2			4		6		8	5	7			3	11	9
13	Nov	5	MERTHYR TOWN	4-0	Vaco 2, Hannah (p), Lamb	7967							10	1		2			4		6		8	5	7			3	11	9
14		12	Charlton Athletic	2-3	Varco, Moule	10530			3				10	1		2			4		6		8	5	7				11	9
15		19	WATFORD	1-1	Robinson	6049			3				10	1		2			4		6			5	7		8		11	9
16	Dec	3	SWINDON TOWN	1-3	Robinson	7479								1		2			4	3	6		10		7	5	8		11	9
17		17	COVENTRY CITY	0-2		5358	1				10				5	2	8		4		6				7	3			11	9
18		24	Gillingham	0-3		4078	1			6						2		9	4		5				7	3	8		11	10
19		27	Millwall	1-2	Robinson	16550				7				1	3	2			4		6		10			5	8		11	9
20		31	Crystal Palace	1-2	Varco	7446				7				1	3	2			4		6		10			5	8		11	9
21	Jan	7	EXETER CITY	2-2	Varco, Lamb	6706				7				1	3	2			4		6		10			5	8		11	9
22		14	Newport County	2-2	Varco, Hannah (p)	2875			3	7				1		2			4		6	5	10				8		11	9
23		21	Torquay United	2-4	Slicer, McGrae	3336			3	7				1		2			4		6	5	10				8		11	9
24		28	WALSALL	1-4	Moule	5730	1		3	4						2			8			6	10	5	7				11	9
25	Feb	4	NORTHAMPTON T	3-4	Varco 2, Robinson	6760	1									2					6	5	8	4	7	3	10		11	9
26		11	Southend United	1-1	Robinson	4671	1									2					6	5	8	4	7	3	10		11	9
27		18	BRIGHTON & HOVE ALB	0-0		8131	1	7				9	10			2			4		6	5				3			11	8
28		25	Bournemouth	1-2	Varco	6041	1	7								2			4		6	5	8			3	10		11	9
29	Mar	3	Bristol Rovers	0-3		7031	1									2			4		6	5	8		7	3	10		11	9
30		10	PLYMOUTH ARGYLE	2-0	Hannah (p), Moule	7211	1									2			4		6	5	8		7	3	10		11	9
31		17	Merthyr Town	1-1	Varco	2317	1						10			2			4		6	5	8		7	3			11	9
32		24	CHARLTON ATHLETIC	0-0		7253				7				1		2			4		6	5	8			3	10		11	9
33		31	Watford	0-2		4412				7		9		1		2			4		6	5				3	10		11	8
34	Apr	6	Brentford	1-3	Varco	11814			3			8		1		2			4			6			7	5	10		11	9
35		7	NEWPORT COUNTY	1-1	Porter	7641								1		2			4		6	5	10		7	3	8		11	9
36		9	BRENTFORD	1-1	Robinson	10848								1		2			4		6	5	10		7	3	8		11	9
37		14	Swindon Town	1-1	Cropper	4980				7			8	1					4	2	6	5	10			3			11	9
38		21	QUEEN'S PARK RANGERS	3-1	Varco 3	4867				4			8	1						2	6	5	10		7	3			11	9
39		28	Coventry City	2-2	Robinson 2	9103							8	1		2			4		6	5			7	3	10		11	9
40		30	MILLWALL	2-0	Varco 2	8979							8	1		2			4		6	5			7	3	10		11	9
41	May	3	Queen's Park Rangers	0-0		4691				4		10		1		2					6	5			7	3	8		11	9
42		5	GILLINGHAM	0-0		6556				4		10		1		2					6	5			7	3	8		11	9
						Apps	10	2	16	13	2	5	12	32	4	40	1	1	35	3	40	21	32	18	32	26	31	3	42	41
						Goals							3			4			2		1		11		3		10		2	29

One own goal

F.A. Cup

	Date		Opponent	Score	Scorers	Att	Allman L	Bradley CM	Campbell AMacE	Cousins WA	Crockford HA	Cropper A	Cropper RW	Dennington C	Ferrari FW	Hannah JH	Hetherington J	Jackson JH	Lamb J	Mason A	McGrae JR	McLaverty B	Moule AS	Pembleton A	Porter EW	Richmond J	Robinson LStJ	Rowe GW	Slicer J	Varco PS
R1	Nov	26	Poole	1-1	Robinson	4490			3					1		2			4		6		8	5	7		10		11	9
rep	Dec	1	POOLE	5-0	Varco 3, Robinson, Moule	5956			3					1		2			4		6		10	5	7		8		11	9
R2		10	Luton Town	0-6		10750								1		2			4	3	6		10	5	7		8		11	9

Notts County

15th in Division Two

	Date	Opponent	Score	Scorers	Att.	Andrews H	Barry LJ	Bisby CC	Connell A	Davies W	Davis AG	Dinsdale N	Fenner T	Ferguson JS	Froggatt F	Gibson H	Haden S	Hilton F	Hopkins GH	Kelly P	Kemp H	Matthews CHW	Mills BR	Mills PC	Plackett S	Smith G	Staniforth C	Stokes A	Streets GH	Taylor GT	Widdowson A
1	Aug 27	BRISTOL CITY	1-2	Staniforth	15302		11	3			10	5						4	1	7			8		6	2	9				
2	Sep 3	Stoke City	0-3		22236		11	3										5	1	8			4		6	2	9			7	10
3	7	Chelsea	0-5		18416		11	3										5	1	8			4		6	2	9			7	10
4	10	SOUTHAMPTON	0-0		9673		11	3								7		5	1						6	2	8	4			10
5	17	Nottm. Forest	1-2	BR Mills	21957		11	3										5	1	8	4		9		6	2	10			7	
6	24	Oldham Athletic	0-0		12417		11	3			8							5	1		4		9		6	2	10			7	
7	Oct 1	GRIMSBY TOWN	3-2	Davis 2, Staniforth	7174			3			8							5	1		4		9		6	2	10			7	
8	6	CHELSEA	0-1		9127			3			10						11	5	1		4		8		6	2	9			7	
9	8	Reading	2-2	BR Mills, Staniforth	11978			3			10						11	5	1		4		8		6	2	9			7	
10	15	BLACKPOOL	3-1	Taylor, Davis, Staniforth	11885			3			10						11	5	1		4		8		6	2	9			7	
11	22	PORT VALE	2-4	Connell, Staniforth	9053			3	8		10						11	5	1		4				6	2	9			7	
12	29	South Shields	3-2	Staniforth 2, Kelly	6379			3			10	5					11	6		8	4					2	9		1	7	
13	Nov 5	LEEDS UNITED	2-2	Staniforth, Hilton (p)	9866			3			10	5					11	6		8	4					2	9		1	7	
14	12	Wolverhampton Wand.	2-2	Davis, Kelly	16100			3			10	5					11	6		8	4					2	9		1	7	
15	19	BARNSLEY	9-0	BR Mills 5, Staniforth 3, Haden	9382			3			10				5		11	6			4		9			2	8		1	7	
16	26	Preston North End	0-4		16041			3			10				5		11	6			4		9			2	8		1	7	
17	Dec 3	SWANSEA TOWN	2-0	Taylor, BR Mills	11618			3			10				5		11	6			4		9			2	8		1	7	
18	10	Fulham	1-2	Staniforth	11562			3			10				5		11	6					9			2	8	4	1	7	
19	17	HULL CITY	1-1	BR Mills	8758			3			10				5		11	6			4		9			2	8		1	7	
20	24	Manchester City	1-3	BR Mills	18362			3	8						5		11	6			4		9			2			1	7	10
21	26	West Bromwich Alb.	2-2	BR Mills, Kemp	14642			3	8						5		11	6	1		4		9			2				7	10
22	27	WEST BROMWICH ALB.	3-0	Widdowson 2, BR Mills	17755			3	8						5		11	6					9		4	2			1	7	10
23	31	Bristol City	2-1	BR Mills 2	6476			3							5		11	6			4		9			2	8		1	7	10
24	Jan 7	STOKE CITY	1-2	Haden	13365			3							5		11	6			4		9			2	8		1	7	10
25	21	Southampton	1-5	BR Mills	10002			3				5					11	6	1		4		9			2				7	8
26	Feb 4	OLDHAM ATHLETIC	2-1	Kemp, Kelly	8678			3							5		11	6	1	8	4		9			2				7	10
27	11	Grimsby Town	0-1		7666			3			10				5		11	6	1	8	4		9			2				7	
28	18	READING	1-1	Fenner	8034			3					8		5	7	11	6	1		4		9			2	10				
29	22	NOTTM. FOREST	1-2	BR Mills	13241			3					8		5		11	6	1		4		9			2	10			7	
30	25	Blackpool	3-3	BR Mills, Staniforth 2	9423			3					8		5	7	11	6	1		4		9			2	10				
31	Mar 3	Port Vale	0-3		9644			3					8				7	5	1		4		9		6	2	10				
32	10	SOUTH SHIELDS	4-1	BR Mills 2, Hilton (p), Taylor	8117			3					7		5		11	6	1		4		9			2	10			8	
33	17	Leeds United	0-6		17643			3		7				1	5		11	6			4	8	9			2	10				
34	24	WOLVERHAMPTON W.	1-2	Haden	13617			3		11				1	5		10	6			4	7	9			2				8	
35	31	Barnsley	0-0		5619	10		3		7				1			11	5		8			9	2	6			4			
36	Apr 6	CLAPTON ORIENT	3-0	BR Mills, Haden, Hilton (p)	13924	10		3		7				1			11	5		8			9	2	6			4			
37	7	PRESTON NORTH END	6-2	Davies 2, Taylor 3, Haden	16226	10		3		7				1	5		11			8				2	6			4		9	
38	9	Clapton Orient	1-0	Taylor	10166	10		3						1	5		11			8		7			6	2		4		9	
39	14	Swansea Town	1-1	Taylor	11566	10		3		7				1	5		11			8					6	2		4		9	
40	21	FULHAM	0-1		7655	10		3		7				1	5		11			8					6	2		4		9	
41	28	Hull City	1-1	Wilson (og)	5284	10		3		7			8	1	5		11	4							6	2				9	
42	May 5	MANCHESTER CITY	2-1	Fenner, Taylor	9907	10		3		7			8	1	5		11	4						2	6					9	
					Apps	8	6	42	4	9	16	5	7	10	24	3	35	38	20	15	28	3	31	4	21	38	27	8	12	34	10
					Goals				1	2	4		2				5	3		3	2		20				14			9	2

LP Price played in games 7 (at 11) and 31 (11)

JA Sullivan played in games 4 (at 9) and 25 (10)

One own goal

F.A. Cup

	Date	Opponent	Score	Scorers	Att.	Andrews H	Barry LJ	Bisby CC	Connell A	Davies W	Davis AG	Dinsdale N	Fenner T	Ferguson JS	Froggatt F	Gibson H	Haden S	Hilton F	Hopkins GH	Kelly P	Kemp H	Matthews CHW	Mills BR	Mills PC	Plackett S	Smith G	Staniforth C	Stokes A	Streets GH	Taylor GT	Widdowson A
R3	Jan 14	SHEFFIELD UNITED	2-3	BR Mills, Taylor	28232			3							5		11	6			4		9			2	8		1	7	10

Nottingham Forest

10th in Division Two

						Barratt PM	Belton J	Boot LGW	Burton N	Dexter A	German AC	Gibson SG	Gordon LW	Graham T	Green H	Harrison A	Hicks TG	Jones C	Langford L	Marsden H	McKinlay W	McLachlan ER	McMillan S	Morgan FG	Price EC	Roe TW	Stocks CW	Sturton TW	Thompson N	Thompson WP	Townsend AH	Wadsworth H	Wallace RS
1	Aug 27	Port Vale	2-2	Stocks, Wadsworth	14524	3			9			7			4	5		10	1								8			2		11	6
2	29	FULHAM	7-0	Burton 3,Jones 2,Stocks,Barratt (p)	11430	3			9			7			4	5		10	1								8			2		11	6
3	Sep 3	SOUTH SHIELDS	7-2	Burton 2, Jones 2, Stocks 2, Gibson	16714	3			9			7			4	5		10	1								8			2		11	6
4	10	Leeds United	0-4		19478	3			9			7			4	5		10	1	2							8					11	6
5	15	Fulham	0-2		9446	3	4					7				5	2	10	1							9	8					11	6
6	17	NOTTS COUNTY	2-1	Gibson, Barratt (p)	21957	2	4		9			7				5	3	10	1								8					11	6
7	24	MANCHESTER CITY	4-5	Roe 3, Jones	12893	2	4					7					3	10	1					5		9	8					11	6
8	Oct 1	Hull City	0-2		8274	2	4					7	6			5	3	10	1							9	8					11	
9	8	PRESTON NORTH END	3-1	Gibson 2, Burton	17056	3	4		9			7				5	2	10	1								8					11	6
10	15	Swansea Town	0-2		14844	2	4		9			7				5	3	10	1								8					11	6
11	22	Reading	2-0	McLachlan, Wadsworth	7785	3	4					7				5		10	1			8				9				2		11	6
12	29	GRIMSBY TOWN	5-2	Burton 2, Jones 2, McLachlan	14546	3	4		9			7				5		10	1			8		6						2		11	
13	Nov 5	Oldham Athletic	1-4	Barratt (p)	6032	3	4		9	1		7				5		10				8								2		11	6
14	12	BLACKPOOL	4-1	Burton, Gibson, Stocks, Barratt (p)	8602	3			9	1		7				4		10						5			8			2		11	6
15	19	Chelsea	1-2	Gibson	28743	3	4		9	1		7				5		11							10		8			2			6
16	26	BRISTOL CITY	1-1	Burton	10040	3	4		9	1		7				5		11							10		8			2			6
17	Dec 3	West Bromwich Albion	3-2	Wadsworth 2, Burton	16674	3	4		9	1		7				5		10				8								2		11	6
18	10	CLAPTON ORIENT	4-3	Gibson 2, Barratt (p), Galbraith (og)	7802	3	4		9	1		7				5		10				8								2		11	6
19	17	Stoke City	3-1	Wadsworth 2, Burton	9093	3	4		9	1		7				5		10				8								2		11	6
20	24	SOUTHAMPTON	1-1	Burton	5572	3	4		9	1		7				5		10				8								2		11	6
21	26	WOLVERHAMPTON W.	3-2	Gibson 2, Burton	12530	3	4		9	1		7				5		10					8	6						2		11	
22	27	Wolverhampton Wan.	0-1		15982	3			9	1		7	6								4		8	5	10					2		11	
23	Jan 7	South Shields	4-3	Stocks 2, Wadsworth 2	4723	3			9	1		7									4		10	5			8			2		11	6
24	21	LEEDS UNITED	2-2	Gibson, Stocks	13133	3	4			1		7				5									10	9	8	6		2		11	
25	Feb 4	Manchester City	3-3	Stocks 2, Jones	30037	3	4		9	1		7				5		10		2							8					11	6
26	11	HULL CITY	1-1	Wadsworth	6617	3			9	1		7						10		2	4			5			8					11	6
27	22	Notts County	2-1	German, Gibson	13241	3	4			1	9	7				5		10						6			8			2		11	
28	25	SWANSEA TOWN	0-2		11687		4		9	1		7				5	3						10				8			2		11	6
29	Mar 5	Preston North End	0-5		10036		4	1				7				5	3	10								9	8			2		11	6
30	10	Grimsby Town	1-2	Burton	7466	3		1	9			7				5		10			4		8				11			2			6
31	17	OLDHAM ATHLETIC	2-1	Harrison, W Thompson (p)	9045	3			9	1		7				5		10			4		8	6						2	11		
32	24	Blackpool	3-5	German,W Thompson (p), Barnett (og)	8977	3				1	9	7				5		10			4			6			8			2	11		
33	29	READING	5-3	Stocks 2, Townsend 2, Harrison	2572	3			9	1		7				5		10			4						8			2	11		6
34	31	CHELSEA	2-2	Townsend, W Thompson (p)	10959	3	4			1		7				9		10						5			8			2	11		6
35	Apr 7	Bristol City	0-0		14575	3	4		9	1		7		6		5		10									8			2	11		
36	9	BARNSLEY	1-1	Jones	11640	3			9	1		7		6		5		10			4						8			2		11	
37	10	Barnsley	1-2	Roe	7688	3				1								10			4	7		5		9	8			2		11	6
38	14	WEST BROMWICH ALB.	0-2		6158	3	4		6	1		7				5		10								9	8			2		11	
39	21	Clapton Orient	2-2	Stocks, Wallace	9451	3			9	1						5		10			4		7				8			2	11		6
40	26	PORT VALE	0-2		3713	3				1						5		10			4		7			9	8			2	11		6
41	28	STOKE CITY	0-2		5382	3	4		11	1						5					8						7		10	2			6
42	May 5	Southampton	1-2	Jones	8244	3			9	1						5		11			4		7		10		8			2			6

I McKennan played at 9 in game 41

	Barratt PM	Belton J	Boot LGW	Burton N	Dexter A	German AC	Gibson SG	Gordon LW	Graham T	Green H	Harrison A	Hicks TG	Jones C	Langford L	Marsden H	McKinlay W	McLachlan ER	McMillan S	Morgan FG	Price EC	Roe TW	Stocks CW	Sturton TW	Thompson N	Thompson WP	Townsend AH	Wadsworth H	Wallace RS
Apps	40	25	2	31	28	2	37	2	2	4	37	8	37	12	3	13	8	9	12	5	9	32	1	1	33	7	30	31
Goals	5			15		2	12				2		10				2				4	13			3	3	9	1

Two own goals

F.A. Cup

						Barratt PM	Belton J	Boot LGW	Burton N	Dexter A	German AC	Gibson SG	Gordon LW	Graham T	Green H	Harrison A	Hicks TG	Jones C	Langford L	Marsden H	McKinlay W	McLachlan ER	McMillan S	Morgan FG	Price EC	Roe TW	Stocks CW	Sturton TW	Thompson N	Thompson WP	Townsend AH	Wadsworth H	Wallace RS
R3	Jan 14	TRANMERE ROVERS	1-0	Wadsworth	17019	3	4		9	1		7											10	5			8			2		11	6
R4	28	Derby County	0-0		22594	3	4		9	1		7				5		10									8			2		11	6
rep	Feb 1	DERBY COUNTY	2-0	Gibson, Stocks	35625	3	4		9	1		7				5		10						6			8			2		11	
R5	18	CARDIFF CITY	2-1	Stocks, W Thompson (p)	30570	3	4		9	1		7				5		10									8			2		11	6
R6	Mar 3	Sheffield United	0-3		52640	3	4		9	1		7				5		10						6			8			2		11	

Oldham Athletic

7th in Division Two

	Date		Opponent	Score	Scorers	Att	Adlam LW	Armitage JH	Brelsford BH	Crompton N	Dyson JM	Goodier E	Grundy H	Hacking J	Hargreaves F	Harris NL	Ivill E	Jones E	Kellard T	King J	Maddison JAB	Malpas E	Naylor J	Porter W	Prince J	Pynegar AE	Stanton C	Taylor G	Trotter W	Watson RH
1	Aug	27	WEST BROMWICH ALB.	3-1	Harris 2, Pynegar	13035	4	5					2	1	10	9	3			7			6			8				11
2		29	Blackpool	2-1	Harris, Watson	16690	4	5					2	1	10	9	3			7			6			8				11
3	Sep	3	Bristol City	1-2	Watson	23694	4	5					2	1	10	9	3			7			6			8				11
4		5	BLACKPOOL	6-0	* see below	14542	4	5					2	1	10	9	3			7			6			8				11
5		10	STOKE CITY	3-1	Harris 2, Trotter	22065	4	5					2	1	10	9	3			7			6			8			11	
6		17	Southampton	2-5	Pynegar, Harris	10360	4	5					2	1	10	9	3			7			6			8			11	
7		24	NOTTS COUNTY	0-0		12417	4	5					2	1	10	9	3			7			6			8				11
8	Oct	1	Manchester City	1-3	Watson	25216		5					2	1	10	9	3			7	4		6			8				11
9		8	Grimsby Town	2-1	Watson 2	10400		5				6	2	1			3			7	4		10			8		9		11
10		15	READING	3-2	Watson 2, Pynegar (p)	14377	4	5					2	1		10	3			7			6			8	9			11
11		22	SOUTH SHIELDS	2-2	Armitage, Pynegar (p)	10723	4	5					2	1		10	3			7			6			8	9			11
12		29	Leeds United	0-1		17615	4	5					2	1		9	3			7			6			10		8		11
13	Nov	5	NOTTM. FOREST	4-1	Pynegar 2, King, Harris	6032	4	5					2	1		9	3			7			6			10		8		11
14		12	Port Vale	0-1		10000	4	5					2	1		9	3			7			6			10		8		11
15		19	WOLVERHAMPTON W.	3-0	Harris 2, King	7350	4	5					2	1		9	3			7			6			10		8		11
16		26	Swansea Town	0-0		12469	4	5					2	1		9	3			7			6			10		8		11
17	Dec	3	FULHAM	4-2	Pynegar 2, Taylor, King	10182	4	5					2	1		9	3			7			6			10		8		11
18		10	Barnsley	1-0	Harris	4944	4	5					2	1		9	3			7			6			10		8		11
19		17	PRESTON NORTH END	0-0		18366	4	5					2	1		9	3			7			6			10		8		11
20		24	Hull City	2-2	Watson, Pynegar	6662	4	5					2	1		9	3			7			6			10		8		11
21		27	CLAPTON ORIENT	5-0	Pynegar 3, Taylor 2	23333	4	5					2	1		9	3			7			6			10		8		11
22		31	West Bromwich Albion	0-0		7357	4	5					2	1			3			7			6			10	9	8		11
23	Jan	7	BRISTOL CITY	4-1	Pynegar 2, Adlam, Watson	12168	4	5					2	1		9	3			7			6			10		8		11
24		21	Stoke City	0-3		13265	4	5					2	1			3			7			6			10	9	8		11
25		31	SOUTHAMPTON	3-1	Stanton 2, King	6365	4			5				1			2			7			6	3		10	9	8		11
26	Feb	4	Notts County	1-2	Stanton	8678	4			5				1			2			7			6	3		10	9	8		11
27		11	MANCHESTER CITY	3-2	Taylor 2, King	25426	4			5				1			2		8	7			6	3		10		8		11
28		18	GRIMSBY TOWN	1-0	Taylor	15701	4			5				1			2			7			6	3		10	9	8	11	
29		25	Reading	0-1		12806	4			5			2	1			3		8	7			6			10		9		11
30	Mar	3	South Shields	3-0	Pynegar 2, King	6186	4			5			2	1		9	3			7			6			10		8		11
31		10	LEEDS UNITED	0-1		22029	4			5			2			9	3			7			6		1	10		8		11
32		17	Nottingham Forest	1-2	Watson	9045	4						2	1		9	3			7		5	6			10		8		11
33		24	PORT VALE	4-1	Taylor 3, Watson	11809	4				8		2	1			3			7		5	6			10		8		11
34		31	Wolverhampton Wan.	1-3	Taylor	14631	4		11		8		2	1			3			7		5	6			10		8		
35	Apr	6	Chelsea	1-2	Pynegar	53309	4			5			2	1		9	3			7			6			10		8		11
36		7	SWANSEA TOWN	0-1		14860	4						2	1		9	3			7	5		6			10		8		11
37		9	CHELSEA	2-1	Watson, Harris	18992					7		2	1		9	3				4		6	5		10		8		11
38		14	Fulham	1-1	Taylor	14394	4				7		2	1		9	3						6	5		10		8		11
39		16	Clapton Orient	0-2		2929	4				8		2	1		9	3			7			6	5		10				11
40		21	BARNSLEY	0-1		7036	4				8		2	1			3			7			6	5		10		9		11
41		28	Preston North End	1-1	Jones	8215	4						2	1		9	3	10		7			6	5				8		11
42	May	5	HULL CITY	5-0	Harris 3, Watson 2	4936	4						2	1		9	3	10		7			6	5				8		11
						Apps	39	24	1	8	6	1	38	41	8	31	42	2	2	40	4	3	42	10	1	40	7	31	3	38
						Goals	1	1								14		1		7			1			19	3	11	1	15

Scorers in game 4: Harris, King, Watson, Naylor, Pynegar (p), Barrett (og)

F.A. Cup

	Date		Opponent	Score	Scorers	Att	Adlam LW	Armitage JH	Brelsford BH	Crompton N	Dyson JM	Goodier E	Grundy H	Hacking J	Hargreaves F	Harris NL	Ivill E	Jones E	Kellard T	King J	Maddison JAB	Malpas E	Naylor J	Porter W	Prince J	Pynegar AE	Stanton C	Taylor G	Trotter W	Watson RH
R3	Jan	14	Blackpool	4-1	Watson 2, King, Stanton	10349	4	5					2	1			3			7			6			10	9	8		11
R4		28	Tottenham Hotspur	0-3		36828	4	5					2	1		9	3			7			6			10		8		11

Plymouth Argyle

3rd in Division Three (South)

	Date	Opponent	Score	Scorers	Att	Black S	Bland WH	Bowden ER	Cann H	Cock JG	Cosgrove F	Craig FG	Davis JAR	Edmunds A	Forbes FJ	Grozier T	Hardie AS	Healy J	Lee AG	Leslie JF	Logan J	Mackay N	Matthews AW	McKenzie FT	Preston R	Price W	Pullen WJ	Richards P	Russell MR	Sloan FJ	Stanbury GH	Titmuss FE
1	Aug 27	MERTHYR TOWN	5-0	Forbes 4, Leslie	11455	11						1			9		6			10			7	5	4				2	8		3
2	31	BRISTOL ROVERS	4-1	Sloan 3, Black	10084	11						1			9		6			10			7	5	4				2	8		3
3	Sep 3	Walsall	1-2	Leslie	13784	11						1			9		6			10			7	5	4				2	8		3
4	7	Bristol Rovers	1-3	Black	9013	11						1			9		6			10			7	5	4				2	8		3
5	10	GILLINGHAM	2-2	Cock, Black	10282	11				9		1			8		6			10			7	5	4				2			3
6	17	Coventry City	1-1	Black	15249	11				9					8		6			10			7	5	4				2		1	3
7	24	NEWPORT COUNTY	2-0	Leslie, Black	10011	11				9					8		6			10			7	5	4				2		1	3
8	Oct 1	Swindon Town	2-2	Black, Cock	6792	11				9					8		6			10			7	5	4				2		1	3
9	8	QUEEN'S PARK RANGERS	3-0	Leslie, Black, Sloan	12343	11									9		6			10	4		7	5					2	8	1	3
10	15	Watford	2-1	Leslie, Black	9016	11									9		6			10	4		7	5					2	8	1	3
11	22	Northampton Town	1-2	Leslie	9434	11									9		6			10	4		7	5					2	8	1	3
12	29	NORWICH CITY	4-2	Leslie, Forbes 3	10912	11				9	2				8		6			10	4		7	5							1	3
13	Nov 5	Torquay United	2-1	Forbes, Black	9172	11				9					8		6			10	4		7	5					2		1	3
14	12	SOUTHEND UNITED	3-2	Forbes, Matthews, Black	10624	11							9		8		6			10	4		7	5					2		1	3
15	19	Brighton & Hove Albion	1-4	Forbes	5552								9		11		6			10	8		7	5	4				2		1	3
16	Dec 3	Brentford	2-0	Black, Logan	7537	11									8		6	7		10	9			5	4				2		1	3
17	10	MILLWALL	3-2	Matthews, Leslie, Bland	16557	11	8								9		6			10			7	5	4				2		1	3
18	17	Millwall	0-2		18567	11	8				2				9		6			10			7	5	4						1	3
19	24	CRYSTAL PALACE	5-1	Fobes, Black 2, McKenzie, Bland	11515	11	8								9		6			10			7	5	4				2		1	3
20	26	Exeter City	0-2		9580		8				3			11	9		6			10			7	5	4				2		1	
21	27	EXETER CITY	1-2	Leslie	14938		8				3			11	9		6		1	10	4		7	5					2			
22	Jan 7	WALSALL	2-1	Matthews, Sloan	7361		4							11	9		6			10			7	5					2	8	1	3
23	14	Merthyr Town	4-1	Forbes, McKenzie, Richards 2	1463									11	8		6			10	4		7	5				9	2		1	3
24	21	Gillingham	1-3	Richards	4473									11	8		6			10	4		7	5				9	2		1	3
25	28	COVENTRY CITY	4-0	Mackay 3, Leslie	4366										11		6			10	4	8	7	5				9	2		1	3
26	Feb 4	Newport County	1-1	Leslie	3502										11		6			10	4	8	7	5				9	2		1	3
27	11	SWINDON TOWN	3-0	Richards, Forbes, Leslie	13052										11		6			10	4	8	7	5				9	2		1	3
28	18	Queen's Park Rangers	1-0	Mackay	17377										11		6			10	4	8	7	5		3		9	2		1	
29	25	WATFORD	0-1		11281	11									7		6			10	4	8		5		3		9	2		1	
30	Mar 3	NORTHAMPTON T	3-3	Richards, Mackay, Leslie	13942		4								11		6	7		10		8		5		3		9	2		1	
31	10	Norwich City	0-2		7211						2				11		6	7		10		8		4		3	5	9			1	
32	17	TORQUAY UNITED	4-1	Richards 3, Matthews	9008	11											6			10		8	7	4		3	5	9	2		1	
33	24	Southend United	0-3		5187	11					2						6		1	10	4		7	5				9	3	8		
34	31	BRIGHTON & HOVE ALB	2-0	Richards, Black	6289	11					2	1					6			10	4		7	5				9	3	8		
35	Apr 6	Charlton Athletic	0-2		9112	11					2	1					6			10	4		7	5				9	3	8		
36	7	Luton Town	1-1	Sloan	10451	11					2	1					6			10	4		7	5				9	3	8		
37	9	CHARLTON ATHLETIC	2-0	Leslie, Black	9686	11					2	1					6			10			7	5	4			9	3	8		
38	14	BRENTFORD	1-0	McKenzie	5940	11					2					7	6		1	10				5	4			9		8		3
39	21	Bournemouth	2-2	Bowden 2	5495	11		9	1		2				7		6			10				5	4					8		3
40	25	BOURNEMOUTH	3-1	Leslie, Richards, Forbes	5519							1			7	11	6			10	4			5				9	2	8		3
41	May 2	LUTON TOWN	4-0	Mackay, Bowden 2, Black	4719	11		9				1					6	7		10		8		5	4				2			3
42	5	Crystal Palace	2-0	Sloan, Craig	12218	11					2	1					6	7				10		5	4			9		8		3
					Apps	29	7	2	1	6	13	12	2	5	33	2	42	5	3	41	21	10	33	42	19	5	2	18	36	17	26	30
					Goals	16	2	4		2		1			14					15	1	6	4	3				10		7		

F.A. Cup

	Date	Opponent	Score	Scorers	Att	Black S	Bland WH	Bowden ER	Cann H	Cock JG	Cosgrove F	Craig FG	Davis JAR	Edmunds A	Forbes FJ	Grozier T	Hardie AS	Healy J	Lee AG	Leslie JF	Logan J	Mackay N	Matthews AW	McKenzie FT	Preston R	Price W	Pullen WJ	Richards P	Russell MR	Sloan FJ	Stanbury GH	Titmuss FE
R1	Nov 26	Gillingham	1-2	Matthews	7900	11							9		8		6			10			7	5	4				2		1	3

Port Vale

9th in Division Two

	Date	Opponent	Score	Scorers	Att	Anstiss HA	Bennett A	Briscoe W	Connelly R	Fishwick AE	Gillespie R	Griffiths PH	Holdcroft GH	Jones R	Kirkham WT	Littlewood SC	Lowe J	Maddock J	Matthews WH	Oakes J	Page T	Rollo D	Rouse VA	Simms J	Smith HW	Smith SJW	Trotter AE	Whitcombe GC	Wootton W
1	Aug 27	NOTTM. FOREST	2-2	Lowe, Briscoe	14524	8	1	6	5						9		7			3	10	2					11	4	
2	31	Bristol City	0-4		20305	8	1	6	5						9		7			3	10	2					11	4	
3	Sep 3	Manchester City	0-1		37583	8	1	6	5						9		7	2		3	10						11	4	
4	10	HULL CITY	1-2	Kirkham	12169	8	1	10	5						9		7	2		3					6		11	4	
5	17	Preston North End	0-4		18129	8			5						9		7	2	1	3	10		6		4		11		
6	19	BRISTOL CITY	5-1	Briscoe, Kirkham 2, Page 2	11319	8		11	5					7	9			2	1	3	10		6					4	
7	24	SWANSEA TOWN	2-0	Kirkham 2	10197	8		11	5					7	9			2	1	3	10		6					4	
8	Oct 1	Fulham	0-4		10560	8			5		11			7	9			2	1	3	10		6		4				
9	8	BARNSLEY	2-1	Simms 2	10010	8			5					4	9		7	2	1	3	10		6	11					
10	15	Wolverhampton Wan.	1-2	Gillespie	18026			4	5		10			7	9			2	1	3	8		6	11					
11	22	Notts County	4-2	Anstiss, Kirkham 2, Trotter	9053	7	1	4	5		10				9			2		3	8		6				11		
12	29	SOUTHAMPTON	4-0	Trotter, Gillespie 2, Kirkham	10679	7	1	4	5		10				9			2		3	8		6				11		
13	Nov 5	Stoke City	2-0	Anstiss, Kirkham	31493	7	1	4	5		10				9			2		3	8		6				11		
14	12	OLDHAM ATHLETIC	1-0	Briscoe	10000	7	1	4	5		10				9			2		3	8		6				11		
15	19	Grimsby Town	0-3		10119	7	1	4	5		10				9			2		3	8		6				11		
16	26	CHELSEA	1-1	Gillespie	14115	7	1	4	5		10				9			2		3	8		6	11					
17	Dec 3	Blackpool	6-1	* See below	7662	7	1	4	5		10				9			2		3	8		6	11					
18	10	READING	3-0	Briscoe, Page, Kirkham	8556	7	1	4	5		10				9			2			8		6	11					3
19	17	Clapton Orient	1-0	Gillespie	9287	7	1	4	5		10				9			2			8		6	11					3
20	24	WEST BROMWICH ALB.	4-1	Simms 3, Gillespie	8216	7	1	4	5		10				9			2		3	8		6	11					
21	26	LEEDS UNITED	1-2	Simms	18869	7	1	4	5		10				9			2		3	8		6	11					
22	27	Leeds United	0-3		32295	8	1		5						9		7	2					6	11			10	4	3
23	Jan 7	MANCHESTER CITY	1-2	Gillespie	14310	7			5		10				9			2	1	3	8		6	11				4	
24	21	Hull City	0-1		7106	7			5		10					9		2	1				6	11	4	8			3
25	Feb 4	Swansea Town	0-2		6745			11	5			7			9			2	1	3	10		6		4	8			
26	6	PRESTON NORTH END	2-0	Littlewood 2	9492	7			5		10					9		2	1	3			6	11	4	8			
27	11	FULHAM	4-1	Littlewood 3, Page	7520	7			5						8	9		2	1	3	10		6		4		11		
28	20	Barnsley	2-4	Gillespie 2	5423	8	1		5		10			7	9			2		3			6		4		11		
29	25	WOLVERHAMPTON W.	2-2	Page, Littlewood	11358	7	1		5		10					9		2		3	8		6		4		11		
30	Mar 3	NOTTS COUNTY	3-0	Gillespie, Littlewood, Maddock (p)	9644				5		10					9	7	2	1	3	8		6		4		11		
31	10	Southampton	3-1	Kirkham, Trotter, Jones	9874	7			5					10	9				1	3			6		4	8	11		2
32	17	STOKE CITY	0-0		21071			11	5	8					9		7	2	1	3	10		6		4				
33	24	Oldham Athletic	1-4	Simms	11809		1		5	8		7			9			2		3	10		6	11	4				
34	31	GRIMSBY TOWN	2-2	Calderwood (og), Simms	9125	10			5	8		7	1		9			2		3			6	11	4				
35	Apr 6	SOUTH SHIELDS	2-3	Page, Simms	11081				5		10	7	1			9		2		3	8		6	11	4				
36	7	Chelsea	0-1		29278				5	8		7	1	4	9					3	10		6	11					2
37	9	South Shields	1-0	Fishwick	4444				5	8	10	7	1		9					3			6	11				4	2
38	14	BLACKPOOL	3-0	Connelly, Gillespie, Griffiths	5321		1		5	8	10	7			9					3			6	11				4	2
39	21	Reading	0-0		7664		1		5		10	7			9					3	8		6	11				4	2
40	26	Nottingham Forest	2-0	Page, Kitchen	3713		1		5	8		7			9					3	10		6	11				4	2
41	28	CLAPTON ORIENT	0-0		5966		1		5	8		7			9					3	10		6	11				4	2
42	May 5	West Bromwich Albion	0-0		9217		1		5	8		7			9					3	10		6	11				4	2

Scorers in game 17: Briscoe, Page, Kirkham, Anstiss, Gillespie, Wright(og)

	Anstiss HA	Bennett A	Briscoe W	Connelly R	Fishwick AE	Gillespie R	Griffiths PH	Holdcroft GH	Jones R	Kirkham WT	Littlewood SC	Lowe J	Maddock J	Matthews WH	Oakes J	Page T	Rollo D	Rouse VA	Simms J	Smith HW	Smith SJW	Trotter AE	Whitcombe GC	Wootton W
Apps	29	24	20	42	9	23	11	4	8	37	6	9	32	14	38	33	2	38	22	15	4	16	14	12
Goals	3		5	1	1	12	1		1	13	7	1	1			8			9			3		

Two own goals

F.A. Cup

	Date	Opponent	Score	Scorers	Att	Anstiss HA	Bennett A	Briscoe W	Connelly R	Fishwick AE	Gillespie R	Griffiths PH	Holdcroft GH	Jones R	Kirkham WT	Littlewood SC	Lowe J	Maddock J	Matthews WH	Oakes J	Page T	Rollo D	Rouse VA	Simms J	Smith HW	Smith SJW	Trotter AE	Whitcombe GC	Wootton W
R3	Jan 14	BARNSLEY	3-0	Simms, Page, Maddock (p)	13162	7		4	5		10				9			2	1	3	8		6	11					
R4	Jan 28	NEW BRIGHTON	3-0	Page, Kirkham, Antiss	10867	7		4	5		10				9			2	1	3	8		6	11					
R5	Feb 18	Blackburn Rovers	1-2	Antiss	43700	7	1		5						8	9		2		3	10		6		4		11		

Portsmouth

20th in Division One

						Clifford G	Cook FC	Davey HH	Davies R	Forward FJ	Foxall H	Haines WWP	Haslam G	Irvine RW	Jarvie J	Mackie J	McColgan J	McIlwaine J	McPhail D	Moffatt WJ	Nichol JB	Rutherford SE	Smith JW	Watson D	Weddle JR
1	Aug 27	Sunderland	3-3	Cook, Mackie, Haines	35106	2	11		4	7	5	9				8	3		1	6				10	
2	31	ASTON VILLA	3-1	Cook, Forward, Watson	32050	2	11		4	7	5	9				8	3		1	6				10	
3	Sep 3	DERBY COUNTY	2-2	Cook, Haines	23489	2	11		4	7	5	9				8	3		1	6				10	
4	5	Aston Villa	2-7	Mackie, Haines	20624	2	11		4	7	5	9				8	3		1	6				10	
5	10	West Ham United	2-4	Watson, Haines	24729	2	11		4	7	5	9				8	3		1	6				10	
6	17	TOTTENHAM HOTSPUR	3-0	Haines, Forward, Cook	26115	2	11		4	7	5	9				8	3		1	6				10	
7	24	LEICESTER CITY	2-0	Watson, Forward	20959	2	11		4	7	5	9				8	3		1	6				10	
8	Oct 1	Liverpool	2-8	Mackie, Cook	25252	2	11		4	7	5	9			1	8	3			6				10	
9	8	ARSENAL	2-3	Haines, Cook	27261	2	11		4	7	5	9				8	3		1	6				10	
10	15	Burnley	0-2		19492	2	11		4	7	5	9				8	3		1	6				10	
11	22	Cardiff City	1-3	Cook	9060	2	11		4	7	5	9				8	3		1	6				10	
12	29	EVERTON	1-3	Foxall	23326	2			4	7	5	9				8	3		1	6		11		10	
13	Nov 5	Manchester United	0-2		13191	2	11		4	7	5	9				8	3		1	6				10	
14	12	BLACKBURN ROVERS	2-2	Haines 2	18078	2	11		4	7		9	5			8	3		1	6				10	
15	19	Bolton Wanderers	1-3	Haines	14302	2	11		4	7		9	5			8	3		1	6				10	
16	26	BIRMINGHAM	2-2	Mackie 2	18549	2	11			7		9	5			8	3		1	6	4			10	
17	Dec 3	Middlesbrough	1-5	Haines	18163	2	11			7		9	5			8	3		1	6	4			10	
18	10	SHEFFIELD WEDNESDAY	0-0		19258	2	11	9	4	7	5					8	3		1	6				10	
19	17	Newcastle United	3-1	Watson, Cook, Forward	19582	2	11	9	4	7	5	8					3		1	6				10	
20	24	HUDDERSFIELD T	2-1	Watson, Davey	21785	2	11	9	4	7	5	8					3		1	6				10	
21	26	Bury	0-4		17230	2	11	9	4	7	5	8					3		1	6				10	
22	27	BURY	1-0	Watson	15819	2	11	9	4	7	5	8					3		1		6			10	
23	Jan 2	Sheffield United	1-3	Davey	23182	2	11	9	4	7	5	8					3		1	6				10	
24	7	Derby County	2-2	Haines, Davies	18611	2	11		4	7	5	9				8	3		1	6				10	
25	21	WEST HAM UNITED	2-1	Smith 2	17656	2	11		4	7		9					3		1	6	5		8	10	
26	Feb 4	Leicester City	2-6	Watson 2	23987	2	11		4	7		9					3		1	6	5		8	10	
27	11	LIVERPOOL	1-0	Watson	17141	2	11			7	5	9					3		1	6	4		8	10	
28	18	SUNDERLAND	3-5	Smith 3	23955	2	11	9		7							3	5	1	6	4		8	10	
29	25	BURNLEY	1-0	Weddle	19666	2	11			7							3	5	1	6	4		8	10	9
30	Mar 3	CARDIFF CITY	3-0	Watson, Weddle, Smith	25157	2	11			7							3	5	1	6	4		8	10	9
31	10	Everton	0-0		29803	2	11			7							3	5	1	6	4		8	10	9
32	17	MANCHESTER UNITED	1-0	Weddle	25400	2	11			7				10			3	5	1	6	4		8		9
33	19	Tottenham Hotspur	3-0	Smith 2, Weddle	12829	2	11			7				10			3	5	1	6	4		8		9
34	28	Arsenal	2-0	Weddle, Smith	15416	2	11			7							3	5	1	6	4		8	10	9
35	31	BOLTON WANDERERS	1-0	Weddle	21846	2	11			7							3	5	1	6	4		8	10	9
36	Apr 7	Birmingham	0-2		32996	2	11			7				10			3	5	1	6	4		8		9
37	9	SHEFFIELD UNITED	4-1	Weddle 2, Cook, Irvine	28023	2	11			7				10			3	5	1	6	4		8		9
38	14	MIDDLESBROUGH	4-1	Smith 2, Weddle, Forward	23897	2	11			7							3	5	1	6	4		8	10	9
39	21	Sheffield Wednesday	0-2		14536	2	11			7							3	5	1	6	4		8	10	9
40	24	Blackburn Rovers	0-6		35516	2	11			7				10			3	5	1	6	4		8		9
41	28	NEWCASTLE UNITED	0-1		28364	2	11			7				10			3	5	1	6	4		8		9
42	May 5	Huddersfield Town	1-4	Cook	11206	2	11			7				10			3	5	1	6	4		8		9
					Apps	42	41	7	24	42	21	26	4	7	1	19	42	15	41	41	21	1	18	35	14
					Goals		10	2	1	5	1	11		1		5							11	10	9

F.A. Cup

						Clifford G	Cook FC	Davey HH	Davies R	Forward FJ	Foxall H	Haines WWP	Haslam G	Irvine RW	Jarvie J	Mackie J	McColgan J	McIlwaine J	McPhail D	Moffatt WJ	Nichol JB	Rutherford SE	Smith JW	Watson D	Weddle JR
R3	Jan 14	WEST HAM UNITED	0-2		27692	2	11	9	4	7	5	8					3		1	6				10	

Preston North End

4th in Division Two

						Cameron K	Carr AG	Chandler SE	Crawford R	Hamilton HH	Hamilton T	Harrison G	James AW	Kendall JW	Metcalfe JA	Morris D	Moss F	Nisbet G	Parry J	Pilkington W	Reid AM	Roberts WT	Robson N	Russell WF	Smith AC	Wade WA	Ward F
1	Aug 27	Fulham	2-2	Roberts, Harrison	25655		1		6		3	11	10		4	5					7	9		8		2	
2	29	HULL CITY	4-2	Harrison 3, Morris	21811		1		6		3	11	10		4	5					7	9		8		2	
3	Sep 3	BARNSLEY	1-2	Morris	20431		1		6		3	11	10		4	5					7	9		8		2	
4	5	Hull City	0-0		8915		1		6		3	11	10		4	5						9		8	7	2	
5	10	Wolverhampton Wan.	3-2	Robson 2, Harrison	17124		1		6		3	11	10		4	5				7		9	8			2	
6	17	PORT VALE	4-0	Oakes (og), Harrison, Roberts 2	18129		1		6		3	11	10		4	5					7	9	8			2	
7	24	South Shields	3-2	Roberts 2, James	6338		1		6		3	11	10		4	5					7	9	8			2	
8	Oct 1	LEEDS UNITED	5-1	James 2, Harrison, Russell, Reid	16966		1		6		3	11	10		4	5					7	9		8		2	
9	8	Nottingham Forest	1-3	Crawford	17056		1		6		3	11	10		4	5					7	9		8		2	
10	15	MANCHESTER CITY	1-0	Reid	30590		1		6		3	11	10		4	5					7	9		8		2	
11	22	Clapton Orient	1-1	James	10533				6		3	11	10	1	4	5					7		9	8		2	
12	29	CHELSEA	0-3		23107				6		3	11	10	1	4	5					7		9	8		2	
13	Nov 5	Blackpool	1-4	Reid	10789		1		6		3	11	10		4	5					7	9		8		2	
14	12	WEST BROMWICH ALB.	3-3	Roberts, Reid, James	15827	8	1		6		3	11	10			5					7	9				2	4
15	19	Bristol City	3-1	Reid, Harison, Roberts	9932		1	8	6		3	11	10			5					7	9				2	4
16	26	NOTTS COUNTY	4-0	Roberts 3, Harrison	16041		1	8	6		3	11	10			5					7	9				2	4
17	Dec 3	Southampton	0-0		10383		1	8	6		3	11	10			5					7	9				2	4
18	10	STOKE CITY	2-0	Morris, Reid	15405		1	8	6		3	11	10			5					7	9				2	4
19	17	Oldham Athletic	0-0		18366		1	8	6		3	11	10			5					7	9				2	4
20	24	GRIMSBY TOWN	3-0	Harrison, James, Roberts	12706		1	8	6		3	11	10			5					7	9				2	4
21	26	SWANSEA TOWN	4-2	Roberts, James 2, Reid	26206		1	8	6		3	11	10			5					7	9				2	4
22	27	Swansea Town	1-0	Reid	15264		1	8	6		3	11	10			5					7		9			2	4
23	31	FULHAM	1-0	James	14816		1		6		3	11	10			5					7	9		8		2	4
24	Jan 7	Barnsley	1-2	Reid	7967		1	8	6		3	11	10			5					7	9				2	4
25	21	WOLVERHAMPTON W.	5-4	Robson 3, James 2	14162		1		6		3	11	10		4	5		8			7		9			2	
26	Feb 4	SOUTH SHIELDS	7-2	* see below	10507		1		6		3	11	10			5		8			7		9			2	4
27	6	Port Vale	0-2		9492		1		6		3	11	10			5		8			7		9			2	4
28	11	Leeds United	4-2	Russell, Reid, Robson 2	24216		1	4		2	3	11	10			5					7		9	8			6
29	25	Manchester City	2-2	James, Russell	59500		1	4	6		3	11	10			5					7		9	8			2
30	Mar 3	CLAPTON ORIENT	0-0		18886			4	6		3	11	10			5	1				7		9	8			2
31	5	NOTTM. FOREST	5-0	Reid, Morris, Harrison 2 (1p), Robson	10036			4	6		3	11	10			5	1				7		9	8			2
32	10	Chelsea	1-2	James	49980			4	6		3	11	10			5	1						9	8	7		2
33	17	BLACKPOOL	2-1	Roberts, James	22341			4	6		3	11	10			5	1					9		8	7		2
34	24	West Bromwich Albion	4-2	James, Harrison (p), Robson 2	24067			4	6		3	11	10			5	1						9	8	7		2
35	31	BRISTOL CITY	5-1	Robson 2, Cameron, Russell 2	14744	10		4	6		3	11				5	1						9	8	7		2
36	Apr 6	READING	4-0	Robson 2, James, Russell	24292			4	6		3	11	10			5	1						9	8	7		2
37	7	Notts County	2-6	James, Robson	16226			4	6		3	11	10			5	1						9	8	7		2
38	9	Reading	1-2	Russell	16661				6	2	3	11	10			5	1						9	8	7		4
39	14	SOUTHAMPTON	1-2	Russell	13069				6	2	3	11	10		4	5	1				7		9	8			
40	21	Stoke City	2-3	Parry, Russell	11403	10			6	2	3				4	5	1		11		7	9		8			
41	28	OLDHAM ATHLETIC	1-1	Robson	8215				6	2	3	11				5	1				7	9	10	8			4
42	May 5	Grimsby Town	6-4	Cameron 3, Robson, Harrison, Reid	8747	8			6	2	3	11				5	1				7	9	10				4
					Apps	4	27	19	41	6	42	41	38	2	16	42	13	3	1	1	33	25	22	25	8	27	26
					Goals	4			1			15	18			4		1	1		13	13	19	9			

Scorers in game 26: Hampson (og), Harrison, Nisbet, Robson 2, Reid, James

Two own goals

F.A. Cup

						Cameron K	Carr AG	Chandler SE	Crawford R	Hamilton HH	Hamilton T	Harrison G	James AW	Kendall JW	Metcalfe JA	Morris D	Moss F	Nisbet G	Parry J	Pilkington W	Reid AM	Roberts WT	Robson N	Russell WF	Smith AC	Wade WA	Ward F
R3	Jan 14	Everton	0-3		37788		1		6		3	11	10			5					7	9		8		2	4

Queen's Park Rangers

10th in Division Three (South)

	Date		Opponent	Score	Scorers	Att	Beats E	Burns JC	Collier JC	Coward WC	Crompton N	Cunningham J	Duthie JF	Eggleton JAE	Gilhooley M	Goddard G	Hawley FW	Johnson JH	Kellard T	Lofthouse J	Mustard J	Neil A	Paterson J	Pierce W	Roberts J	Rounce GA	Stephenson J	Swan J	Sweetman SC	Turner W	Woodward JH	Young J
1	Aug	27	NEWPORT COUNTY	4-2	Goddard 2 (1p), Lofthouse, Swan	15489			4			1			5	9				11		8					7	10	2	6		3
2	Sep	1	GILLINGHAM	3-3	Goddard 2, Lofthouse	9241			4			1			5	9				11		8					7	10	2	6		3
3		3	Swindon Town	2-0	Swan, Johnson	9659			4			1			5			9		11		8		3			7	10	2	6		
4		7	Gillingham	2-1	Johnson, Neil	5499			4			1			5			9		11		8		3			7	10	2	6		
5		10	BRENTFORD	2-3	Lofthouse 2	18826			4			1				9	5			11		8		3			7	10	2	6		
6		17	WATFORD	2-1	Swan, Goddard	13950			4			1				9	5			11		8		3			7	10	2	6		
7		21	Bournemouth	2-1	Lofthouse, Goddard	4440			4			1				9	5			11		8		3			7	10	2	6		
8		24	Charlton Athletic	0-1		12823			4			1					5	9		11		8		3			7	10	2	6		
9	Oct	1	BRISTOL ROVERS	4-2	Goddard 3, Collier	8448			4			1				9	5			11		8		3			7	10	2	6		
10		8	Plymouth Argyle	0-3		12343			4			1				9	5			11		8					7	10	2	6		3
11		15	MERTHYR TOWN	0-0		11406			4			1				9	5			11	7	8		3				10	2	6		
12		22	Crystal Palace	1-1	Lofthouse	7115			4			1	10	5		9				11	7	8		3					2	6		
13		29	MILLWALL	0-1		16960			4			1	10	5		9				11	7	8		3					2	6		
14	Nov	5	Luton Town	1-0	Goddard	7695			4			1		5		9		10			7		8	3	11				2	6		
15		12	EXETER CITY	0-1		8291			4			1		5		9					7	10	8	3	11				2	6		
16		19	Torquay United	0-1		2235			4			1	10	5		9				11		8					7		2	6		3
17	Dec	3	Northampton Town	0-1		9737						1	4	5		9		10		11	7	8		2						6		3
18		17	Brighton & Hove Albion	3-1	Goddard 2, Lofthouse	5835						1	4	5		9				11	8	10		2			7			6		3
19		24	BOURNEMOUTH	2-0	Goddard, Mustard	6260						1	4	5		9				11	8	10		2			7			6		3
20		27	Coventry City	0-0		8975						1	4	5		9				11	8	10		2			7			6		3
21	Jan	7	SWINDON TOWN	0-1		9981						1	4	5		9				11	8	10		2			7			6		3
22		14	SOUTHEND UNITED	3-2	Burns, Mustard, Young (p)	7294		8				1		5		9		10		11	7	4		2						6		3
23		21	Brentford	3-0	Goddard 2, Burns	10430		8				1		5		9		10		11	7	4		2						6		3
24		28	Watford	3-3	Lofthouse 2, Goddard	5597		8				1		5		9		10		11	7	4		2						6		3
25	Feb	4	CHARLTON ATHLETIC	3-3	Goddard 2, Burns	10830		8				1		5		9		10		11	7	4		2						6		3
26		11	Bristol Rovers	4-0	Goddard 2, Johnson, Lofthouse	6862		8				1		5		9		10		11	7	4		2						6		3
27		18	PLYMOUTH ARGYLE	0-1		17377		8				1		5		9		10		11	7	4		2						6		3
28		25	Merthyr Town	4-0	Goddard 3, Rounce	2869						1		5		9				11	7	4		2		8		10		6		3
29	Mar	3	CRYSTAL PALACE	2-0	Swan, Goddard	16468								5		9				11	7	4		2		8		10		6	1	3
30		10	Millwall	1-6	Beats	18689	9	8						5						11	7	4		2				10		6	1	3
31		17	LUTON TOWN	3-2	Johnson, Burns, Lofthouse	11217		8					6	5				9		11		4		2		10	7				1	3
32		24	Exeter City	0-4		5657		8						5		9				11		4		2		10	7			6	1	3
33		31	TORQUAY UNITED	2-3	Coward, Rounce	5839		8		7		1			5	9				11		4		2		10				6		3
34	Apr	6	Newport County	6-1	*See below	5918		8		7		1			5	9				11		4		2		10				6		3
35		7	Southend United	0-7		8126		8		7		1			5	9				11		4		2		10				6		3
36		9	WALSALL	1-1	Young (p)	8082		8		7		1			5	9				11		4		2		10				6		3
37		10	Walsall	2-2	Lofthouse, Rounce	6419		8		7		1			5	9				11		4		2		10				6		3
38		14	NORTHAMPTON T	0-4		8399		8		7		1		5		9		10				4		2	11					6		3
39		21	Norwich City	1-3	Johnson	4867						1	6	5				9			8	4		2	11	10	7					3
40		26	COVENTRY CITY	1-5	Rounce	4095				7		1	6	5				9		11	8	4		2		10						3
41		28	BRIGHTON & HOVE ALB	5-0	Johnson 2, Rounce, Lofthouse, Young (p)	5394		8						5				9		11	7	4		2		10				6	1	3
42	May	3	NORWICH CITY	0-0		4691					5			6				9	10	11	7	4		2		8					1	3
						Apps	1	16	16	7	1	36	11	26	9	33	7	17	1	38	23	41	2	38	4	13	18	14	16	38	6	30
						Goals	1	5	1	2						26		7		13	2	1				6		4				4

Scorers in game 34: Goddard 2, Burns, Young (p), Coward, Rounce.

F.A. Cup

	Date		Opponent	Score	Scorers	Att	Beats E	Burns JC	Collier JC	Coward WC	Crompton N	Cunningham J	Duthie JF	Eggleton JAE	Gilhooley M	Goddard G	Hawley FW	Johnson JH	Kellard T	Lofthouse J	Mustard J	Neil A	Paterson J	Pierce W	Roberts J	Rounce GA	Stephenson J	Swan J	Sweetman SC	Turner W	Woodward JH	Young J
R1	Nov	30	ALDERSHOT	1-2	Johnson	4709			4			1		5		9		10		11	7	8							2	6		3

After game on Nov 26 abandoned in the second half with QPR leading 1-0

Reading

18th in Division Two

	Date	Opponent	Score	Scorers	Att.	Baggett WJ	Batten HG	Braithwaite E	Davey HH	Dennington LA	Duckworth JC	Eggo RM	Evans DG	Evans S	Girvan H	Goodwin HB	Inglis W	Johnstone W	Knox W	Lindsay T	McConnell WH	McDonald M	Messer AT	Nimmo J	Richardson F	Robson JC
1	Aug 27	CHELSEA	1-2	Davey	24529		8		9		1	2	6	7	3		4						5		10	11
2	30	Grimsby Town	3-3	Batten, Davey 2	13431		10		9		1	2	6	7	3		4						5		8	11
3	Sep 3	Clapton Orient	0-3		18593		10		9		1	2	6	7	3		4						5		8	11
4	10	WEST BROMWICH ALB.	1-4	Davey	16238			8	9		1	2	6	7			4	10			3		5			11
5	14	GRIMSBY TOWN	2-2	Davey 2	6295			8	9		1	2	6	7			4	10			3		5			11
6	17	Bristol City	1-4	Davey	22480			8	9	4	1	2	6	7				10			3		5			11
7	24	STOKE CITY	1-1	Richardson	12522		10				1	2	6				4	8			3	7	5		9	11
8	Oct 1	Southampton	0-0		7010						1	2	6	7			4	9			3	8	5		10	11
9	8	NOTTS COUNTY	2-2	Johnstone 2	11978		6				1	2		7			4	9			3	8	5		10	11
10	15	Oldham Athletic	2-3	McDonald 2	14377		6	8	9		1	2					4	10			3	7	5			11
11	22	NOTTM. FOREST	0-2		7785	10	8				1	2	6		3		4	9				7	5			11
12	29	Manchester City	1-4	Robson	33717		8	9			1	2	6				4	10			3	7	5			11
13	Nov 5	HULL CITY	3-0	Johnstone, Braithwaite, Davey	9935		8	9			1	2	6				4	10			3	7	5			11
14	12	Leeds United	2-6	Davey 2	17257			9			1	2	6				4	10	7		3		5		8	11
15	19	SOUTH SHIELDS	5-1	Robson 2, Davey 3	6141			9			1	2	6				4	10	7		3		5		8	11
16	26	Barnsley	0-2		7181			9			1	2	6				4	10	7		3		5		8	11
17	Dec 3	WOLVERHAMPTON W.	2-1	Richardson 2	9550		8				1	2	6			7	4	9			3		5		10	11
18	10	Port Vale	0-3		8556		8				1		6		2	7	4	9			3		5		10	11
19	17	FULHAM	2-1	Lindsay, McDonald	8472						1	2	6			7	4	9		11	3	8	5		10	
20	24	Swansea Town	1-0	Lindsay	9030						1	2	6			7	4	9		11	3	8	5		10	
21	26	Blackpool	1-3	Goodwin	13233						1	2	6			7	4	9		11	3	8	5		10	
22	27	BLACKPOOL	1-0	McDonald	11841		10				1	2	6			7	4	9		11	3	8	5			
23	31	Chelsea	0-0		26525		10				1	2	6			7	4			11	3	8	5		9	
24	Jan 7	CLAPTON ORIENT	4-0	Richardson 2, Lindsay, Batten	10533		10				1	2	6			7	4			11	3	8	5		9	
25	21	West Bromwich Albion	3-5	McDonald, Richardson 2	16104		10				1	2	6			7	4			11	3	8	5		9	
26	Feb 4	Stoke City	1-4	D Evans	11609		10				1	2	6		3	7	4	9		11		8	5			
27	11	SOUTHAMPTON	0-0		11428						1	2				7	4	9			3	8	5	6	10	11
28	15	BRISTOL CITY	3-2	Johnstone 2, Goodwin	6287						1	2				7	4	9			3	8	5	6	10	11
29	18	Notts County	1-1	Richardson	8034						1	2			3	7	4	9				8	5	6	10	11
30	25	OLDHAM ATHLETIC	1-0	Richardson	12806	8					1	2				7	4	9			3		5	6	10	11
31	Mar 10	MANCHESTER CITY	1-1	Johnstone	13313	8					1	2	6			7	4	9			3		5		10	11
32	17	Hull City	1-0	Baggett	6493	8					1	2	6			7	4	10			3		5		9	11
33	24	LEEDS UNITED	0-1		13098	8					1	2	6			7	4	10			3		5		9	11
34	29	Nottingham Forest	3-5	Robson 2, Baggett	2572	8		10			1	2	6			7	4				3		5		9	11
35	31	South Shields	0-0		3301	8		10			1	2	6			7	4				3	9	5			11
36	Apr 6	Preston North End	0-4		24292	8					1	2	6			7	4	9		11	3	10	5			
37	7	BARNSLEY	1-1	Richardson	10659	8		10			1	2	6			7	4			11	3		5		9	
38	9	PRESTON NORTH END	2-1	Johnstone, Robson	16661	8					1	2	6		3	7	4	9					5		10	11
39	14	Wolverhampton Wan.	1-2	Richardson	10357	8					1	2		11	3	7	4	9					5	6	10	
40	21	PORT VALE	0-0		7664	8					1	2		11	3	7	4					10	5	6	9	
41	28	Fulham	0-1		18918	8					1	2		11	3	7	4					10	5	6	9	
42	May 5	SWANSEA TOWN	0-0		7771	8		10			1	2	6		3		4		7	11			5		9	
					Apps	14	16	13	7	1	42	41	33	11	12	25	41	30	4	11	31	22	42	7	31	28
					Goals	2	2	1	13				1			2		7		3		5			11	6

F.A. Cup

	Date	Opponent	Score	Scorers	Att.	Baggett WJ	Batten HG	Braithwaite E	Davey HH	Dennington LA	Duckworth JC	Eggo RM	Evans DG	Evans S	Girvan H	Goodwin HB	Inglis W	Johnstone W	Knox W	Lindsay T	McConnell WH	McDonald M	Messer AT	Nimmo J	Richardson F	Robson JC
R3	Jan 14	GRIMSBY TOWN	4-1	Richardson 2, Batten, McDonald	19007		10				1	2	6			7	4			11	3	8	5		9	
R4	28	LEICESTER CITY	0-1		27243		10				1	2	6			7	4			11	3	8	5		9	

Rochdale

13th in Division Three (North)

	Date	Opponent	Score	Scorers	Att	Barber J	Bertram W	Braidwood E	Brown WJ	Christie AG	Clennell J	Halkyard C	Hall J	Holroyd E	Hopkins AD	Hughes R	Martin H	Miles U	Mittell JL	Moody JH	Murray AF	Parkes D	Plane E	Schofield R	Stephenson J	Tompkinson WV	Ward F	Webster W	Whitehurst AJ	Wood WC
1	Aug 27	Barrow	3-1	Bertram, Barber, Whitehurst	7783	10	8	4	2	6						11				1		5				7	3		9	
2	30	STOCKPORT COUNTY	2-1	Bertram, Hughes	10253	10	8	4	2	6						11				1		5				7	3		9	
3	Sep 3	NELSON	1-0	Whitehurst	9869	10	8	4	2	6						11				1		5				7	3		9	
4	10	Wigan Borough	2-1	Bertram, Whitehurst	5275	10	8	4	2	6							11			1		5				7	3		9	
5	17	Rotherham United	1-3	Whitehurst	4911		8	4	2	6			10				11			1		5				7	3		9	
6	24	SOUTHPORT	5-1	*See below	6264		8	4	2	6			10			11				1		5				7	3		9	
7	Oct 1	Durham City	2-3	Tompkinson, Gurkin (og)	2354		8	4	2	6			10			11				1		5				7	3		9	
8	8	WREXHAM	3-0	Tompkinson 2, Whitehurst	7493		8	4	2	6			10			11				1		5				7	3		9	
9	15	Chesterfield	3-1	Hughes, Whitehurst 2	5439		8	4	2	6			10			11				1		5				7	3		9	
10	22	LINCOLN CITY	0-3		5229	9	8	4	2	6			10			11				1		5				7	3			
11	29	Hartlepools United	2-0	Parkes, Hughes	4086		8	4	2	6	10					11				1		5				7	3		9	
12	Nov 12	New Brighton	1-2	Bertram	4409	6	8	4	2		10					11				1		5				7	3		9	
13	19	BRADFORD CITY	3-3	Russell (og), Tompkinson, Whitehurst	5952	6	8	4			10				2		11			1		5				7	3		9	
14	Dec 3	CREWE ALEXANDRA	4-0	Whitehurst 2, Tompkinson, Martin	3991	6		4			8		10		2		11			1		5				7	3		9	
15	17	DARLINGTON	4-1	Whitehurst 2, Tompkinson, Hughes	3912	6	8	5		4	10				2	11				1						7	3		9	
16	24	Doncaster Rovers	2-5	Whitehurst, Bertram	5291	6	8	5		4	10				2	11				1		3				7			9	
17	27	Bradford Park Avenue	1-4	Bertram	21762	6	8	5		4	10	3			2	11				1						7			9	
18	31	BARROW	3-0	Tompkinson 2, Clennell	3973	6	8	5		4	10				3	11				1					2	7			9	
19	Jan 2	Stockport County	1-5	Tompkinson	10571	6	8	5		4	10				3	11				1					2	7			9	
20	3	BRADFORD PARK AVE.	0-4		5481	6	8	5	3	4	10						11						1		2	7			9	
21	7	Nelson	3-6	Whitehurst 2, Clennell	2539	6	8	5		4	10				3	11							1		2	7			9	
22	14	Ashington	1-5	Whirehurst	1223	6	8			4	10					11						5			2	7	3		9	1
23	21	WIGAN BOROUGH	3-0	Bertram, Whitehurst 2	3626	6	8			4	10					11			1			5			2	7	3		9	
24	Feb 4	Southport	1-3	Tompkinson	2731	6	8			4							11		1			5		10	2	7	3		9	
25	11	DURHAM CITY	1-0	Bertram	1458	6	8			4							11		1			5		10	2	7	3		9	
26	18	Wrexham	1-2	Whitehurst	4157		10			4		6	8				11		1		2	5				7	3		9	
27	25	CHESTERFIELD	5-1	Whitehurst 4, Bertram	2602		8			4		6	10				11		1		2	5				7	3		9	
28	28	ROTHERHAM UNITED	2-1	Whitehurst, Hall	1885		8	4				6	10				11		1		2	5				7	3		9	
29	Mar 3	Lincoln City	1-3	Whitehurst	5760		8	4				6	10				11	7	1			5			2		3		9	
30	10	HARTLEPOOLS UNITED	0-1		2582		8			4		6	10				11	7	1			5			2		3		9	
31	17	Accrington Stanley	0-1		3885	10	8					6	4			11		7	1			5			2		3		9	
32	24	NEW BRIGHTON	0-0		2404	6	8	4								11			1			5			2	7	3	10	9	
33	31	Bradford City	2-2	Miles, Hughes	10565	6		4								11		9	1			5			2	7	3	10	8	
34	Apr 6	Tranmere Rovers	0-3		10053	6	8	4								11			1			5			2	7	3	10	9	
35	7	ASHINGTON	2-2	Bertram, Whitehurst	3309	6	8	5		4							11	9	1						2	7	3		10	
36	9	TRANMERE ROVERS	1-2	Whitehurst	3069		8			4			6			11			1			5		10	2	7	3		9	
37	10	Halifax Town	1-1	Whitehurst	3595	5	8			4			6				11	7	1						2	10	3		9	
38	14	Crewe Alexandra	1-1	Miles	2887		8			4			6				11	7	1		5				2	10	3		9	
39	21	HALIFAX TOWN	2-2	Murray, Whitehurst	2099	5	8			4			6			11			1		3				2	7		10	9	
40	28	Darlington	0-1		2708	5	8		2	4			6			11			1						3	7		10	9	
41	May 1	ACCRINGTON STANLEY	3-2	Whitehurst 2, Bertram	1443	5	8		2	4			6	11		7			1						3			10	9	
42	5	DONCASTER ROVERS	1-0	Webster	1768	5	8		2	4			6				11								3	7		10	9	
					Apps	29	40	27	16	33	13	7	20	1	8	26	16	7	19	19	5	29	2	3	22	38	32	7	41	1
					Goals	1	13				2		1			5	1	2			1	2				11		1	32	

Scorers in game 6: Whitehurst, Parkes, Bertram 2, Tompkinson

Played in game 42: A Monks (1).

Two own goals

F.A. Cup

	Date	Opponent	Score	Scorers	Att	Barber J	Bertram W	Braidwood E	Brown WJ	Christie AG	Clennell J	Halkyard C	Hall J	Holroyd E	Hopkins AD	Hughes R	Martin H	Miles U	Mittell JL	Moody JH	Murray AF	Parkes D	Plane E	Schofield R	Stephenson J	Tompkinson WV	Ward F	Webster W	Whitehurst AJ	Wood WC
R1	Nov 26	CROOK TOWN	8-2	Whitehurst 4, Clennell 3, Martin	4139	6		4			8		10		2		11			1		5				7	3		9	
R2	Dec 10	Darlington	1-2	Bertram	7571	6	8	4	3		10				2		11			1		5				7			9	

Rotherham United

14th in Division Three (North)

	Date		Opponent	Score	Scorers	Att	Atter J	Bailey H	Best J	Chilton C	Clayton J	Davies A	Dransfield E	Hall T	Hemingway CF	Higginbottom E	Jackson R	Lievesley EF	Mountney CT	Parkin A	Phillips WM	Reed E	Saville W	Scott JW	Sellars W	Snee JE	Taylor A	Turner J	Webb GJH
1	Aug	27	Stockport County	0-2		11546	1	4		9	8				10	6	2				7	5		11				3	
2		29	TRANMERE ROVERS	2-1	Clayton, Scott	4200	1	4		9	8				10	6	2				7	5		11				3	
3	Sep	3	BARROW	3-0	Bailey, Chilton, Phillips	4227	1	4		9	8				10	6	2				7	5		11				3	
4		10	Nelson	1-6	Scott	4881	1	4		9	8				10	6	2				7	5		11				3	
5		17	ROCHDALE	3-1	Scott 2, Parkin	4911	1	6			8				10		2			9	7	5	4	11				3	
6		24	Doncaster Rovers	0-2		7764	1	6			8				10		2			9	7	5	4	11				3	
7	Oct	1	Southport	1-1	Scott	2977	1	6		9	8						2	10				5	4	11			7	3	
8		8	DURHAM CITY	1-1	Scott	4520	1	6			8				9		2	10				5	4	11			7	3	
9		15	Wrexham	2-3	Clayton, Phillips	7139	1	6			8				9		2	10			7	5		11		4		3	
10		22	HARTLEPOOLS UNITED	5-0	Clayton 3, Phillips, Scott	2395	1	6			8					9	2	10			7	5		11		4		3	
11		29	Accrington Stanley	1-3	Scott	4930	1	6			8					9	2	10			7	5		11		4		3	
12	Nov	5	WIGAN BOROUGH	6-0	Hall 4, Hemingway, Lievesley	3819	1	6			8			9	7	3	2	10				5		11		4			
13		12	Lincoln City	1-4	Lievesley	5819	1	6			8			9	7	3	2	10				5		11		4			
14		19	NEW BRIGHTON	0-0		4135	1			6	8			9			2	10			7	5		11		4		3	
15	Dec	3	HALIFAX TOWN	0-0		4965	1				8			9			2	10	5	7		6		11		4		3	
16		17	ASHINGTON	1-1	Scott	4420	1	6			8		2	9				10			7	5		11		4		3	
17		24	Darlington	1-4	Lievesley	3409	1	6			8		2	9				10			7	5		11		4		3	
18		26	CHESTERFIELD	1-2	Hall	6748	1	6			8		2	9				10			7	5		11		4		3	
19		27	Chesterfield	5-2	Phillips, Scott, Lievesley 2, Hall	5227	1	6			8		2	9				10			7	5		11		4		3	
20		31	STOCKPORT COUNTY	0-1		3625	1	6			8		2	9				10				5		11	7	4		3	
21	Jan	2	Tranmere Rovers	0-2		5576	1	6			8		2	9	10							5		11	7	4		3	
22		7	Barrow	1-1	Hemingway	2804	1	6			8				9		2	10				5		11	7	4		3	
23		21	NELSON	4-3	Higginbottom, Clayton, Scott, Lievesley	4505	1	6			8					9	2	10				5		11	7	4		3	
24	Feb	4	DONCASTER ROVERS	2-1	Bailey, Clayton	11530	1	6			8				9		2	10				5		11	7	4		3	
25		8	Crewe Alexandra	2-3	Hemingway, Scott	2169	1	6			8				9		2	10				5		11	7	4		3	
26		11	SOUTHPORT	1-1	Higginbottom	4155	1	6			8					9	2	10				5		11	7	4		3	
27		18	Durham City	4-1	Scott 2, Parkin, Lievesley	2037		6	1		8						2	10		9		5		11	7	4		3	
28		25	WREXHAM	0-1		5665		6	1		8				10	11	2			9		5			7	4		3	
29		28	Rochdale	1-2	Scott	1885		6	1		8						2			9	10	5		11	7	4		3	
30	Mar	3	Hartlepools United	3-1	Scott, Parkin 2	4190	1	6		4	10						2			9		5		11	7	8		3	
31		10	ACCRINGTON STANLEY	2-1	Chilton, Scott	3763	1	6		8	10						2			9		5		11	7	4		3	
32		14	Bradford City	1-3	Scott	3821	1	6		8	10						2	10				5		11	7	4		3	
33		17	Wigan Borough	0-0		3281	1	6			8				11		2	10		9		5			7	4		3	
34		24	LINCOLN CITY	2-4	Clayton, Lievesley	4339	1	6		4	8			9			2	10				5			7			3	11
35		31	New Brighton	1-1	Lievesley	3240	1	6			8			9			2	10				5			7	4		3	11
36	Apr	7	CREWE ALEXANDRA	2-0	Phillips, Lievesley	3625	1	6			8			9	11		2	10			7	5				4		3	
37		9	BRADFORD PARK AVE.	1-0	Clayton	6288	1	6			8			9	11		2	10			7	5				4		3	
38		10	Bradford Park Avenue	1-3	Phillips	14311	1	6			8			9	11		2	10			7	5				4		3	
39		14	Halifax Town	0-0		3171	1	6			8		2		11		9	10			7	5				4		3	
40		21	BRADFORD CITY	0-0		2775	1	6			8	10			11		2	9				5			7	4		3	
41		28	Ashington	0-6		1464	1	6			8	10			11		2		5	9					7	4		3	
42	May	5	DARLINGTON	3-1	Hemingway, Parkin, Sellars	2058	1	6			8	10		4	11		2			9		5			7			3	
						Apps	39	40	3	10	42	3	7	16	23	11	36	29	2	11	19	41	4	31	19	32	2	40	2
						Goals		2		2	9			6	4	2		10		5	6			18	1				

F.A. Cup

	Date		Opponent	Score	Scorers	Att	Atter J	Bailey H	Best J	Chilton C	Clayton J	Davies A	Dransfield E	Hall T	Hemingway CF	Higginbottom E	Jackson R	Lievesley EF	Mountney CT	Parkin A	Phillips WM	Reed E	Saville W	Scott JW	Sellars W	Snee JE	Taylor A	Turner J	Webb GJH
R1	Nov	26	Spennymoor United	1-1	Scott	4776	1				8			9		6	2	10			7	5		11		4		3	
R1	Dec	1	SPENNYMOOR UNITED	4-2	Lievesley 2, Phillips, Hall	5045	1	6			8			9			2	10			7	5		11		4		3	
rep		10	Bradford City	3-2	Phillips, Clayton, Lievesley	9503	1	6			8		2	9				10			7	5		11		4		3	
R3	Jan	14	EXETER CITY	3-3	Scott 2, Hemingway	15425	1	6			8				9		2	10				5		11	7	4		3	
rep		18	Exeter City	1-3	Hall	11805	1	6			8			9			2	10				5		11	7	4		3	

Sheffield United

13th in Division One

	Date	Opponent	Score	Scorers	Att	Alderson JT	Birks L	Blair JG	Boyle TW	Cawthorne H	Chandler A	Dunne J	Gillespie W	Green GH	Johnson H	Johnson M	King S	Matthews V	Mercer AS	Mercer DW	Mordue T	Partridge AE	Phillipson TW	Pickering J	Sampy T	Shankly J	Stevenson AB	Tunstall FE	Turnbull G	Webster WG
1	Aug 27	LIVERPOOL	1-1	Johnson	21667	1	3			4	2		10	6	9		5		8	7								11		
2	29	Leicester City	1-3	Johnson	27117		3			4	2		10	6	9		5		8			7						11	1	
3	Sep 3	Arsenal	1-6	Partridge	30910	1	3			4	2		10	6	9		5				8	7						11		
4	5	LEICESTER CITY	1-1	Johnson	13096	1	3						10	6	9		5		8			7			4			11		2
5	10	BURNLEY	5-2	Johnson 3, Tunstall 2	17479	1	3						10	6	9		5		8	7					4			11		2
6	17	Bury	0-1		14732	1	3				2		10	6	9		5		8	7					4			11		
7	24	SHEFFIELD WEDNESDAY	1-1	Tunstall	42512	1	3		8		2		10	6	9		5					7			4			11		
8	Oct 1	ASTON VILLA	0-3		12327	1	3				2		10	6	9		5		8			7			4		11			
9	8	Sunderland	1-0	Johnson	18854	1	3				2	9		6	8	10		5		7					4			11		
10	15	DERBY COUNTY	1-0	Dunne	24862	1	3				2	9		6	8	10		5		7					4			11		
11	22	Newcastle United	0-1		12376	1	3				2	8		6	9	10		5		7					4			11		
12	29	BIRMINGHAM	3-1	Tunstall 2 (1p), Johnson	17128	1	3				2	8		6	9	10		5		7					4			11		
13	Nov 5	Middlesbrough	0-3		22061	1	3				2	8		6		10		5		7				9	4			11		
14	12	HUDDERSFIELD T	1-7	Tunstall	22163	1	3					8		6	9	10		5		7					4			11		2
15	19	Tottenham Hotspur	2-2	Gillespie, Partridge	19147	1	3			4	2		10	6	9			5	8			7						11		
16	26	CARDIFF CITY	3-4	Blair, Partridge, Tunstall (p)	22999	1	3	8		4	2		10	6	9			5				7						11		
17	Dec 3	Everton	0-0		36141	1	3	8		4	2	9	10	6				5				7						11		
18	10	MANCHESTER UNITED	2-1	Partridge, Tunstall	11984	1	3	8		4	2			6				5			10	7				9		11		
19	17	Blackburn Rovers	0-1		12588	1	3	8		4	2			6				5			10	7				9		11		
20	24	BOLTON WANDERERS	4-3	Gillespie, Blair, Tunstall, Johnson	10503	1	3	8			2		10	6	9			5				7			4			11		
21	26	WEST HAM UNITED	6-2	Tunstall, Johnson 5	23591	1	3	8			2		10	6	9			5				7			4			11		
22	27	West Ham United	1-1	Johnson	20434	1	3				2	8	10	6	9			5				7			4			11		
23	31	Liverpool	1-2	Blair	13797	1	3	8			2		10	6	9			5				7			4			11		
24	Jan 2	PORTSMOUTH	3-1	Tunstall, Johnson 2	23182	1	3	8			2		10	6	9			5				7			4			11		
25	7	ARSENAL	6-4	Johnson 4, Partridge, Gillespie	18158	1	3	8			2		10	6	9			5				7			4			11		
26	21	Burnley	3-5	Blair, Johnson, Partridge	12716	1	3	8			2		10	6	9			5				7			4			11		
27	Feb 4	Sheffield Wednesday	3-3	Blair 2, Partridge	41646	1		8			2		10	6	9		3	5				7			4			11		
28	11	Aston Villa	0-1		27231	1	3	8			2		10	6	9			5				7			4			11		
29	25	Derby County	1-2	Tunstall (p)	14257	1	3	8			2		10	6	9			5				7			4			11		
30	Mar 10	Birmingham	1-4	Partridge	22860	1	3	8			2		10	6				5				7			4	9		11		
31	12	BURY	3-1	Tunstall, Partridge 2	6712	1	3	8			2		10	6	9			5				7			4			11		
32	17	MIDDLESBROUGH	4-1	Gillespie, Johnson, Tunstall, Phillipson	26328	1	3				2		10	6	9			5				7	8		4			11		
33	31	TOTTENHAM HOTSPUR	3-1	Johnson 2, Phillipson	17495	1	3						10	6	9		2	5				7	8		4			11		
34	Apr 7	Cardiff City	2-2	Johnson 2	11283	1	3				2		10	6	9			5		7			8		4			11		
35	9	Portsmouth	1-4	Johnson	28023	1	3	8					10	6	9		2	5				7			4		11			
36	14	EVERTON	1-3	Gillespie	26252	1	3						10	6	9			5				7	8		4			11		2
37	16	SUNDERLAND	5-1	Johnson 2, Matthews, Tunstall 2	8545	1	3				2		10	6	9			5				7	8		4			11		
38	21	Manchester United	3-2	Tunstall 2, Partridge	27137	1	3				2		10	6	9			5				7	8		4			11		
39	23	NEWCASTLE UNITED	1-1	Johnson	16895	1	3						10	6	9		2	5				7	8		4			11		
40	28	BLACKBURN ROVERS	2-3	Johnson, Phillipson	25239	1	3						10	6	9		2	5				7	8		4			11		
41	30	Huddersfield Town	1-0	Johnson	22380	1	3	8					10	6	7			5					9		4			11		2
42	May 5	Bolton Wanderers	1-1	Tunstall (p)	7958	1	3	6					10	2				5				7	9	8	4			11		
					Apps	41	41	18	1	8	32	8	34	42	36	6	13	34	7	10	3	31	10	2	34	3	2	40	1	5
					Goals			6				1	5		33			1				11	3					19		

F.A. Cup

	Date	Opponent	Score	Scorers	Att	Alderson JT	Birks L	Blair JG	Boyle TW	Cawthorne H	Chandler A	Dunne J	Gillespie W	Green GH	Johnson H	Johnson M	King S	Matthews V	Mercer AS	Mercer DW	Mordue T	Partridge AE	Phillipson TW	Pickering J	Sampy T	Shankly J	Stevenson AB	Tunstall FE	Turnbull G	Webster WG
R3	Jan 14	Notts County	3-2	Johnson 2, Tunstall	28232	1	3	8			2		10	6	9			5				7			4			11		
R4	28	WOLVERHAMPTON WAND.	3-1	Johnson 2, Partridge	34120	1	3	8			2		10	6	9			5				7			4			11		
R5	Feb 18	Sheffield Wednesday	1-1	Partridge	57076	1	3	8			2		10	6	9			5				7			4			11		
rep	22	SHEFFIELD WEDNESDAY	4-1	Partridge, Johnson 3	59447	1	3	8			2		10	6	9			5				7			4			11		
R6	Mar 3	NOTTM FOREST	3-0	Dexter (og), Johnson, Gillespie	52640	1	3	8			2		10	6	9			5				7			4			11		
SF	24	Huddersfield Town	2-2	Johnson 2	69260	1	3	8			2		10	6	9			5				7			4			11		
rep	26	Huddersfield Town	0-0	(aet)	53749	1	3	8			2		10	6	9			5				7			4			11		
rep2	Apr 2	Huddersfield Town	0-1		69360	1	3	8					10	6	9		2	5				7			4			11		

SF at Old Trafford, replay at Maine Road, replay 2 at Goodison Park

Sheffield Wednesday

14th in Division One

	Date		Opponent	Score	Scorers	Att	Allen JWA	Blenkinsop E	Brown JH	Burridge BJH	Felton W	Froggatt F	Harper EC	Hill H	Hodgkiss T	Hooper M	Kean FW	Kirkwood D	Leach TJ	Marsden W	Marson F	Mellors RD	Powell S	Prince A	Rimmer EJ	Seed JM	Smith N	Strange AH	Trotter JW	Walker T	Wilkinson J	Williams DR	Wilson C
1	Aug	27	Everton	0-4		39485		3	1		2						5		4	6						8		10	9		11	7	
2		29	MANCHESTER UNITED	0-2		17944		3	1	6	2						5		4							8		10	9		11	7	
3	Sep	3	CARDIFF CITY	3-3	Allen, Hooper, Trotter	19218	10	3		4	2	5				7				6	11	1				8			9				
4		7	Manchester United	1-1	Trotter	18759		3		4	2	5		10		7				6	11	1				8			9				
5		10	Blackburn Rovers	1-3	Allen	17877	10	3		4	2			8		7			5	6	11	1							9				
6		17	BOLTON WANDERERS	3-0	Trotter 2, Marsden	19111	10	3		4	2					7	5			6	11	1						8	9				
7		24	Sheffield United	1-1	Trotter	42512	10	3		4	2					7	5			6	11	1						8	9				
8	Oct	1	Middlesbrough	3-3	Hooper 2, Allen	22230	10	3		4	2					7	5			6	11	1						8	9				
9		8	BIRMINGHAM	2-3	Allen, Trotter	19974	10	3		4	2					7	5			6	11	1				8			9				
10		15	Newcastle United	3-4	Allen, Hooper, Harris (og)	29886	10	3		6	2					7	5		4			1				8			9		11		
11		22	ARSENAL	1-1	Hooper	12698	10	3		6	2					7	5		4			1				8			9		11		
12		29	Burnley	1-3	Hooper	16366		3	1	4	2					7	5			6						10		8	9		11		
13	Nov	5	BURY	4-0	Hill, Seed, Trotter, Wilkinson	16808		3	1	4				8		7	5			6						10			9	2	11		
14		12	Liverpool	2-5	Kean, Wilkinson	24253		3	1	4				8		7	5			6						10			9	2	11		
15		19	LEICESTER CITY	1-2	Trotter	15969		3	1	4				8		7	5			6						10			9	2	11		
16		26	Derby County	6-4	Harper 3, Hill, Wilkinson, Collin (og)	16067		3	1				9	8		7	5		4	6						10				2	11		
17	Dec	3	WEST HAM UNITED	2-0	Harper, Hooper	22796		3	1				9	8		7	5		4	6						10				2	11		
18		10	Portsmouth	0-0		19258		3	1				9	8		7	5		4	6						10				2	11		
19		17	SUNDERLAND	0-0		19755		3	1				9	8		7	5			6						10	4			2	11		
20		24	Aston Villa	4-5	Hooper 2, Harper, Seed	12345		3	1				9	8		7	5		4							10	6			2	11		
21		26	Huddersfield Town	0-1		21336		3	1				9	8		7	5		4							10	6			2	11		
22		27	HUDDERSFIELD T	0-5		41824			1		3		9	8		7			5							6	4	10		2	11		
23		31	EVERTON	1-2	Marsden	18354		3	1							7	5		4	8							6	10	9	2	11		
24	Jan	7	Cardiff City	1-1	Seed	9208		3	1					8		7	5			6						10	4		9	2	11		
25		21	BLACKBURN ROVERS	4-1	Harper 2, Hill, Hooper	36094		3	1				9	8		7	5			6						10	4			2	11		
26	Feb	4	SHEFFIELD UNITED	3-3	Wilkinson 2, Harper	41646		3	1				9			7	5			6						10	4		8	2	11		
27		11	MIDDLESBROUGH	2-3	Hooper 2	15631		3	1				9			7	5	8		6						10	4			2	11		
28		25	NEWCASTLE UNITED	0-0		25462		3	1	6			9			7	5								11	10	4			2			8
29		29	Bolton Wanderers	0-2		9786		3	1	6			9			7	5								11	8	4			2			10
30	Mar	7	Birmingham	0-1		12076		3	1	6						7			5				9		11	8	4			2			10
31		10	BURNLEY	5-0	Rimmer 2, Wilson 2, Trotter	12401			1	6					2	7			5						11	8	4		9	3			10
32		17	Bury	2-4	Hooper, Trotter	14185			1						2	7	4		5						11	8	6		9	3			10
33		24	LIVERPOOL	4-0	Hooper, Rimmer, Seed, Trotter	12255	10	3	1							7	4		5	6					11	8			9	2			
34		31	Leicester City	2-2	Prince, Trotter	18634	10	3	1										5	6				7	11	8	4		9	2			
35	Apr	6	Tottenham Hotspur	3-1	Hooper 2, Seed	26432	10	3	1							7			5	6					11	8	4		9	2			
36		7	DERBY COUNTY	2-2	Seed, Trotter	28566		3	1							7			5	6					11	8	4	10	9	2			
37		10	TOTTENHAM HOTSPUR	4-2	Hooper 3, Seed	15900	10	3	1							7	4		5						11	8		6	9	2			
38		14	West Ham United	2-1	Allen 2	14580	10	3	1							7			5						11	8	4	6	9	2			
39		21	PORTSMOUTH	2-0	Allen, Trotter	14536	10	3	1							7			5						11	8	4	6	9	2			
40		28	Sunderland	3-2	Hooper 2, Trotter	19339	10	3	1							7			5	6					11	8		4	9	2			
41	May	2	Arsenal	1-1	Seed	15818	10	3	1							7			5	6					11	8		4	9	2			
42		5	ASTON VILLA	2-0	Allen, Trotter	36636	10	3	1							7			5	6					11	8		4	9	2			
						Apps	17	39	33	18	13	2	12	14	2	39	28	1	25	28	7	9	1	1	15	37	19	15	30	30	20	2	5
						Goals	9						8	3		21	1			2				1	3	8			16		5		2

Two own goals

F.A. Cup

	Date		Opponent	Score	Scorers	Att	Allen JWA	Blenkinsop E	Brown JH	Burridge BJH	Felton W	Froggatt F	Harper EC	Hill H	Hodgkiss T	Hooper M	Kean FW	Kirkwood D	Leach TJ	Marsden W	Marson F	Mellors RD	Powell S	Prince A	Rimmer EJ	Seed JM	Smith N	Strange AH	Trotter JW	Walker T	Wilkinson J	Williams DR	Wilson C
R3	Jan	14	BOURNEMOUTH	3-0	Harper 2, Seed	26797		3	1				9	8		7	5			6						10	4			2	11		
R4		28	Swindon Town	2-1	Harper, Seed	17474		3	1				9	8		7	5			6						10	4			2	11		
R5	Feb	18	SHEFFIELD UNITED	1-1	Wilkinson	57076		3	1				9			7	5			6						10	4	8		2	11		
rep		22	Sheffield United	1-4	Hooper	59447		3	1				9			7	5			6						10	4	8		2	11		

South Shields

Bottom of Division Two: Relegated

	Date	Opponent	Score	Scorers	Att	Atkinson F	Brown RR	Conaty T	Cook C	Davies J	Dunn GA	Gibson TD	Grenyer A	Hampson W	Hardy JJ	Henderson SJ	Hunter C	Hutchinson D	Loftus JL	Matthewson TJ	Maycock R	Neilson A	Oxberry J	Parker R	Phizacklea JR	Ramage A	Scott G	Shevlin P	Smith JW	Smith WH	Stevenson J	Taylor A	Turnbull RA	Wilkinson TW	Wilson H
1	Aug 27	LEEDS UNITED	1-5	Ramage	9826					6								4		7			10		3	9	11	1	8		5				2
2	Sep 3	Nottingham Forest	2-7	Scott, Oxberry	16714	2				4		9	6							7			10		3		11	1	8						5
3	5	Wolverhampton Wan.	1-2	J Smith	10971					4		9	6							7			10		3		11	1	8	2					5
4	10	MANCHESTER CITY	0-1		7623					4		9	6	2						7			10		3		11	1	8						5
5	12	WOLVERHAMPTON W.	2-2	J Smith, Oxberry	4873					4			6	3					10	7			9				11	1	8	2	5				
6	17	Hull City	0-1		10252					4			6	3					10	7			9				11	1	8	2					5
7	24	PRESTON NORTH END	2-3	Loftus, Oxberry	6338					4			6						10	7			9		3		11	1		2	8				5
8	Oct 1	Swansea Town	3-6	Oxberry 3	3697					6		8							10	7			9		3		11	1	4	2					5
9	8	FULHAM	2-1	J Smith, Mathewson	6253					4				3		6			10	7			9				11	1	8	2					5
10	15	Barnsley	0-0		10611											6			10	7			9		3		11	1	8	2	5				4
11	22	Oldham Athletic	2-2	Oxberry 2	10723											6			10	7			9		3		11	1	8	2	5				4
12	29	NOTTS COUNTY	2-3	Oxberry 2	6379											6			10	7			9		3		11	1	8	2	5				4
13	Nov 5	Southampton	5-3	* see below	9787								6		5	4				7			9		3		11	1	8	2	10				
14	12	GRIMSBY TOWN	1-2	Stevenson	6430								6			4				7			9		3		11	1	8	2	10				5
15	19	Reading	1-5	Oxberry	6141								6		5					7			9	10	3			1	8	2				11	4
16	26	CLAPTON ORIENT	2-2	Oxberry, Loftus	5771								6		5				8	7			9	10	3					2		1		11	4
17	Dec 3	Chelsea	0-6		28719										6		5		10	7				9	3			1	8	2				11	4
18	10	BLACKPOOL	2-2	Oxberry, Parker	5130									2	6		5			7			9	10	3		11		8			1			4
19	17	West Bromwich Albion	0-3		11711						3		6	2	5					7			9	10			11		8			1			4
20	24	BRISTOL CITY	1-3	J Smith	4232						3		6	2	5					7			9	10			11		8			1			4
21	27	Stoke City	1-3	J Smith	13990			4					6	3	5								10	9			11		8	7		1			2
22	31	Leeds United	0-3		12952									2	5	4		6				11	8			9				7	10	1			3
23	Jan 2	STOKE CITY	2-3	Wilson, Oxberry	6480										5	4		6				11	8		3	9				7	10	1			2
24	7	NOTTM. FOREST	3-4	Stevenson, Oxberry, Loftus	4723										5	4		6	10				9		3		11			7	8	1			2
25	21	Manchester City	0-3		29200					6				2		4	5		10	7			9				11				8	1			3
26	Feb 4	Preston North End	2-7	Scott, Oxberry	10507			5		6				2		4			10	7			9				11		8			1			3
27	11	SWANSEA TOWN	3-1	Oxberry 3	3572					6				2		4	5		10	7			9				11		8			1			3
28	18	Fulham	0-2		15626					6				2		4	5		10	7			9				11		8			1			3
29	22	HULL CITY	1-0	Cook	4322				9	6				2			5		10	7			8		3		11					1			4
30	25	BARNSLEY	0-0		5513				9	6			4	2			5		8	7			10				11					1			3
31	Mar 3	OLDHAM ATHLETIC	0-3		6186				9	6				2			5		10	7					3		11				8	1			4
32	10	Notts County	1-4	Stevenson	8117			5	9	6				2					10	7					3		11	1			8				4
33	17	SOUTHAMPTON	2-1	Loftus, Parker	2650					6				2			5		10			11		9	3			1		7	8				4
34	24	Grimsby Town	1-4	Stevenson	7868		4			6				2			5		10	7				9	3		11	1			8				
35	31	READING	0-0		3301					6				2			5			7	9			10	3		11	1			8				4
36	Apr 6	Port Vale	3-2	Maycock, Loftus 2	11081					6				2			5		10	7	9			8	3		11	1							4
37	7	Clapton Orient	2-2	Wilson, Matthewson	11019					6				2			5		10	7	9			8	3		11	1							4
38	9	PORT VALE	0-1		4444					6				2			5		10	7	9			8	3		11	1							4
39	14	CHELSEA	2-1	Grenyer, Matthewson	3395					4			6	2			5			7	9	11		10	3			1			8				
40	21	Blackpool	1-4	Maycock	8539					4			6	2			5		10	7	9			11				1			8		3		
41	28	WEST BROMWICH ALB.	2-3	Stevenson, Scott	5514					4	2		6				5			7	9			10	3		11	1			8				
42	May 5	Bristol City	1-1	Stevenson	5607					4			6				5			7	9			10	3		11	1			8				2
					Apps	1	1	3	4	27	3	4	18	25	11	13	18	4	25	37	8	4	29	17	29	3	34	27	22	19	21	15	1	3	36
					Goals				1				1			1			6	3	2		21	2		1	4		6		6				2

Scorers in game 13: Henderson, Oxberry 2, Scott, J Smith

F.A. Cup

	Date	Opponent	Score	Att	Atkinson F	Brown RR	Conaty T	Cook C	Davies J	Dunn GA	Gibson TD	Grenyer A	Hampson W	Hardy JJ	Henderson SJ	Hunter C	Hutchinson D	Loftus JL	Matthewson TJ	Maycock R	Neilson A	Oxberry J	Parker R	Phizacklea JR	Ramage A	Scott G	Shevlin P	Smith JW	Smith WH	Stevenson J	Taylor A	Turnbull RA	Wilkinson TW	Wilson H
R3	Jan 14	Middlesbrough	0-3	25682					6				2		4	5		10	7			9				11				8	1			3

Southampton

17th in Division Two

	Date	Opponent	Score	Scorers	Att.	Adams W	Allen T	Bradford JA	Bullock J	Coundon C	Cribb SR	Ellison JW	Harkus GC	Henderson WJ	Hough E	Keeping AME	Luckett W	Mackie J	Mitton J	Murphy W	Petrie C	Rawlings WE	Robinson E	Rowley RWM	Shelley FA	Swinden JF	Taylor SJT	Taylor T	Thompson GH	Woodhouse S
1	Aug 27	STOKE CITY	3-6	Rawlings 2, S Taylor	12107	3	1						5	7	2					11		9		8	4		10			6
2	29	Clapton Orient	0-2		13711		1	3					5	7	2					11		9		8	4		10			6
3	Sep 3	Leeds United	0-2		19479		1	3			11		5	7	2				6		10	9		8	4					
4	5	CLAPTON ORIENT	1-3	Petrie	7982		1	3			11		5	7	2				6		10	9		8	4					
5	10	Notts County	0-0		9673			3		7	11		5		2				6		10	9		8	4				1	
6	17	OLDHAM ATHLETIC	5-2	Rawlings 2, S Taylor 2, Murphy	10360			3		7			5		2					11		9		8	4		10		1	6
7	24	Grimsby Town	2-2	S Taylor 2	11298			3		7			5		2					11		9			4		10	8	1	6
8	Oct 1	READING	0-0		7010			3		7			5		2				6	11		9			4		10	8	1	
9	8	Blackpool	0-1		11875			3		7			5		2				6	11		9		8	4		10		1	
10	15	CHELSEA	2-4	Petrie 2	14724			3		7			5		2				6	11	10	9		8	4				1	
11	22	WOLVERHAMPTON W.	4-1	Rowley 2, Rawlings 2	5794			5		7			4		2	3				11		9		8			10		1	6
12	29	Port Vale	0-4		10679			5		7			4		2	3				11		9		8			10		1	6
13	Nov 5	SOUTH SHIELDS	3-5	Rawlings 2, S Taylor	9787		1	5					4		2	3				11	8	9		7			10			6
14	12	Barnsley	1-0	Rowley	7621		1	5		7			4		2	3				11		9		8			10			6
15	19	FULHAM	5-2	Rawlings 2, Bradford, Rowley, Murphy	4619		1	5		7			4		2	3				11		9		8			10			6
16	26	Hull City	0-1		8081		1	5		7			4		2	3				11		9		8			10			6
17	Dec 3	PRESTON NORTH END	0-0		10383		1	5		7			4		2	3				11		9		8			10			6
18	10	Swansea Town	0-2		10676		1	5		7			4		2	3				11	8	9					10			6
19	17	MANCHESTER CITY	1-1	S Taylor	10013		1	2		7			5			3				11	8	9			4		10			6
20	24	Nottingham Forest	1-1	Rawlings	5572		1	2					5	7		3				11	8	9			4		10			6
21	26	Bristol City	0-3		17702		1	3					5	7	2					11	8	9			4		10			6
22	27	BRISTOL CITY	3-2	Rawlings 2, Bullock	10132		1		9					7	2	3			5	11		8			4		10			6
23	31	Stoke City	1-2	Dixon (og)	6399		1		9				5	7		3				11		8	2		4		10			6
24	Jan 7	LEEDS UNITED	1-4	Murphy	13966		1	5	9				4	7	2	3				11		8					10			6
25	21	NOTTS COUNTY	5-1	Luckett 2, Rawlings 2, Bullock	10002		1	2	9				5			3	7			11		8			4		10			6
26	31	Oldham Athletic	1-3	Bullock	6365		1	2	9				5			3	7			11		8			4		10			6
27	Feb 4	GRIMSBY TOWN	5-0	S Taylor 2, Rawlings, Bullock, Murphy	7180		1	2	9				5			3	7			11		8			4		10			6
28	11	Reading	0-0		11428		1		9				5	7	2	3				11		8			4		10			6
29	18	BLACKPOOL	2-0	Rawlings, Bullock	12229		1	2	9				5	7		3				11		8			4		10			6
30	25	Chelsea	2-0	Rawlings 2	46567		1	2	9				5	7		3				11		8			4		10			6
31	Mar 3	Wolverhampton Wan.	1-2	Rawlings	13363		1	2	9				5	7		3				11		8			4		10			6
32	10	PORT VALE	1-3	S Taylor	9874		1		9			2	5	7		3	11					8			4		10			6
33	17	South Shields	1-2	Bullock	2650		1	2	9	7	11		5			3		8							4		10			6
34	24	BARNSLEY	6-1	Mackie 3, Woodhouse, Petrie, Cribb	10528		1	2			11		5	7		3		8			10			9	4					6
35	31	Fulham	0-1		9316		1	2			11		5	7		3		8			10			9	4					6
36	Apr 7	HULL CITY	2-0	Mackie, Cribb	11955		1	2	9		11		5	7		3		8			10				4					6
37	9	WEST BROMWICH ALB.	3-2	Mackie, Bullock, Cribb	18000		1	3	9		11		5	7	2			8			10				4					6
38	10	West Bromwich Albion	1-2	Bullock	10500		1		9		11		5	7	2			8	4		10				3					6
39	14	Preston North End	2-1	Mackie, Petrie	13069		1	2	9				5	7	3		11	8			10				4					6
40	21	SWANSEA TOWN	0-2		8820			2	9				5	7		3				11				8	4		10		1	6
41	28	Manchester City	1-6	T Taylor	42361		1	2			11		5	7		3								9	4	8		10		6
42	May 5	NOTTM. FOREST	2-1	Rowley, T Taylor	8244			2					5	7		3	11							9	4	8		10	1	6
					Apps	1	32	36	17	15	10	1	41	23	25	28	6	7	8	29	15	32	1	20	33	2	30	4	10	36
					Goals			1	8		3						2	6		4	5	20		5			10	2		1

One own goal

F.A. Cup

	Date	Opponent	Score	Scorers	Att.	Adams W	Allen T	Bradford JA	Bullock J	Coundon C	Cribb SR	Ellison JW	Harkus GC	Henderson WJ	Hough E	Keeping AME	Luckett W	Mackie J	Mitton J	Murphy W	Petrie C	Rawlings WE	Robinson E	Rowley RWM	Shelley FA	Swinden JF	Taylor SJT	Taylor T	Thompson GH	Woodhouse S
R3	Jan 14	Cardiff City	1-2	Rawlings	23000		1	2	9				5			3	7			11		8			4		10			6

Southend United

7th in Division Three (South)

No	Date	Opponent	Score	Scorers	Att	Andrews JH	Bailey JH	Baron FJ	Bell TG	Boyce TD	Brophy TJ	Clenshaw LJ	Daykin HR	Dixon T	Donoven AE	Falconbridge GH	Fell JW	French JP	Frew J	Hick WM	Horne A	Jarvie J	Moore WR	Morris H	Plum SL	Purdy A	Robinson W	Rosier HL	Sayer SC	Wilson J	Woodward JH
1	Aug 27	LUTON TOWN	1-0	Hick	11186		8		3	1				4	10		11		5	9	7				6			2			
2	31	Bournemouth	3-2	Hick 2, Bailey	5874		8		3	1				4	10		11		5	9	7				6			2			
3	Sep 3	Millwall	1-5	Horne	15690		8		3	1				4	10		11		5	9	7				6			2			
4	7	BOURNEMOUTH	3-0	Hick 3	5631		8		3					4	10		11		5	9	7				6			2			1
5	10	CRYSTAL PALACE	6-1	Donoven 4, Hick, Horne	6808		8		3					4	10		11		5	9	7				6			2			1
6	17	Exeter City	2-3	Hick, Bailey	6309		8			1	3			4	10		11		5	9	7				6			2			
7	24	TORQUAY UNITED	1-0	Donoven	8546		8		3					4	10		11		5	9	7		1		6			2			
8	Oct 1	Norwich City	1-2	Horne	9079		8				3			4	10		11		5	9	7		1		6			2			
9	8	NORTHAMPTON T	2-0	Sayer, Horne	8768						3			4	10		11		5	9	7		1		6			2	8		
10	15	Coventry City	1-6	Hick	11059				3					4	10		11		5	9	7		1		6			2	8		
11	22	MERTHYR TOWN	2-1	Fell, Hick	3774				3		6			4		10	11		5	9	7		1					2	8		
12	29	Walsall	1-0	Hick	7897				3		6			4		10	11		5	9	7		1					2	8		
13	Nov 5	GILLINGHAM	1-2	Hick	6756				3		6			4		10	11		5	9	7		1					2	8		
14	12	Plymouth Argyle	2-3	Hick 2	10624				3		6					10	11		5	9	7		1	4				2	8		
15	19	BRISTOL ROVERS	2-1	Hick, Falconbridge	4421				3		6					10	11		5	9	7		1	4				2	8		
16	Dec 3	WATFORD	3-0	Donoven, Hick, Fell	5320				3					6	10	8	11			9	7		1	4			5	2			
17	24	Newport County	2-3	Bailey, Baron	3837		8	9	3					4	6	10	11		5		7		1					2			
18	26	BRENTFORD	3-2	Horne, Baron, Fell	3540		8	9	3					4	6	10	11				7		1				5	2			
19	31	Luton Town	0-0		5402		8		3					4	6	10	11		5	9	7		1					2			
20	Jan 7	MILLWALL	0-1		9767		8		3		4				6	10	11		5	9	7		1					2			
21	14	Queen's Park Rangers	2-3	Donoven, Hick	7294		8		3		4				6	10	11			9	7		1				5	2			
22	21	Crystal Palace	1-4	Horne	10606		8		3	1				4	6	10	11	2		9	7					5					
23	Feb 4	Torquay United	3-3	Hick 2, Bailey	3419	6	8		3							10	11			9	7		1	4		5		2			
24	11	NORWICH CITY	1-1	Horne	4671	6	8		3							10	11			9	7		1	4		5		2			
25	15	EXETER CITY	1-2	Horne	2603		8		3					6			11		5	9	7		1	4				2	10		
26	18	Northampton Town	1-2	Hick	13133		8							6			11	2	5	9	7		1	4				3	10		
27	25	COVENTRY CITY	3-2	Baron 2, Horne	5979		8	9	3					6		10	11		5		7		1	4				2			
28	Mar 3	Merthyr Town	3-2	Baron 2, Horne	2289			9	3	1				6	10		11		5		7			4				2	8		
29	10	WALSALL	2-1	Baron, Donoven	4736			9	3	1				6	10		11		5		7			4				2	8		
30	14	SWINDON TOWN	1-1	Dixon	3159			9	3					6	10	8	11		5		7	1		4				2			
31	17	Gillingham	0-1		6240	6		9					11	4	10			2	5			1		7				3	8		
32	24	PLYMOUTH ARGYLE	3-0	Baron 2, Morris	5187	6		9				11		4	10			2	5			1		7				3	8		
33	26	Charlton Athletic	2-1	Donoven, Morris	2210	6						11		4	10			2	5	9		1		7				3	8		
34	31	Bristol Rovers	3-1	Baron 2, Morris	4764	6		9				11		4	10			2	5			1		7				3	8		
35	Apr 6	Brighton & Hove Albion	0-1		11742	6		9				11		4	10			2	5			1		7				3	8		
36	7	QUEEN'S PARK RANGERS	7-0	Hick 3, Donoven, Morris, Dixon, Clenshaw	8126	6						11		4	10			2	5	9		1		7				3	8		
37	9	BRIGHTON & HOVE ALB	0-1		10407	6						11		4	10			2	5	9		1		7				3	8		
38	14	Watford	1-1	Hick	5048	6						11		4		10		2		9		1		7			5	3	8		
39	21	CHARLTON ATHLETIC	1-2	Donoven	4501	6		9				11		4	10			2	5			1		7				3	8		
40	23	Brentford	2-2	Clenshaw, Baron	4889			9				11		4	10				5	8		1		7				3	6	2	
41	28	Swindon Town	1-0	Andrews	4899	6	8					11		4	10					9		1		7				3	5	2	
42	May 5	NEWPORT COUNTY	5-1	Morris 2, Bailey, Clenshaw, Hick	4796	6	8					11		4	10					9		1		7				3	5	2	

	Andrews JH	Bailey JH	Baron FJ	Bell TG	Boyce TD	Brophy TJ	Clenshaw LJ	Daykin HR	Dixon T	Donoven AE	Falconbridge GH	Fell JW	French JP	Frew J	Hick WM	Horne A	Jarvie J	Moore WR	Morris H	Plum SL	Purdy A	Robinson W	Rosier HL	Sayer SC	Wilson J	Woodward JH
Apps	13	21	12	26	7	10	11	1	36	31	17	30	11	33	31	30	13	20	23	10	3	4	41	23	3	2
Goals	1	5	12				3		2	11	1	3			25	10			6					1		

F.A. Cup

Round	Date	Opponent	Score	Scorers	Att	Andrews JH	Bailey JH	Baron FJ	Bell TG	Boyce TD	Brophy TJ	Clenshaw LJ	Daykin HR	Dixon T	Donoven AE	Falconbridge GH	Fell JW	French JP	Frew J	Hick WM	Horne A	Jarvie J	Moore WR	Morris H	Plum SL	Purdy A	Robinson W	Rosier HL	Sayer SC	Wilson J	Woodward JH
R1	Nov 26	WELLINGTON TOWN	1-0	Hick	5000	6			3		2					10	11		5	9	7		1	4					8		
R2	Dec 10	Gillingham	0-2		10215				3					6	10	8	11		5	9	7		1	4				2			

Southport

8th in Division Three (North)

	Date	Opponent	Score	Scorers	Att	Banner HS	Beadles GH	Devine J	Foster I	Halsall W	Hamilton W	Hughes J	James AF	Jones GW	Jones RH	Laws JM	Lowe H	Marshall WH	Martin JC	Newnes J	Openshaw JE	Parsons J	Rimmer A	Robinson W	Saxton J	Shaw GR	Sinclair T	Tait T	Warburton W	Worrall JE
1	Aug 27	Tranmere Rovers	0-1		8495		9	3		1			10	7		11		8	5						4		6			2
2	30	BRADFORD PARK AVE.	2-1	Beadles, Sinclair	6457		9	3		1	8		10	7		11			5						4		6			2
3	Sep 3	STOCKPORT COUNTY	4-0	Worrall (p), Sinclair, Beadles, G Jones	6845		9	3		1	8		10	7		11			5						4		6			2
4	5	Bradford Park Avenue	3-5	Beadles, James 2	10429		9	3		1	8		10	7		11			5						4		6			2
5	10	Barrow	1-3	Parsons	6154			3		1	8		10	7		11			5			9			4		6			2
6	17	NELSON	1-2	Marshall	5406		9	3		1	7		10	11				8	5	4							6			2
7	24	Rochdale	1-5	Hamilton	6264			3		1	9		10	7		11		8	5						4		6			2
8	Oct 1	ROTHERHAM UNITED	1-1	Parsons	2977			3		1			10	7		11		8	5			9			4		6			2
9	8	Darlington	1-3	Beadles	4789		9	3		1	8			7		11		10	5						4		6			2
10	15	Durham City	0-0		2389		9	3		1	8			7		11		10	5						4		6			2
11	22	ACCRINGTON STANLEY	5-0	Marshall 2, Parsons, G Jones, Hamilton	2655			3		1	8			7		11		10	5			9			4		6			2
12	29	Wigan Borough	3-1	Marshall 2, Hamilton	4247			3		1	8			7		11		10	5						4		6	9		2
13	Nov 5	DONCASTER ROVERS	1-2	Worrall (p)	2840			3		1	8			7		11		10	5						4		6	9		2
14	12	Hartlepools United	1-2	Beadles	2429		8	3		1	4			7		11		10	5								6	9		2
15	19	LINCOLN CITY	3-1	Tait 2, Beadles	3113		8	3		1				7		11		10	5						4		6	9		2
16	Dec 3	BRADFORD CITY	5-1	Beadles 2, Marshall, Tait, Laws	3841		8	3		1				7		11		10	5						4		6	9		2
17	17	CREWE ALEXANDRA	3-2	Marshall 2, Beadles	3326		8			1	7					11	3	10	5						4		6	9		2
18	24	Ashington	3-1	Beadles, Tait 2	1703		8	3		1				7		11		10	5						4		6	9		2
19	26	WREXHAM	4-1	Laws 2, Beadles, Marshall	6705		8	3		1	7					11		10	5						4		6	9		2
20	27	Wrexham	0-3		6998		8	3		1	7					11		10	5			9			4		6			2
21	31	TRANMERE ROVERS	0-1		3899		8			1	7		10			11	3		5						4		6	9		2
22	Jan 7	Stockport County	3-6	Beadles, Tait, Worrall (p)	10384		8			1	7					11	3	10		5					4		6	9		2
23	21	BARROW	4-0	Laws, Tait, Marshall, Worrall (p)	3051		8	3		1	7					11		10	5						4		6	9		2
24	Feb 4	ROCHDALE	3-1	Devine, Marshall 2	2731	7	8	3		1						11		10	5						4		6	9		2
25	11	Rotherham United	1-1	Tait	4155	7	8	3		1						11		10	5						4		6	9		2
26	15	New Brighton	1-0	Tait	2871		8	3		1	7		10			11				5					4		6	9		2
27	18	DARLINGTON	2-0	Hamilton, Tait	4293		8	3		1	7					11		10	5						4		6	9		2
28	25	DURHAM CITY	3-1	Beadles, Hamilton, Marshall	3142		8	3		1	9					11		10	5						4	7	6			2
29	Mar 3	Accrington Stanley	1-4	Beadles	4593		8	3		1	9			7		11		10	5						4		6			2
30	10	WIGAN BOROUGH	2-1	Beadles, Marshall	3890		8	3	7	1		9				11		10	5						4		6			2
31	17	Doncaster Rovers	1-0	Beadles	6622		10	3		1	8	9		7		11			5						4		6			2
32	20	Nelson	1-1	Hughes	3583		10	3		1	8	9				11			5	4			7				6			2
33	24	HARTLEPOOLS UNITED	0-2		2518		10	3	7	1	8	9				11			5	4							6			2
34	26	Halifax Town	0-1		1792		10			1	8	9				11	3		5	4			7				6			2
35	31	Lincoln City	0-2		4427		10			1		9		7		11	3		5		8				4		6			2
36	Apr 6	CHESTERFIELD	2-1	Dennis (og), Beadles	4369	7	9			1			8			11	3		5					10			6		4	2
37	7	HALIFAX TOWN	3-1	Beadles 2, James	3524	7	9			1			8			11	3		5					10			6		4	2
38	9	Chesterfield	2-5	Hamilton 2	3515		8				7		10		1	11	3		5				9		4		6			2
39	14	Bradford City	0-2		9072		10	3			7	9	8		1	11				5					4		6			2
40	21	NEW BRIGHTON	4-2	Beadles, Hamilton, Robinson 2	2139		9	3		1	7		8			11			5					10	4		6			2
41	28	Crewe Alexandra	1-0	Beadles	2552		9	3		1	7	8	5			11								10	4		6			2
42	May 5	ASHINGTON	3-3	Laws, Beadles 2	1749		10	3		1	7	9	5			11							8		4		6			2
					Apps	4	36	34	2	40	31	9	17	20	2	41	8	24	37	7	1	4	4	4	35	1	42	15	2	42
					Goals		23	1			8	1	3	2		5		13	1			3		2			2	10		4

One own goal

F.A. Cup

	Date	Opponent	Score	Scorers	Att	Banner HS	Beadles GH	Devine J	Foster I	Halsall W	Hamilton W	Hughes J	James AF	Jones GW	Jones RH	Laws JM	Lowe H	Marshall WH	Martin JC	Newnes J	Openshaw JE	Parsons J	Rimmer A	Robinson W	Saxton J	Shaw GR	Sinclair T	Tait T	Warburton W	Worrall JE
R1	Nov 26	Denaby United	3-2	Tait 2, Marshall	5150		8	3		1				7		11		10	5						4		6	9		2
R2	Dec 10	Bradford Park Avenue	2-0	Marshall, Tait	9226		8	3		1						11		10	5						4	7	6	9		2
R3	Jan 14	FULHAM	3-0	Horler (og), Tait 2	8000		8	3		1	7					11		10	5						4		6	9		2
R4	Jan 28	MIDDLESBROUGH	0-3		11000		8	3		1	7					11		10	5						4		6	9		2

Stockport County

3rd in Division Three (North)

	Date	Opponent	Score	Scorers	Att	Boardman B	Bocking W	Bond S	Broome AH	Burgess G	Burgess H	Cawley E	Duffus JM	Fielding HL	Hayes WE	Helliwell E	Hooker E	James RW	Jobson JT	Johnston WG	Kay G	Kirby N	Malloy W	Newton F	Newton W	Odenrode H	Pearson AV	Ramsden CW	Scullion JP	Scurr TW	Smith J	Turner JA	Whitelaw J	Wilson W
1	Aug 27	ROTHERHAM UNITED	2-0	Johnstone, Smith	11546	7	2				9				1	6			5	8					4					11	10			3
2	30	Rochdale	1-2	H Burgess	10253	7	2				8				1	6			5						4				9	11	10			3
3	Sep 3	Southport	0-4		6845		2		8		9				1	6			5				7		4					11	10			3
4	10	DURHAM CITY	2-1	H Burgess, Fielding	8690	7	2			3	9			11	1	6				8	5				4						10			
5	17	Wrexham	0-1		7211		2							11	1	6		7	5	8					4				9		10			3
6	24	CHESTERFIELD	3-0	H Burgess (p), Helliwell 2	6252	8	2				9			11	1	6			5	10			7		4									3
7	Oct 1	Bradford Park Avenue	0-2		9838	8	2				9				1	6	4		5	10			7				11							3
8	8	TRANMERE ROVERS	1-0	Jobson	8283	8	2							11	1	6	4		5	10			7								9			3
9	15	Lincoln City	0-2		7468	8	2						9	11	1	6	4		5				7								10			3
10	22	HALIFAX TOWN	3-0	Boardman, Duffus, Smith	9291	8	2						9	11	1	6			5						4	7					10			3
11	29	Bradford City	2-2	Odenrode, Smith	13582	8	2						9	11	1	6			5						4	7					10			3
12	Nov 5	NEW BRIGHTON	0-0		6382	8	2						9	11	1	6			5						4	7					10			3
13	12	Crewe Alexandra	0-3		4185	8	2				9			11	1	6			5						4	7					10			3
14	19	ASHINGTON	3-0	Smith, Duffus, Jobson	6590	7	2				8		9		1				5						4		6			11	10			3
15	Dec 3	DONCASTER ROVERS	2-1	Smith (p), Duffus	9760	7	2				8		9		1		6		5						4					11	10			3
16	17	ACCRINGTON STANLEY	3-3	Smith 3	4020		2				8				1	6			5				7		4				10	11	9			3
17	24	Hartlepools United	1-2	Smith	2033	8	2									6			5				7		4		11		10		9	1		3
18	26	BARROW	4-0	Smith 3, H Burgess	8697		2				8					6			5				7		4		11		10		9	1		3
19	27	Barrow	3-2	Wilson, Scullion, H Burgess	6225		2				8					6			5				7		4		11		10		9	1		3
20	31	Rotherham United	1-0	Smith	3625	7	2				8					6			5						4		11		10		9	1		3
21	Jan 2	ROCHDALE	5-1	Smith 3, F Newton, Scullion	10571		2				8						6		5						4		11		10	7	9	1		3
22	7	SOUTHPORT	6-3	Smith 5, Ramsden	10384		2				8						6		5						4			7	11		9	1	10	3
23	14	Wigan Borough	3-1	Smith, Ramsden, Bocking (p)	3843		2				8						6		5						4			7	11		9	1	10	3
24	21	Durham City	2-1	Whitelaw, H Burgess	1781		2				8						6		5						4			7	11		9	1	10	3
25	28	LINCOLN CITY	2-0	Whitelaw, Scullion	7478		2				8						6		5						4			7	11		9	1	10	3
26	Feb 4	Chesterfield	1-1	Dennis (og)	4768		2				8						6		5						4			7	11		9	1	10	3
27	11	BRADFORD PARK AVE.	2-2	Smith 2	15775		2				8						6		5						4			7	11		9	1	10	3
28	18	Tranmere Rovers	2-5	Scullion, Whitelaw	8943		2				8						6				5				4			7	11		9	1	10	3
29	27	WREXHAM	5-0	Smith 4, Ramsden	4120		2				8								5						4		6	7	11		9	1	10	3
30	Mar 3	Halifax Town	3-1	H Burgess, Scullion, Smith	4770		2				8								5						4		6	7	11		9	1	10	3
31	10	BRADFORD CITY	3-0	Ramsden, Smith, H Burgess	9984		2				8								5						4		6	7		11	9	1	10	3
32	17	New Brighton	0-0		4876		2				8								5						4		6	7	11		9	1	10	3
33	24	CREWE ALEXANDRA	1-0	Smith	9766		2				8								5			11			4		6	7			9	1	10	3
34	31	Ashington	1-4	Ramsden	2053	11	2				8								5					10	4		6	7			9	1		3
35	Apr 6	NELSON	8-0	* see below	8430	10	2				8								5						4		6	7		11	9	1		3
36	7	WIGAN BOROUGH	1-1	Bocking (p)	8840	10	2				8			11					5						4		6	7			9	1		3
37	9	Nelson	4-0	H Burgess, Bocking (p), Smith 2	5441	10	2				8	4							5								6	7		11	9	1		3
38	14	Doncaster Rovers	2-0	Ramsden 2	5872	10	2				8	4							5								6	7		11	9	1		3
39	21	DARLINGTON	4-0	Pearson, Smith 2, H Burgess	6921	10	2				8	4							5								6	7		11	9	1		3
40	23	Darlington	1-3	Brooke (og)	1925	10	2	6			8								5						4			7		11	9	1		3
41	28	Accrington Stanley	0-1		5225	10	2				8								5						4		6	7		11	9	1		3
42	May 5	HARTLEPOOLS UNITED	2-2	H Burgess, Smith	4991	10	2				8								5						4		6	7		11	9	1		3
					Apps	24	42	1	1	1	35	3	6	10	16	18	12	1	40	6	2	1	9	1	36	4	20	21	18	15	40	26	12	41
					Goals	3	3				12		3	1		2			2	1					1	1	1	9	5	1	38		3	1

Scorers in game 35: Ramsden 2, Boardman 2, Scurr, Smith 2, H Burgess

Two own goals

F.A. Cup

	Date	Opponent	Score	Scorers	Att	Boardman B	Bocking W	Bond S	Broome AH	Burgess G	Burgess H	Cawley E	Duffus JM	Fielding HL	Hayes WE	Helliwell E	Hooker E	James RW	Jobson JT	Johnston WG	Kay G	Kirby N	Malloy W	Newton F	Newton W	Odenrode H	Pearson AV	Ramsden CW	Scullion JP	Scurr TW	Smith J	Turner JA	Whitelaw J	Wilson W
R1	Nov 26	OSWESTRY TOWN	5-2	Smith 2 (1p), Scurr, Pearson, Duffus	9368	7	2				8		9		1				5						4		6			11	10			3
R2	Dec 10	Crewe Alexandra	0-2		9064	7	2				8		9		1				5						4		6			11	10			3

Stoke City

5th in Division Two

No.	Date		Opponents	Result	Scorers	Att.	Archibald RF	Armitage L	Bussey W	Cull JE	Davies HA	Dixon RH	Eastwood CM	Eyres J	Godfrey T	Jackson W	Johnson RK	Lister R	McGrory R	Sellars H	Shirley JH	Spence W	Watson H	Williams JJ	Williams R	Williamson TR	Wilson C
1	Aug	27	Southampton	6-3	Williamson, Eyres, Wilson, Davies 2, Archibald	12107	11	4			8	1	6	10					2			3		7		5	9
2		31	West Bromwich Albion	4-2	Wilson 3, Armitage (p)	15453	11	4			8	1	6	10					2			3		7		5	9
3	Sep	3	NOTTS COUNTY	3-0	Archibald, Wilson 2	22236	11	4			8	1	6	10					2			3		7		5	9
4		5	WEST BROMWICH ALB.	1-1	Wilson	20614	11	4			8	1	6	10					2			3		7		5	9
5		10	Oldham Athletic	1-3	Wilson	22065	11	4			8	1	6	10					2			3		7		5	9
6		17	GRIMSBY TOWN	0-0		15216	11	4			8	1	6	10					2			3		7		5	9
7		24	Reading	1-1	Wilson	12522	11	4			8	1				6	10		2			3		7		5	9
8	Oct	1	BLACKPOOL	2-0	Davies 2	9293	11	4			8	1				6	10		2			3		7		5	9
9		8	Chelsea	0-1		41472	11				8	1				6	10		2	4		3		7		5	9
10		15	CLAPTON ORIENT	2-0	Wilson, Williams	15009	11	4			8	1					10		2	6		3		7		5	9
11		22	BARNSLEY	0-0		8323	11	4			8	1					10		2	6		3		7		5	9
12		29	Wolverhampton Wan.	2-1	Wilson 2	17247	11	4			8	1					10		2	6		3		7		5	9
13	Nov	5	PORT VALE	0-2		31493	11	4			8	1					10		2	6		3		7		5	9
14		12	Fulham	5-1	Shirley 2, Barrett (og), Davies, Wilson	10773		4		7	8	1						11	2	6	10	3				5	9
15		19	SWANSEA TOWN	1-1	Sellars	9938	11	4		7	8	1							2	6	10	3				5	9
16		26	Manchester City	0-4		36456	11	4			8	1							2	6	10	3		7		5	9
17	Dec	3	HULL CITY	3-1	Wilson, Armitage, Johnson	9638	11	7			8	1			4		10		2	6		3				5	9
18		10	Preston North End	0-2		15405	11	7			8	1			4		10		2	6		3				5	9
19		17	NOTTM. FOREST	1-3	Wallace (og)	9093	11	7	8			1	6		4		10		2			3				5	9
20		24	Leeds United	1-5	Williamson	12889	11	4			10	1							2	6		3	5	7		8	9
21		27	SOUTH SHIELDS	3-1	Sellars, Bussey 2	13990	11	4	8		10	1							2	6		3	5	7			9
22		31	SOUTHAMPTON	2-1	Wilson, Bussey	6399	11	4	8	7	10	1							2	6		3				5	9
23	Jan	2	South Shields	3-2	Cull, Archibald, Davies	6480	11	4	8	7	10	1							2	6		3				5	9
24		7	Notts County	2-1	Wilson 2	13365	11	4	8	7	10	1							2	6		3				5	9
25		21	OLDHAM ATHLETIC	3-0	Bussey 2, Wilson	13265	11		8	7	10	1			4				2	6		3				5	9
26	Feb	4	READING	4-1	Davies 2, Cull, Bussey	11609	11	4	8	7	10	1					9		2	6		3				5	
27		11	Blackpool	1-3	Wilson	8744	11	4	8	7	10	1							2	6		3				5	9
28		20	CHELSEA	1-0	Bussey	15770	11	4	8	7	10	1					9		2	6		3				5	
29		25	Clapton Orient	2-3	Campbell (og), Wilson	20084	11	4	8	7	10	1							2	6		3				5	9
30	Mar	6	Grimsby Town	2-1	Wilson, Sellars	8279	11				10				4	5	8		2	6		3		7	1		9
31		10	WOLVERHAMPTON W.	2-2	Wilson, Davies	13264	11			7	10	1			4		8		2	6		3				5	9
32		17	Port Vale	0-0		21071	11	4	8		10	1							2	6		3		7		5	9
33		19	Barnsley	1-3	Williams	4658	11	4	8		10	1							2	6		3		7		5	9
34		24	FULHAM	5-1	Armitage (p), Davies, Wilson 3	10120	11	4	8	7	10	1							2	6		3				5	9
35		31	Swansea Town	1-1	Armitage	10893	11	4	8	7	10	1							2	6		3				5	9
36	Apr	6	Bristol City	0-4		21503	11	4	8			1							2	6	10	3		7		5	9
37		7	MANCHESTER CITY	2-0	Archibald, Wilson	29455	11	4	8	7	10	1							2	6		3				5	9
38		9	BRISTOL CITY	1-0	Wilson	13765	11	4	8	7	10	1							2	6		3				5	9
39		14	Hull City	0-1		4848	11	4	8	7	10	1							2	6		3				5	9
40		21	PRESTON NORTH END	3-2	Wilson 2, Archibald	11403	11	4	8	7	10	1							2	6		3				5	9
41		28	Nottingham Forest	2-0	Wilson, Davies	5382	11	4	8	7	10	1							2	6		3				5	9
42	May	5	LEEDS UNITED	5-1	Wilson 2, Bussey, Archibald, Cull	12401	11	4	8	7	10	1							2	6		3				5	9
						Apps	41	38	21	19	40	41	7	6	6	4	14	1	42	33	4	42	2	20	1	40	40
						Goals	6	4	8	3	11			1			1			3	2			2		2	32

Three own goals

F.A. Cup

Rd	Date		Opponents	Result	Scorers	Att.	Archibald RF	Armitage L	Bussey W	Cull JE	Davies HA	Dixon RH	Eastwood CM	Eyres J	Godfrey T	Jackson W	Johnson RK	Lister R	McGrory R	Sellars H	Shirley JH	Spence W	Watson H	Williams JJ	Williams R	Williamson TR	Wilson C
R3	Jan	14	GILLINGHAM	6-1	Wilson 2, Williamson, Archibald, Bussey, Davies	14855	11		8	7	10	1			4				2	6		3				5	9
R4		28	BOLTON WANDERERS	4-2	Archibald, Davies, Wilson 2	23050	11	4	8	7	10	1							2	6		3				5	9
R5	Feb	18	Manchester City	1-0	Wilson	73668	11	4	8	7	10	1							2	6		3				5	9
R6	Mar	3	Arsenal	1-4	Wilson	41974	11	4	8	7	10	1							2	6		3				5	9

Sunderland

15th in Division One

	Date	Opponent	Score	Scorers	Att	Allan AMcI	Andrews A	Bartley J	Bell JC	Clunas WMcL	Cresswell F	Death WG	Dowsey J	Ellis WT	England EE	Gurney R	Halliday D	Hargreaves L	Henderson GB	Lilley T	Marshall RS	McGorian IM	McInroy A	Murray W	Oakley JE	Parker CW	Ramsay SH	Robinson GH	Thomson RW	Whelan W	Wilks A	Wood A	Wright D
1	Aug 27	PORTSMOUTH	3-3	Halliday, Marshall, Ellis	35106	5	6			4				11			9			3	8		1		2						7		10
2	Sep 1	West Ham United	4-2	Halliday 2, Marshall, Wright	19037	5	6			4							9	11			8		1	2					3		7		10
3	3	Leicester City	3-3	Halliday 2, Ellis	28977	5	6			4				11			9				8		1	2					3		7		10
4	7	BIRMINGHAM	4-2	Clunas, Halliday, Marshall, Wilks	23007	5				4				11			9				8		1	2	3					6	7		10
5	10	LIVERPOOL	2-1	Halliday, Hargreaves	29479	5	6			4							9	11			8		1	2	3						7		10
6	17	Arsenal	1-2	Halliday	45561	5	6		1	4							9	11			8			2	3						7		10
7	24	BURNLEY	2-3	Halliday, Wilks	22420	5			1	4							9	11			8			2	3					6	7		10
8	Oct 1	Bury	3-5	Halliday 3	10233	5	6			4				11			9				8		1	2	3						7		10
9	8	SHEFFIELD UNITED	0-1		18854	5	6			4				11			9				8		1	2	3						7		10
10	15	Aston Villa	2-4	Clunas, Wright	38116	5	6			4				11			9				8		1	2	3						7		10
11	22	Tottenham Hotspur	1-3	Ellis	19039		6							11	3		9					4	1	2		5					7	8	10
12	29	HUDDERSFIELD T	3-0	Cresswell, Ramsay, Wright	22070	5	6		1		10				3			11						2		4	8				7		9
13	Nov 5	Newcastle United	1-3	Marshall	44780	5	6		1						3		9	11			8			2		4					7		10
14	12	MANCHESTER UNITED	4-1	Halliday 3, Marshall	13319	5		6	1						3		9	11			8			2		4					7		10
15	19	Everton	1-0	Hargreaves	35993			6	1	4					3		9	11			8			2		5					7		10
16	26	BOLTON WANDERERS	1-1	Halliday	20406			6	1	4					3		9	11			8			2		5					7		10
17	Dec 3	Blackburn Rovers	0-0		16175	5		6	1		10				3		9	11			8			2		4					7		
18	10	CARDIFF CITY	0-2		16450			6	1		10	7			3		9	11	5		8			2		4							
19	17	Sheffield Wednesday	0-0		19755		6		1	4					3		9	11	5		8			2							7		10
20	24	MIDDLESBROUGH	1-0	Ramsay	23633		6			4					3		9	11	5				1	2			8				7		10
21	26	Birmingham	1-1	Ramsay	20120		6			4					3		9	11	5				1	2			8				7		10
22	Jan 2	WEST HAM UNITED	3-2	Halliday 2, Hargreaves	27542		6			4					3		9	11	5				1	2			8				7		10
23	7	LEICESTER CITY	2-2	Halliday, Ramsay	20770		6			4					3		9	11	5				1	2			8				7		10
24	21	Liverpool	5-2	* see below	28243		6			4							9	11	5		8		1	2			10		3		7		
25	Feb 4	Burnley	0-3		11442		6			4		11					9		5		8		1	2			10		3		7		
26	11	BURY	1-0	Clunas	13586			6		4			8				9	11	5				1	2					3		7	10	
27	18	Portsmouth	5-3	Halliday 4, Dowsey	23955			6		4			8				9	11	5				1	2					3		7		10
28	25	ASTON VILLA	2-3	Hargreaves 2	29444			6		4			8				9	11	5				1	2					3		7		10
29	Mar 10	Huddersfield Town	2-4	Halliday, Hargreaves	17497	5			1	4			8				9	11						2					3	6	7		10
30	14	ARSENAL	5-1	Gurney 3, Halliday, Wilks	9478					4						8	9	11					1	2		5			3	6	7		10
31	17	NEWCASTLE UNITED	1-1	Gurney	40071					4						8	9	11					1	2		5			3	6	7		10
32	28	TOTTENHAM HOTSPUR	0-0		9244					4						8	9	11					1	2		5			3	6	7		10
33	31	EVERTON	0-2		15407					4						8	9	11					1	2		5			3	6	7	10	
34	Apr 6	DERBY COUNTY	0-1		27431		6			4	10	11	8			9			5				1	2					3		7		
35	7	Bolton Wanderers	2-1	Halliday 2	18064		6			4	10	11	8				9		5				1	2					3		7		
36	9	Derby County	0-1		24226		6			4	10	11	8				9		5				1	2					3		7		
37	14	BLACKBURN ROVERS	1-0	Halliday	12577	5	6			4		11				8	9						1	2					3		7		10
38	16	Sheffield United	1-5	Wright	8545		6			4	11		8			10			5				1	2					3		7		9
39	21	Cardiff City	1-3	Hargreaves	10268	5	6					9	8					11				4	1	2					3		7		10
40	25	Manchester United	1-2	Halliday	9545	5	6			4		11				8	9						1	2					3		7		10
41	28	SHEFFIELD WEDNESDAY	2-3	Halliday 2	19339	5	6		1	8					3	10	9	11						2		4					7		
42	May 5	Middlesbrough	3-0	Death, Halliday, Wright	41997	5	6			4		11			3		9	10					1	2				7					8

Scorers in game 24: Hargreaves 2, Halliday, Marshall, Riley (og)

	Allan AMcI	Andrews A	Bartley J	Bell JC	Clunas WMcL	Cresswell F	Death WG	Dowsey J	Ellis WT	England EE	Gurney R	Halliday D	Hargreaves L	Henderson GB	Lilley T	Marshall RS	McGorian IM	McInroy A	Murray W	Oakley JE	Parker CW	Ramsay SH	Robinson GH	Thomson RW	Whelan W	Wilks A	Wood A	Wright D
Apps	20	27	8	12	35	7	9	9	7	15	9	38	28	15	1	19	2	30	41	8	13	7	1	19	7	40	3	32
Goals					3	1	1	1	2		4	33	9			6						4				3		5

One own goal

F.A. Cup

	Date	Opponent	Score	Scorers	Att	Allan AMcI	Andrews A	Bartley J	Bell JC	Clunas WMcL	Cresswell F	Death WG	Dowsey J	Ellis WT	England EE	Gurney R	Halliday D	Hargreaves L	Henderson GB	Lilley T	Marshall RS	McGorian IM	McInroy A	Murray W	Oakley JE	Parker CW	Ramsay SH	Robinson GH	Thomson RW	Whelan W	Wilks A	Wood A	Wright D
R3	Jan 14	NORTHAMPTON TOWN	3-3	Halliday, Hargreaves, Wright	25484		6			4					3		9	11	5		8		1						2		7		10
rep	19	Northampton Town	3-0	Halliday 2, Clunas	21148		6			4							9	11	5		8		1	2			10		3		7		
R4	28	Manchester City	1-2	Halliday	38658		6			4							9	11	5		8		1	2					3		7	10	

Swansea Town

6th in Division Two

	Date	Opponent	Res	Scorers	Att	Collins J	Deacon H	Ferguson FSB	Fowler J	Gunn K	Hanford H	Hiles WR	Hole WJ	Lewis WL	Lloyd CJ	McPherson L	Milne WE	Morley EB	Nicholas DS	Sampy WE	Sykes WJ	Thomas G	Thompson L	Williams BD	Woodward TG
1	Aug 27	Blackpool	2-2	Fowler 2	15771	4	8	1	9				7	10		6	3		11		5			2	
2	29	Manchester City	4-7	Lewis 2, Deacon, Hiles (p)	34316	4	8	1	9			11	7	10		6	3				5			2	
3	Sep 3	FULHAM	2-1	Lewis, Hole	14617	4	8	1					7	9		10	3		11		5			2	6
4	5	MANCHESTER CITY	5-3	McPherson 3 (1p), Lewis 2	17554	4	8	1					7	9		10	3		11		5			2	6
5	10	Barnsley	3-3	Lewis, Thomas, Nicholas	13643	4	8	1						9		10	3		11		5	7		2	6
6	17	WOLVERHAMPTON W.	6-0	McPherson 3 (1p), Fowler 3	16692	4		1	9				7	8		10	3		11		5			2	6
7	24	Port Vale	0-2		10197	4		1	9				7	8		10	3		11		5			2	6
8	Oct 1	SOUTH SHIELDS	6-3	McPherson, Lewis 3, Fowler 2	3697	4		1	9				7	8		10	3		11		5			2	6
9	8	Leeds United	0-5		18097	4		1	9				7	8		10	3		11		5			2	6
10	15	NOTTM. FOREST	2-0	Fowler, Deacon	14844	4	8	1	9				7	10		6		3	11		5			2	
11	22	West Bromwich Albion	2-5	Deacon, Lewis	15245	4	8	1	9				7	10		6		3	11		5			2	
12	29	CLAPTON ORIENT	5-0	Lewis 2, Deacon 2, McPherson	12562	4	8	1						9		10	3		11		5	7		2	6
13	Nov 5	Chelsea	0-4		41220	4	8	1	9				7			10	3		11		5			2	6
14	12	BRISTOL CITY	1-1	McPherson	13600	4	8	1	9				7			10	3		11		5			2	6
15	19	Stoke City	1-1	Fowler	9938	4	8	1	10				7	9		6	3		11		5			2	
16	26	OLDHAM ATHLETIC	0-0		12469	4	8	1	10				7	9		6	3		11		5			2	
17	Dec 3	Notts County	0-2		11618	5	8	1	10				7	9		6	3		11					2	4
18	10	SOUTHAMPTON	2-0	McPherson, Fowler	10676	4	8	1	10			11		9		6	3				5	7		2	
19	17	Grimsby Town	2-1	Deacon, Hiles	9581	5	8	1	9			11		10		6	3					7		2	4
20	24	READING	0-1		9030	5	10	1	9			11	7	8		6	3							2	4
21	26	Preston North End	2-4	Deacon, Lewis	26206		8	1			5	11	7	9		6	3		10					2	4
22	27	PRESTON NORTH END	0-1		15264		8	1			5	11	7	9		6	3		10					2	4
23	31	BLACKPOOL	1-0	Lewis	9185		10	1	9			11	7	8		6	3			5				2	4
24	Jan 7	Fulham	2-3	Fowler, Lewis	15008		10	1	9				7	8		6	3		11	5				2	4
25	21	BARNSLEY	3-0	Thompson 2, Lewis	6420		4	1	9				7	8		6	3		11				10	2	5
26	Feb 4	PORT VALE	2-0	Fowler 2	6745		8	1	9						4	6	3		11	2		7	10		5
27	11	South Shields	1-3	Hole	3572			1	9				7	8	4	6	3		11				10	2	5
28	18	LEEDS UNITED	1-1	Thompson	13444		4	1	9				7	8		6	3		11				10	2	5
29	25	Nottingham Forest	2-0	Lewis, Fowler	11687		4	1	9				7	8		6	3		11				10	2	5
30	Mar 3	WEST BROMWICH ALB.	3-2	McPherson, Thompson, Lewis	15355		4	1	9				7	8		6	3		11				10	2	5
31	10	Clapton Orient	1-1	Thompson	11508		4	1	9				7	8		6	3		11				10	2	5
32	17	CHELSEA	0-0		15653		10	1	9				7	8		6	3		11		5			2	4
33	24	Bristol City	1-2	Lewis	17123		10	1	9				7	8		6	3		11		5			2	4
34	31	STOKE CITY	1-1	Fowler	10893		10	1	9				7	8		6	3		11		5			2	4
35	Apr 6	Hull City	2-0	Gunn, McPherson (p)	8877		8	1		10			7	9		6	3		11		5			2	4
36	7	Oldham Athletic	1-0	Gunn	14860		8	1		10			7	9		6	3		11		5			2	4
37	9	HULL CITY	2-0	Lewis, Nicholas	15732		8	1		10			7	9		6	3		11		5			2	4
38	14	NOTTS COUNTY	1-1	Lewis	11566	4	8	1		10			7	9		6	3		11		5			2	
39	21	Southampton	2-0	Lewis, Gunn	8820		8	1		10			7	9	6	5	3		11					2	4
40	28	GRIMSBY TOWN	3-2	Lewis 2, Deacon	9208		8	1		10			7	9	6	5	3		11					2	4
41	30	Wolverhampton Wan.	1-1	Lewis	8972		8	1		10			7	9	6	5	3		11					2	4
42	May 5	Reading	0-0		7771		8	1		10			7	9	6	5	3		11					2	4
					Apps	21	37	42	28	8	2	7	37	39	6	42	40	2	37	3	24	5	7	41	34
					Goals		8		15	3		2	2	25		12			2			1	5		

F.A. Cup

	Date	Opponent	Res	Scorers	Att	Collins J	Deacon H	Ferguson FSB	Fowler J	Gunn K	Hanford H	Hiles WR	Hole WJ	Lewis WL	Lloyd CJ	McPherson L	Milne WE	Morley EB	Nicholas DS	Sampy WE	Sykes WJ	Thomas G	Thompson L	Williams BD	Woodward TG
R3	Jan 14	Wrexham	1-2	Hole	12000		4	1	9				7	8		6	3		11				10	2	5

Swindon Town

6th in Division Three (South)

	Date		Opponent	Score	Scorers	Att	Archer AAE	Bew DC	Bourne JT	Chivers W	Cooper R	Daniel CH	Denyer AEC	Dickinson W	Eddleston J	Flood CW	Humphries B	Jeffries CE	Johnson S	Low D	Morris DH	Nash EM	O'Neill H	Roberts CL	Thom A	Thompson F	Walker J	Weale RH	Weston AM	Wylie T
1	Aug	27	Bournemouth	0-2		10208	6	5	1				7	2	8					4	9			10	11	3				
2		29	COVENTRY CITY	6-0	Morris 4, Eddleston 2	8846	6	5	1				7	2	8					4	9			10		3	11			
3	Sep	3	QUEEN'S PARK RANGERS	0-2		9659	6	5	1				7		8					4	9			10	11				3	2
4		5	Coventry City	0-4		9553	3		1	4			7		9	8	5		6					10			11			2
5		10	Watford	5-2	Dickinson 2 (2p), Thom, Morris 2	10483	6	5	1				7	2	10	8				4	9				11					3
6		17	CHARLTON ATHLETIC	2-2	Dickinson (p), Morris	8077	6	5	1					2	10	8				4	9				11			7		3
7	Oct	1	PLYMOUTH ARGYLE	2-2	Morris 2	6792		5	1					2	10				6	4	9			8	11			7	3	
8		8	Merthyr Town	2-8	Morris, Roberts	5418	6	5	1				7	2	10				6		9			8	11				3	
9		15	WALSALL	5-0	Morris 3, Eddleston, Roberts	6938	6						7	2	10		5			4	9	1		8	11				3	
10		22	Millwall	3-3	Morris 2, Roberts	8338	6						7	2	10		5			4	9	1		8	11				3	
11		29	LUTON TOWN	4-2	Roberts, Morris, Dickinson (p), Thom	7580	6						7	2	10		5			4	9	1		8	11				3	
12	Nov	5	Brentford	4-1	Eddleston 2, Thom, Morris	9527	6						7	2	10		5			4	9	1		8	11				3	
13		12	CRYSTAL PALACE	3-3	Morris 2, Thom	7608	6						7	2	10		5			4	9	1		8	11				3	
14		19	Exeter City	0-0		6310	6						7	2	10		5			4	9	1		8	11				3	
15	Dec	3	Norwich City	3-1	Roberts 2, Low	7479	6						7	2	10		5			4	9	1		8	11				3	
16		24	BRIGHTON & HOVE ALB	4-3	Dickinson (p), Morris, Thom 2	7455	6						7	2	10		5			4	9	1		8	11					3
17		26	Newport County	3-1	Morris, Thom, Eddleston	3610	6						7	2	10		5			4	9	1		8	11					3
18		27	NEWPORT COUNTY	4-1	Dickinson (p), Roberts, Morris 2	9715	6						7	2	10		5			4	9	1		8	11					3
19	Jan	7	Queen's Park Rangers	1-0	Denyer	9981	6						7	2	10		5			4	9	1		8	11					3
20		21	WATFORD	4-0	Roberts, Archer, Morris 2	6356	6						7	2	10		5			4	9	1		8	11					3
21	Feb	4	BRISTOL ROVERS	2-1	Dickinson (p), Morris	5403	6						7	2	10		5			4	9	1		8	11					3
22		11	Plymouth Argyle	0-3		13052	6						7	2	10		5			4	9	1		8	11					3
23		18	MERTHYR TOWN	1-2	Eddleston	6464	6						7	2	10		5			4	9	1		8			11			3
24		25	Walsall	2-1	Eddleston, Morris	7591	6						7	2	10		5			4	9	1		8			11			3
25	Mar	3	MILLWALL	3-0	Morris 2, Roberts	11716	6						7	2	10		5			4	9	1		8			11			3
26		10	Luton Town	1-2	Morris	6973	6						7	2	10		5			4	9	1		8			11			3
27		14	Southend United	1-1	Thom	3159	6						7	2	10		5			4	9	1			11		8			3
28		17	BRENTFORD	1-1	Walker	6500	6						7	2	10		5			4		1		8	11		9			3
29		21	BOURNEMOUTH	3-2	Morris, Denyer, Roberts	2685	6	5					7	2	10					4	9	1		8	11					3
30		24	Crystal Palace	0-1		8373	6	5				9	7	2	10					4		1		8	11					3
31		31	EXETER CITY	3-0	Morris, Eddleston, Denyer	2999	6	5					7	2	10					4	9	1		8	11					3
32	Apr	6	Gillingham	1-0	Roberts	7930		5					7	2	10				6	4	9	1		8	11					3
33		7	Northampton Town	0-3		14174		5					7	2	10				6	4	9	1		8	11					3
34		9	GILLINGHAM	6-1	Morris, Denyer, Eddleston 2 (1p), Walker, Roberts	7901	6	5					7	2	10					4	9	1		8			11			3
35		14	NORWICH CITY	1-1	Morris	4980	6	5					7		10					4	9	1	2	8			11			3
36		18	Bristol Rovers	0-1		5445	6	5					7		10			11	3	4	9	1		8		2				
37		21	Torquay United	1-2	Thom	2808	5					9	7		10				6	4		1		8	11	2			3	
38		25	NORTHAMPTON T	4-0	Morris, Roberts, Eddleston, Denyer	5289	6	5					7		10					4	9	1		8		2		11		3
39		28	SOUTHEND UNITED	0-1		4899	6	5					7		10				3	4	9	1		8		2		11		
40		30	Charlton Athletic	1-3	Daniels	2900		5			6	9	7		10				3	4		1				2	8	11		
41	May	2	TORQUAY UNITED	2-2	Morris, Eddleston	2528	6	5					7	2	10				3	4	9	1					11	8		
42		5	Brighton & Hove Albion	2-4	Morris 2	5757		5			4			2	10				6		9	1		8	11			7	3	
						Apps	37	20	8	1	2	3	39	34	42	3	21	1	11	39	37	34	1	37	29	7	12	7	12	25
						Goals	1					1	5	7	13					1	38			13	9		2			

F.A. Cup

	Date		Opponent	Score	Scorers	Att	Archer AAE	Bew DC	Bourne JT	Chivers W	Cooper R	Daniel CH	Denyer AEC	Dickinson W	Eddleston J	Flood CW	Humphries B	Jeffries CE	Johnson S	Low D	Morris DH	Nash EM	O'Neill H	Roberts CL	Thom A	Thompson F	Walker J	Weale RH	Weston AM	Wylie T
R1	Nov	26	Newport County	1-0	Morris	9600	6						7	2	10		5			4	9	1		8			11		3	
R2	Dec	10	CRYSTAL PALACE	0-0		16360	6						7	2	10		5			4	9	1		8	11				3	
rep		14	Crystal Palace	2-1	Morris 2	8500	6						7	2	10		5			4	9	1		8	11					3
R3	Jan	14	CLAPTON ORIENT	2-1	Morris 2	19079	6						7	2	10		5			4	9	1		8	11					3
R4		28	SHEFFIELD WEDNESDAY	1-2	Morris	17494	6						7	2	10		5			4	9	1		8	11					3

Torquay United

Bottom of Division Three (South)

			Opponent	Score	Scorers	Att	Bayes AWC	Budd HR	Clark W	Connor JCT	Cook G	Daniel W	Davis CF	Good HJ	Gough CWM	Griffiths LH	Jones J	Knapman L	Mackey JA	Mackrill PA	McGovern IT	Millsom L	Orrick G	Pattison JW	Price JW	Ringland R	Smith GH	Thomas A	Thomson D	Turner HL	Wellock M	Wragge F
1	Aug	27	EXETER CITY	1-1	Turner (p)	10749				6	2						9		7		10	1					3		11	8	4	5
2		29	Millwall	1-9	Thomson	6204				6	2						9		7		10	1					3		11	8	4	5
3	Sep	3	Merthyr Town	3-1	Jones 2, Thomson	4644				4		6	5			10	9		7			1			2		3		11	8		
4		7	MILLWALL	0-1		5413	1			4		6	5				9		7						2		3		11	8	10	
5		10	Norwich City	0-4		12887	1			4		6	5				9		7						2		3		11	10	8	
6		17	NORTHAMPTON T	1-5	Turner	4625	1			4					6	8	9		7						2		3		11	10	5	
7		24	Southend United	0-1		8546	1				2	6			4		9		7	3									11	10	8	5
8	Oct	1	BRIGHTON & HOVE ALB	1-1	Jones	2156	1				2	5			4		9		7	3									11	10	8	5
9		8	Bournemouth	1-1	Wellock	5781	1				2	6			4		9		7	3									11	10	8	5
10		15	BRENTFORD	2-1	Turner (p), Pattison	4185	1				2	6			4		9		7	3				11						10	8	5
11		22	CHARLTON ATHLETIC	1-2	Daniel	4816	1				2	6			4		9		7	3	8			11						10		5
12		29	Bristol Rovers	1-5	Wellock	6824	1				2	6	4				9		7	3				11						10	8	5
13	Nov	5	PLYMOUTH ARGYLE	1-2	Jones	9172	1				2	10	5		4		9		7					11	3					8		6
14		12	Watford	2-1	Daniel, Turner	6929	1				2	10	5		4		9		7					11	3					8		6
15		19	QUEEN'S PARK RANGERS	1-0	Jones	2235	1				2	10	5		4		8		7		11				3					9		6
16	Dec	3	NEWPORT COUNTY	1-1	Wellock	3489	1				2		5		4		8		7				11		3					9	10	6
17		10	Walsall	0-4		3610	1				2	6			4		9		7				11		3					8	10	5
18		17	GILLINGHAM	1-1	Turner (p)	2992	1	9			2	6			4				7				11		3					8	10	5
19		27	CRYSTAL PALACE	0-2		3353					2	6			4		8		7			1			3	9			11	10		5
20		31	Exeter City	0-5		8224	1			6	2		5		4									7	3	9			11	10	8	
21	Jan	7	MERTHYR TOWN	2-2	Jones, Ringland	3234	1			6	2				4		8		7		10				3	9		11				5
22		14	Coventry City	1-5	Ringland	6878	1			6	2				4	10	8	7						11	3	9						5
23		21	NORWICH CITY	4-2	Turner 3, Ringland	3336	1			6	2				4				7		10			11	3	9				8	5	
24		28	Northampton Town	4-4	Mackey, Turner, Pattison, Ringland	4832	1			6	2				4				7		10			11	3	9				8	5	
25	Feb	4	SOUTHEND UNITED	3-3	Ringland 2, McGovern	3419	1			6	2				4				7		10			11	3	9				8	5	
26		11	Brighton & Hove Albion	0-3		7430	1			6	2				4				7		10			11	3	9				8	5	
27		18	BOURNEMOUTH	2-2	Ringland 2	4236	1			6	2			5	4				7		10			11	3	9				8		
28		25	Brentford	2-1	Pattison, Ringland	8355	1			6				5	4				7		10			11	2	9				8	3	
29	Mar	3	Charlton Athletic	0-1		8290	1			6				5	4				7		10			11	3	9				8	2	
30		10	BRISTOL ROVERS	0-0		4078	1			6				5	4				7		10			11	3	9				8	2	
31		14	Crystal Palace	2-3	Mackey, Pattison	4842	1			6				5	4				7		10			11	3					8	2	9
32		17	Plymouth Argyle	1-4	Russell (og)	9008	1							5	4				7		8			11	3			10		9	2	6
33		24	WATFORD	1-1	Turner	3750	1			6				5	4				7		10			11	3	9				8	2	
34		31	Queen's Park Rangers	3-2	Turner, Griffiths 2	5839	1	10	6				5	4		9			7					11						8	2	3
35	Apr	6	Luton Town	0-5		10397	1	10	6				5	4		9			7					11						8	2	3
36		7	COVENTRY CITY	2-3	Budd, Griffiths (p)	3275	1	10	6				5	4		9			7		8			11							2	3
37		9	LUTON TOWN	0-4		2994	1	10			3		5	6	4	8			7						2	9		11				
38		14	Newport County	2-2	Budd, Griffiths	3199	1	10		4	2		5	6		9			7					11						8		3
39		21	SWINDON TOWN	2-1	Griffiths 2	2808		10		6	2		5	4		9			7			1		11						8		3
40		28	Gillingham	1-4	Pattison	3868	1			6	2		5	4		9			7		10			11						8		3
41	May	2	Swindon Town	2-2	Griffiths 2	2528	1			4	2		5	6		9			7					11				10		8		3
42		5	WALSALL	1-1	Mackey	3365	1			4	2		5	6		9			7					11				10		8		3
						Apps	37	7	3	24	29	15	18	16	28	12	20	1	40	6	18	5	3	26	26	14	6	5	11	38	27	27
						Goals		2				2				8	6		3		1			5		9			2	11	3	

One own goal

F.A. Cup

Did not enter.

Tottenham Hotspur

21st in Division One: Relegated

No	Date	Opponent	Score	Scorers	Att	Armstrong JW	Barnett FW	Bellamy WR	Blair JG	Britton J	Clay T	Dimmock JH	Elkes AJE	Evans A	Forster M	Grimsdell A	Handley CHJ	Hartley F	Helliwell S	Lindsay AF	Lowdell AE	NichollsJH	O'Callaghan E	Osborne FR	Poynton C	Richardson J	Sanders AW	Skitt H	Smith B	Spiers CH	Thompson A	Townley JC
1	Aug 27	BIRMINGHAM	1-0	O'Callaghan	37408							11	10	9	2					6	4	1	8	7	3			5				
2	31	Middlesbrough	1-3	Dimmock(p)	29113							11	10	9	2					6	4	1	8	7	3			5				
3	Sep 3	Newcastle United	1-4	O'Callaghan	41038		7	11					10	9	2					6	4	1	8			3		5				
4	10	HUDDERSFIELD T	2-2	Lindsay, Dimmock	27983				9	1		11	10		2		7			6	4		8			3		5				
5	12	MIDDLESBROUGH	4-2	Blair 3, Dimmock(p)	19219				9	1		11	10		2	6							8	7		3		5	4			
6	17	Portsmouth	0-3		26115				9	1		11	10		2	6							8	7		3		5	4			
7	22	LEICESTER CITY	2-1	Osborne, Blair	9436				9	1		11	10		2	6							8	7		3		5	4			
8	24	Manchester United	0-3		13952			11	9	1			10		2	6			5				8	7		3			4			
9	Oct 1	EVERTON	1-3	Townley	7716			11		1					2	6				9	4		8	7		3		5				10
10	8	Cardiff City	1-2	Townley	21811			11		1			9		2	6					4		8	7		3		5				10
11	15	BLACKBURN ROVERS	1-1	Osborne	23020					1	2	11	9			6	10				4		8	7		3		5				
12	22	SUNDERLAND	3-1	Dimmock 2, Osborne	19039					1	2	11	10			6	7				4		8	9		3		5				
13	29	Derby County	1-1	Grimsdell	15963					1	2	11	10			6	7				4		8	9		3		5				
14	Nov 5	WEST HAM UNITED	5-3	O'Callaghan 2,Osborne,Elkes,Handley	35099					1		11	10		2	6	7				4		8	9		3		5				
15	12	Aston Villa	2-1	Osborne 2	30759					1		11	10		2	6	7				4		8	9		3		5				
16	19	SHEFFIELD UNITED	2-2	Osborne, Elkes	19147					1		11	10		2	6	7				4		8	9		3		5				
17	Dec 3	BURNLEY	5-0	Osborne 2,O'Callaghan,Handley,Dimmock	20404						2	11	10			6	7				4		8	9		3		5		1		
18	10	Bury	2-1	O'Callaghan 2	12204						2	11	10			6	7				4		8	9		3		5		1		
19	17	LIVERPOOL	3-1	Elkes 2, Osborne	21234						2	11	10			6	7				4		8	9		3		5		1		
20	24	Leicester City	1-6	Handley	19987						2	11	10			6	7				4		8	9		3		5		1		
21	26	Bolton Wanderers	1-4	Elkes	25229						2	11	10		3		7			6	4		8	9				5		1		
22	31	Birmingham	2-3	O'Callaghan, Womack (og)	11603	10					2	11			3		7			9			8					5	4	1		
23	Jan 2	Arsenal	1-1	O'Callaghan	13518	10						11			2	6	7			9	4		8			3		5		1		
24	7	NEWCASTLE UNITED	5-2	Osborne 4, Dimmock	34731	10						11			2	6	7				4		8	9		3		5		1		
25	21	Huddersfield Town	2-4	O'Callaghan, Osborne	17892						2	11	10		3	6					4		8	9				5		1	7	
26	Feb 4	MANCHESTER UNITED	4-1	Armstrong 2, Dimmock, O'Callaghan	23545	10					2	11			3	6	7				4		8	9				5		1		
27	6	BOLTON WANDERERS	1-2	Armstrong	18183	9					2	11	10				7			6	4		8			3		5		1		
28	11	Everton	5-2	O'Callaghan 4, Dimmock	29149	10					2	11				6	7			9	4		8			3		5		1		
29	25	Blackburn Rovers	1-2	O'Callaghan	20890	10					2	11				6	7				4		8	9		3		5		1		
30	Mar 5	CARDIFF CITY	1-0	Dimmock	15559	10					2	11			3	6	7				4		8	9	5					1		
31	10	DERBY COUNTY	1-2	Armstrong	22458	10					2	11			3	6	7				4		8	9	5					1		
32	17	West Ham United	1-1	Osborne	33908							11			2	6		10		7	4		8	9	3			5		1		
33	19	PORTSMOUTH	0-3		12829	9						11			2	6		10		7	4		8		3			5		1		
34	24	ASTON VILLA	2-1	Grimsdell(p), Lindsay	21537		7					11			2	6	10			9	4		8		3			5		1		
35	28	Sunderland	0-0		9224		7					11			2	6	10			9	4		8		3			5		1		
36	31	Sheffield United	1-3	Handley	17495		7					11			2	6	10			9	4		8		3			5		1		
37	Apr 6	SHEFFIELD WEDNESDAY	1-3	Lindsay	26432		7					11			2	6				9	4		8	10	3			5		1		
38	7	ARSENAL	2-0	O'Callaghan 2	39193							11			2	6	7						8	9	3		10	5	4	1		
39	10	Sheffield Wednesday	2-4	O'Callaghan, Osborne	15900							11			2	6	7			10			8	9		3		5	4	1		
40	14	Burnley	2-2	Osborne, Dimmock	10906							11			2	6			5				8	9	3				4	1	7	10
41	21	BURY	1-4	Lindsay	15618							11			2	6				10	4		8	9	3			5		1	7	
42	28	Liverpool	0-2		31780	10						11			2	6				9	4		8		3			5		1	7	

PC Austin played at 6 in game 22

	Armstrong JW	Barnett FW	Bellamy WR	Blair JG	Britton J	Clay T	Dimmock JH	Elkes AJE	Evans A	Forster M	Grimsdell A	Handley CHJ	Hartley F	Helliwell S	Lindsay AF	Lowdell AE	NichollsJH	O'Callaghan E	Osborne FR	Poynton C	Richardson J	Sanders AW	Skitt H	Smith B	Spiers CH	Thompson A	Townley JC
Apps	11	5	4	5	13	16	38	22	3	32	35	26	2	2	19	34	3	42	31	14	24	1	38	8	26	4	3
Goals	4			4			11	5			2	4			4			19	18								2

One own goal

F.A. Cup

Rd	Date	Opponent	Score	Scorers	Att	Armstrong JW	Barnett FW	Bellamy WR	Blair JG	Britton J	Clay T	Dimmock JH	Elkes AJE	Evans A	Forster M	Grimsdell A	Handley CHJ	Hartley F	Helliwell S	Lindsay AF	Lowdell AE	NichollsJH	O'Callaghan E	Osborne FR	Poynton C	Richardson J	Sanders AW	Skitt H	Smith B	Spiers CH	Thompson A	Townley JC
R3	Jan 14	Bristol City	2-1	O'Callaghan, Osborne	36260	10						11			2	6	7				4		8	9		3		5		1		
R4	28	OLDHAM ATHLETIC	3-0	Handley, O'Callaghan, Dimmock	36828	10					2	11			3	6	7				4		8	9				5		1		
R5	Feb 18	Leicester City	3-0	O'Callaghan 2, Dimmock	47296	10					2	11				6	7			9	4		8			3		5		1		
R6	Mar 3	Huddersfield Town	1-6	O'Callaghan	52390	10					2	11				6	7				4		8	9		3		5		1		

Tranmere Rovers

5th in Division Three (North)

	Date		Opponent	Score	Scorers	Att.	Bamber J	Barton EV	Bedford F	Beswick SMcA	Bevan HF	Briggs AL	Campbell IH	Cartman HR	Charlton WG	Evans HP	Flanagan J	Gray M	Gray RA	Jackson G	Jones TI	Kelly C	Lewis JJ	Littlehales H	Naylor TH	O'Connor JP	Rimmer EJ	Stuart TAM	Thirkell P	Urmson F	Waring T	Yates WJ
1	Aug	27	SOUTHPORT	1-0	Flanagan	8495	5					1		7	8	4	9				10		6				11		3			2
2		29	Rotherham United	1-2	Charlton	4200	5					1			8	4					10		6			7	11		3		9	2
3	Sep	3	Durham City	3-1	Waring 2, Jones	2842	5	4				1	6		8						10					7	11		3		9	2
4		10	WREXHAM	2-1	Rimmer, Lewis	8677	5					1	4	7	8						10		6				11		3		9	2
5		17	Chesterfield	2-2	Waring, Charlton	5681	5					1	4	7	8						10		6				11		3		9	2
6		24	BRADFORD PARK AVE.	2-2	Waring 2	5370	5					1	4	7	8						10		6				11		3		9	2
7	Oct	1	New Brighton	1-0	Waring	9228	5					1	4	7	8						10		6				11		3		9	2
8		8	Stockport County	0-1		8283	5					1	4	7	8						10		6				11		3		9	2
9		15	BARROW	5-0	Waring 2, Cartman, Rimmer, Charlton	5666	5					1	4	7	8						10		6				11		3		9	2
10		22	CREWE ALEXANDRA	3-3	Charlton 2, Littlehales	3817	5					1	4	7	8								6	10			11		3		9	2
11		29	Halifax Town	2-2	Rimmer, Charlton	9503	5					1	4	7	8								6	10	3		11				9	2
12	Nov	5	BRADFORD CITY	2-1	Rimmer, Waring	4882	5					1	4	7	8								6	10	3		11				9	2
13		12	Ashington	0-3		1785	5	4				1		7	8								6	10	3		11				9	2
14		19	DARLINGTON	3-1	Charlton 2, Waring	4099	5					1	4	7	8								6	10			11		3		9	2
15	Dec	3	WIGAN BOROUGH	5-2	Waring 3, Rimmer, Cartman	4448	5					1	4	7	8								6	10			11		3		9	2
16		17	HARTLEPOOLS UNITED	1-2	Littlehales	4878	5					1	4	7	8								6	10			11		3		9	2
17		24	Lincoln City	1-1	Waring	5363	5					1	4	7	8								6	10			11		3		9	2
18		27	NELSON	1-1	Rimmer	8946	5					1	4	7	8								6	10			11		3		9	2
19		31	Southport	1-0	Littlehales	3899	5					1	4	7	8				6					10			11		3		9	2
20	Jan	2	ROTHERHAM UNITED	2-0	Littlehale, Rimmer	5576						1	4	7	8								6	10			11	5	3		9	2
21		7	DURHAM CITY	11-1	* see below	5205	5					1	4	7							8		6	10			11		3		9	2
22		21	Wrexham	0-2		4792	5		7			1	4									8	6	10	2		11		3		9	
23		28	CHESTERFIELD	6-3	Rimmer 2,Charlton,Bedford,Littlehales,Waring	4162	5		7			1	4		8			6						10	2		11		3		9	
24	Feb	4	Bradford Park Avenue	2-6	Bedford, Charlton	13815	5		7			1	4		8				6					10	2		11		3		9	
25		11	NEW BRIGHTON	4-0	Waring 2, Littlehales, Charlton	6664	5					1	4		8						7		6	10			11		3		9	2
26		15	Accrington Stanley	3-2	Littlehales, Flanagan, Charlton	2017	5					1	4		8		9				7		6	10			11		3			2
27		18	STOCKPORT COUNTY	5-2	Flanagan, Charlton, Urmston, Jones 2	8943	5					1	4		8		9				7		6	10					3	11		2
28		25	Barrow	1-2	Littlehales	5119	5				8	1	4				9				7		6	10					3	11		2
29	Mar	3	Crewe Alexandra	3-2	Flanagan, Littlehales, Bevan	5307	5				10	1	4				9				7		6	8					3	11		2
30		10	HALIFAX TOWN	2-2	Charlton, Flanagan	5858	5					1	4		8		9				7		6	10					3	11		2
31		17	Bradford City	1-3	Jones	9717	5					1	4		8		9				7		6	10					3	11		2
32		24	ASHINGTON	5-3	Charlton 3, Littlehales, Flanagan	3749	5					1	4		8		9				7		6	10					3	11		2
33		31	Darlington	7-3	Jones 2, Flanagan 3, Charlton, Littlehales	4989	5					1	4		8		9				7		6	10					3	11		2
34	Apr	6	ROCHDALE	3-0	Flanagan, Urmston, Bevan	10053					10	1	5		8		9				7		6	4					3	11		2
35		7	ACCRINGTON STANLEY	3-2	Littlehales, Charlton, Jones	6169		4				1	5		8		9				7		6	10					3	11		2
36		9	Rochdale	2-1	Charlton, Flanagan	3069	5					1	4		8		9				7		6	10					3	11		2
37		14	Wigan Borough	0-1		2682	5					1	4		8		9				7		6	10					3	11		2
38		21	DONCASTER ROVERS	0-0		4072	5					1	4		8		9				7		6	10					3	11		2
39		24	Nelson	5-3	Charlton 2, Flanagan, Jones 2	1126	5					1	4		8		9				7		6	10					3	11		2
40		28	Hartlepools United	0-2		2132	5	4				1			8		9			3	7		6	10						11		2
41	May	1	Doncaster Rovers	2-5	Littlehales, Flanagan	4056	5	4				1			8		9			2	7		6	10					3	11		
42		5	LINCOLN CITY	2-2	Beswick 2	4029	5			9		1	4		8						7		6	10					3	11		2

Scorers in game 21: Waring 6, Nicholson (og), Jones, Cartman, Littlehales 2

	Bamber J	Barton EV	Bedford F	Beswick SMcA	Bevan HF	Briggs AL	Campbell IH	Cartman HR	Charlton WG	Evans HP	Flanagan J	Gray M	Gray RA	Jackson G	Jones TI	Kelly C	Lewis JJ	Littlehales H	Naylor TH	O'Connor JP	Rimmer EJ	Stuart TAM	Thirkell P	Urmson F	Waring T	Yates WJ
Apps	39	5	3	1	3	42	37	19	38	2	17	1	2	2	28	1	38	33	6	2	26	1	38	16	24	38
Goals			2	2	2			3	22		13				10		1	15			9			2	23	

One own goal

F.A. Cup

	Date		Opponent	Score	Scorers	Att.	Bamber J	Barton EV	Bedford F	Beswick SMcA	Bevan HF	Briggs AL	Campbell IH	Cartman HR	Charlton WG	Evans HP	Flanagan J	Gray M	Gray RA	Jackson G	Jones TI	Kelly C	Lewis JJ	Littlehales H	Naylor TH	O'Connor JP	Rimmer EJ	Stuart TAM	Thirkell P	Urmson F	Waring T	Yates WJ
R1	Nov	26	Shirebrook	3-1	Charlton 2, Waring	7031	5					1	4	7	8								6	10			11		3		9	2
R2	Dec	10	HALIFAX TOWN	3-1	Bamber, Rimmer 2	8554	5					1	4	7	8								6	10			11		3		9	2
R3	Jan	14	Nottingham Forest	0-1		17019	5					1	4	7	8								6	10			11		3		9	2

18th in Division Three (South)

	Date	Opponent	Score	Scorers	Att	Adams WE	Beck HA	Bedford L	Bradford JW	Caesar WC	Edwards WJT	Fairhurst DL	Fereday DT	Groves E	Hill WT	Hughes H	Lake WH	Lane MAE	Lansdale A	McClure A	Plunkett AETB	Reeve FD	Robson G	Springell GW	Staley HE	Wait H	Walker DJ	Walters F	White HA
1	Aug 27	Bristol Rovers	2-5	Robson, Lane	12181	3			6	5	7			2		10		9					8	11	4	1			
2	29	WATFORD	2-0	Edwards, Lane	7744	3			6	5	7			2				9					8	11	4	1		10	
3	Sep 3	PLYMOUTH ARGYLE	2-1	Hughes, Robson	13784	3	5		6		7			2		10		9					8	11	4	1			
4	7	Watford	0-4		6459	3	5		6	4	7			2		10		9					8	11		1			
5	10	Merthyr Town	2-3	Lane, Walters	3066	3	5		6	4	7			2				9					8	11		1		10	
6	17	NORWICH CITY	1-1	Lane	9885	3	5		6		7			2				9					8	11	4	1		10	
7	24	GILLINGHAM	7-4	Hebdon (og), Hughes 2, Lane 4	6923	3	5		6		7			2		10		9					8	11	4	1			
8	Oct 1	Coventry City	1-0	Edwards	13662	3	5		6		7			2		10		9					8	11	4	1			
9	8	NEWPORT COUNTY	0-3		11738	3	5		6		7			2		10		9					8	11	4	1			
10	15	Swindon Town	0-5		6938		5		6		7	3		2				9					8	11	4	1	10		
11	22	Brighton & Hove Albion	0-0		2737				6	5	7	2		3				9						11	4	1	8	10	
12	29	SOUTHEND UNITED	0-1		7897				6	5	7	2		3				10						11	4	1	8		9
13	Nov 5	Northampton Town	0-1		11340				6	5	7	2		3									8	11	4	1	10		9
14	12	BOURNEMOUTH	2-3	Blair (og), Lane	3917	5	6			4	7	2			3			9					10	11		1			8
15	Dec 3	Millwall	1-7	Springell	15338	3	6		4			2		5		10		9				7	8	11		1			
16	5	Brentford	2-3	Lake, Lane	2202		6					2	7	5			10	9	11		3		8		4	1			
17	10	TORQUAY UNITED	4-0	Lake 2, Lane 2	3610		6					2	7	5			10	9	11		3		8		4	1			
18	17	Exeter City	0-3		5206		6					2	7	5			10	9	11		3				4	1		8	
19	27	CHARLTON ATHLETIC	1-0	Lane	6244		6					2	7	5			10	9			3			11	4	1	8		
20	31	BRISTOL ROVERS	1-2	Walker	2967		6					2	7	5			10	9	11		3				4	1	8		
21	Jan 7	Plymouth Argyle	1-2	Lane	7361		6					2	7	5			10	9	11		3				4	1	8		
22	14	CRYSTAL PALACE	1-1	Walker	4297		6					2	7	5			10	9			3			11	4	1	8		
23	21	MERTHYR TOWN	2-2	Lansdale, Lane	4747		6					2	7	5			10	9	11		3				4	1	8		
24	28	Norwich City	4-1	Lane 2, Lake, Robson	5730	3			6			2	7	5			10	9					8	11	4	1			
25	Feb 4	Gillingham	0-2		4296	3			6			2	7	5			10	9					8	11	4	1			
26	9	Charlton Athletic	3-1	Lane 2, Robson	4647			7	6			2		5			10	9			3		8	11	4	1			
27	11	COVENTRY CITY	7-0	Lane 2, Lake, Bradford 2, Robson 2	5878			7	6			2		5			10	9			3		8	11	4	1			
28	18	Newport County	1-4	Lane	5561			7	6			2		5			10	9			3		8	11	4	1			
29	25	SWINDON TOWN	1-2	Robson	7591			7	6			2		5			10	9			3		8	11	4	1			
30	Mar 3	BRIGHTON & HOVE ALB	3-3	Robson, Lane 2 (1p)	6170			7	6			2		5		4	10	9			3		8	11		1			
31	10	Southend United	1-2	Robson	4736			7	6			2		5		4		9			3		8	11		1			10
32	17	NORTHAMPTON T	1-1	Lane	7800			7	6			2		4				9		5	3		8	11		1			10
33	24	Bournemouth	1-3	Lake	4549			7	6			2		4			10	9		5	3		8	11		1			
34	31	BRENTFORD	4-2	Lane 3, Bradford (p)	4750			7	6			2		4		10		9		5	3		8	11		1			
35	Apr 7	Crystal Palace	1-5	Lane (p)	12530			7	6			2		4		10		9		5	3		8	11		1			
36	9	Queen's Park Rangers	1-1	Hughes	8082	2		7	6					4		10		9		5	3		8	11		1			
37	10	QUEEN'S PARK RANGERS	2-2	Lane 2	6419	2			6					4		10		9	11	5	3		8			1		7	
38	14	MILLWALL	2-5	Robson, Lane	6302			7	6			2		4		10		9	11	5	3		8			1			
39	21	Luton Town	1-4	Hughes	6118			11	6			2		4		10		9		5	3		7			1	8		
40	23	LUTON TOWN	4-1	Lane 3 (1p), Robson	3666			7	6			2		4		10		9		5	3		8	11		1			
41	28	EXETER CITY	5-1	Walker 3, Lane, Bedford	5843			7	6			2		4				9		5	3		8	11		1	10		
42	May 5	Torquay United	1-1	Walker	3365			7	6			2		4				9		5	3		8	11		1	10		
					Apps	15	18	16	33	8	14	31	10	41	1	16	16	41	8	11	25	1	34	33	25	42	12	6	5
					Goals			1	3		2					5	6	36	1				11	1			6	1	

Two own goals

F.A. Cup

	Date	Opponent	Score	Scorers	Att	Adams WE	Beck HA	Bedford L	Bradford JW	Caesar WC	Edwards WJT	Fairhurst DL	Fereday DT	Groves E	Hill WT	Hughes H	Lake WH	Lane MAE	Lansdale A	McClure A	Plunkett AETB	Reeve FD	Robson G	Springell GW	Staley HE	Wait H	Walker DJ	Walters F	White HA
R1	Nov 26	Bristol Rovers	2-4	White, Groves	8000	3	6				7	2		5		10							8	11	4	1			9

Watford

15th in Division Three (South)

	Date		Opponent	Score	Scorers	Att	Armstrong W	Daniels AWC	Davison JW	Foster CJ	Fuller EW	Groome JPG	Hewett JT	Hills WR	Jewett G	Kirkpatrick J	Leaver J	Mingay HJ	Morris H	Parker RR	Prior G	Sheppard W	Slade R	Smith FW	Vanner HJ	Warner J	Wilbourn H	Wilkinson GG	Woodward A	Yates J	Yates W
1	Aug	27	COVENTRY CITY	3-1	Sheppard 2, Warner	10151		11			6			7	9	3	5		4		2	10				8					1
2		29	Walsall	0-2		7744		11			6			7	9	3	5		4		2	10				8					1
3	Sep	3	Newport County	2-3	Groome 2	7362		11		8	6	9		7		3	5		4		2	10									1
4		7	WALSALL	4-0	Hills, Foster, Sheppard, Groome	6459		11		8	6	9		7		3	5				2	10		4							1
5		10	SWINDON TOWN	2-5	Wylie (og), Sheppard	10483		11		8		9		7		3	5				2	10		4					6		1
6		17	Queen's Park Rangers	1-2	Hills	13950		11	3			9		7			5		6			10	2	4		8					1
7		24	LUTON TOWN	1-0	Sheppard	12903		11	3	8				7	9		5		6			10	2	4							1
8	Oct	1	CHARLTON ATHLETIC	1-2	Foster	5350		11	3	8	6			7			5					10	2	4		9					1
9		8	Bristol Rovers	1-3	Sheppard	7247	9	11	3		6			7			5					10	2	4		8					1
10		15	PLYMOUTH ARGYLE	1-2	Warner	9016		11	3			9		7			5		6		2	10		4		8					1
11		22	Exeter City	3-3	Warner, Sheppard, Daniels	5750		11		9				7		3			6		2	10		4		8			5		1
12		29	CRYSTAL PALACE	2-1	Sheppard, Daniels	7346		11		9				7		3			6		2	10		4		8			5		1
13	Nov	5	Millwall	2-4	Foster, Warner	13302		11		9			1	7		3			6		2	10		4		8			5		
14		12	TORQUAY UNITED	1-2	Parker	6929		11					1	7		3			6	9	2	10		4		8			5		
15		19	Norwich City	1-1	Sheppard	6049		11	3	8	6			7				1		9	2	10		4					5		
16	Dec	3	Southend United	0-3		5320		11	3		6			7	4		5	1		9	2	10				8					
17		10	Coventry City	3-2	Sheppard, Groome, Warner	7448		11	3		5	9	1	7	6				4		2	10				8					
18		17	Bournemouth	0-1		3798		11	3		5	9	1	7	6				4		2	10				8					
19		24	BRENTFORD	1-1	Sheppard	5226		11	3		5		1	7	6				4	9	2	10				8					
20		27	Gillingham	3-0	Sheppard 3	3310		11	3		5	9	1	7	6				4		2	10				8					
21	Jan	7	NEWPORT COUNTY	2-3	Goome 2	5972		11	3		5	9	1	7	6				4		2	10				8					
22		14	BRIGHTON & HOVE ALB	3-3	Sheppard 2, Groome	5912		11	3		5	9	1	7	6				8		2	10		4							
23		21	Swindon Town	0-4		6356		11	3		5	9	1	7	6						2	10		4		8					
24		28	QUEEN'S PARK RANGERS	3-3	Sheppard 2, Warner	5597		11	3		5		1	7	6					9	2	10		4		8					
25	Feb	4	Luton Town	2-3	Sheppard, Warner	8012		11	3		5		1	7	6					9	2	10		4		8					
26		11	Charlton Athletic	2-0	Warner, Sheppard	5464		11	3		5		1	7	6					9		10	2	4		8					
27		18	BRISTOL ROVERS	2-1	Parker, Daniles	7246		11			5		1	7					6	9	3	10	2	4		8					
28		25	Plymouth Argyle	1-0	Groome	11281		11	3		5	9	1	7	6						2	10				8				4	
29	Mar	3	EXETER CITY	3-2	Groome, Morris 2	7951		11	3		5	9	1		6				7		2	10				8				4	
30		10	Crystal Palace	1-2	Smith	9851		10	3	9	5		1		6				7		2			4		8	11				
31		17	MILLWALL	0-3		13727		11	3	9	5		1		6				7		2	10		4		8					
32		24	Torquay United	1-1	Warner	3750		11	3		5		1		6				7	9	2	10		4		8					
33		31	NORWICH CITY	2-0	Warner, Daniels	4412		10	3		5		1		6				7	9	2			4		8	11				
34	Apr	7	Brighton & Hove Albion	1-1	Sheppard	7969		11	3		5		1		6				7	9	2	10		4		8					
35		9	MERTHYR TOWN	1-1	Sheppard	8360		11	3		5		1		6				7	9	2	10		4		8					
36		10	Merthyr Town	1-3	Warner	2590		11	3	7	5		1		6					9	2	10		4		8					
37		14	SOUTHEND UNITED	1-1	Daniels	5048		11	3		5		1		6				7		2	10		4		8		9			
38		18	NORTHAMPTON T	2-0	Sheppard, Sheppard	4221		11	3	7	5		1						6			10	2	4		8		9			
39		21	Northampton Town	0-5		6255		11	3	7	5		1						6			10	2	4		8		9			
40		28	BOURNEMOUTH	2-0	Groome 2	5102		11	3	7	5	9	1								2	10		4		8			6		
41	May	2	GILLINGHAM	5-3	Sheppard 2, Groome 2, Warner	3645		11	3		5	9	1								2	10		4	7	8			6		
42		5	Brentford	1-1	Groome	4775		11	3		5	9	1						7		2	10		4		8			6		

	Armstrong W	Daniels AWC	Davison JW	Foster CJ	Fuller EW	Groome JPG	Hewett JT	Hills WR	Jewett G	Kirkpatrick J	Leaver J	Mingay HJ	Morris H	Parker RR	Prior G	Sheppard W	Slade R	Smith FW	Vanner HJ	Warner J	Wilbourn H	Wilkinson GG	Woodward A	Yates J	Yates W
Apps	1	42	32	15	34	16	28	28	24	9	11	2	28	13	35	40	8	31	1	36	2	3	9	2	12
Goals		6		3		14		2					2	2		25		1		12					

One own goal

F.A. Cup

	Date		Opponent	Score	Scorers	Att	Armstrong W	Daniels AWC	Davison JW	Foster CJ	Fuller EW	Groome JPG	Hewett JT	Hills WR	Jewett G	Kirkpatrick J	Leaver J	Mingay HJ	Morris H	Parker RR	Prior G	Sheppard W	Slade R	Smith FW	Vanner HJ	Warner J	Wilbourn H	Wilkinson GG	Woodward A	Yates J	Yates W
R1	Nov	30	BRIGHTON & HOVE ALB.	1-2	Parker	6058		11	3	8	6			7				1		9	2	10		4					5		

West Bromwich Albion

8th in Division Two

	Date	Opponent	Score	Scorers	Att.	Ashmore GSA	Baugh RH	Bromage E	Byers JE	Blytheway GS	Carter JH	Chambers H	Cookson J	Corbett FJ	Edwards J	Evans JT	Finch EAR	Fitton GA	Fryer ER	Glidden TW	Howarth N	James GC	Magee TP	Pearson HF	Poxton JH	Rix J	Rooke EIH	Shaw GE	Short JS	Sproson T	Wilson C
1	Aug 27	Oldham Athletic	1-3	Cookson	13035		2		11		8		9			5				7	6		4					3		1	10
2	31	STOKE CITY	2-4	Cookson, Byers	15453		2		11		8		9			5				7	6		4					3		1	10
3	Sep 3	GRIMSBY TOWN	3-1	Carter 2, Wilson	16521				11		8		9			5	2		6	7			4					3		1	10
4	5	Stoke City	1-1	Cookson	20614	1					8		9			5	2	11	6	7			4					3			10
5	10	Reading	4-1	Cookson, Fitton, Glidden, Wilson	16238	1					8		9			5	2	11	6	7			4					3			10
6	17	BLACKPOOL	6-3	Cookson 6 (1p)	19605	1					8		9			5	2	11	6	7			4					3			10
7	24	Chelsea	1-1	Carter	44724	1					8		9			5	2	11	6	7			4					3			10
8	Oct 1	CLAPTON ORIENT	4-1	Fitton, Carter, Glidden, Cookson	19994	1					8		9			5	2	11	6	7			4					3			10
9	8	Wolverhampton Wan.	1-4	Evans	40816	1					8					5	2	11	6	7		9	4					3			10
10	15	Bristol City	1-0	Glidden	24442	1					8					5	2	11	6	9			7				4	3			10
11	22	SWANSEA TOWN	5-2	Fitton, Carter 2, Cookson, Wilson	15245	1					8		9			5	2	11	6	7			4					3			10
12	29	Fulham	1-3	Cookson	20577	1					8		9			5	2	11	6	7			4					3			10
13	Nov 5	BARNSLEY	1-1	Wilson	18129	1					8		9			5	2			7			4		11		6	3			10
14	12	Preston North End	3-3	Cookson, Glidden 2	15827	1					8		9			5	2			7			4		11		6	3			10
15	19	HULL CITY	1-1	Glidden	8857	1					8		9			5	2		6	7			4		11			3			10
16	26	Leeds United	2-1	Carter 2	23690	1				7	8					5	2		6	9			4		11			3			10
17	Dec 3	NOTTM. FOREST	2-3	Carter, Glidden	16674	1				7	8					5	2		6	9			4		11			3			10
18	10	Manchester City	1-3	Glidden	29747	1				7	8		9			5	2		6	10			4		11			3			
19	17	SOUTH SHIELDS	3-0	Glidden, Evans, Cookson	11711				11	7	8		9			5	2		6	10			4	1				3			
20	24	Port Vale	1-4	Cookson	8216				11	7	8		9			5	2		6	10			4	1				3			
21	26	NOTTS COUNTY	2-2	Cookson, Poxton	14642					7	8		9			5	2			10	6		4	1	11			3			
22	27	Notts County	0-3		17755						8		9			5	2		4	7	6			1	11			3			10
23	31	OLDHAM ATHLETIC	0-0		7357	1				7	8		9			5	2	11		10	6		4					3			
24	Jan 7	Grimsby Town	6-0	Cookson 4, Short, Blytheway	12242	1				7			9			5	2	11		8	6		4					3	10		
25	21	READING	5-3	Inglis (og), Cookson 4	16104	1				7			9			5	2	11		8	6		4					3	10		
26	28	Blackpool	3-4	Cookson 2, Short	8102	1				7			9			5	2	11		8	6		4					3	10		
27	Feb 4	CHELSEA	3-0	Short 2, Carter	23718	1					8		9			5	2	11		7	6		4					3	10		
28	11	Clapton Orient	0-0		11443	1					8		9			5	2	11		7	6		4					3	10		
29	18	WOLVERHAMPTON W.	4-0	Cookson 2, Carter, Wilson	37342	1					8		9			5	2	11		7	6		4					3			10
30	25	BRISTOL CITY	0-0		23142						8		9			5	2	11		7	6		4	1				3	10		
31	Mar 3	Swansea Town	2-3	Cookson 2	15355						8		9			5	2	11		7	6		4	1				3	10		
32	10	FULHAM	4-0	Cookson, Chambers, Glidden 2	17662	1					8	10	9			5	2	11		7	6		4					3			
33	17	Barnsley	4-2	Carter, Cookson 2, Glidden	8144	1		11			8	10	9			5	2			7	6		4					3			
34	24	PRESTON NORTH END	2-4	Carter, Cookson	24067	1		11			8		9			5	2			7	6		4					3	10		
35	31	Hull City	1-1	Bromage	7964	1		11				10	9	3	8	5				7	6		4					2			
36	Apr 7	LEEDS UNITED	0-1		23644	1		11			8	10	9			5	2			7	6		4					3			
37	9	Southampton	2-3	Glidden, Carter	18000	1		11			8		9				2			7	6		4				5	3	10		
38	10	SOUTHAMPTON	2-1	Cookson, Short	10500			11			8		9				2			7	6		4	1			5	3	10		
39	14	Nottingham Forest	2-0	Cookson, Carter	6158			11		7	8	10	9				2				6		4	1			5	3			
40	21	MANCHESTER CITY	1-1	Chanbers	15409			11			8	10	9				2			7	6		4	1			5	3			
41	28	South Shields	3-2	Bromage, Dunn (og), Cookson	5514			11		7	8	10	9				2				6		4	1			5	3			
42	May 5	PORT VALE	0-0		9217			11		7	8	10	9				2						4	1		6	5	3			
					Apps	28	2	10	5	13	38	8	38	1	1	36	39	19	17	39	23	1	41	11	8	1	9	42	10	3	19
					Goals			2	1	1	15	2	38			2		3		13					1				5		5

Two own goals

F.A. Cup

	Date	Opponent	Score	Scorers	Att.	Ashmore GSA	Baugh RH	Bromage E	Byers JE	Blytheway GS	Carter JH	Chambers H	Cookson J	Corbett FJ	Edwards J	Evans JT	Finch EAR	Fitton GA	Fryer ER	Glidden TW	Howarth N	James GC	Magee TP	Pearson HF	Poxton JH	Rix J	Rooke EIH	Shaw GE	Short JS	Sproson T	Wilson C
R3	Jan 14	Arsenal	0-2		43322	1							9			5	2	11		8	6		4					3	10		

Played at 7: Taylor

West Ham United

17th in Division One

							Baillie DA	Barrett JW	Cadwell AF	Campbell J	Collins JFA	Cox WC	Earl AT	Earle SGJ	Gibbins WVT	Hebden JT	Henderson W	Hodgson T	Horler GH	Hufton AE	Jackson W	Johnson WJ	Loughlin J	Moore WGB	Norrington CJ	Robson GC	Ruffell JW	Smith H	Smith WA	Tate IH	Watson VM	Yews TP
1	Aug	27	Derby County	3-2	Barrett, Gibbins, Watson	18538		5	6		4		3	8	10	2				1							11				9	7
2	Sep	1	SUNDERLAND	2-4	Ruffell 2	19037		5	6		4		3	8		2				1				10			11				9	7
3		3	HUDDERSFIELD T	4-2	Earle 2, Loughlin, Yews	23925	1	5	6		4		3	8		2						10	9				11					7
4		10	PORTSMOUTH	4-2	Loughlin 2, Earle, Ruffell	24729		5	6		4		3	8	10	2				1			9				11					7
5		17	Leicester City	3-2	Earle, Ruffell, Yews	25482		5	6		4			8		3	2			1			10				11				9	7
6		24	LIVERPOOL	3-1	Earle, Gibbins, Ruffell	26876		5	6		4			8	9	3	2			1			10				11					7
7	Oct	1	Arsenal	2-2	Earle, Gibbins	34931		5	6		4			8	9	3	2			1			10				11					7
8		8	BURNLEY	2-0	Gibbins 2	27467		5	6		4			8	9	3	2			1			10				11					7
9		15	Bury	1-3	Ruffell	20110		5	6		4				10	3	2			1			8				11				9	7
10		22	Everton	0-7		20151	1	5	6		4				10	3	2						8				11				9	7
11		29	MANCHESTER UNITED	1-2	Watson	21972	1	5			4	6		8		2			3								11	10			9	7
12	Nov	5	Tottenham Hotspur	3-5	Barrett, Earle, Ruffell	35099	1	5			4	6		8	9	2			3					10			11					7
13		12	CARDIFF CITY	2-0	Watson, Yews	18189	1	5			4	6	2	8	10										3		11				9	7
14		19	Blackburn Rovers	0-1		14040	1	5			4	6	2	8	10										3		11				9	7
15		26	MIDDLESBROUGH	4-5	Yews 2, Gibbins, Watson	14666	1	5			4	6	2	8	10										3		11				9	7
16	Dec	3	Sheffield Wednesday	0-2		22796	1	5			4	6	2	8	10										3		11				9	7
17		10	BOLTON WANDERERS	2-0	Watson 2	18926		5			4	6	2	8										10	3		11			1	9	7
18		17	Birmingham	2-1	Ruffell, Yews	18206		5			4	6	2		9									10	3		11			1	8	7
19		24	NEWCASTLE UNITED	5-2	Gibbins 3, Ruffell 2	19296		5			4	6	2		9									10	3		11			1	8	7
20		26	Sheffield United	2-6	Gibbins, Yews	23591		5			4	6	2		9						11			10	3					1	8	7
21		27	SHEFFIELD UNITED	1-1	Yews	20434		5			4	6	2	8	9						11				3					1	10	7
22		31	DERBY COUNTY	2-2	Ruffell, Watson	17702		5		9	4	6	2		10										3		11			1	8	7
23	Jan	2	Sunderland	2-3	Gibbins 2	27542		5			4	6	2		9									10	3		11			1	8	7
24		7	Huddersfield Town	2-5	Watson, Yews	10972		5			4	6	2		9					1				10			11		3		8	7
25		21	Portsmouth	1-2	Gibbins	17656			6		4	5	3		9		2			1				10			11				8	7
26	Feb	4	Liverpool	3-1	Ruffell 2, Watson	23897			6		4	5	3	8			2			1				10			11				9	7
27		11	ARSENAL	2-2	Watson 2	28086			6		4	5	3	8			2			1				10			11				9	7
28		18	Burnley	0-0		14663			6		4	5	3	8			2			1				10			11				9	7
29		25	BURY	1-2	Ruffell	19903			6		4	5	3	8			2			1				10			11				9	7
30	Mar	3	EVERTON	0-0		31997		5			4	6	3		9		2			1				10			11				8	7
31		10	Manchester United	1-1	Earle	21577			6		4	5	3	8	9		2			1				10			11					7
32		12	LEICESTER CITY	4-0	Watson 3, Yews	6211	1		6		4	5	3	8			2							10			11				9	7
33		17	TOTTENHAM HOTSPUR	1-1	Ruffell	33908		3	6		4	5		8			2			1				10			11				9	7
34		24	Cardiff City	5-1	Earle 2, Watson 2, Yews	14529		5	6		4		3	8			2			1				10			11				9	7
35		31	BLACKBURN ROVERS	4-3	Ruffell 2, Earle, Moore	12504	1	5	6		4		3	8				2						10			11				9	7
36	Apr	6	ASTON VILLA	0-0		31469		5	6		4		3	8				2		1				10			11				9	7
37		7	Middlesbrough	2-2	Moore, Ruffell	21860		5	6		4		3	8				2		1				10			11				9	7
38		9	Aston Villa	0-1		31059		5	6		4		3	8	10			2		1							11				9	7
39		14	SHEFFIELD WEDNESDAY	1-2	Barrett	14580		5	6		4		3	8	10			2		1				11							9	7
40		21	Bolton Wanderers	0-4		8520		3	6		4	5	2	8						1				10			11				9	7
41		28	BIRMINGHAM	3-3	Barrett 2, Loughlin	17917		10	6		4	5	2	8						1			9		3		11					7
42	May	5	Newcastle United	1-3	Gibbins	17909			6		4	5	2		10					1			9		3	8	11					7
						Apps	10	34	27	1	42	26	33	31	25	12	16	5	2	25	2	1	10	23	13	1	39	1	1	7	33	42
						Goals		5						11	14								4	2			18				16	11

F.A. Cup

							Baillie DA	Barrett JW	Cadwell AF	Campbell J	Collins JFA	Cox WC	Earl AT	Earle SGJ	Gibbins WVT	Hebden JT	Henderson W	Hodgson T	Horler GH	Hufton AE	Jackson W	Johnson WJ	Loughlin J	Moore WGB	Norrington CJ	Robson GC	Ruffell JW	Smith H	Smith WA	Tate IH	Watson VM	Yews TP
R3	Jan	14	Portsmouth	2-0	Gibbins, Ruffell	27692			6		4	5	3		9		2			1				10			11				8	7
R4		28	Huddersfield Town	1-2	Gibbins	27525			6		4	5	3	8	9		2			1							11				10	7

Wigan Borough

20th in Division Three (North)

	Date	Opponent	Score	Scorers	Att	Barrowman W	Bryce J	Collier S	Cooke GH	Dickinson W	Fenner T	Finney J	Fisher W	Glover CE	Humpish AE	Lawson D	Mandy JT	McGuire J	Moran J	Potter AE	Riddell JH	Robb D	Shaw GR	Tillbrook C	Walker JR	Welsby A	Wilson TH	Winter W	Yates GH
1	Aug 27	HARTLEPOOLS UNITED	0-2		6385				11	9	7			3				10	2	6		4		8			5	1	
2	29	Lincoln City	1-4	Fenner	5518		3			10	9				11		7	8	2	6		4					5	1	
3	Sep 3	Accrington Stanley	4-2	Fenner 3, Mandy	8331		3			8	9				7		11	10	2	6		4					5	1	
4	7	LINCOLN CITY	1-3	Potter	4260		3			8	9				7		11	10	2	6		4					5	1	
5	10	ROCHDALE	1-2	Fenner	5275						9				10		11	8	2	6	3	4	7				5	1	
6	17	DONCASTER ROVERS	1-1	Mandy	3325					8	9				10		11		2	6	5	4	7				3	1	
7	24	Darlington	0-1		5921				7	8	9				6		11	10		3	5	4					2	1	
8	Oct 1	ASHINGTON	0-0		1696					8	9				7		11	10	2	3	5	6					4	1	
9	8	Crewe Alexandra	2-1	McGuire, Mandy	4005					8	7				10		11	9	2	3		6				4	5	1	
10	15	HALIFAX TOWN	1-3	McGuire	4989					8	7				10		11	9	2	3	6					4	5	1	
11	22	Durham City	0-3		789					8	7		6		10		11	9	2	3						4	5	1	
12	29	SOUTHPORT	1-3	Dickinson (p)	4247					10	8		4			7	11	9	2	3		5				6		1	
13	Nov 5	Rotherham United	0-6		3819								4		8	7	11		2	3		5			10	6		1	9
14	12	WREXHAM	3-0	Mandy, Fenner, Cooke	3426				11		9				8	7	10		2	3	5	4				6		1	
15	19	Chesterfield	0-0		2354				11	8	9					7	10		2	3	5	4				6		1	
16	Dec 3	Tranmere Rovers	2-5	Dickinson, Fenner	4448				11	8	9					7	10		2	3	5	4				6		1	
17	10	NELSON	4-2	Dickinson, Fenner 3	2736				11	8	9				4	7	10		2	3	5					6		1	
18	17	Barrow	2-6	Riddell, Dickinson	4110				11	8	9				4	7	10		2	3	5					6		1	
19	26	Bradford City	0-3		13748				11	8	9			2	4	7	10			3	5					6		1	
20	27	BRADFORD CITY	2-2	Mandy, Dickinson	4100				11	8	9			2	4	7	10			3	5					6		1	
21	31	Hartlepools United	1-1	Dickinson	3546					8	9			2	4	7	11			3	5				10	6		1	
22	Jan 7	ACCRINGTON STANLEY	2-0	Dickinson 2	2756				11	8	9			2	4	7	10			3	5					6		1	
23	14	STOCKPORT COUNTY	1-3	Fenner	3843				11	8	9			2	4	7	10			3	5					6		1	
24	21	Rochdale	0-3		3626					8	9			2	4	7	11			3					10	6	5	1	
25	28	Doncaster Rovers	1-4	Fenner	6264					8	9			2	4	7	11			3					10	6	5	1	
26	Feb 1	BRADFORD PARK AVE.	1-3	Dickinson	2406					8	9			2	4	7	11			3		6			10		5	1	
27	4	DARLINGTON	0-3		2000				11	8	10				4	7	9		3	6	5						2	1	
28	11	Ashington	3-6	Fenner, Cooke, Yates	1380				11	10	8				4		7		2	3	5	6						1	9
29	18	CREWE ALEXANDRA	2-1	Dickinson, Lawson	3259	1				10					8	7	11		2	3	5	6					4		9
30	25	Halifax Town	2-2	Humpish, Yates	2678	1				10			7		8		11		2	3	5	6					4		9
31	Mar 3	DURHAM CITY	3-0	Dickinson 3	4060					10					8	7	11		2	3	5	6					4	1	9
32	10	Southport	1-2	Yates	3890	1				10					8	7	11		2	3	5	6					4		9
33	17	ROTHERHAM UNITED	0-0		3281	1				10					8	7	11		2	3	5	6					4		9
34	24	Wrexham	1-5	Mandy	2374	1			11	8						7	10		2	3	5	6					4		9
35	31	CHESTERFIELD	3-2	Mandy, Humpish, Yates	3299			1							10	7	11		2	3	5	6			8		4		9
36	Apr 6	NEW BRIGHTON	2-2	Walker, Yates	4858			1	11						10	7	1		2	3	5				8	6	4		9
37	7	Stockport County	1-1	Lawson	8840			1	11	8		10				7			2	3	5					6	4		9
38	9	New Brighton	1-2	Dickinson	4128			1	11	8					10	7			2	3	5					6	4		9
39	14	TRANMERE ROVERS	1-0	Mandy	2682			1	11	8					10	7	9		2	3		6				4	5		
40	21	Bradford Park Avenue	1-5	Welsby	11236			1	11	9				2	10					3	5	6			8	7	4		
41	28	BARROW	1-0	Dickinson (p)	3355			1		8					10	7	11			3	5	6				4	2		9
42	May 5	Nelson	3-3	Mandy 2, Dickinson	2183			1		8					10	7	9		2	3	5	6				4	11		
					Apps	5	3	8	19	37	27	1	4	10	36	28	38	11	31	42	30	27	2	1	8	24	29	29	13
					Goals				2	16	11				2	2	11	2		2	1				1	1			5

F.A. Cup

	Date	Opponent	Score	Scorers	Att	Barrowman W	Bryce J	Collier S	Cooke GH	Dickinson W	Fenner T	Finney J	Fisher W	Glover CE	Humpish AE	Lawson D	Mandy JT	McGuire J	Moran J	Potter AE	Riddell JH	Robb D	Shaw GR	Tillbrook C	Walker JR	Welsby A	Wilson TH	Winter W	Yates GH
R1	Nov 26	Rhyl Athletic	3-4	Dickinson, McLean (og), Fenner	4500				11	8	9					7	10		2	3	5	4				6		1	

Wolverhampton Wanderers

16th in Division Two

No	Date	Opponent	Score	Scorers	Att	Baker JE	Baxter TW	Botto LA	Bowen TG	Bryce F	Canavon A	Chadwick W	Charnley S	Cock DJ	Fox WV	George FN	Green F	Harrington JW	Higham F	Kay AE	Lees HH	Legge AE	MacDougall AL	Marshall WH	Phillipson WT	Pritchard TF	Richards DT	Richards WE	Rotton WH	Shaw HV	Watson EG	Weaver RW	Weaver W	Williams LH	Williams WJ
1	Aug 27	MANCHESTER CITY	2-2	Phillipson, W Weaver	22600							10		8		1		7	4	6					9					3	2		11		5
2	Sep 3	Hull City	0-2		11050							8			3	1			4	6	10				9			7			2		11		5
3	5	SOUTH SHIELDS	2-1	Chadwick, Phillipson	10971							8			3	1				6	10				9			7			2		11		5
4	10	PRESTON NORTH END	2-3	Chadwick 2	17124				4			8	5		3	1				6	10				9			7			2		11		
5	12	South Shields	2-2	Chadwick 2	4873							10	5			1				6	8		4		9			7		3	2		11		
6	17	Swansea Town	0-6		16692							10	5		3	1				6	8		4		9			7			2		11		
7	24	FULHAM	3-1	Chadwick 2, Watson	11685				8			10			3	1			4	6					9	5		7			2		11		
8	Oct 1	Barnsley	2-2	Chadwick. Higham	9082				8			10			3	1			4	6					9	5		7			2		11		
9	8	WEST BROMWICH ALB.	4-1	Chadwick 2, Bowen, Phillipson	40816				8			10			3	1			4	6					9	5		7			2		11		
10	15	PORT VALE	2-1	Cock, W Weaver	18026				8			10		9	3	1			4	6						5		7			2		11		
11	22	Southampton	1-4	Bowen	5794				8			10			3	1			4	6						5		7			2		11		
12	29	STOKE CITY	1-2	W Weaver	17247				8			10			3	1		7	4	6		9				5					2		11		
13	Nov 5	Bristol City	1-4	Rotton	14384							10			3	1			4	6		8				5		7	9		2		11		
14	12	NOTTS COUNTY	2-2	Chadwick, Green	16100			1				10					9		4	6						5		7		3	2	8	11		
15	19	Oldham Athletic	0-3		7350			1				10					9		4	6						5		7		3	2	8	11		
16	26	BLACKPOOL	2-4	Phillipson, W Richards	13200			1				10							4	6					9	5		7		3	2	8	11		
17	Dec 3	Reading	1-2	Chadwick	9550	4					1	10			3			7				8	6			5					2	9	11		
18	10	GRIMSBY TOWN	0-1		7431	4					1	10		9	3			7					6			5					2	8	11		
19	17	Chelsea	0-2		24340		11		10		1				6			7					4		9	5				3	2	8			
20	24	CLAPTON ORIENT	5-3	* see below	6023		11		8		1	10			3			7		6			4		9	5					2				
21	26	Nottingham Forest	2-3	Bowen, Phillipson	12530		11		8		1				3			7		6			4		9	5			10		2				
22	27	NOTTM. FOREST	1-0	Baxter	15982	4	11		8		1				3			7					6		9	5			10		2				
23	31	Manchester City	0-3		25991		11		8		1				3			7		6			4		9	5			10		2				
24	Jan 7	HULL CITY	1-1	Bowen	12106		11		8		1				3		10	7		6			4		9	5					2				
25	21	Preston North End	4-5	Phillipson 2, Chadwick, Charnley	14162		11		8	1		10	4		3								6		9	5		7			2				
26	Feb 4	Fulham	0-7		12981	4	11		8	1		10			3								6		9	5					2	7			
27	11	BARNSLEY	2-1	Phillipson, Watson	7151	4	11				1						10			6					9	5		7		3	2	8			
28	18	West Bromwich Albion	0-4		37342	4	11		8		1	10	5							6					9			7		3	2				
29	25	Port Vale	2-2	Chadwick, R Weaver	11358		11				1	10							4	6						5	8	7		3		9		2	
30	Mar 3	SOUTHAMPTON	2-1	Chadwick, R Weaver	13363		11	1				10							4	6					8	5		7		3		9		2	
31	10	Stoke City	2-2	Chadwick, R Weaver	13264		11	1				10							4	6					8	5		7		3		9		2	
32	17	BRISTOL CITY	5-2	R Weaver 3, Chadwick, Marshall	15492		11	1				10							4	6				8		5		7		3		9		2	
33	24	Notts County	2-1	R Weaver 2	13617		11	1				10							4	6				8		5		7		3		9		2	
34	31	OLDHAM ATHLETIC	3-1	R Weaver 2, Chadwick	14631		11	1				10							4	6				8		5		7		3		9		2	
35	Apr 7	Blackpool	0-3		18030		11	1				10						7	4	6				8		5				3		9		2	
36	9	LEEDS UNITED	0-0		25251		11	1									10	7	4	6				8		5				3		9		2	
37	10	Leeds United	0-3		29821	4	11	1									10	7		6				8		5				3		9		2	
38	14	READING	2-1	Harrington, Marshall	10357	4	11	1									10	7		6				8		5				3		9		2	
39	21	Grimsby Town	1-0	Baxter	7248	4	11	1				10						7		6				8		5				3		9		2	
40	28	CHELSEA	1-2	R Weaver	16727	4	11	1				10						7		6				8		5				3		9		2	
41	30	SWANSEA TOWN	1-1	Marshall	8972		11	1				10								6				8		5	4	7		3		9		2	
42	May 5	Clapton Orient	0-0		12891		11	1				10			3					6				8		5	4	7				9		2	
					Apps	10	24	16	16	2	11	33	5	3	22	13	7	16	20	36	5	3	12	11	22	35	3	25	4	21	28	22	18	14	3
					Goals		4		5			19	1	1			1	1	1					3	9			1	1		2	11	3		

Scorers in game 20: Baxter 2, Bowen, Chadwick, Phillipson

Played in one game: W Boswell (game 11, at 9), J Bradford (3, at 4)

F.A. Cup

Rd	Date	Opponent	Score	Scorers	Att	Baker JE	Baxter TW	Botto LA	Bowen TG	Bryce F	Canavon A	Chadwick W	Charnley S	Cock DJ	Fox WV	George FN	Green F	Harrington JW	Higham F	Kay AE	Lees HH	Legge AE	MacDougall AL	Marshall WH	Phillipson WT	Pritchard TF	Richards DT	Richards WE	Rotton WH	Shaw HV	Watson EG	Weaver RW	Weaver W	Williams LH	Williams WJ
R3	Jan 14	CHELSEA	2-1	Baxter, Phillipson	32134		11		8		1	10			3			7	4				6		9	5					2				
R4	28	Sheffield United	1-3	Phillipson	34120	4	11		8		1	10			3			7					6		9	5					2				

Wrexham

11th in Division Three (North)

	Date	Opponent	Score	Scorers	Att	Beever A	Bellis GA	Bingham HW	Condon B	Crompton W	Davies HC	Evans AR	Graham RH	Gunson JG	Harris WJ	Jones A	Jones RT	Lawrence E	Longmuir AM	Lucas A	Lumberg AA	Read E	Regan EGP	Robson ER	Rogers W	Smith AH	Smith FC	Smith J	Woodhouse RT
1	Aug 27	Chesterfield	1-0	Bellis	7164		5						6	11		2			7		3		4	1			9	10	8
2	31	CREWE ALEXANDRA	2-0	C Smith, J Smith	5259		5						6	11		2			7		3		4	1			9	10	8
3	Sep 3	BRADFORD PARK AVE.	1-1	Gunson	7579		5						6	11		2			7		3		4	1			9	10	8
4	5	Crewe Alexandra	1-1	Woodhouse	4158		5				11					2		6	7		3		4	1			9	10	8
5	10	Tranmere Rovers	1-2	Rogers	8677	3	5						6	11		2			7				4	1	9			10	8
6	14	HARTLEPOOLS UNITED	3-2	J Smith, Woodhouse, Rogers	2927	3	5						6	11		2			7				4	1	9			10	8
7	17	STOCKPORT COUNTY	1-0	Gunson	7211		5						6	11		2			7		3		4	1			9	10	8
8	24	Barrow	2-2	Longmuir, J Smith	4426		5						3	11		2		6	7				4	1	9			10	8
9	Oct 1	NELSON	5-2	Woodhouse 3, Bellis, Longmuir	4828		5						3	11		2		6	7				4	1	9			10	8
10	8	Rochdale	0-3		7493	6	5						3	11		2			7				4	1	9			10	8
11	15	ROTHERHAM UNITED	3-2	A Jones (p), Gunson, Harris	7139		5		9				6	11	8	2			7		3		4	1					10
12	22	DONCASTER ROVERS	1-2	Woodhouse	3536		5		9	3			6	11	8	2			7				4	1					10
13	29	Darlington	3-1	Longmuir, Woodhouse, Rogers	6692		5			3			6	11		2			7				4	1	8		9		10
14	Nov 5	ASHINGTON	5-1	Rogers 2, C Smith 3	3531		5			3			6	11		2			7				4	1	8		9		10
15	12	Wigan Borough	0-3		3426		5			3	11		6			2			7				4	1	8		9		10
16	19	ACCRINGTON STANLEY	0-1		2070		5			3			6	11		2			7				4	1	8		9		10
17	Dec 3	LINCOLN CITY	1-0	Woodhouse	4400		5	11					6		9	2			7		3		4	1				10	8
18	17	BRADFORD CITY	1-0	C Smith	4072		5			3			6	11		2			7				4	1			9	10	8
19	24	Halifax Town	1-4	Longmuir	3032		5			3			6	11		2			7				4	1			9	10	8
20	26	Southport	1-4	Gunson	6705		5						6	11		2			7		3		4	1	8		9	10	
21	27	SOUTHPORT	3-0	C Smith, Gunson 2	6998		5						6	11		2					3		4		7	1	9	10	8
22	31	CHESTERFIELD	1-2	C Smith	2399		5						6	11		2					3		4		7	1	9	10	8
23	Jan 7	Bradford Park Avenue	0-2		13060		5						6	11		2			7		3		4	1			9	10	8
24	21	TRANMERE ROVERS	2-0	Gunson, C Smith	4792		5						6	11	8	2			7		3		4			1	9		10
25	Feb 4	BARROW	5-0	Woodhouse, Longmuir, Gunson 3	2438		5						6	11	8	2			7		3			1	4		9		10
26	11	Nelson	0-4		2721		5						6	11	8	2			7		3			1	4		9		10
27	18	ROCHDALE	2-1	R Jones, Harris	4157		5						6	11	9	2	8		7		3			1	4				10
28	25	Rotherham United	1-0	Woodhouse	5665		5					1	6	11		2			7		3		4		8		9		10
29	27	Stockport County	0-5		4120		5					1	6	11		2			7		3		4		8		9		10
30	Mar 3	Doncaster Rovers	1-1	Longmuir	8519		5						6	11		2			7		3		4	1	8		9		10
31	7	New Brighton	0-0		3020		5						6	11		2			7	1	3		4		8		9		10
32	10	DARLINGTON	1-2	Longmuir (p)	3794		5						6	11	9	2			7	1	3		4		8				10
33	17	Ashington	1-2	Rogers	1369		5	11					6		8	2		4		1	3				7		9		10
34	24	WIGAN BOROUGH	5-1	Woodhouse, J Smith 2, C Smith, Wilson (og)	2374		5						6	11		2					3		4	1	7		9	10	8
35	31	Accrington Stanley	0-2		3188		5						6	11		2			7		3		4	1			9	10	8
36	Apr 6	DURHAM CITY	4-0	Longmuir (p), Bellis 2, C Smith	3767		5						6	11		2			7		3		4	1			9	10	8
37	7	NEW BRIGHTON	0-2		4296								6	11		2			7		3	5	4	1	9			10	8
38	9	Durham City	1-1	C Smith	2399								6	11		2			7		3	5	4	1			9	10	8
39	14	Lincoln City	0-5		4005		5						6	11		2			7		3		4	1			9	10	8
40	21	Hartlepools United	2-4	C Smith 2	1542		5						6	11		2		10	7		3		4	1			9		8
41	28	Bradford City	0-2		6844		5	11								2		6	7		3		4	1	10		9		8
42	May 5	HALIFAX TOWN	2-0	Woodhouse, Gunson	1726		5							11		2		6	7		3		4	1	10		9		8

	Beever A	Bellis GA	Bingham HW	Condon B	Crompton W	Davies HC	Evans AR	Graham RH	Gunson JG	Harris WJ	Jones A	Jones RT	Lawrence E	Longmuir AM	Lucas A	Lumberg AA	Read E	Regan EGP	Robson ER	Rogers W	Smith AH	Smith FC	Smith J	Woodhouse RT
Apps	3	40	3	2	7	2	2	39	37	9	42	1	7	38	3	30	2	38	34	25	3	31	23	41
Goals		4							11	2	1	1		8						6		13	5	12

One own goal

F.A. Cup

	Date	Opponent	Score	Scorers	Att	Beever A	Bellis GA	Bingham HW	Condon B	Crompton W	Davies HC	Evans AR	Graham RH	Gunson JG	Harris WJ	Jones A	Jones RT	Lawrence E	Longmuir AM	Lucas A	Lumberg AA	Read E	Regan EGP	Robson ER	Rogers W	Smith AH	Smith FC	Smith J	Woodhouse RT
R1	Nov 26	Durham City	1-1	Gunson	3690		5			3			6	11	8	2			7				4	1	9				10
rep	30	DURHAM CITY	4-0	Woodhouse 2, Gunson 2	3804		5			3			6	11	9	2			7				4	1	8				10
R2	Dec 10	CARLISLE UNITED	1-0	C Smith	7522		5			3			6	11		2			7				4	1	8		9		10
R3	Jan 14	SWANSEA TOWN	2-1	Longmuir, Gunson	12000		5						6	11	8	2			7		3		4			1	9		10
R4	28	BIRMINGHAM	1-3	Gunson	12228		5						6	11	8	2			7		3				4	1	9		10

F.A. Challenge Cup 1927/28

Round One

	Accrington Stanley v. Lincoln City	2-5
	Aldershot v. Queen's Park Rangers	2-1
	Bath City v. Southall	2-0
	Botwell Mission v. Peterborough & Fletton Utd.	3-4
	Bradford City v. Workington	6-0
	Bristol Rovers v. Walsall	4-2
	Carlisle United v. Doncaster Rovers	2-1
	Coventry City v. Bournemouth	2-2
	Crewe Alexandra v. Ashington	2-2
	Darlington v. Chesterfield	4-1
	Dartford v. Crystal Palace	1-3
	Denaby United v. Southport	2-3
	Durham City v. Wrexham	1-1
	Exeter City v. Aberdare Athletic	9-1
	Gainsborough Trinity v. Stockton	6-0
	Gillingham v. Plymouth Argyle	2-1
	Halifax Town v. Hartlepools United	3-0
	Ilford v. Dulwich Hamlet	4-0
	Kettering Town v. Chatham	2-0
	Luton Town v. Clapton	9-0
	Merthyr Town v. Charlton Athletic	0-0
	Nelson v. Bradford Park Avenue	0-3
	Newport County v. Swindon Town	0-1
	Northampton Town v. Leyton	8-0
	Northfleet United v. London Caledonians	0-1
	Poole v. Norwich City	1-1
	Rhyl Athletic v. Wigan Borough	4-3
	Rochdale v. Crook Town	8-2
	Shildon v. New Brighton	1-3
	Shirebrook v. Tranmere Rovers	1-3
	Southend United v. Wellington Town	1-0
	Spennymoor United v. Rotherham United	1-1
	Stockport County v. Oswestry Town	5-2
	Watford v. Brighton & Hove Albion	1-2
r	Ashington v. Crewe Alexandra	0-2
r	Bournemouth v. Coventry City	2-0
r	Charlton Athletic v. Merthyr Town	2-1
r	Norwich City v. Poole	5-0
r	Rotherham United v. Spennymoor United	4-2
r	Wrexham v. Durham City	4-0

Round Two

	Bournemouth v. Bristol Rovers	6-1
	Bradford City v. Rotherham United	2-3
	Bradford Park Avenue v. Southport	0-2
	Charlton Athletic v. Kettering Town	1-1
	Crewe Alexandra v. Stockport County	2-0
	Darlington v. Rochdale	2-1
	Exeter City v. Ilford	5-3
	Gainsborough Trinity v. Lincoln City	0-2
	Gillingham v. Southend United	2-0
	London Caledonians v. Bath City	1-0
	Luton Town v. Norwich City	6-0
	New Brighton v. Rhyl Athletic	7-2
	Northampton Town v. Brighton & Hove Albion	1-0
	Peterborough & Fletton Utd. v. Aldershot	2-1
	Swindon Town v. Crystal Palace	0-0
	Tranmere Rovers v. Halifax Town	3-1
	Wrexham v. Carlisle United	1-0
r	Crystal Palace v. Swindon Town	1-2
r	Kettering Town v. Charlton Athletic	1-2

Round Three

	Arsenal v. West Bromwich Albion	2-0
	Birmingham v. Peterborough & Fletton Utd.	4-3
	Blackburn Rovers v. Newcastle United	4-1
	Blackpool v. Oldham Athletic	1-4
	Bolton Wanderers v. Luton Town	2-1
	Bristol City v. Tottenham Hotspur	1-2
	Burnley v. Aston Villa	0-2
	Cardiff City v. Southampton	2-1
	Charlton Athletic v. Bury	1-1
	Huddersfield Town v. Lincoln City	4-2
	Hull City v. Leicester City	0-1
	Liverpool v. Darlington	1-0
	London Caledonians v. Crewe Alexandra	2-3
	Manchester City v. Leeds United	1-0
	Manchester United v. Brentford	7-1
	Middlesbrough v. South Shields	3-0
	Millwall v. Derby County	1-2
	New Brighton v. Corinthians	2-1
	Nottingham Forest v. Tranmere Rovers	1-0
	Notts County v. Sheffield United	2-3
	Port Vale v. Barnsley	3-0
	Portsmouth v. West Ham United	0-2
	Preston North End v. Everton	0-3
	Reading v. Grimsby Town	4-0
	Rotherham United v. Exeter City	3-3
	Sheffield Wednesday v. Bournemouth	3-0
	Southport v. Fulham	3-0
	Stoke City v. Gillingham	6-1
	Sunderland v. Northampton Town	3-3
	Swindon Town v. Clapton Orient	2-1
	Wolverhampton Wan. v. Chelsea	2-1
	Wrexham v. Swansea Town	2-1
r	Bury v. Charlton Athletic	4-3
r	Exeter City v. Rotherham United	3-1
r	Northampton Town v. Sunderland	0-3

Round Four

	Arsenal v. Everton	4-3
	Aston Villa v. Crewe Alexandra	3-0
	Bury v. Manchester United	1-1
	Cardiff City v. Liverpool	2-1
	Derby County v. Nottingham Forest	0-0
	Exeter City v. Blackburn Rovers	2-2
	Huddersfield Town v. West Ham United	2-1
	Port Vale v. New Brighton	3-0
	Reading v. Leicester City	0-1
	Sheffield United v. Wolverhampton Wan.	3-1
	Southport v. Middlesbrough	0-3
	Stoke City v. Bolton Wanderers	4-2
	Sunderland v. Manchester City	1-2
	Swindon Town v. Sheffield Wednesday	1-2
	Tottenham Hotspur v. Oldham Athletic	3-0
	Wrexham v. Birmingham	1-3
r	Blackburn Rovers v. Exeter City	3-1
r	Manchester United v. Bury	1-0
r	Nottingham Forest v. Derby County	2-0

Round Five

	Arsenal v. Aston Villa	4-1
	Blackburn Rovers v. Port Vale	2-1
	Huddersfield Town v. Middlesbrough	4-0
	Leicester City v. Tottenham Hotspur	0-3
	Manchester City v. Stoke City	0-1
	Manchester United v. Birmingham	1-0
	Nottingham Forest v. Cardiff City	2-1
	Sheffield Wednesday v. Sheffield United	1-1
r	Sheffield United v. Sheffield Wednesday	4-1

Round Six

	Arsenal v. Stoke City	4-1
	Blackburn Rovers v. Manchester United	2-0
	Huddersfield Town v. Tottenham Hotspur	6-1
	Sheffield United v. Nottingham Forest	3-0

Semi Finals

	Blackburn Rovers v. Arsenal	1-0 N
	Huddersfield Town v. Sheffield United	2-2 N
r	Huddersfield Town v. Sheffield United	0-0eN
r2	Huddersfield Town v. Sheffield United	1-0 N

Final

	Blackburn Rovers v. Huddersfield Town	3-1 N